Peter Woll   BRANDEIS UNIVERSITY

BEHIND THE SCENES IN

American Government

Personalities and Politics

Fifth Edition

LITTLE, BROWN AND COMPANY
Boston   Toronto

Library of Congress Cataloging in Publication Data
Main entry under title:

Behind the scenes in American government.

  Bibliography: p.
  1. United States — Politics and government — 20th century — Addresses, essays, lectures. 2. Politicians —United
States — Addresses, essays, lectures.
3. Statesmen — United States — Addresses, essays,
lectures. I. Woll, Peter, 1933–
JK271.B533 1985   320.973   84-21303
ISBN 0-316-95171-4

Library of Congress Catalog Card No. 84-21303

ISBN 0-316-95171-4

9–8–7–6–5–4–3–2–1
ALP

Published simultaneously in Canada
by Little, Brown & Company (Canada) Limited

Printed in the United States of America

For Rochelle Jones

PREFACE

This book is designed as a supplementary text for introductory American government courses. It is also an exciting complement to a wide range of courses that analyze parties and political campaigning, interest groups and lobbyists, the media and political consultants, the presidency, Congress, the courts, and the bureaucracy.

Politics is, by any measure, fascinating. But this fascination is not often conveyed to students because many books and courses concentrate on structures and processes at the expense of the individuals who constitute the life-blood of politics. And it is, after all, the people in politics who shape its character, just as they themselves are shaped by it. This book illustrates how character and personality influence politics, and the ways in which political institutions and processes, such as the presidency and political campaigning, affect the personalities and actions of those who are directly, and sometimes indirectly, involved. Vignettes of famous politicians, pressure group leaders, journalists and political consultants, members of Congress, White House staffers and presidential advisers, Supreme Court justices, and top-level bureaucrats comprise the book. By introducing students to the colorful and powerful personalities who are to be found in politics, I hope to make American government the lively subject that it should be.

The fifth edition, just off the presses after the dramatic and exciting presidential and congressional elections in 1984, presents fresh profiles of the contestants for the White House and, in the Democratic party, of leading contenders for the presidential nomination. At the outset, as the text examines political parties and politicians, Elizabeth Drew sets the stage with her classic *New Yorker* selection that describes the grueling process of running for the presidential nomination in a time of party reforms that require candidates to campaign at the grass-roots level in primaries and at the party level caucuses throughout the nation. Although the Democrats in 1984 retreated somewhat from the grassroots reforms of the 1970s, by reducing the number of primaries and adding "super-delegates," members of Congress and state and local elected officials who became 14 percent of the convention delegates, the race for the nomination was just as exhausting as ever. A new selection by a team of *Time* reporters examines how the fatigue factor affected Walter Mondale, Gary Hart, and Jesse Jackson in the final laps of the nomination race.

Nowhere can the effect of personality and style upon politics be better seen than in Jesse Jackson's historic race for the presidency. A fresh first-hand account of his campaign depicts how his masterful oratorical skills and political techniques influenced both party and national politics.

Running for the presidency has changed since the days when local party bosses, such as Chicago Mayor Richard J. Daley, were important power brokers because of their ability to deliver enough votes to swing their states. Daley remains the paradigm of the big city boss and an important part of our political history, which is the reason for the retention of Mike Royko's classic account of Daley and his machine. How that machine has continued to shape Chicago politics into the mid-1980s is the subject of a new selection following Royko.

As the book turns from portraits of politicians in the electoral process to lobbyists and interest groups, a new portrayal of Florida Congressman Claude Pepper, champion of America's elderly, illustrates how a member of Congress can become an interest group leader and its chief Washington lobbyist. Nicholas von Hoffman describes a scene familiar to the Capitol Hill community as he writes about the Monocle's power lunch, where lobbyists, members of Congress and their staffers, and an occasional cabinet secretary meet to plan strategies while they enjoy gastronomic delights.

While politicians and political insiders confront each other directly as they play the political game, they all know that effective use of the media is essential to maintain and expand their political bases. Elected officials, lobbyists, and top-level bureaucrats seek expert advice from political consultants within and without government to polish the images they project to their constituencies. New vignettes in this edition portray the wizardry of Patrick Caddell, the champion of anti-establishment candidates that included Gary Hart in 1984, and, in a first person account, the challenges and dilemmas of presidential press secretary Jody Powell during the Iranian hostage crisis.

A major reason for Ronald Reagan's success with the public has been his mastery of the electronic media and skillful press relations, which are described in a new selection on Reagan's "magical" style. He was called "The Man in the Teflon Suit" because criticism of his actions did not seem to stick to him as a person. The presidency chapter also includes a fresh profile of Walter Mondale, describing how he used his time out of office to build the political base that enabled him to become the presidential nominee of his party.

It is not only the character and style of the incumbent that determines presidential performance but also the personalities and political skills of White House staffers. In this edition, George Reedy and John Dean continue to describe the role of White House aides and their behind-the-scenes machinations as they struggle for power.

At the other end of Pennsylvania Avenue, powerful politicians of many political stripes dot the Capitol Hill landscape. *New Yorker* prize-winning author John McPhee contributes a fresh portrait of New Jersey Senator Bill Bradley, who was identified by the *Wall Street Journal* after the 1984 national party convention to be a rising political star. McPhee focuses on the former New York Knick star's "homestyle" manner of relating to his constituents. The subject of another new and lively selection is the Washington team of Elizabeth and Robert Dole, the Secretary and the Senator, powerful insiders who in marriage still respect the separation of powers. Finally, added to the Congress chapter is a vignette of Wisconsin Congressman Les Aspin that not only illustrates how the former political outsider became a powerful insider on Capitol Hill, but also describes how his successful political career was built. Complementing and balancing these new selections are the ever-popular portrayals of: Lyndon B. Johnson's style as majority leader, by Roland Evans and Robert Novak; the contrasting styles of Senators Robert Byrd and Edward Kennedy, by Laurence Leamer; Russell Long, by Aaron Latham; and House Speaker Thomas P. (Tip) O'Neill by Jimmy Breslin.

In Chapter Six, is the popular selection by Bob Woodard and Scott Armstrong that gives a behind-the-scenes account of the Supreme Court's abortion decision along with Earl Warren's firsthand description of the interplay of personalities on the Court when it confronted the desegregation cases.

The book's concluding chapter on the bureaucracy retains Sanford Unger's classic piece on J. Edgar Hoover ("The King"), and the selection by Jonathan Alter that portrays prominent political entrepreneurs in the bureaucracy, including Admiral Hyman Rickover.

An underlying theme of this book is that the personalities and styles of people in high positions in politics do shape the political process. However, many political scientists, including our first — the framers of the Constitution — believe that structural arrangements can shape and determine human behavior. The framers of our system of government were not particularly concerned with the deeper psychological variants in human beings; they delved into psychopolitics only to the extent of accepting the premise that persons, particularly those entering the political process, are likely to be motivated by self-interest rather than by the national interest.

Thus the framers carefully constructed our system of separation of powers and of checks and balances for the purpose of controlling the baser side of human nature. The safeguards they established offered protection against unbridled political ambition, the pursuit of self-interest in the political process, and the possibility of tyranny. The map of our political system, devised by men such as Alexander Hamilton and James Madison, resembled a military map, with defensive and offensive positions being taken by the armies — the branches of government — and with differing weapons being provided to the combatants. Balancing the forces would ensure that victory would not be certain on any one side, and that after the forces grew exhausted by their perpetual and often futile combat they would seek not unconditional surrender but a negotiated peace settlement. By carefully controlling the conditions of political warfare, the framers hoped to limit governmental power and to shape policy in the people's interest.

James Madison in *Federalist 51* succinctly stated the framers' views on human nature and how it should be controlled within government:

> But the greatest security against a gradual concentration of the several powers in the same department, consists in giving to those who administer each department, the necessary constitutional means, and personal motives, to resist encroachments of the others. The provision for defense must in this, as in all other cases, be made commensurate to the danger of attack. Ambition must be made to counteract ambition. The interest of the man must be connected with the constitutional rights of the place. It may be a reflection on human nature, that such devices should be necessary to control the abuses of government. But what is government itself, but the greatest of all reflections on human nature? If men were angels, no government would be necessary. If angels were to govern men, neither external nor internal controls on government would be necessary. In framing a government, which is to be administered by men over men, the great difficulty lies in this: you must first enable the government to control the governed; and in the next place oblige it to control itself. A dependence on the people is, no doubt, the primary control on the government; but experience has taught mankind the necessity of auxiliary precautions.

The relatively simple governmental model established by the framers to control political evil and at the same time to provide effective government has undergone many changes over the more than a century and a half since the Constitution was ratified. Before the end of the nineteenth century the presidency had developed imperial powers, due not only to historical circumstances but also to the character of the men who had occupied the office from the beginning. Thomas Jefferson, who opposed a strong presidency while he was in Paris at the time the Constitution was framed, ironically changed his mind after his election to the presidency in 1800. The forceful and determined character of Abraham Lincoln helped not only to save the Union but also to establish precedents for the growth of presidential power. The personalities of presidents Theodore Roosevelt, Woodrow Wilson, Franklin D. Roosevelt, Harry S. Truman, John F. Kennedy, Lyndon B. Johnson, Richard M. Nixon, Jimmy Carter, and Ronald Reagan all had a profound effect on the institution of the presidency. Just as presidential character helped to build up the office, it also was responsible for bringing it into temporary disrepute after Watergate. No one would deny that the personality of Richard Nixon played a significant role in the Watergate affair, particularly in the way it was handled in the White House, nor that the personality of Gerald Ford helped to restore dignity to the White House.

Just as the transformations in the presidency have been shaped by the personalities of the men who have held the office, so have changes in other political institutions. Congress is a venerable and highly structured institution, but it too has an important personal dimension, found in the personalities of its leaders and the chairmen of its committees. Legislative styles and policies frequently depend on the characters of congressmen. Congress is composed of men and women who are not simply conduits for the few electoral demands that exist, but who act as they are motivated by their consciences and by their psychological needs for power and status within the institution.

The courts and the bureaucracy were designed to be more nearly neutral politically than were the president and the Congress and such obvious political advocates as parties and pressure groups. The judiciary was to dispense justice impartially and independently of the political arms of government, and the bureaucracy was to administer the laws. But here, too, the characters and personalities of judges and bureaucrats influence how justice is carried out and how laws are implemented.

I would like to thank Donald Palm, whose perceptive and timely editorial judgments and recommendations creatively shaped the fifth edition of this book. Billie Ingram skillfully and efficiently guided the manuscript through the production process. I greatly appreciate Neil Sullivan's enduring interest in the book and recommendations for it. Rochelle Jones, to whom the book is dedicated, continues to help keep the author abreast of the Washington political scene. Her suggestions for this as for previous editions have been invaluable and reflect her enthusiasm and originality in many ways. Finally, no acknowledgments would be complete for any of my books without thanks to Barbara Nagy, who for years has made my writing enjoyable.

CONTENTS

CHAPTER ONE

POLITICAL PARTIES AND POLITICIANS   1

1

Elizabeth Drew
Running   3
The candidates and their campaign staffs speak for themselves in describing the personal effect of the grueling presidential primary process in this New Yorker *selection by Elizabeth Drew.*

2

Kurt Andersen
Campaign 1984: Facing the Fatigue Factor   24
Walter Mondale became forgetful, Gary Hart looked haggard, and Jesse Jackson was exhausted as they ran full tilt for the Democratic presidential nomination. A team of Time *reporters gives a lively account of the race and examines the important question of whether or not the exhausting process of running is a true test of the candidate's ability to govern.*

3

Evan Thomas
Campaigning with Jesse Jackson: Pride and Prejudice   29
Bold, charismatic, dedicated, driven, and flamboyant are among the adjectives that describe Jesse Jackson. As the first serious black candidate for the presidency, he changed political history. A lively Time *cover story depicts Jackson's masterful political style, his soaring rhetoric and media skills, which, combined with his charismatic personality, made him a major political force.*

4   Lou Cannon
     Ronald Reagan: A Political Perspective   43

Ronald Reagan was finishing high school on the eve of the stock market crash of 1929 and the Great Depression that followed. Franklin Roosevelt became his political idol, and for most of his life he backed liberal causes. He trained for a career in radio, but his talent and handsome appearance helped him to become a highly successful Hollywood actor. His stage presence and mastery of the media led him to the White House in 1980.

5   Mike Royko
     The Boss   62

The inner workings of one of the last big-city machines and its powerful boss, Mayor Richard J. Daley of Chicago, are described in Mike Royko's best selling expose of city politics, The Boss.

6   E. R. Shipp
     Will Loyalty Win the Ward Again?   79

The legacy of the Daley machine continued to affect Chicago politics after the Mayor's death in 1976. A special New York Times report describes the 1984 battle for the post of ward committeeman, which pitted an old-time machine candidate against a Hispanic community activist who had made an impressive showing the year before by garnering 42 percent of the vote in an election for alderman against an organization candidate who had served under Daley.

CHAPTER TWO

PRESSURE GROUPS AND LOBBYISTS   83

7   Albert R. Hunt
     The Washington Power Brokers   84

Thomas Boggs, Jr., a member of a distinguished political family, has become one of the most influential lob-

byists in the nation's capital. Albert R. Hunt, a prize-winning Wall Street Journal reporter, gives a lively account of Boggs's style, which has made him a Capitol Hill insider and an accepted member of Washington's political establishment.

8

Steven Emerson
Dutton of Arabia   91

Fred Dutton was an aspiring young lawyer in California when historian Arthur Schlesinger, Jr., noticed his political column in the Los Angeles Times and recruited him for Adlai Stevenson's presidential campaign. That was the beginning of a meteoric political career. Dutton joined the Kennedy administration in the early 1960s and later became one of the most influential power brokers in Washington. In the 1980s his time and political skills are devoted to the representation of Saudi Arabia, whose interests he assiduously protects and advances as he plays the Washington power game.

9

John Egerton
Congressman Claude Pepper: Courtly Champion of America's Elderly   103

If the elderly had a union, Florida Congressman Claude Pepper would be its leader and chief Washington lobbyist. That members of Congress may become national advocates of interests that transcend their districts is illustrated in this portrayal of a veteran congressman whose Capitol Hill career spans almost fifty years.

10

Nicholas von Hoffman
The Washingon Monocle: Scene of the Power Lunch   114

Monumental egos breed monumental appetites as well as a thirst for power. The Monocle hosts the power lunch on Capitol Hill as Washington's political players

*gather to see and be seen while they plan strategies
and enjoy gastronomic delights.*

11 The Reverend Jerry Falwell and the Tide of Born Again   122

*Jerry Falwell, the Lynchburg, Virginia, evangelist,
forged religion and politics into a significant political
force in the 1980s. A special* Newsweek *story depicts
the character and style of the leader of a nation-wide
movement that is attempting to use the ballot box to
turn many fundamentalist Christian beliefs into public
policy.*

CHAPTER THREE

THE MEDIA AND POLITICAL CONSULTANTS   133

12 Ralph Whitehead
For Whom Caddell Polls   136

*The chief wizard of political pollsters and consultants
is Patrick Caddell, the champion of anti-establishment
candidates. He is a backroom general whose keen political insights and plots of voter attitudes shape his
tactical advice. He was a major force behind Gary
Hart's unusually strong bid for the presidential nomination in 1984.*

13 Sidney Blumenthal
**Richard Viguerie: The Postmaster General
of the Right**   144

*Richard Viguerie is the undisputed master of the di-
rect-mail consultants. He is the force behind the National Conservative Political Action Committee
(NCPAC), and numerous other political causes. This
lively portrayal of one of the chief architects of the
New Right is taken from Sidney Blumenthal's timely
book,* The Permanent Campaign.

14   Jody Powell
The Right to Lie   157
*A former presidential press secretary reveals, in a se-
lection taken from his provocative book,* The Other
Side of the Story, *how he manipulated the media to
protect the national interest and individual lives during
the Iranian hostage crisis.*

CHAPTER FOUR

THE PRESIDENCY   173

15   Steven R. Weisman
Ronald Reagan's Magical Style   175
Ronald Reagan is The Man in the Teflon Suit, *because
nothing sticks to him. Even Americans who disagreed
with his policies liked him for his upbeat and optimistic approach to the presidency. His positive style and
mastery of the media deflected public criticism, giving
him more leeway than most presidents to make mistakes.*

16   Charles R. Babcock
The Rewards of Losing: Mondale Out of Office   191
*Politicians, especially those who have occupied the
White House, can enrich themselves far more easily
out of than in office. Unlike most defeated politicians,
losing vice presidents may, as Walter Mondale did, not
only replenish the family coffers but also build and
strengthen their political base to make a run for the
presidency.*

17   George E. Reedy
The White House Staff: A Personal Account   199
*One of Lyndon B. Johnson's most astute staffers de-
picts the rarified atmosphere of the White House and
its impact upon the personal staff of the president.
The selection is from George Reedy's provocative
book,* The Twilight of the Presidency.

18 John Dean
My First Day at the White House 205

John Dean describes, in his best-seller, Blind Ambition, *his tour of the White House on the first day in his new job as a Nixon aide. Uppermost in his mind was how to achieve the symbols and reality of power as a member of the president's inner circle.*

19 David Wise
Why the President's Men Stumble 211

Presidential character and style is always reflected in the president's relationship with his staff and cabinet officials. He sets the tone for his administration and the boundaries of his subordinates' power. Nevertheless, the indiscreet behavior of the president's men has often embarrassed the White House. This selection, by a prize-winning investigative reporter, takes the reader behind the scenes of the White House from the administration of Franklin D. Roosevelt to that of Ronald Reagan. An assessment is made of why scandal rocks some presidencies, while others avoid it.

CHAPTER FIVE

THE CONGRESS 225

20 John McPhee
Senator Bill Bradley: Open Man 229

New Jersey Senator Bill Bradley has the right stuff. The former New York Knicks star also has an engaging and effective homestyle, described by best-selling author John McPhee.

21 Douglas B. Feaver
The Secretary and the Senator 240

Robert and Elizabeth Dole have become a Washington political item, an exception to the old adage that politics makes strange bedfellows. Both have had distin-

*guished political careers in their own right. Now a
team, they are reaching ever-new heights of political
power.*

22 Roland Evans and Robert Novak
The Johnson System 248
In their masterly book, Lyndon B. Johnson: The Exercise of Power, *Roland Evans and Robert Novak picture
Johnson as the consummate politician who ruled the
Senate with an iron hand as majority leader. His overwhelming personality and highly individualistic style
made a lasting imprint on friends and foes alike.*

23 Laurence Leamer
**Robert Byrd and Edward Kennedy:
Two Stories of the Senate** 255
*Edward Kennedy is a star, and Robert Byrd is a tactician. Kennedy's individualistic style is in sharp contrast
to Byrd's emphasis on collegiality. Both, in different
ways, have achieved power and status in the Senate,
as described in this selection from Laurence Leamer's
book on leading Washington personalities,* Playing for
Keeps.

24 Aaron Latham
Russell Long 264
In this provocative piece from New York *magazine,
Aaron Latham describes how Senator Russell Long, the
son of "Kingfish" Huey Long, has conquered the Senate and the House of Representatives through a personal style that wins respect, admiration, and sometimes grudging assent from his colleagues.*

25 Jimmy Breslin
The Politician 275
*The Massachusetts politician, a vanishing breed, is
brought to life by Jimmy Breslin in this portrayal of*

Thomas P. ("Tip") O'Neill, a streetwise, commonsense politician, whose instincts have led him to a position of dominance in the House of Representatives. The vignette is from Jimmy Breslin's best-seller, How the Good Guys Finally Won.

26 Fred Kaplan
Going from Outsider to Insider on Capitol Hill: Les Aspin and the Case of the MX   286
A former outsider and gadfly becomes a major force in shaping defense policy by learning how to play the Capitol Hill's power game.

CHAPTER SIX

THE COURTS   291

27 Bob Woodward and Scott Armstrong
The Brethren and the Abortion Decision   294
Clashing personalities and intrigue on the Supreme Court may affect the outcome of important cases that have a nationwide impact. In their best-selling book, The Brethren, *Bob Woodward and Scott Armstrong write about the impact of personalities on the Court's decision to guarantee women the right to obtain abortions.*

28 Earl Warren
A Case of Emotional Impact   314
Earl Warren, hero to some, villain to others, helped to shape the Supreme Court during a crucial period in its history. His character molded his beliefs, which surfaced in his major court opinions. The force of his personality and style more than once persuaded colleagues to his point of view. This selection, from The Memoirs of Earl Warren, *is a personal account by the former Chief Justice of his role on the Supreme Court as it faced a number of difficult decisions, including the desegregation cases of 1954.*

CHAPTER SEVEN

THE BUREAUCRACY 321

29   Sanford J. Ungar
The King: J. Edgar Hoover 323

The bulldog face of J. Edgar Hoover was not a facade. The man behind the mask had an iron will and a quick temper, as is vividly illustrated in this selection from Sanford J. Ungar's definitive book, F.B.I.

30   Jonathan Alter
The Powers That Stay 347

Top-level bureaucrats must be consummate politicians to maintain their power. Many of the most successful, such as Admiral Hyman Rickover and J. Edgar Hoover, were political entrepreneurs, while others, such as Deputy Defense Secretary Frank Carlucci, learned to serve and often manipulate many masters. This entertaining selection from the Washington Monthly *describes the games that bureaucrats play.*

POLITICAL PARTIES
AND POLITICIANS

Chapter One

In classical democratic theory, political parties are supposed to bridge the gap between people and government. They are to be the principal policymakers, presenting contrasting choices to the electorate so that, by voting, people can participate in the choice of government programs. It is important that a political party have control over its candidates and officeholders, because a party that has a majority in the legislature and controls the executive will then be able to carry out its platform.

Although political parties in an ideal situation are suited to presenting meaningful and realistic policy choices for the electorate, they also serve the personal goals of their active members, which may have nothing at all to do with implementing one public policy instead of another. Roberto Michels, the great European political sociologist of the early twentieth century, draws from German sociologist Max Weber to define the political party as:

> A spontaneous society of propaganda and of agitation seeking to acquire power, in order to procure thereby for its active militant adherents chances, ideal and material, for the realization of either objective aims or of *personal advantages,* or of both. Consequently, the general orientation of the political party, whether in its personal or impersonal aspect, is that of *machtstreben* (striving to power).[1]

In this chapter we will be concerned with the personal motives of active party members. These motives affect the organization and orientation of political parties at national, state, and local levels. The drive for power may completely overshadow party policy. American party leaders are more interested in power than in ideology, and therefore will often shape their policy promises in accordance with the wishes of the majority of the electorate. And, in the absence of any clear electoral desires, which is a common situation, party leaders themselves must determine their actions, which are usually directed toward expanding their power and status in both the party and the government.

[1] Alfred De Grazia, trans., Roberto Michels' *First Lectures in Political Sociology* (Minneapolis: University of Minnesota Press, 1949), p. 134. Italics added.

Their personalities often determine the kinds of decisions they will make, and the way in which they conduct their offices. At the lower levels of parties, particularly in city party machines, the orientation of adherents is often economic security as much as a drive for power. Policy is almost completely irrelevant at these lower echelons.

E ACH POLITICAL PARTY DETER-mines for itself the procedures for the selection of candidates. Since 1968 both major parties have undergone a democratization process that has resulted in expanding grass-roots participation in party affairs through various new procedures, the most important of which is the in-crease in the number of national con-vention delegates selected through state primaries. In 1980 the number of states adopting the primary method for the selection of delegates and for the determination of presidential prefer-ences of the electorate expanded to thirty-five, a remarkable number by any past standards. The Democratic party in particular pushed the primary selection method after the debacle of the 1968 convention, which numer-ous party members believed to have been boss controlled.

The dissatisfaction of party leaders with the delegate rules of the Demo-cratic party led to a rules change for 1984, providing that party officials, in-cluding two-thirds of the Democrats in Congress, were seated and con-trolled 14 percent of the delegate votes. Primaries continued to be cru-cial, but grass-roots control was less emphasized than in the 1970s. The number of primaries was reduced to twenty-eight.

Party procedures for delegate se-lection to national conventions are, of course, institutional. What effect do these rules have on the personalities of the candidates? Do they help to de-termine what types of people will run for the nomination? What other ef-fects do they have on individuals dur-ing the preconvention campaign, and later, after they have run for nomina-tion? The comments of those who have run, or who have been involved in nominating campaigns, are not en-couraging. All observers seem to agree that the campaigns have a deep and adverse impact on the psyche and physical condition of those who are running, and often on campaign staffs. The primary campaigns breed para-noia, uncertainty, physical fatigue and sleeplessness, and unnerving ten-sions due to tight scheduling. Partici-pants in the nominating process uni-versally describe it as "grueling," "inhuman," and "crazy." The condi-tions of campaigning make the large number of aspirants for the presi-dency all the more remarkable.

The following selection tells what it means to run for the presidential nomination, and describes the effect of the selection procedures on the candidates as well as the effects of the candidates' personalities on the pro-cess.

1 Elizabeth Drew
RUNNING

In selecting those who might occupy the most important office in this country — the presidency — we put our potential leaders through a process that is both strange and brutal. The people who might make crucial decisions about war and peace, about our taxes, who will have enormous effect on the quality of our lives, our social order, the civility of our public discourse, undergo an experience from which few human beings could emerge whole. Some do not. The evidence of the damaging nature of modern political campaigns — the scarred veterans, the burnt-out cases, the bitterness — is all about. "They never come out of it the same," one senator said of colleagues of his who had run for the presidential nomination or the presidency. Moreover, the pressures on those who undertake presidential campaigns are growing. In 1960, John F. Kennedy ran in only seven primaries. Now, as a result of subsequent political reforms, there are twenty-nine Democratic primaries. In addition, the Democrats' reform rules have led to more open processes for choosing delegates by convention or caucus in the other states. As politics has become more open, the growth in participation has led to growth in demands on candidates. Other developments have added to the strains a campaign imposes on the candidate. One is the growth in the variety and skill of pressure groups. Another is the education of the populace — which is increasingly well informed about politics. Intensified coverage by the press intensifies the stress. One mistake and a candidate can be destroyed. Those relatively modern inventions — television and the jet plane — have added not to the politicians' ease but to the demands that are put upon them or that they put upon themselves. One gets the impression that the entire presidential selection process is about to snap, and that new forms and styles must emerge.

Curiously, the questions of why people run and why the race often leaves such deep scars may have common answers. Running for the presidency appears to have an impact on the ego that is unlike that of any other endeavor. *Homo candidatus* might be said to undergo a unique human experience. There are some exceptions, but many candidates for the presidency seem to react with strikingly similar emotions — even those who enter the race with the best of motives, who are thoughtful people, who care deeply about their country. They feel an extraordinary exhilaration in making the race — a great lift, an unparalleled expansion of self-esteem. It is as if the limits on ambition and ego were removed.

All this is reinforced by aides and backers who are themselves susceptible to expansion of ego and fantasies of power. They are investors in power, who stand to gain if the candidate wins. The aides and other investors fuel a candidate's ambition and flog him on. After a while, the candidate, caught in a web of ambition (his own and others'), begins to believe that he can win — has to believe it in order to go through what he does — and begins to picture himself in the Oval Office. In the deepest fatigue, he continues to function on an unnatural flow of energy — a kind of high. It is the only way to get through it. Set against this is the devastation of losing — the deflated self-esteem, the bitterness, the sheer physical difficulty of adjusting to the sudden cessation of activity. Two years after his unsuccessful race for the presidency was over, one former candidate told a Senate colleague, "I still wake up nights campaigning."

Almost every campaign eventually generates uncommon stress: There is infighting among the staff and the reaction of an exhausted candidate to that infighting; failures in staff work (often caused by rivalries); unfair attacks by opponents; the necessity of appealing for money and other forms of help from people whom one holds in low esteem or people who may exact an exorbitant price — not just in commitments to policies but also in promises of federal appointment or demands on a candidate's time. There are constant pressures to take various positions on issues — to win one constituency but do it in a way that does not lose another. There are pressures to be something one is not — to change everything from one's haircut to one's personality. There is pressure to be shallow, sensational, so as to get press attention. Aides grow quarrelsome and suspicious. And all the while the candidate is being asked to undertake more than human flesh can endure. Understandably, the self-pity that is endemic among politicians — who feel overworked, underappreciated, and misunderstood — reaches great intensity in the candidate for national office. As a result of the pressures, candidates get derailed from their strategies — if they ever had them. Concentration on substance — even for those who wish to engage in it — becomes increasingly difficult. Planning for what one would actually do if one should win the presidency becomes almost out of the question.

A losing campaign as often as not leaves an atmosphere of bitter recrimination. Political defeat really is an orphan. Former aides and advisers go about telling how it could have been otherwise if this or that piece of advice had been followed. Participants in campaigns write whole score-settling books. Candidates go through self-doubt, rationalization, and examination of the "but for"s that stood between them and victory. The "but for" exercises prompt them, often successfully, to run again; having experienced the stratosphere of a presidential campaign, many — most, it seems — find it difficult to readjust to previous routines. Of course, good things also happen to people who run in presidential campaigns. They can receive a political education that is unequaled. They can learn unforgettable lessons about their country — about issues, about constituencies. They can learn about the mood of the people and the subtleties of that mood. They can gain a better understanding of where they can lead people — if they choose to — of how to lead them by gaining their trust and unlocking their higher aspirations and motivations. And they are given some preparation for the pressures involved in trying to govern a complicated nation. But — in the very nature of contemporary campaigning — the costs seem to outweigh the benefits. Good people can get through campaigns and survive, but at a heavy price — for them and for us. And some good people — after a close look — count themselves out. Campaigns have become a screening process that does not always screen out, or in, the right qualities.

Conversations with former candidates for the presidential nomination and for the presidency and with several former campaign aides give one a striking picture of what can happen to a candidate who seeks the highest office. "It leaves scar tissue," one former campaign manager said. "There's no way it can't have a deep impact on the candidate's psyche and physical condition. For a person in public life, it is the aspiration to the ultimate. There is no way a losing candidate can pick himself up and pretend nothing has happened to him. Even though you haven't lost your public position, you feel you're a loser. It hurts. You wonder what you did wrong. There are all the self-doubts. The system rewards success. There is no second place."

Another man who has participated in several campaigns said, "Everyone at the end of a campaign has blown off at his staff every night — thinks his mother is going to vote against him and his wife is trying to subvert him."

"It's the way they lay their egos on the line," said Mark Shields, a heavyset, thirty-eight-year-old man who has worked in several campaigns. "It's a terribly vulnerabilizing experience."

I asked Shields at lunch one day to tell me something about how campaigns work.

"Most of them don't work," he replied. "Everybody in the business is an amateur. Everybody looks at the last campaign. Most people have only one good campaign in them or maybe, if they're lucky, two. It's a total absorption of emotional, psychic, physical energy. It's not like being in the Senate. The Senate is bad preparation for a presidential campaign. A senator can say 'Let's have hearings on tire safety' or something else and issue a press release and in three months hold hearings and issue another press release. In a presidential campaign, issues are thrust upon you — a Middle East crisis, a public employees' strike. The press wants to know what you would do. That's more like the presidency. You get too many easy answers as a senator. A senator can make statements, offer testimony, send a letter to the Internal Revenue Service. He can be for housing, but he doesn't have to say where it's going to be built. He can't do that in a presidential campaign." Shields continued, "The toughest thing in running for president is to understand the fact that there are millions of people who are going to make a judgment about you who don't know you. And then you have to ask people you don't like for their help — that's tough. How many fools can you suffer in one day? And how many speeches can you give? How many days can you take away from home and still feel good? Can you resist trying to be your own campaign manager? All day, you'll get complaints about those dopes who did this and that. How good are you at raising money? How many people can you be nice to? Can you convince other people that you are worth their time and money?"

Another former campaign manager told me, "The physical, emotional, and energy strain is so staggering that you end up with a person whose emotional and physical level has to be beyond human — it has to be animal. Look at the candidate as a person. Quite often, he's a husband; he's a father; there are problems at home. There are financial problems, if he's honest. Quite often, there are arguments with the family, or there is a distance from the family — an emotional acceptance of a dreadful circumstance. There is a terrible emotional drain on the candidates. They are like an automobile whose lights have been left on overnight — and just maybe you can start it. The whole thing is excruciating. I wish to Christ you could spend just one whole day on the inside of a difficult campaign. At the end of the day, the candidate used to look at me with red eyes and say, '*For what?* How much more do I have to do?'"

"A lot of them go into a presidential campaign with the idea that the United States might be one big congressional district or state," said a man who was active in the 1972 campaign. "They begin by thinking they can wander around the country the way they wandered around the state. Then the shock sets in. Frankly, what it takes out of them is a great deal. Most normal people can concentrate on only one thing at a time. The candidate has to realize that the only thing he can handle is being an articulate, good candidate. He can't think about whether the mail is going out or the money is coming in. The biggest thing is fatigue. The staff sits around and says, 'Can the candidate do this?' or 'Can the candidate do that?' The candidate can hardly walk."

An aide to one of the current candidates, when I asked him what candidates have to go through, replied, "They have to go through a whole lot of — a lot of running around. You really have to want to be president. We run our guy; we really run him. You just have to come to grips with the fact that your life is not your own for some period of time. We run him a lot harder than we should. He's good about it, but every once in a while it has an adverse impact on his performance. He begins to answer questions too long; his speeches become too long; he becomes less precise."

"Here is a truism about politics," said one former campaign manager. "Candidates' wives hate schedulers and advance men. They always think their husband is being overscheduled."

One day in October, I asked George McGovern to give me some of his impressions of what it was like to go through a campaign. We talked during lunch in the senators' dining room in the Capitol. McGovern began by talking about his experience in 1972. Understandably, he said he thinks that the system of primaries and state caucuses is "pretty good," but he feels that the general election gives all the advantages to the incumbent. "I suppose I reflect the bias of someone who won in the selection process and lost so disastrously in the general election," he said. Still, McGovern has some things to say about running for the presidency that illuminate what a candidate goes through.

"I think running for the presidency is different from anything else," McGovern said. "Maybe it isn't that it's so different but that the stakes are so much higher. You always know when you're in a presidential campaign that a slip of the tongue or an ill-advised statement can be devastating. In a statewide race, you have time to make up for such a thing. But in a presidential campaign it's as if you were always in the seventh game of the World Series — one error and it could all be over. The sense of excitement and tension is always there — day and night. It's physically exhausting on the one hand and exhilarating on the other. You literally live for months on the flow of adrenalin. I was tired, but I went at a pace that couldn't be sustained at any other time. It couldn't be sustained by the staff, by the press — they had to be rotated. The great weakness is that there is seldom any opportunity for reflection. Even when there is a rest time scheduled, your mind and your emotions are racing ahead, and you're anxious for some scheduler to give you something to do, so you don't have to go through the pain of thinking about what you're doing. And there's always some scheduler with extra things for you to do."

McGovern continued, "One of the cruellest things that go on in presidential politics is the struggle for the candidate's body. It goes on from the county chairman to the campaign manager. The handshaking tours have to be drastically curtailed. They're really a lot of baloney. They don't add very much to the process in terms of the candidate's security and the candidate's dignity, and they really don't make sense. The candidate arrives at the airport and sometimes spends half an hour shaking hands with the first three rows of people. Candidates do it for two reasons: one, to show how democratic they are; two, to inflate their egos. It's pretty heady stuff to have dozens of people waving their hands in the air to touch you. It makes you feel you're some sort of gift to them. But it really doesn't contribute to the education of the public or the candidate." Candidates also go through the handshaking routine because it gives them a chance to show their popularity to television audiences.

McGovern offered an example of the kind of incident that can cause havoc in a campaign and irritate a candidate's already raw nerves. Toward the end of his election campaign, he decided to interrupt his scheduled appearances in various towns and "media markets" to do some nationwide telecasts. (This decision itself was much disputed within the McGovern campaign. One former McGovern campaign official still talks of it as "disastrous," causing as it did the unmaking of so many commitments, and he blames other McGovern advisers for the decision.) "The first television address was highly successful," McGovern recalls. "It was on the Vietnam war. The second was on economic problems. I had numerous meetings with economists and staff members who were traveling with me, and I cleared it at one o'cock in the afternoon, and we dispatched it back here to be put on the TelePrompTer at the Capitol, in time for the taping at nine o'clock. Well, when we landed and I was all made up and ready to go at seven o'clock, there was nothing on the TelePrompTer. The staff back here had decided they didn't like the speech and were fighting about it. So, after fuming for an hour, I said, 'I want that speech I cleared this afternoon.' But there was no time to rehearse or go over it. I was mad; I was exhausted; I was unnerved. That kind of thing happened a dozen times; it draws every ounce of energy out of you."

Edmund Muskie now has sufficient seniority in the Senate to have an elegant hideaway office in the Capitol — actually, Sam Ervin's former hideaway. As we sat there — in a high-ceilinged room with chandeliers, brown leather furniture, and a spectacular view of the Mall leading to the Washington Monument — Muskie, relaxed, sometimes with one of his long legs slung over an arm of his chair, talked about his 1972 campaign for the Democratic nomination. He offered a number of insights into the experiences of a candidate.

"The most difficult problem — and I wish I'd seen it in advance as well as I do in retrospect — is for the candidate to control his campaign and be himself and be sure the campaign reflects that," Muskie said. "People don't buy an organization — they buy a candidate, his philosophy, his character, his goals. But the campaign starts to overwhelm the candidate." Referring to his role as vice-presidential candidate on Hubert Humphrey's ticket, Muskie continued, "In 1968, I went in at the top. It was a new experience, a liberating experience, and the organization responded to me pretty well. It was a pretty good start. Odd as it may seem, the bad start for 1972 was the election eve speech" — the televised speech he gave on the eve of the 1970 congressional elections, which was in sharp contrast to a poorly delivered speech on law and order by Richard Nixon, and increased the talk of Muskie as the probable candidate in 1972. "All of a sudden, I was the frontrunner — without the resources, without the organization. There was a tidal wave of people wanting to respond, to be involved, and we didn't have the physical capacity to handle it. Being frontrunner made me defensive, overprotective, and too damn structured. I suddenly got up there on a high wire and wasn't sure enough of myself to take it and handle it naturally. People have reported that my staff acted as if I were already president." In a characteristically different perception, or assessment of blame, some members of Muskie's campaign staff say that it was Muskie who acted as if he were already president. Muskie remarked, "People in Maine say, 'You weren't the Ed Muskie we knew.' I suspect that's still some of my problem in Maine." Muskie is up for reelection to the Senate in 1976. This is seen as a reason for him to remain out of at least the early primaries next year, even if, as many people believe, he would like another chance at the presidency. If he does not face substantial opposition in seeking reelection to the Senate seat and if the situation seems opportune, he could still enter some of the later presidential primaries. In the meantime, he can stand apart from the melee and win national attention as chairman of the Senate Budget Committee while other candidates battle it out.

I asked Muskie what his major problem was in 1972.

"The pressures on your time and energy," he replied. "That's always the problem — so many people seeking access to the candidate. And then there is the physical need to get around the country and get exposure. Those are the pressures that the staff sees and responds to. They have a very useful tool — the white space on the calendar. When the white space is full, they've done their job. The candidate has his own priorities in regard to where he should go and whom he should see and finding time to think through a program for the country. The staff doesn't consider this. Their candidate is a mechanical man who can find the time to think through his positions on abortion and the gay movement, on the economy. These are the things the candidate doesn't get time to think through. I look at these guys who are running now, and wonder how they can do it. The press wants instant responses to everything, and if you don't give them instant responses they believe that you haven't thought it through, that you don't have any answer. Those are the kinds of things that frustrated me. Unless you've got the time to think, to formulate your own policy, you've missed the essence of it, the excitement of it, and you've become a frenetic thing moving around the landscape proving you've got more energy, more charisma, more instant answers than anyone else."

Muskie paused, and then continued, "The exposure to crowds is exhilarating, and is useful if you don't overdo it. I can understand why President Ford likes it; he probably didn't have much as a congressman from Michigan. It gives you some feeling that people respond to you, they think they need you, they can believe in you. There's nothing like that to give a man the adrenalin flow that permits him to believe in himself. But we do overdo it. We need to change the balance, to get more of a dialogue. Think back to Franklin D. Roosevelt and Al Smith. We didn't have the jet plane. There wasn't this constant rush to get around the country and get near the people. It was so much more leisurely and there was so much more communication. FDR and Truman traveled on trains; they didn't plunge through crowds. Television is supposed to reduce the expenditure of energy. It seems to have done the opposite. I wonder whether, if the candidates could get together and agree on a pace and a style, it wouldn't work just as well. Or if one candidate did it — reduced the running around — I'm not sure it wouldn't take."

I asked Muskie about the problem of raising money.

"That's going to continue to be a problem," he answered. Like several politicians, Muskie has misgivings about the new law to reform financing of campaigns, which limits individual contributions to a thousand dollars and requires presidential candidates, in order to get federal matching funds, to raise at least five thousand dollars, in contributions of no more than two hundred and fifty dollars, in each of twenty states. (The new law, which is under review by the Supreme Court, also sets limits on how much may be spent in each state.) It was far easier for some politicians to go to fewer contributors for larger sums — which is precisely what the new law is designed to prevent. Therefore, while from some politicians' point of view the old money-raising system had its difficulties, some of them don't like the new one much better. "It costs a lot of money to raise money from the grass roots," Muskie said. "The methods, such as mass mailing, can be overused and lose their productiveness. You'll have every candidate in the land sending letters." Muskie laughed, and added, "We'll have to raise the postal rates." Of his own experience in raising money in 1972, Muskie said, "I'd spend days and days going to see one individual — traveling to New York, traveling to Chicago, to see one guy who was a potential contributor. Being the front runner was very costly. We had to keep it going for two years. You have a tremendous organization to keep going, and at the first signs of stumbling the money starts drying up. That's what brought us down eventually. The New Hampshire and Florida primaries were tremendously expensive and didn't raise much money. We had to spend money we'd raised in New York and California. Wisconsin was pretty tough. In Illinois you can raise the money, but Pennsylvania — when the outcome of that primary was disappointing we had to fold. It was a classic case of too much too soon, of peaking too soon. Adlai Stevenson" — the Democratic senator from Illinois and son of the former presidential candidate — "used to say, 'Cut off and run from the Senate floor.' That would be easier to do this year than then."

I asked Muskie why, given the strains he had described, people run for the presidency — especially more than once.

"It's a very heady business, really, to suddenly find yourself near the top, and to breathe constantly the atmosphere of those who simply take it for granted that you're going to be the next president of the United States — not just the staff but also the press and your foes," Muskie replied. "It does things to you. You begin subconsciously to believe it yourself. You begin to consider the heavy responsibilities you have before you announce your position on something. It was the source of a lot of my difficulty, I fear, but at the same time it was a rather wonderful feeling. It would be nice if you could go through an experience like that on a trial-run basis — psychologically, mentally, physically — before you actually do it. In so many ways, I could do it much better now. But that's true of so much of life — you can't live it twice. The really invigorating parts of a campaign are the exposure to crowds and the all too scarce opportunities that you have to actually sit down with people and thrash out policies for the country — the chance to get into it and get good brains you can bounce off of. And so much of what we did of that ended up in the Democratic platform in 1972. I know I was perceived as not being issue-oriented, but I think the problem was that we tried to cover too much. We weren't identified with *an* issue, and people want to associate you with one issue or stand. George McGovern created that; George Wallace created that. What I was trying to do apparently isn't doable. I was trying to project the image of someone who could reach out to all segments of the Democratic party and establish a common cause with them. I managed to come out second with all of them."

Muskie laughed, and continued, "I came out fourth in the Florida primary. A Yankelovich survey a couple of days later showed I was the only one who could get more Democratic votes than Nixon there. And I'll tell you a historical footnote about New Hampshire. There was this game about the percentage by which I had to win New Hampshire. After starting out with 60 percent, the press settled on 50 percent. I got 46 percent, and it was decided I'd lost. Later, it was found that I actually got forty-nine and nine-tenths percent of the vote. I just found that out this spring. I got some satisfaction out of that, but it wasn't of any practical use."

Muskie continued, "Right after the *Manchester Union Leader* incident, I was not aware that it bore the seeds of disaster." His public display of emotion when, shortly before the New Hampshire primary, he attacked the *Union Leader* for printing a story taken to be critical of Mrs. Muskie and broke down and, according to some press reports, cried, was considered nearly fatal to his election chances. "As a matter of fact, my understanding as I went through New Hampshire was that it made a very favorable impression," Muskie told me. "I thought it was a bit of a triumph. That shows you how the candidate's perception can be off. I also found out later that the press had a different perception of what happened from mine. The press thought I cried. I didn't. I was madder than hell, and I choked. Up to that point, I was perceived as able, controlled, disciplined, stable, strong, and the image of that incident undermined what had been my basic strength. Which comes back to my basic point — you have to be yourself and have to be seen as that, or you're sunk. The more people there are who see what you are and decide they're for you, the firmer your base is. There's a lot of accident to it. Take my 1970 election eve speech. That did more than anything in my political life, but there was a lot of chance to it — the juxtaposition with the president. Unless there is that kind of fortuitous circumstance, then I guess you have to run around to get known, unless someone comes out of the first primary with a big margin. Then the press will give him big coverage — and he may become another George McGovern, or an Ed Muskie and stumble. The press is another problem. It's so easy to become defensive, guarded, suspicious about the press, and also to regard it as conspiratorial in a loose kind of way. And I'm sure I felt all those things in 1972. But that's a mistake. A candidate tends to overlook the fact that most of the members of the press never get a chance to meet him and talk to him and get to know him, so they write what they can or pay attention to those they believe to have access, or they want to be sensational and get attention for themselves. It must be very difficult for reporters to cover this passing scene. They don't have as direct access as we do to the facts on which we have to act."

Muskie returned to talking about the 1972 primaries. "We decided to start in New Hampshire and Forida on successive days," he recalled. "It was tough to do both states well. In Florida I never could catch up, and in New Hampshire it was an effort to get up to the standard the press had set. I was discouraged the night of the Florida primary, and sort of had a feeling that the whole thing had ended. Illinois, the next week, was a great primary. We never got credit for it." Muskie defeated Eugene McCarthy, his only real challenger, in the Illinois primary. "We did consider bypassing Wisconsin. The governors and senators who were supporting me met and opposed that. I think my instincts were right — to avoid another vulnerable situation, with Humphrey and McGovern coming from neighboring states. And I did not do well in multicandidate races. So Illinois was the only good primary, and now, historically, New Hampshire. Really, anyone who can do 50 percent in New Hampshire — especially in a five-candidate field — is doing pretty goddam well."

Walter Mondale's face gets a pained expression when he is asked about his experience as a potential Democratic candidate in 1976. Re-elected in Minnesota to his Senate seat by a wide margin in 1972, proclaimed a presidential candidate by Hubert Humphrey that election night, Mondale spent a year exploring his chances as the Democratic nominee. On November 21, 1974, he announced that he was withdrawing, because, he said, "I found that I did not have the overwhelming desire to be president which is essential for the kind of campaign that is required." The interesting thing is that he was taken at his word. In the rather cynical political community, the word might well have been that Mondale had pulled out because he wasn't getting anywhere, but it was widely accepted that no such conclusion about his chances could yet be drawn and that Mondale had pulled out for exactly the reason he said he did — that he couldn't stand it.

One day this fall, I asked Mondale to talk about his excursion into presidential politics. He had been talking easily about other matters, and it was clear that he would have preferred to continue to do so. But he agreed, reluctantly, to cooperate with my inquiry into the presidential-nominating process.

"The presidency is the most important office in the world," Mondale said. "The nominating system was unstudied and unanticipated by those who wrote the Constitution. There has been almost no study of it by a president, by Congress. It has just grown. Its growth has been malignant, almost. It's anarchy."

I asked what the process does to a candidate.

"Lots of things," Mondale replied. "One, fatigue. Look at the schedules, travel times, time changes, the absence of weekends for rest. It's not just the physical fatigue; it's the emotional pressure of it all. At every event you have to do exceedingly well — good isn't enough. You might never be seen there again. You have to be up for every meeting, be properly briefed, speak well. So the emotional, psychological pressure, which is hard to define, is worse than the physical fatigue, which is terrible. I was going through the easy, nice time when you can pick your schedule. What are these characters going to do when they get to the primary and caucus time — one primary or caucus on one coast and one on another? One on the Canadian border and one on the Mexican border — all with different rules?"

Mondale went on, "Then, you have the problem of money. You spend days and days and days pleading for money — answering questions, trying to make a good impression on people who have it. Even with the new limits on contributions, you have to do this. You need movers and shakers who can go out and help raise money in thousand-dollar quantities. When you get through with all this, you've got the conflict between what you have to do to be nominated and what you have to do to be a decent president. Some of it's the same. Some of the conflict and emotional pressure is a necessary test for the presidency. I'm not for the greenhouse approach. You can't be inaccessible and be a candidate, and by being accessible you may learn more than you'll ever learn again. But the way you spend your time is irrelevant to issue development. It's a different life style. Politicians have to be persuasive and able to move people, but when you get to the national scene it's theatre. When you're running for the House or the Senate, you have to grow well on a number of people. When you're running for president, it's like a series of one-night stands in vaudeville — you have to have a good act every night. The good act may carry you farther than the good program."

Mondale continued, "The feeling that bothered me more than anything else was that we were in the control of events we were unable to stop or do anything about. Experts are coming and telling you what you have to do, what positions you have to take — usually it's what they want. Then there are the people who want you to get a speech coach and cut your hair differently. None of that's very important. What's really important is that the goddam news media won't pay you much attention until you've become big. You have to spend years on the road until you get enough percentage points in the polls. The national media won't give you a break until then, and their eyes turn glassy when you talk to them about it. They don't want to hear about it. That's because their business isn't electing presidents — it's competing with their competitors. The result is that the nation is denied a look at new leadership. If you want to get on the evening news, you have to escalate your rhetoric in order to merit the time. If you're saying something rational and restrained, that's not news. That's one of the reasons politicians look so bad. They're always saying something wild. The news programs don't want to put someone unknown on because their competitor might be putting someone well known on. It's understandable, but why shouldn't there be some national forum where who our next president might be is considered and among those considered are those who are not well known but who have great merit? Now there's no adequate forum for that. So what I had to ask myself was whether I wanted to go through all that was involved not just for two years but maybe for ten years — to get on that lifetime presidential cycle that some get on. I didn't want to do it. I had to think about whether you should also have some time to be with friends, family, to fish, to have a little balance in your life, or whether the oneness of purpose should consume your life."

One man who has run for presidential office said to me, "Rich people — you have to go to rich people. These were the worst, most humiliating experiences of my life. There is a certain feeling that they know best, that they're expert. Here I've spent twenty years in government, and some jerk whose father made a lot of money is lecturing me. He doesn't know up from down and he's lecturing me on everything. One time, I was talking with a car dealer. He said, 'You have to smash through with an issue.' I said, 'What issue?' He said, 'I'm not going to get into that.' He makes a lot of money, so he's a political expert. You spend too much time listening to people who have money. Not that they shouldn't be listened to, but they shouldn't have that special access to a politician's ear."

A manager of one 1972 campaign, when I asked him what campaigns were really like, was fairly vehement in his response.
"You start with the basic proposition that, regardless of appearances, campaigns are, by their nature, disorganized, impossible to control," he said. "The better you appear to be doing, the more you attract the parasites, the so-called professionals, for whom you grow to have enormous disdain. There's no such thing as a professional in this business.
"Campaigns generate a king-of-the-mountain atmosphere: a contest to see who can become closest to the candidate — at the expense of someone else, which is the only way to do it. The interests of the candidate diminish at the hands of the staff. This has been true of every campaign I've heard about. The candidate has zero time; his life is no longer his own; he doesn't own his soul. Everyone is telling him what to do. The media managers tell him they need more time. You can't attract the kind of support and ideas you need from intellectuals without giving them time. The fund raisers demand time. The speech writers are in constant dispute. The upshot is that long-range planning is impossible. I've left out the constituencies that demand access — labor groups, women's groups, blacks, state leaders. And I haven't mentioned the grass-roots people or the schedulers. You have inherent chaos and conflict among all these warring groups, all of whom see in the candidate their tool to power, and want access, so that when Armageddon is won they will be up there with the heavenly angels."
I asked this man what to watch for in campaigns.
"Look for the obvious gap between the desire for an appearance of harmony and the undertones of conflict," he said. "This is symptomatic of all campaigns. There are always people on the edge of departure be-

cause they don't have access to the candidate. That's what matters. Then, there are the professionals, the hustlers. They hire out for pay, but they don't give any pleasure. They don't give a damn about the candidate. They bounce from one campaign to another. They flood the office with memos, and the memos just happen to leak out.

"There is an enormous distance between having a strategy and having the ability to carry it out. Things aren't what they appear. The successes, failures; the harmony, disharmony; getting money, not getting money; having grass-roots followers or not — campaign managers always want to give the impression that they are on top of all of that. The truth is that they are not. The difference in whether they are or not is marginal and accidental."

I asked this man whether he or his candidate had had much time to stop and think.

"The problem amounts to more than that," he replied. "The problem is the system in a country as large as this, with differences in the rules of each state. It's the uncertainty about your allies and the question of whether they have their own axes to grind — whether they are using the candidate. You have to look at the local staff as well as at the national one. You get involved in the selection of campaign posters and pictures. It's a great shell game. It's a silly-ass system."

I asked him if it is possible to run a campaign and think through a program for governing.

He said, "No. No one knows what's going on. No one can monitor a campaign, because it is moving too fast. Almost every campaign tries to set up a system for gathering information — someone responsible for organized labor, a group responsible for blacks, and so on. You do that in the headquarters and in the states. The financial community is a constituency that has to be serviced — they have their views on how to run absolutely everything. If you try to get endorsements from political figures, you do it at the cost of also getting enemies, and then the endorsers want to run your campaign in their own communities, and do it in a way which may be in their own interest instead of the candidate's. It would be almost impossible to describe the day of a campaign manager. To say it's enervating understates the case badly. You feel like a punching bag that Muhammad Ali has been using for two weeks. You're pummelled by staff, by grass-roots, local people. To see to noon the next day is a feat of uncommon accomplishment. When someone asks at 11 P.M. 'What did you do today?' it's amazing if you can remember ten minutes."

Picking up an earlier theme, he continued, "I've overlooked the other constituencies — young people, the elderly. And you can't go on the assumption that labor's labor. There are all sorts of divisions within what is referred to as 'labor.' There's another constituency of the Democratic party — the 'elder statesmen.' They drive you bananas. It's devastating. They can be ignored only at the staff's peril or the candidate's peril. They're the Washington lawyers who have been around, and there are also people in every state — an ex-party chairman, ex-governor, ex-university president. Multiply this by every city and county in the United States and you begin to get the picture. They have something to offer, but they are not involved in the campaign. Some take you back to a campaign twenty years ago and insist that that's the way yours should be; some think everything you're doing is wrong."

I asked this man what effect all these elements had had on his candidate in 1972.

"As it grew clear that we wouldn't win, he became very concerned about what it meant to his capacity for continuing in public life," the campaign manager replied. "He would ask, 'Can I continue to be effective?' He would say, 'I've let people down.' It took an enormous toll. He wondered what his old constituents would think. There was lost time with the family to be made up. You either win or lose. That's all there is to it. You win because you're brilliant or clever or had superb media or great staff. He who lost had a lousy campaign, lousy staff, bad media. You start out saying, 'What does it take to get the voters to vote for me in New Hampshire, and what does it take to get them to vote for me in Florida the following week, and what will it take in Wisconsin?' By and large, people in Democratic primaries vote their strongest emotions, their insides: 'Send them a message.' What a way to pick the leader of this country! The whole system stinks. Crazy. Crazy. Crazy."

Power struggles and ego bruises occur in any competitive situation — a business, a university, a church hierarchy — and perhaps it is only fitting that they seem to be most intense where the stakes are the highest: in the race for the presidency of the United States. But their intensity seems to have grown — as have other problems, such as candidate fatigue — with the changes that have taken place in presidential campaigns since 1960. In 1960, styles changed, and after that so did the rules — formal and informal. The dilemma is that many of the changes are for the better, but at great cost to the candidate's time and energy. In 1960, John Kennedy won the nomination by having won a few primaries and having had major states "delivered" at the convention by those who controlled the states' party machinery: John Bailey and Abraham Ribicoff in Connecticut; David Lawrence and William Green in Pennsylvania; Michael DiSalle in Ohio; Richard Daley in Illinois. The party bosses could not deliver to a candidate with no support or stop a candidate with overwhelming support, but they were in a position to have a decisive effect on the outcome of a convention. It was probably the candidacy of Barry Goldwater for the Republican nomination in 1964 that began to change the rules of the game. Goldwater's grass-roots organizing — a kind of guerrilla action by private individuals against the party hierarchy — showed new ways to win state caucuses and primaries, and established a model that was followed by Eugene McCarthy in 1968 and by George McGovern in 1972 and is being adopted by a number of the current Democratic candidates. At the same time, after its 1968 convention the Democratic party began to establish ground rules for state caucuses and primaries. One result is that the processes are more open and democratic, and invite more participation by citizens. Another is a drastic change in the nature of campaigns.

In recent campaigns for both the nomination and the election, a number of practices have developed. To win in the primaries or the caucuses, candidates must — or think they must — build extensive organizations of people who will attend the caucuses, canvass, and get out the vote. In order to become known or to get coverage, candidates chase from "media market" to "media market" — preferably hitting three in one day, with at least two of the three in different states. If there is no particular reason for a candidate to turn up in an area, a reason must be devised. Finding the reason for a candidate to appear in Pittsburgh a fifteenth time can require some imagination. If there is doubt that the media will see fit to cover what the candidate has to say, or if he has nothing new to say, a "media event" may be concocted: the candidate rushes into a supermarket, holds up a package of hamburger, and decries the rise in the price of meat; the candidate milks a cow, descends into a coal mine. During his 1972 presidential campaign, George McGovern stopped at a farm in Iowa so that he could be photographed on the porch of an old farmhouse discussing farm problems, and then, for good measure, proceeded, with the camera crews, to the farm's cornfield and pigpen, to be photographed there. What such events do to the dignity of the candidates and also of politics, and how much they contribute to the enlightenment of the electorate, is questionable. In any case, they are part of what consumes a candidate's time, drains his energy, and exposes his nerves.

In late September, I had a talk with Kenneth O'Donnell, who was one of John Kennedy's chief political advisers. O'Donnell is now a businessman in Boston, but, like so many who have been in politics, he still hears its siren song.

"We entered only seven primaries in 1960," O'Donnell pointed out. "It was a very different ballgame. We had religion as an issue, age as an issue, and an incumbent vice-president as our opponent. Then we had a beautiful candidate. Geez, we had a candidate. Now you're in a different situation. You have to divide the candidates into different groups. There are those who wait for the convention. Teddy Kennedy can,

Muskie can, Humphrey can — they're known. Then, you have guys like Sargent Shriver, Morris Udall, Birch Bayh — they have to run. Henry Jackson is in that position."

Shifting back to the subject of campaigns, O'Donnell said, "You know what they care about in the party? Who's going to be sheriff. If I'm sitting with Richard Daley, I'm looking for a candidate who helps the ticket — who elects me attorney general. I care about who's going to be the sheriff, the judge, the D.A. Do you know how much they cared in West Virginia who was going to be president? Zero. Now everybody's talking about SALT and détente — nobody cares about that in Boston. They care about busing and about jobs. About themselves. It's a terrible, horrendous course, you know. People expect you to do things every day. I don't think the fact that you went to three hot dog plants in the morning makes you a better president. We did it, and it was almost embarrassing. John Kennedy opened his Wisconsin campaign at five o'clock in the morning at an Oscar Mayer plant. Do you think anyone cared? But if you don't do it people think you're lazy and arrogant. If you do it, it means you're willing to work, that's all. Estes Kefauver began it. But people do want to see the candidate and ought to see the candidate."

I asked O'Donnell where he would draw the line.

"I don't know," he replied. "There's a great deal of talk about the question of whether there should be a national primary or regional primaries. That's something we have to think more about. First, you have to get name recognition. The average guy in the street says, 'Who's Birch Bayh?' People say, 'Who's Scoop Jackson?' That's what the problem is. Everybody knows Ted Kennedy's name. They don't know if he's Jack Kennedy or Bob Kennedy or Ted Kennedy. In 1960, between Kennedy and Humphrey, it came down to who could lead the country. We haven't had that since. In 1968, the war was the issue, and Humphrey was trapped. In 1972, McGovern beat Humphrey in the primaries, but he did it in a way that lost him the election. This is a brand-new situation, and nobody knows what it's about. As of now, nobody knows anything."

Among the truisms heard currently is that within the Democratic party in 1968 and 1972 the Vietnam war was a galvanizing issue, which stirred people into working for Eugene McCarthy and George McGovern, but that no such issue exists now. In those years, it was the cause more than the personalities that defined the Democratic struggle; at present there is no similar compelling cause. It has been the case that those wings of the major parties which are most driven by ideology — for the Republicans, the right; for the Democrats, the left — work hardest in the primaries and caucuses, and thus the results are skewed toward those wings. It was this phenomenon that caused the Republicans to nominate Gold-

water, the Democrats to nominate McGovern — each losing disastrously in the general election. Nixon won the Republican nomination
in 1968 by spreading himself across the "middle" of the party, and now
several Democrats are trying to figure out how to win the nomination
without committing what has come to be known as "the McGovern mistake." The search is for a potion that will arouse nonideological passion.

Fred Dutton is a Washington lawyer who has been involved in the
presidential campaigns of Adlai Stevenson, John Kennedy, Robert Kennedy, and George McGovern. During the Kennedy administration, he
worked in the White House and the State Department. He is an unconventional man, and tends to think about politics in terms of mood and
style rather than of mechanics. He is one of the people in Washington
who are consulted by politicians and journalists for a sense of what to
do or of what is going on. Over lunch one day, I asked Dutton to talk to
me not about "who's ahead" but about campaigns.

"The present campaign styles were set by Nixon and Kennedy in 1960,"
he said. "Both were bright young politicians at the top of their form.
The Eisenhower period had burned itself out. Robert Montgomery, as
an adviser to Eisenhower, had been toying with TV. Kennedy and Nixon
set the new style: standing at microphones, no heavy podium — all sorts
of new techniques. They recognized that the idea was to sell themselves,
to put across a style. We are still in the dregs of 1960. There is nothing
creative. The current candidates are rote figures, automatons, responding in a hack way to 1960. The big changes came when Roosevelt made
effective use of the radio, and Kennedy and Nixon used their new techniques in 1960. In fairness, campaign styles haven't changed very often.
The early presidents — Jefferson and the others — offered themselves
to the voters in a lofty manner; they spoke from on high, were relaxed,
cool. The first big change in style was by Andrew Jackson after he lost
in 1824; in 1828 he campaigned like crazy, and personalized contact with
the public. In the process, he expanded the electoral base. National political conventions began early in the 1830s, and then we started to get
the bunting, the torchlight parades, keynote addresses. That was the
beginning of P.R. in politics; of slogans — guys like William Henry Har-
rison and Zachary Taylor running on slogans. It was one of the most
creative periods in politics, but it came about because the candidates
couldn't come to grips with the emerging issues — the diverging economies of the North and the South, slavery. The slogans and the hoopla
were to divert attention from substantive questions. In 1896, Mark Hanna,
trying to get William McKinley elected, organized county chairmen and
outside groups and sent them out on trains to Ohio to see McKinley.
Mark Hanna is generally considered the first expert in organizational
politics. Roosevelt was the first guy who used the radio effectively; TV

wasn't really used with any imagination until 1960. Kennedy and Nixon pulled out all the stops, and we got to the jet planing and the three stops a day. The problem is that style — the communication of the implicit — has become self-conscious. Everything has become organized, unspontaneous. The implicit and the explicit, the word and the picture should go together. What has happened is that they have diverged, and there is so much that is clearly phony. It is as if Kennedy, instead of relying on his good looks, had worried about getting his picture taken in front of the Statue of Liberty, as Lyndon Johnson did. The Statue of Liberty is a good thing. The Statue of Liberty with a politician in front of it is a phony. By the time Scoop Jackson makes a tour in California, all the humanity and spontaneity are gone. Everything is overorganized. It's the bureaucratization of politics. My guess is that in the next round we're going to get back to substantive people. Someone is going to have to get himself across as a real person. Campaigns should change. The country is going through a withdrawal. It's tired. I tell potential candidates, 'Don't be frenetic. Don't run around the country. Don't do three stops a day. You may have to get around and see power brokers and groups, but take the heat out of it. It's too frenetic.' Then they ask how they would get on television and in the papers. I tell them, 'Get some ideas; get good people around you.' They don't need the daily TV or press story. The real political animal needs to see his name in the paper. They lose all quality control. If they get on Cronkite or Chancellor three times a year with something classy it's better than fifty times a year."

Dutton continued, "People are looking for more spiritual qualities in their leaders. The guy who is going to break through is going to have fresh proposals, and is not going to fit the political stereotypes. All that the candidates are doing now, at a time when people hate politicians, is acting like politicians. These guys who are staying above the battle — the Hubert Humphreys, the Muskies, the Gaylord Nelsons — are being smarter. Mondale was very shrewd. He saw what kind of person he did not want to be, that he would get cut up by the meat grinder, that it was a demeaning process that would make him a lesser man. His was a shrewder judgment than people thought. The best strategy now is to stay out of it and take the chance that nobody will emerge from the primaries and caucuses in a position to win the convention. Muskie and Humphrey can sit it out, make thoughtful speeches. Like de Gaulle in 1946, going off to the side and waiting to be called. It's one of the oldest tricks in politics."

Early this November, Humphrey, who was being widely touted as the possible Democratic nominee — as was Muskie four years ago — told Jules Witcover, of the *Washington Post*, "It's my judgment that right now the person that has no ambition, no declared ambitions, is more credible," and he added, "He's freer. You don't have to go around weighing every word as you inevitably do when you become a candidate. . . . The minute you get in it, you're just another one of them."

Dutton went on, "I favor the reform rules, but they are making politics more organizational, when what we need is more free form. And if the result is that apathy and cynicism become even greater, we may be worse off than ever. You have more midgets, more faceless people, surrounding campaigns. And the kinds of people you have around in the campaign can determine much more about a presidency than you think. Nixon ran a Byzantine, secretive campaign and the same kind of administration."

I asked Dutton if that was not a question of the character of the candidate himself.

He replied, "It's the individual verifying himself in the campaign and then in office. How good is he at putting together a staff? Can he move from state politics to shark-infested national politics?"

I asked Dutton if he felt that campaigns call for the wrong qualities in people.

He replied, "The White House operation is more like a campaign than people think: the number of hardball questions that come in to a president every hour; how much thought goes into a speech. Campaigns are highly imperfect schools for the White House. They are learning exercises. You learn that some issues go and some don't. You don't go out there to preach at people, you go out there to lead. You have to find out where you can lead them. How much stamina do you have? How much can you take the stress of a complicated society? The White House is a hurly-burly job. If you can't stand the strains, you shouldn't be in that league; you should do something else — be a senator, a preacher, a philosopher. A campaign is a frenetic, superficial, compulsive, neurotic process. Can you come across on current technology — not by being handsome but by coming across? Do you understand the mood of the country? The good candidate learns how far he can go, what his stamina is, what the good camera angles are. If you can't reconcile differences within your campaign staff, can't make decisions, you probably can't do those things in the White House. If you can't slow down the pace of a campaign, you can't slow down the pace in the White House. If you can't structure your emotional or decisional process in a campaign, you can't do it in the White House. Ninety-five to ninety-nine percent of those who run don't think beyond the point of winning; they don't think about accumulating the authority and power to do things once they are in office. Just winning the election is not enough; you also have to come out of it with the power to govern. The candidates run as if they were running for sheriff, yet the next day one of them is going to take over the White House. Eventually, we'll move to new political forms, and then those will become trite, too."

THE GROWTH OF PRESIDEN-
tial primaries, hailed by their advocates as a return to grass-roots
democracy, continued unabated in the
1970s and peaked in 1980, when thirty-
four states and the District of Columbia held primaries for the selection of
delegates to the national nominating
conventions. Democratic party leaders, however, who had had their
doubts about the grass-roots process
all along because they were largely
excluded from it, took charge to
change the rules for delegate selection after President Jimmy Carter's
defeat in 1980. Many congressional
Democrats, joined by state and local
party leaders, felt that Carter, like
McGovern before him, was unrepre-
sentative of the party's mainstream.
Primaries generally attract a relatively
low turnout of party activists who neither represent broad party membership nor the wider electorate whose
support is necessary for victory in November. The Democratic National
Committee (DNC) provided that for
the 1984 convention 14 percent of the
delegates would represent the party
leadership and would be chosen
through regular party channels rather
than by primary. House and Senate

party caucuses selected two-thirds of
their members to attend the convention. All members of the DNC were
also delegates, as were governors,
mayors, and other leaders chosen by
state and local party organizations.

The moderate backlash against the
grass-roots selection of presidential
candidates also led to the reduction
in the number of primaries to twenty-
eight in 1984; however, the primary
states still controlled the majority of
delegates, forcing all serious candidates for the nomination to run in
them. Moreover, candidates always
campaign in the remaining states that
hold caucuses for the selection of
delegates. A victory in the Iowa caucuses, for example, is as important as
winning the New Hampshire primary
to establish candidates' credibility.
Energy and resources must be poured
into caucus as well as primary states.

The following selection depicts the
exhausting campaigns of Walter Mondale, Gary Hart, and Jesse Jackson for
the 1984 Democratic presidential
nomination. Little has changed from
Elizabeth Drew's description, in the
previous selection, of the physical and
emotional demands of campaigning.

2

Kurt Andersen
CAMPAIGN 1984: FACING THE
FATIGUE FACTOR

The Denver reporter, who had not seen Gary Hart for weeks, thought he looked terrible — haggard, pale, tapped out. "Don't you badly need a rest?" he asked when the candidate arrived in Colorado last week as the votes were being counted in Pennsylvania. Hart hemmed, hawed, then rasped almost plaintively, "Tomorrow will be the first day we've had off since Christmas." Back in Philadelphia, Walter Mondale, the eventual victor, had turned peevish during his last go-round of a day with reporters. Would he predict his margin of victory, a newsman asked. "No," snapped an irritated Mondale. Is something wrong? asked the next questioner. "Nothing." barked Mondale. Then he caught himself and apologized. "I am getting what is known as punchy," he said. "I don't think I've been home in five weeks."

Four weeks, in fact. But none of the three men who remain in the race for the Democratic nomination can be blamed if they lose track of a few days here, a week or so there. Even Jesse Jackson, the youngest of them, is exhausted. "He doesn't sleep," jokes a Jackson aide. "He just faints a while." Hart, forty-seven, Mondale, fifty-six, and Jackson, forty-two, have been on the road for more than a year. Since January they have had to go at a ferocious pace, running an electoral marathon at sprinters' speeds. It shows. The survivors often look drawn and ashen, and all have made blunders because of fatigue. Indeed, the intensity of this year's primary rigors, physical and emotional, may be unprecedented. Says one drained journalist, a veteran who is trooping after Jackson: "There has never been anything like this. Never."

The candidates are enjoying a bit of a respite right now. But during the high-pitched seven weeks from Iowa's caucuses to Pennsylvania's primary, each roared in and out of hundreds of towns, eating perfunctorily and exercising hardly at all. Sleep comes a few hours at a time in stuffy rooms and cramped airplane seats. The adrenaline gushes all day long. Every remark, every intellectual twitch or tic is scrutinized, recorded, analyzed. In the frenzy of political combat, the candidate must improvise crucial strategic moves, keep his facts straight and try to look presidential to boot. Senator John Glenn said he was "perpetually tired" two months before the first primary. Fellow dropout George McGovern seemed well rested, even twinkly, while he was in the race. Still, he says, "Fatigue is public enemy No. 1. It has become a most serious problem in American politics."

The standard campaign day just before any primary includes a couple of events in each of five cities. Mondale may hold one season record: The day before Super Tuesday, he hit eight Southern cities in eighteen hours. During one twenty-four hour period before the Pennsylvania primary, Jackson flew aboard a twelve-seat turboprop plane from Pittsburgh to Madison, Wisconsin, to Milwaukee to New Orleans. Along the way he delivered five speeches and slept about five hours. Two weeks ago, Jackson made a campaign appearance that ended at 10:30 P.M. in Albany. He then traveled to Harrisburg, Pennsylvania, and went to an antinuclear rally from 4 to 6 the next morning, after that attending a meeting of black state legislators at 10 A.M.

For the two front runners, last Monday's schedules were typically tough. Mondale awoke at dawn in Wilkes-Barre and toured a dress factory. He flew to Erie for a runway press conference, then to Pittsburgh for another runway press conference. In Harrisburg, Mondale waited as usual for the press to shuffle out of the 727 ("How many more?" he croaked as the reporters filed by), so that the TV news cameramen could get a clear shot of him disembarking. For the 100 supporters gathered on the tarmac, he recited his routine speech, then climbed back up the ramp. On to Philadelphia for a fourth runway press conference ("Vice-President Mondale, what is your favorite color?"), and then to Washington for a fund-raising dinner.

Hart's Monday, meanwhile, publicly began at the Philadelphia docks for a 7:30 A.M. mingle with longshoremen. He flew off to Allentown and Bethlehem to stroll through a steel plant and hold a press conference, but engine problems kept him from leaving for Pittsburgh on time. While a pair of small Learjets were being hired, Hart felt obliged to caper around for photographers (he posed in a cockpit wearing dark glasses and pilot's cap) and to discuss the Democrats' alleged indulgence of black anti-Semitism. At Pittsburgh's airport (four hours after Mondale had touched down there), he met with a group of old people bused out for the occasion, then submitted to three separate television interviews and a twenty-minute radio call-in show. During his hour in Erie, Hart gave another press conference and, growing ever more hoarse with bronchitis, addressed a rally. From there he flew to Trenton, New Jersey, drove back into Pennsylvania for a nighttime rally in a shopping mall, and finally returned at 11 P.M. to Philadelphia — where the day had begun.

The ceaseless scurrying would tax anyone. The more ineffable pressures the candidates face, to regain or maintain momentum, to remain intellectually focused but not rigid, are at least as burdensome. Frequent high-stakes televised debates (eight so far) have been an extra drain on emotional resources. "The debates are particularly difficult," says Oliver ("Pudge") Henkel, Hart's campaign manager. "It's a major change of pace from the rest of the campaign. It is so intense that there's invariably a letdown afterward."

The advanced stages of candidate fatigue are obvious. "I can tell," Mondale says. "My syntax starts going first." Press Secretary Maxine Isaacs notes that his looks go too: "He gets big bags under his eyes." Other aides say Mondale gets grouchy as long days wind down.

A bushed candidate is more prone to mistakes and misstatements. Usually the bungles are minor. When Mondale was asked in Pennsylvania about Hart's proposal for a $10-per-bbbl. tax on imported oil, he rambled numbly, "It's a question of, ah . . . ah . . . ." He stopped. "I can't think of the name. I'm getting a little tired. I'll get back to it." Yet Mondale, who is rather too buttoned down in public, sometimes loosens up when he is fatigued. Campaigning in upstate New York, he joked that as vice-president he had channeled so much federal money to Rochester, he was afraid he would be investigated.

Jackson fell asleep during two recent interviews. When he is groggy he tends to mix up his trademark parallel constructions. "Jails at their worst," he proclaimed in Ference, Alabama, "are better than schools at their best." Hart last week mistakenly referred to his "nineteen-year-old son"; John Hart is eighteen. The senator (who seems to have a knack for muffing ages) made an odd joke last week about how old he feels. "When we started, I was twenty," he told a little girl who asked if it was difficult running for presedent. "Now I feel like I'm ninety-five."

Hart, perhaps the most driven of the three, has probably committed more serious tactical blunders because of exhaustion. "Gary Hart has been suffering from extreme fatigue since Super Tuesday," contends McGovern. "The errors he made during the Illinois primary were a direct result of fatigue." In Illinois, Hart looked foolish when he accused Mondale of broadcasting unfair advertisements, which, it turned out, did not exist; a Hart commercial attacking a powerful local Democrat aired for two days even after Hart had disclaimed it. Said Press Secretary Kathy Bushkin at the time: "Gary's fatigued now and he's delegating decisions that he used to make before."

Hart and Mondale smoke cigars, but none of the candidates admit to any special relaxation techniques. Indeed, Jackson seems determined to stay cranked up. "I have never known him to rest," says Frank Watkins, his press secretary, "except when he was ordered by the doctor to go to the hospital [for exhaustion, in 1979]." Mondale, before his defeat in New Hampshire, could afford three quiet hours a day in his hotel room; now he relies on naps in transit. Lately, Hart's handlers have tried to schedule only three major campaign events a day. "It's surprising to me," says Henkel, "that Gary is holding up so well, that his psyche is largely intact after this roller-coaster ride."

Roller-coaster ride, shooting the rapids, demolition derby — almost any metaphor involving gut-churning ups and downs or collisions is apt. Candidates seem to think the electorate wants to see them endure incredible campaign pressures. Yet it is unclear whether surviving such a regimen is a measure of presidential mettle. Henkel, new to national politics, thinks not. "The Democratic party has to face up to the punishment this process inflicts on its people," he says. "These four or five months of extremely intense activity are not the best test of a candidate's ability." Hart, however, has no real complaints. And Mondale, who quit a presidential candidacy once before, approves of the campaign's intensity. "I think it tests much of the same qualities needed in a president," he says, such as "decision making under fire, the ability to unify and persuade."

Pushed and inspected for unrelenting months, all the candidates last week had some R. and R. On Wednesday, Mondale had a relatively calm day in Phoenix, joking with a winner's swagger about his fatigue. "I'm not tired," he said. "But the Smithsonian called and wanted my eyeballs." Hart, still troubled by bronchitis and a nasty cough, spent the time at home in Denver, resting up and swallowing antibiotics. "The day off helped a lot," Hart said on Thursday — in between high-pressure public appearances in Missouri, right back on the campaign trail.

BOLD, CHARISMATIC, DEDI-cated, driven, and flamboyant are among the adjectives that describe Jesse Jackson. He stands before his black audiences as a role model, asking them to repeat after him, "I am somebody!" His campaign for the Democratic presidential nomination mobilized blacks in unprecedented numbers, making their voice heard in party politics as it had never been before. Many successful black politicians had preceded him at the local level, but Jackson was the first black candidate to make a serious run for the presidency.

Jesse Jackson's political roots are in the 1960s, when he participated in sit-ins and protest marches while attending the all-black North Carolina Agricultural and Technical College in Greensboro. Clearly adept at politics, he became president of the student body, and led the 1963 student sit-ins in Greensboro.

Although politics became his chosen profession, Jackson might well have gone in another direction. A natural athlete, he became a star three-letter man in high school on the football, basketball, and baseball teams. Both the New York Giants and the Chicago White Sox recruited him, the Giants outbidding the Sox with an offer of $6,000. Jackson, however, noting that the star white player from his Greenville, North Carolina, high school was offered $95,000 by the White Sox, refused the contract and accepted an athletic scholarship at the University of Illinois instead. There, the football coach told him that blacks were supposed to be linemen, not quarterbacks. Jackson characteristi-cally would have none of that, and he transferred to Greensboro after his freshman year, where he soon became the quarterback of the football team.

Jackson decided to be a minister in 1965, a year after his graduation from college. Black ministers are political as well as religious leaders, who shape both the content and style of black politics. Jackson soon became a protégé of the Reverend Martin Luther King, Jr., and an active participant in the civil rights movement. He went on the Selma march with King in 1965 and was with him when he was assassinated three years later. He helped King organize Operation Bread Basket in Chicago, an economic boycott by blacks of businesses they believed practiced discrimination. Jackson's extraordinary activity and success in leading the black community in Chicago provided him with the political base to establish Operation PUSH (People United to Serve Humanity) to boost the education and opportunities of ghetto children.

Whatever position Jackson occupies, he is always a master of the media, a consummate stylist who knows how to attract media and therefore public attention. Long before he ran for the presidency his name was a household word in the white as well as the black community. While he headed PUSH, one journalist wrote, "Jesse Jackson's staged entrances into page one politics are small masterpieces of showmanship. In the Middle East, at Camp David, wherever cameramen gather, he descends as if on wires, deus ex video. He stays just long enough to spin off a few provocative quotes, in self-contained twenty-second snippets, shrewdly timed to accommodate the editors in the cutting room. Then he is up and away back to his Chicago base. . . ."[1] Both style and substance helped Jackson to change the face of presidential politics in 1984. His campaign is the subject of the following selection.

3 Evan Thomas
CAMPAIGNING WITH JESSE JACKSON: PRIDE AND PREJUDICE

There is the Jesse Jackson that blacks revere. He is the embodiment of black pride, an incandescent force glowing beside dull white politicians, demanding respect and "our fair share." He is the powerbroker who is ignored or patronized at great risk.

There is the Jesse Jackson that many whites distrust and some even fear. He is the former black radical, the civil rights leader who threatened white businessmen with economic boycotts, the presidential candidate who called Jews "Hymie" and New York City "Hymietown." In his shadow, neither embraced nor disavowed, stands Minister Louis Farrakhan, leader of the Nation of Islam, a Black Muslim sect, who has praised Hitler and seemed to threaten a black reporter with death.

In recent weeks, these conflicting perceptions of Jesse Jackson have come to overshadow his remarkable achievements in the Democratic primaries. Almost overnight, he shattered the prevailing wisdom that a black could not make a credible run for the presidency. He has spurred an unprecedented black voter turnout, outlasted five more politically experienced white rivals, and picked up enough delegates and prestige to play a major role at the Democratic convention in July. Says former Democratic National Committee Chairman Robert Strauss: "Jesse Jackson has had a larger impact on American politics than either he or anyone else anticipated." But as his successes multiplied, so did concerns about his candidacy. Would he raise the arm of the Democratic nominee in San Francisco, or stalk angrily from the convention hall? Would he bring out the black vote for Democrats in November, or sit sulking on the sidelines? Would his efforts lead to black political power or white backlash?

The Jackson campaign, unavoidably, has brought questions of race

[1]Clarence Page, "Jesse Jackson — 'I am somebody!' . . . But Who?" *The Washington Monthly*, February 1980, p. 26.

back to the forefront of American politics. The candidate himself has not used race in a demagogic way, as George Wallace did in 1968. Indeed, Jackson has tried to add other colors to his Rainbow Coalition. But the electorate is polarized nevertheless, with blacks voting overwhelmingly for Jackson and whites voting overwhelmingly for white candidates. "A certain latent racism has come out," says Garry Wills, Henry Luce Professor of American Culture and Public Policy at Northwestern University. "People say, 'Whenever I hear somebody stir up crowds, I think of Hitler.' That kind of comment shows a blindness to black style, and it's most often said by people who've never heard a black church service."

Jackson's appeals to black pride, almost by definition, are racially charged. In effect, he is asking blacks to vote for him because he is black. The white majority would quickly condemn a white candidate who practiced such overt racial politics. But with blacks, the situation is far more delicate. Sensitive to the victimization of blacks throughout American history, whites tend to be reticent about criticizing them, especially on racial matters.

Because of his color, and because he was never given a realistic chance of winning the nomination, Jackson has been treated differently from the other candidates. His rivals dealt with him gingerly, hoping not to alienate potential black support in the fall. The press concentrated on his vivid campaign style and rarely challenged his positions on the issues. He did not come under intense press scrutiny until his "Hymie" remark touched off conflicting charges of white and black racism. "Jesse hasn't injected racism into politics. His campaign has only brought to the surface things that were there long before," insists Ernest Green, one of Jackson's closest advisers. "To make that accusation is a classic case of blaming the victim for the crime."

Whoever was to blame, the flaring of the racial issue was like jiggling political nitroglycerin. Avoiding an explosion became as important to Democrats as choosing their presidential nominee. Their best hope was that the debate would be constructive and clear the air for the fall. Racism in the United States is less obvious than in the past but it has hardly gone away, and some thought that a candid discussion of the issue could strengthen the party. As Hodding Carter, an official in the Carter administration and a crusader for civil rights as a Mississippi newspaper editor in the 1960s, wrote last week, "We ought to thank Mr. Jackson for running. Not because he should or shouldn't be president, but because his candidacy has helped to put race and things racial back in public view where they belong."

Getting the public's attention has been a Jackson trademark from the time he first worked for Martin Luther King, Jr. in 1966. Over the years, as a preacher, a civil rights leader and now a politician, he has kept the same goal: instilling in blacks a sense of self-worth. The message he gave black teen-agers as he toured the country during the late 1970s for his PUSH (People United to Serve Humanity) for Excellence, Inc., program was identical to the one delivered by white middle-class parents to their teen-age children, except that it came from a black man wearing an Afro haircut and speaking in rhyme. "Down with dope! Up with hope!" Jackson would shout. "Less than your best is a sin! You are not a man because you can make a baby! It takes a man to raise one!" By the end of these exhortations, schoolchildren would line up to sign pledges that they would study for two hours every school night, without radio or TV.

In recent years, Jackson has stressed an additional message: that the path to black success was through the polling place. With the same evangelical style, he intoned to audiences, "There's a freedom train acoming. But you got to be registered to ride!" Then and there he would march listeners to the courthouse to sign voter rolls. Even Farrakhan, who has claimed that the American political process was too "corrupt" to deserve black votes, enrolled.

At rally after rally, Jackson cried, "Hands that picked cotton will pick the president! From the guttermost to the uttermost! From the outhouse to the White House!" And the audiences would pick up the chant: "Run, Jesse, run! Run, Jesse, run!" Jackson, forty-two, finally heeded the chant — against the wishes of many black leaders. Esablished black politicians like Atlanta Mayor Andrew Young, Los Angeles Mayor Tom Bradley, and Harlem Congressman Charles Rangel feared that Jackson would split the liberal vote for Mondale and thereby nominate the more conservative John Glenn. They feared that Jackson knew too little about conventional politics, that he was too freewheeling and flamboyant. They feared he would fail and embarrass an entire race. Not a few whites agreed.

They were wrong. Early polls showed that Jackson could take only about 40 percent of the black vote. But in the most recent three big primaries — Illinois, New York, and Pennsylvania — Jackson won between 74 percent and 89 percent of the black vote. In New York, he came within two percentage points of beating Gary Hart. Many political experts predicted that Jackson would have about 150 delegates with him going into the Democratic convention. It now appears that he could have twice that many. "Whether I win or lose," Jackson declares, "American politics will never be the same."

Jackson has overcome a lack of funds (he has raised about $2 million, compared with about $15 million for Mondale and $3 million for Hart) and a campaign organization that does not deserve the name. The black church is Jackson's base and a principal source of his funds (collected by passing the hat to parishioners, who drop in wrinkled dollar bills as

Jackson exhorts, "Don't make change, just drop it in the bucket!"). On the Jackson campaign, schedules are merely suggestions, and Secret Service agents joke that the candidate runs on "J.S.T." — Jesse Standard Time. Although he has not bought a single television advertisement, he has become a fixture on the evening news, sopping up a fortune's worth of "free media."

A major breakthrough for Jackson occurred when the eight Democratic contenders squared off for their first national debate, which came before the New Hampshire primary. Jackson more than held his own; he was poised, reasonable, and witty. He added to his credibility as a candidate by playing peacemaker when Hart and Mondale squabbled at the New York debate. Says Minerva Johnican, a Memphis city councilwoman and Hart supporter: "Jesse really surprised a lot of people. Previously, other black leaders thought he was an opportunist, out for himself and himself only. I think the perception of Jackson has changed."

Jackson has extraordinary appeal among young blacks, but he has also been able to win over middle-class and older blacks, many of whom were dubious. They see him as an alternative to Michael Jackson and "Mr. T" of television's *The A-Team* as a black role model for their children. Says retired schoolteacher Jessie Adderley, seventy-five, mother of the late jazz musician Cannonball Adderley and grandmother of Brown and Yale students: "Black youngsters looking at Reverend Jackson will have the feeling now they have a chance. Maybe now they will buckle down and apply themselves."

The dream of growing up to be president one day may be a cliché, but until Jackson came along it was only a white cliché. More immediately, Jackson has inspired black adults to run for local office. They were winning on the local level already, especially in cities (four of the six largest have black mayors), but Jackson for the first time has demonstrated black political power on the national level.

Although few have voted for Jackson, many whites say they admire him. In New York, where he polled only 7 percent of the white vote, Jackson was seen as an "attractive, forceful leader" by two out of three voters, a higher positive rating than given to either Hart or Mondale, according to a Harris poll. Said pollster Louis Harris: "Jackson might be president if he were white."

That Jackson cannot win the Democratic nomination does not discourage blacks from supporting him. By voting for him, blacks cast "a vote of confidence in themselves," says Albert McDaniel, forty-four, an administrator for a skills-training school in Chicago. "Jackson is saying you have to judge winning in more than one way. The rise of pride among people who never gave a thought to voting — that's winning. People renewing hope in the Democratic system — that's a definite win."

Blacks know that if Jackson goes to the Democratic Convention with enough delegates, he can extract important concessions from the party. Many blacks do not trust white Democrats, no matter how liberal their voting records, to push their interests. Indeed, with the party preoccupied with cutting the federal deficit, issues of vital importance to blacks — affirmative action, teenage unemployment, the black underclass — are hardly discussed by white candidates. Says Max Palevsky, a liberal activist in Los Angeles: "The Democrats have lost their way and become a not too articulate reflection of the Republicans. Instead of sweeping these issues under the rug, Jackson is lifting the rug up."

A vote for Mondale or Hart, Jackson tells voters, means "getting off a Republican elephant and onto a Democratic donkey going in the same direction, just a little slower. We need a new direction. It is better to lose an election going in the right direction than win going in the wrong direction." Some blacks carry that logic to its literal conclusion. Asked if she feared that a vote for Jackson would actually help Reagan, Chicago Secretary Selestine Humphrey answered, "I don't want to see Reagan back, but if that's the price black people have to pay for some respect, I say let's pay it." The message to white Democrats is that black voters can no longer be taken for granted because they have "nowhere else to go." Says Jackson: "We had to break the dependency syndrome. We moved from a relationship born of paternalism to one born of power."

Having taken Jackson lightly at first, neither heeding him nor holding him accountable, many whites were unsettled by his soaring prominence. They scrutinized his calls for racial pride, looking for overt signs of racism. Unfortunately, Jackson provided one. A foolish and offensive remark, spoken in an unguarded moment, set off a chain of events that threatened to overwhelm Jackson's accomplishments with controversy and bitterness.

"Let's talk black talk," Jackson said to two black reporters on January 25 as he waited for a flight at Washington's National Airport. It was in the course of that conversation that Jackson dropped his "Hymie" bombshell. One of the reporters, Milton Coleman of the *Washington Post*, passed on the remark to a white colleague, Rick Atkinson, who used it in the thirty-seventh paragraph of a story about Jackson's foreign policy. Jackson at first insisted that he had no recollection of making the remark, then apologized in a synagogue two days before the New Hampshire primary.

The controversy had almost subsided when Farrakhan, the Muslim leader who has been making appearances with Jackson and furnishing him with bodyguards, declared on a radio sermon, "We're going to make an example of Milton Coleman! What do [we] intend to do? At this point no physical harm . . . One day soon we will punish you with death!" As a gratuitous aside, Farrakhan allowed that Hitler was "a very great man" albeit a "wicked" one.

Until his incendiary words burst into national headlines, Farrakhan, fifty, was — to whites, at least — the obscure leader of a fringe movement. A onetime nightclub singer known as the Charmer, Farrakhan in 1955 joined the puritanical (no smoking or drinking) Nation of Islam, a black separatist group founded by Elijah Muhammad in the 1930s. Once 250,000-members strong, the Nation of Islam split apart upon Muhammad's death in 1975. His son Imam W. Deen Muhammad renamed the group the American Muslim Mission, rejected many of his father's teachings, and began admitting whites. Farrakhan formed his own faction, keeping the Nation of Islam name and prophesying that one day white "devils" would be incinerated by holy fire, leaving Black Muslims to rule the earth. Farrakhan can claim only between 5,000 and 10,000 followers, but his influence is spread by a weekly radio show. Says he: "I never dreamed that my words, spoken not on his platform but on my own, on my own radio show, paid for with our own money, would be taken and used by the media to bring me to public attention."

Farrakhan, in the tradition of Elijah Muhammad, speaks in an apocalyptic tongue that many whites find frightening but that many blacks do not take seriously. "I don't represent violence," Farrakhan insisted to *Time.* "Not at all, and I'm not antiwhite, I'm against that which whites have done to blacks . . . we're antioppression, antityranny, antiexploitation." By any standard, however, his remarks were outrageous in a presidential campaign, and they demanded a quick denunciation from Jackson. None was forthcoming. Instead, Jackson commented that Coleman and Farrakhan were "two very able professionals caught in a cycle that could be damaging to their careers." He later stated that Farrakhan's apparent death threat was "counterproductive" and "wrong," but he complained that the pressures to disavow Farrakhan were a "form of harrassment" by the white media. Why not badger President Reagan to reject his endorsement by the Ku Klux Klan? Jackson asked reporters. The furthest Jackson would go was to demote Farrakhan from "surrogate" to "supporter."

Jackson's "Hymie" slur and his failure to repudiate Farrakhan caused outrage in several respected quarters. The *New Republic,* a leading liberal magazine with a strong pro-Israel slant, editorialized that Jackson's "potential for blighting the future of interracial politics and for wounding the Democratic party now seems great indeed." Carl T. Rowan, the most widely circulated black columnist, warned that Jackson might be stirring a white backlash that would help reelect Reagan, "in which case Jackson is going to have to face the conscience-searing question: Why, in his stubborn embrace of a few black demagogues, he has made it so easy for the Reaganites to appeal to white racism?"

Jewish leaders were skeptical of Jackson to begin with. Sympathetic to the demand for a Palestinian homeland, Jackson was borne aloft by Arabs shouting, "Arafat! Jackson!" on a trip to the Middle East in 1979. He was also quoted as saying that he was "tired of hearing about the Holocaust" — a comment that he says was taken out of context. Today many Jewish leaders are convinced that Jackson is anti-Semitic. Although Jews and black leaders have had their differences — particularly on the use of racial quotas, which are anathema to Jews but favored by many blacks as a cure for historic discrimination — the two groups have often worked together politically. Jewish voters, for example, were supportive of black mayoral candidates in Los Angeles, Chicago, and Philadelphia. The conflict with Jackson threatens to scuttle that affinity.

The Republicans naturally hope that Jackson will drive Jewish voters right out of the Democratic party. Vice-President George Bush, acting in his role of GOP stalking horse for 1984, was quick to condemn not only Farrakhan and Jackson but Mondale and Hart, neither of whom made much of an issue of the ethnic slurs in order to avoid offending black voters. Bush's ploy was "a great political stroke," admitted a Mondale aide. "It was simple, crude, and effective."

The Republicans are also counting on Jackson to push other threatened whites into the GOP column. Conservative Jesse Helms even invokes Jackson's name in fund-raising solicitations (in one letter, twenty-four times). Republican strategists predict that Jackson will register more whites for the Republicans than blacks for the Democrats. Each side aims to sign up about 2 million new voters, but that represents far more of a challenge for blacks, since there are 49 million unregistered whites compared with 7 million unenrolled blacks. Says Lamarr Mooneyham, president of the North Carolina Moral Majority: "If I could afford to pay Jesse, I'd bring him down here every month."

Such a backlash would confirm the worst fears of many mainstream black leaders, who feel that Jackson is ill-versed in the delicate art of building interracial coalitions. Jackson has never held an elected office. Whereas mayors like Young and Bradley needed to court white votes to win elections, Jackson has opted for confrontation, forging all-black protest blocs to demand concessions. At Operation PUSH, he organized boycotts of white businesses in order to win more contracts and jobs for minorities. In the process he was able to wring concessions from such companies as Anheuser-Busch, Coca-Cola, and Kentucky Fried Chicken. Another group under the PUSH umbrella is proving to be a political liability in quite a different way. Last month federal auditors demanded that PUSH-EXCEL return $708,431 of over $3 million in U.S. Department of Education grants awarded between 1978 and 1981. The government claims that PUSH authorities have failed to account for the money properly. Says Jackson casually: "It's really a dispute between auditors and accountants."

By personality and disposition, Jackson is not a perfect choice to make the first significant black bid for the presidency.[1] He is frequently blustery, volatile, and egotistical. But he is the only black leader with the drive and audacity to mount such an extraordinary political campaign. Revolutions of all kinds — political, economic, social — are often led by rough-edged men, and Jackson is unexceptional in their company. The established order is invariably unnerved by firebrands with fiercely held views, especially if those views stir the masses. The press is equally "traumatized," says Jackson, who has grown cool to even the black reporters who trail him. No longer does he indulge in "Let's talk black talk" off-the-record sessions. "I don't trust you all on that level," he tells black reporters he once confided in.

Jackson is better at inspiring hopes and dreams than he is at designing specific programs to help the poor. His critics are biting on this score. Says elections expert Richard Scammon, a conservative Democrat: "Jesse Jackson is a black George Wallace — a Rodney Dangerfield. He wants respect. It's a scream for attention. He has no real program. He doesn't know what he's doing." In private, one of Jackson's Democratic rivals is almost as caustic. "There's still one speech Jackson hasn't given yet," he says. "We still haven't seen his agenda."

Jackson does have an agenda, which, like those of his Democratic opponents, is constrained by the federal budget deficit. He would raise $50 billion from a one- or two-year surtax ranging from 1 percent on incomes of $25,000 to 10 percent on incomes over $90,000. He would save another $80 billion by cutting defense outlays by 20 percent. But if Jackson reduces the deficit by $70 billion, as he proposes, and fulfills his intention to spend $50 billion to rebuild the nation's infrastructure (roads, bridges, water systems, mass transit), he would have only $10 billion left to fight poverty. That amount would not come close to restoring the $25 billion cut from programs affecting the poor by the Reagan administration in 1981.

Jackson's foreign policies are radically noninterventionist, with a pro–Third World tilt. Like Hart and Mondale, he favors a freeze on building and deploying nuclear weapons. He would cut American military forces in Europe and Japan in half over five years, arguing that allies should pay for more of their own defense, which he says now costs the United States $150 billion a year. Critics note correctly that his defense planks would tempt Soviet adventurism, but Jackson dismisses such talk as alarmist. To ease cold war tensions and revive arms-control talks, he would "aggressively negotiate" with the Soviets.

A greater believer in his own powers as a negotiator, especially after

[1] He is not the first black candidate. Congresswoman Shirley Chisholm ran for the Democratic nomination in 1972, winning 152 delegates. Abolitionist Frederick Douglass won a single, complimentary vote at the 1888 Republican Convention.

arranging the release of downed Navy Lieutenant Robert Goodman from Syria last January, Jackson wants to establish a "dialogue" with Palestinian leaders on the issue of an independent Palestinian state, which he advocates. "I've always supported Israel's right to exist with security," Jackson says. "But unless you can talk with adversaries, you cannot help the ally." He would try to curtail United States investments in South Africa, while increasing foreign aid to other African nations. Jackson is unconvinced that Cuba and Nicaragua are fomenting revolution in Central America. He favors "normalizing" relations with the Marxist-led Sandinista regime in Nicaragua, which he says is "on the right side of history," and withdrawing all troops from the region. On the other hand, he does not rule out sending United States troops to the Persian Gulf in the event of a Soviet invasion, and he favors covert United States support of Afghan rebels against the Soviets.

Jackson has a vastly different world view than his Democratic rivals. He says that he was "born in occupied territory, having lived all my developing years under apartheid." (He grew up in South Carolina.) His Third World sympathies make him highly skeptical of United States involvement abroad ("too often we are aligned with the landed gentry, the dictator, the oppressor"), and sometimes too forgiving of the excesses of revolutionary causes. He condemns United States covert operations in Central America as "a form of terrorism," but finds such lawless regimes as Muammar Gaddafi's Libya and the Khmer Rouge in Cambodia merely "distasteful."

Jackson's real issue, the one he cares about most deeply, is voting rights. Although Southern states have long since stopped using literacy tests and police dogs to keep blacks from voting, Jackson claims that they have found more subtle methods of disenfranchisement. Most offensive to him is the "runoff primary" system used in ten Southern states. If no candidate wins a majoirty in a primary, the system forces a second, runoff primary between the two leaders. Blacks can sometimes win the first round, says Jackson, but usually not the second. Without second primaries, he claims, the South would send fifteen more blacks to Congress, and elect scores of blacks to state and local offices. He has made abolishing dual primaries his "litmus test issue."

His demand has puzzled some election experts, provoked defiance by Southern party leaders, and struck fear in the heart of the Democratic National Committee. The experts say that dual primaries do not necessarily discriminate against blacks. A study of nearly 200 state elections in Texas, for example, did not disclose a single instance of a candidate's losing because of his race or ethnicity. Georgia Democratic Party chairman Bert Lance says he is prepared to "go to the wall" to defend the system. Party leaders have a more immediate concern: that Jackson will angrily stalk out of the convention if his demands are not met, taking with him the Democrats' chance to win back the White House.

That fear probably is exaggerated. Jackson sloughs it off as "negative hype and speculation" by the media. Says he: "I am not going to tear up the Democratic party." He vows to be a "healer," not a "spoiler." Last week he called on DNC chairman Charles Manatt, and to Manatt's huge relief promised that he would not bolt the party at the convention. He never intended to, he says. The idea of a walkout was "Manatt's magnificent obsession." It is in Jackson's interest to compromise, and he knows it. If he wants to be the undisputed leader of American blacks — his real goal, many believe, and one that he is on the verge of attaining — he cannot afford to be a renegade. He has to show that he can deliver black votes in November, that he can put a Democratic president in his debt.

At the same time, Jackson must show his black supporters that he has exacted a price for his allegiance. In addition to opposing second primaries, Jackson wants to change party rules that hinder minority candidates by, for instance, requiring that they win 20 percent of the vote in a congressional district to qualify for delegates. Jackson points out that to date he has won 17 percent of the popular vote, yet holds only 7 percent of the delegates. Responding to Jackson's claim that he was "robbed" of 220 delegates, Manatt promised to ask state chairmen to consider allocating Jackson unpledged convention delegates. Meanwhile, Jackson came up with another idea that could touch off debate: automatic voter registration at the age of eighteen. Such a system would demand a philosophical change in the United States, where voting is considered a privilege, not a requirement.

Mondale — or Hart, if he should suddenly surprise — can probably work out a deal with Jackson on most of his demands. (Exception: his 20 percent defense cut, which neither of the major candidates could even consider and which Jackson is unlikely to press.) Last week the Jackson and Mondale camps worked in private to come up with an overall compromise that both sides could live with. It appeared possible that Jackson would agree to abolishing dual primaries only where they can be proved discriminatory, in return for changes at the local level, like reapportioning local election districts, that could put more blacks in state and city offices.

Party leaders are still worried about how the deal will look. If Mondale, say, seems to be snubbing Jackson, he risks offending a very prideful man and losing black support. But if he too eagerly embraces Jackson, he risks turning off large slices of the white electorate. Says one Mondale fund raiser: "The first question Jews ask me is whether Jesse

Jackson is going to be on the ticket as vice-president. The second question is whether Jackson is going to have a cabinet job." Jackson has shown no interest in either, but that has not let Mondale off the hook. Says Scammon: "If Mondale panders to Jackson at the convention, white Southerners and white blue-collar workers would turn away, in addition to the Jews."

Both sides are eager to cut their deal in private, and before the party faithful gather in San Francisco. Jackson could lose leverage if Mondale locks up the nomination before the convention, an increasingly likely prospect. As for Mondale, he cannot afford to be seen on bended knee in public. To beat President Reagan, the party needs a well choreographed but restrained love feast. Says Texas Democratic chairman Robert Slagle: "I'm in absolute horror of a brokered convention. The last thing we need this year is to be playing *Let's Make a Deal* on national TV."

Much depends on how Jackson handles himself in the weeks ahead. If he is intemperate in his public utterances, if he locks himself into unrealistic demands, he could wound the Democratic nominee, discredit himself and further divide the races. But if he reaches a rapprochement with the party's candidate, then campaigns for him in a temperate and intelligent way, Jackson could greatly enlarge the role of blacks in national politics. In that way, Jesse Jackson's candidacy could turn out to be a powerful and positive force, a reminder of the diversity and promise of American politics.

Campaigning in Free Verse

As Always, Jesse Jackson was late — three hours behind schedule this time — as his motorcade sped through downtown Baltimore on a chilly, misty afternoon last week. The procession of cars, vans, and buses wove in and out of rush-hour traffic, red and blue lights flashing and police sirens wailing. Clots of office worders gathered outside the trendy shops and restaurants of Harborplace to watch. The caravan zipped by them and into East Baltimore, an area of sagging row houses, many disfigured by broken or boarded-up windows.

The streets initially were empty, but when the motorcade turned into North Bond, a crowd of 400 people came into view several blocks ahead. Many who had made the mistake of thinking Jackson would keep his schedule had turned out early and been waiting four or even seven hours to greet their hero, but their spirits had not been dimmed. When a navy blue Chrysler New Yorker pulled to a halt and the candidate leaped out, the crowd surged over wooden police barricades chanting, "Win, Jesse, win!" Jackson, smiling broadly, strode into the throng, surrounded by apprehensive Secret Service agents who formed

4

a circle around him; one kept a tight grip on the back of Jackson's raincoat so that he could yank the candidate down immediately if any danger arose. None did; Jackson's admirers obviously wanted only to touch and be touched. A young man dressed in a dirty sweatshirt and blue jeans held his open right hand in front of him and exclaimed in wonder, "I shook his hand! I shook the man's hand!"

Jackson worked his way through the crowd and into a campaign headquarters ("outreach center," in his terminology), and campaign workers arranged the scene for his speech. An aide pointed to the spot where the candidate would stand and shouted, "Rainbow, rainbow!" It was a signal to another assistant to plunge into the predominantly black throng and look for whites who could be brought up front to stand near Jackson, so that photographs would show the preacher as leader of a multiracial rainbow coalition.

There was nothing artificial about the response when Jackson emerged to speak. His talks are not connected discourses but collections of applause lines that bring shouts of "All right! . . . Talk it up, Jesse! . . . Yessir!" building steadily. He begins slowly, his voice strong but not strident, his phrases short. He gathers speed and volume, often breaking into a cadence that scans well as impromptu free verse:

> Yesterday was a day
>> Of mixed emotions for me.
>> Jesus was crucified on Friday,
>> Resurrected on Sunday.
>> That's great joy
>> Because the stone was rolled away.
>> But for the poor of Baltimore,
>> For the malnourished of our nation,
>> For the poor mothers
>> Who cannot get prenatal care,
>> For children who cannot get
>> A breakfast program or lunch programs,
>> For the youth who can't get a skill.
>> They were crucified on Friday,
>> Crucified on Saturday,
>> Crucified on Sunday,
>> Crucified on Monday.
>> The hands are still bleeding,
>> The thorns are still on their heads.
>> I say it's time for the poor
>> To realize resurrection,
>> To stop the hammers, stop the nails,
>> Wheel the stone away.

So it went last week, on the streets of East Baltimore, on the campus of the largely black University of Maryland Eastern Shore in the town of Princess Anne, in the tiny Ebenezer African Methodist Episcopal Church in Oxon Hill, Maryland, later in Texas at a San Antonio barrio and a West Dallas project, and on Friday night in the Mount Canaan Baptist Church in Shreveport, Louisiana. To dramatize his appeal to the poor, Jackson has taken to sleeping some nights in their homes rather than in hotels. Last Monday he stayed with William Jarrard, an unemployed white Baltimorean who bears an ironic resemblance to Archie Bunker; Wednesday in the San Antonio home of Hortencia Cabrera, mother of fourteen. To call attention to industrial pollution, Jackson on Wednesday also visited the West Dallas housing project apartment of Sarah Dean, whose five-year-old daughter Africia suffers from lead poisoning believed to be caused by a nearby smelter.

Staying in private homes may also serve to stretch skimpy campaign funds, but the practice adds to the already legendary chaos of the Jackson drive. Jackson's schedules are haphazard at best, and difficulty in finding the homes of the poor is making him even later than usual. In Baltimore, campaign workers had to hire a cab to lead a motorcade of aides and reporters to pick up Jackson at Jarrard's home Tuesday morning, and borrow $12 from a reporter to pay the fare. Even then, aide Frank Watkins had to stop the caravan of vans and buses to ask exact directions from two children playing on a nearby sidewalk.

In Dallas, campaign workers did manage to line up a fleet of Cadillac limousines, which hauled reporters around Wednesday in a procession that looked disconcertingly like a funeral cortege. But on Thursday morning someone mistook the motorcade's destination for its point of origin, and the limousines gathered in Fort Worth while journalists and campaign workers waited for them at the Loews Anatole Hotel in Dallas. Jackson aides rounded up two church buses to get the tour under way — ninety minutes late. But one bus broke down and limped onto a goat farm near the town of Grand Prairie; reporters and camera crews had to hire a fleet of taxis to chase after the candidate. All of which seemed apt for a major campaign that has generated more excitement with less money and organization than any other in memory. In a self-satisfied moment, Jackson put it this way: "If Hart or Mondale had my budget, they could not compete. And if I had their budgets, they could not compete."

R ONALD REAGAN'S VICTORY seemed assured by election eve, 1980. A Massachusetts bartender told a questioner who was conducting his own straw poll that he was going to vote Republican for the first time in his life. That, by itself, was an almost certain sign of a Reagan victory. More sophisticated pollsters, including Patrick Caddell in the Carter camp, knew as well that the die was already cast, that Carter would lose.

Reagan's victory was explained in many ways. Some, especially liberal Democrats, said that it was a vote against Carter. They confidently predicted that the Reagan phenomenon would be short lived, that Democrats would gain in both the House and the Senate in the 1982 elections, and that the party could once again win the White House in 1984.

Reagan's mastery of the media was more widely believed to have been the cause of his success. He had been an actor, after all, and knew how to appeal on television to popular emotions. His image, more than his views on major issues of public policy, was given credit for his victory. During the 1980 presidential campaign Garry Wills wrote that Reagan was the man on the white horse who would save the nation from its past foibles. Wills stressed Reagan's image and style. He was, suggested Wills, "the first serious counter-authority [to government] with an air of authority; the charismatic leader without a vision, just a role."[1] Reagan, concluded Wills, was "both Henry Aldrich and Grandpa Walton, our remembered and our present selves, our fantasy of afternoons with popcorn and the 'real' world of TV politics. Where so little is stable, the emptiness at the center looks eternal. Reagan is the calm eye of history's hurricane; and we hope, by moving with it, never to slip toward the edges into chaos."[2]

While most commentators concentrated upon Reagan's media skills and image to explain his victory, journalist Jeff Greenfield, a TV commentator himself, concluded that Reagan won by following the more traditional rules of politics. He had a superb political organization, and his program offered a clear and apparently popular choice for the electorate.[3]

The Greenfield thesis about Reagan echoed the views of the late political scientist V. O. Key, Jr., who wrote:

Voters are not fools. To be sure, many individual voters act in odd ways indeed; yet in the large, the electorate behaves about as rationally and responsibly as we should expect, given the clarity of the alternatives presented to it and the character of the information available to it. In American presidential campaigns of recent decades the portrait of the American electorate that develops from the data is not one of an electorate straitjacketed by social determinants or moved by subconscious urges triggered by devilishly skillful propagandists. It is rather one of an electorate moved by concern about

[1] Garry Wills, "Ron and Destiny: Where Will He Lead Us, This Embodiment of Our Everyday Experience?" *Esquire,* August 1980, p. 37.

[2] Ibid.

[3] Jeff Greenfield, *The Real Campaign* (New York: Summit Books, 1982).

central and relevant questions of public policy, of governmental performance, and of executive personality.[4]

Whether voters chose Reagan because of his style, program, or a combination of both, remained conjecture during the first two years of his administration. There was no doubt, however, that Reagan had a program that he intended to carry out. His clarion call to the Conservative Political Action Conference a year after he had been in office reveals his determination: "Fellow citizens, fellow conservatives, our time is now. Our moment has arrived. We stand together shoulder to shoulder in the thickest of the fight."[5] The president had already achieved remarkable success in reducing taxes and government expenditures, but to change the face of government in the way that he wanted far more needed to be done.

Reagan's actions as president, particularly his direct confrontation of the Washington political establishment, which he carefully courted but whose powers he wanted to diminish, surprised political pundits. Reagan apparently meant what he said during his campaign, which made him a political novelty. The following selection, by a journalist who has closely followed Reagan's political career since its inception, depicts his character and style and examines the underlying forces that have shaped him.

Lou Cannon
RONALD REAGAN: A POLITICAL PERSPECTIVE

He seemed to many, from beginning to end, a most unlikely leader of the nation. As the United States of America entered the complex, computer age of the 1980s, Ronald Wilson Reagan reached backward and spoke to the future in the accents of the past. His suits were as out of date as his metaphors, most of which derived from the Great Depression or World War II. He quoted freely from the Founding Fathers and from his early hero, Franklin Delano Roosevelt. He viewed Soviet expansionism much as Roosevelt had viewed Nazi aggression. When others protested that he saw the world in stark and simple terms, Reagan would say: "For many years, you and I have been shushed like children and told there are no simple answers to complex problems that are beyond

[4]V. O. Key, Jr., *The Responsible Electorate* (Cambridge, Mass.: The Belknap Press of Harvard University Press, 1966), pp. 7–8.

[5]*National Journal,* May 2, 1981, p. 779.

our comprehension. Well, the truth is there *are* simple answers — just not easy ones."

By the historical standards of the American presidency, Reagan seemed an even more unlikely leader. Though he was vigorous and athletic, he was sixty-nine years old and would be seventy within a month of taking the presidential oath of office. The age showed in the dewlapped wrinkles of his neck. It showed in the Reagan campaign schedules, which were generously endowed with "staff time" that was the euphemistic reference to Reagan's afternoon nap. And Reagan in other ways seemed singularly unprepared for the office which he and others have ritualistically referred to as "the most important in the free world."

He had not held public office in six years. He had no foreign policy experience. He had never worked in Washington. He was a divorced man espousing the values of the family, a wartime stateside noncombatant advocating military preparedness, a fiscal conservative who as governor of California had sponsored the largest tax increases in the state's history.

But despite all this and the majority party and the White House incumbency against him, Reagan was a formidable candidate with an appeal that reached beyond his natural, conservative constituency. He was larger than the sum of his parts. Some said this was because he was a superb television performer whose skills were honed by years of professional experience. Others said he was a lucky politician (as some had said of Jimmy Carter), with the good fortune to face overrated opponents at the time they were most vulnerable. But there was another reason, and it was more important than the others. It was that whatever Reagan lacked in complexity or youth or consistency, he made up for in an unremitting vision of America. The vision was the thing. It was a vision frozen in time, which made it more powerful than transitory visions. Reagan believed in it, which made it even more powerful. A close personal aide, Michael K. Deaver, said this about Reagan's belief: "He's resolved something, his being or what he is, a long time ago. He seems to know what is right."

And whether Reagan did, in fact, know what was right, his vision of America was what made this aging, out-of-date exactor credible to other Americans. Reporters and Reagan aides would smile at one another and head for the press buses when Reagan approached his standard tearjerker ending of the basic speech he used in early 1980. They would laugh outright when Reagan, for the thousandth time, quoted John Winthrop aboard "the tiny Arabella" in 1630 as telling his followers that they should be "as a city on a hill."

"The eyes of all mankind are still upon us," Reagan would conclude. "Our party came into being more than one hundred years ago, born of a great crisis at that time. We led this nation through that crisis. We are being called upon again. Let us keep our rendezvous with destiny, let us build a shining city upon a hill."

This was part of Reagan's vision, and the audience did not laugh at it. Most of the people who heard the speech applauded. A few of them cried. And they came back for the equally simplistic and more materialistic versions of the vision: "At the heart of our message should be five simple familiar words. No big economic theories. No sermons on political philosophy. Just five short words: family, work, neighborhood, freedom, peace."

Historically, Reagan's vision was rooted in small-town Midwestern America of the early twentieth century — then the real and symbolic heartland of the nation. His values were shaped in a day when most Americans lived not in the great, cluttered urban landscapes of our time but in towns and small cities surrounding a more pastoral land. When he was trying out self-characterizations early in the 1980 campaign, Reagan briefly referred to himself as a "Main Street Republican," a phrase intended to show that he was not a boardroom candidate like John Connally or an Ivy Leaguer like George Bush. The phrase, quietly discarded after the primaries because Reagan's advisers thought it made the candidate seem partisan and out of date, was an appropriate description of Reagan. Like all persons, he is a product of his time and region, his experience and his culture. For Reagan it was small-town Illinois, the quintessential Main Street celebrated in Middle America and satirized by Sinclair Lewis's famous novel of the same name. "Main Street is the climax of civilization," Lewis wrote in the preface to his novel, which appeared in 1920 when Reagan was nine years old. Lewis meant these words sardonically but Reagan would accept them as literal truth. In his autobiography, *Where's The Rest of Me?*, Reagan describes his childhood as "a rare Huck Finn-Tom Sawyer idyll."

"Reagan was shaped by the small towns of the Midwest, and that explains in large part the simple moral and conservative approach he brought to public life," wrote early biographer Bill Boyarsky in *The Rise of Ronald Reagan.* "Where Lewis satirized the Midwest communities, Reagan glorifies them. He enthusiastically accepts the values that Lewis criticized. As a result, he is deeply respectful of business; determinedly conservative; mistrusting of change; unintellectual and slightly suspicious of higher education . . . convinced that, as his father said, 'All men were created equal and man's own ambition determines what happens to him the rest of his life.' "

Reagan's father, John Reagan, known as Jack, was a gregarious, nomadic, hard-drinking Irish-American whose own life seems to have fallen far short of his ambition. He was a Catholic in a Protestant land and in Reagan's childhood a fierce opponent of the Ku Klux Klan, which was at the time a national force in American politics. In his autobiography,

Reagan related how his father, then a traveling salesman, was told by a small-town hotel clerk that he would appreciate the accommodations because Jews weren't permitted there. "I'm a Catholic," Reagan quotes his father as saying, "and if it's come to the point where you won't take Jews, you won't take me, either." Jack Reagan then stalked out, spent a cold winter night in his car and became seriously ill.

At the time his second son Ronald was born, Jack was working as a clerk in the Pitney General Store in Tampico. Jack's ambition was to own his own store, a goal briefly realized but quickly crushed by the Depression. Ronald Reagan still seems troubled by what happened to his father. When he announced his presidential candidacy on November 13, 1979, Reagan repeated an oft-told story of Christmas Eve in 1931 when Reagan and his older brother Neil were home from college.

Their father received a special delivery letter he hoped would be a bonus. It was instead a "blue slip" telling him that he had been fired.

Ronald Reagan was born in a five-room flat above the Pitney General Store on February 6, 1911. For the first nine years of his life he lived in a procession of Illinois cities and towns: Chicago, Galesburg, Monmouth, Tampico again, and finally Dixon, the place Reagan still calls his hometown and where he lived until he was twenty-one. His mother, and the anchor of the Reagan family, was Nelle Wilson Reagan. She was a do-gooder, a lifelong member of the Christian Church who practiced what she preached. Reagan and his older brother remember many instances of her finding food or jobs for needy persons. Sometimes the Reagan home became — in a day when the phrase was unknown — a halfway house for released convicts.

Reagan was a prodigy. Born with a remarkable memory, he learned to read at an early age and dazzled his mother, who encouraged him to read newspapers aloud to her friends. Reagan recalls reading an account of the Preparedness Day bombing in San Francisco on July 22, 1916, when he was five years old.

There were other ways in which the Reagan home was avant-garde for Dixon. The Reagan boys called their parents by their first names and they called the boys by their nicknames — "Dutch" for Ronald and "Moon" for Neil. The Reagans were the town Democrats in a place and time devotedly Republican. Both Jack and Nelle participated in amateur theatricals, which stimulated the imagination of their children and which made both of them talk about an acting career.

But there also was the dark side of Jack Reagan's alcoholism. Even the relentlessly cheerful Reagan autobiography, written in 1965 with one eye to his coming political career, cannot disguise Reagan's feelings about his father's drinking. "I was eleven years old the first time I came home to find my father flat on his back on the front porch and no one there to lend a hand but me," Reagan writes. "He was drunk, dead to the world.

I bent over him, smelling the sharp odor of whiskey from the speakeasy. I got a fistful of his overcoat. Opening the door, I managed to drag him inside and get him to bed. In a few days, he was the bluff, hearty man I knew and loved and will always remember."

Children are stronger than we expect them to be, and there is no evidence that Jack Reagan's alcoholism cast any permanent blight on the lives of his sons. Ronald Reagan would not drink at all for many years, and he was repelled by the Hollywood cocktail circuit. But by all accounts, including his own, he grew up to be a resolute, cheerful young man, hardworking and unintellectual, interested in football and girls and theatricals. Athletic and well built, Reagan enjoyed the role of local lifeguard, and the varying numbers of persons he saved from drowning became an obligatory part of his political biography. Most of all, he enjoyed talking. He had a nonstop gift of gab that had been encouraged by his mother's showing off of his precocious reading ability. As a freshman at tiny Eureka College, Reagan's fiery speechmaking made him the leader of a student strike (over Depression-cancelled classes that would have prevented some students from graduating), which cost the college president his job. He developed a consuming interest, which has never left him, in the medium of radio, which Franklin Roosevelt was then using to carry the gospel of the New Deal to the countryside. At Eureka, Reagan would listen for hours to sports broadcasts, sometimes interspersed with Roosevelt's "fireside chats." Thirty-five years later, as governor of California, Reagan would use the fireside chats as his model for broadcast and televised reports to the people on the public issues of the day.

The Depression and Hollywood stand with Main Street as the shaping symbols in the life of Ronald Reagan. Reagan still considers the Depression as the single most important influence upon him. The Depression cost his father a partnership in a Dixon shoe store. It sent his mother to work in a dress shop for fourteen dollars a week. Reagan, then working his way through Eureka, sent fifty dollars a week home so that his parents could continue to get credit at the local grocery store. But there were many others in as difficult a predicament, or worse. Often, in his days as governor, when Reagan was asked whether he had been poor as a child, he replied with the bromide that "we were poor but we didn't think of ourselves as poor." Sometimes he used the line when he was talking about limiting welfare, the way out for the modern poor. As a historical reference, however, Reagan's statement is an accurate one. What had happened to the Reagans had happened to America.

In his senior year at Eureka, Reagan won an acting award for his role in *Aria de Campo*, an antiwar play by Edna St. Vincent Millay, and he had thoughts of an acting career. But he had no job and he returned to Dixon, uncertain of his future and thinking of radio as an entry into show business. Reagan applied for work at several Chicago radio stations and was turned down. Then, in the fall of 1932, came a chance to broadcast University of Iowa football games for WHO, the NBC affiliate in Des Moines. Reagan had been a starting guard at Eureka, and he loved football. From his first broadcast, he gave a tense and evocative account of what was going on on the field of play below. When baseball season began, Reagan's proclivity for nonstop talking plunged him into the since-lost art of recreating baseball games from the laconic summaries of the action furnished by Western Union telegraph. At a time when everyone listened to radio, Dutch Reagan became a sportscasting star.

He used radio as his springboard to Hollywood. In 1937 he accompanied the Chicago Cubs to Catalina Island off the Southern California coast for spring training, and a friend arranged a screen test for him at Warner Brothers. Reagan passed easily and Hollywood proved even more suitable for Reagan's talents than had radio. Starting out on low-budget pictures, where his ability to quickly memorize scripts proved an enormous asset, Reagan advanced to become "the Errol Flynn of the B's." He made thirty-one movies in five years, progressing from his $200-a-week starting salary to the princely figure of $1,650 a week in 1941. Popular and invariably cast as a good guy, Reagan had mastered his craft and seemed to be rising to the pinnacle of stardom. Though burdened with "B" pictures, he won critical acclaim for performances in *Brother Rat* (where Eddie Albert made his debut and where Reagan met his first wife, Jane Wyman), in *Knute Rockne* (where Reagan plays the doomed Notre Dame football player George Gipp and Pat O'Brien plays Rockne), in *Dark Victory* (with Humphrey Bogart) and, especially in *King's Row*, where the cast included Claude Rains, Robert Cummings, and Charles Coburn.

King's Row, the story of a small Southern town more malevolent than Dixon, was Reagan's best picture. He portrayed Drake McHugh, a playboy whose legs are amputated by sadistic surgeon Coburn as revenge for the seduction of his daughter. "Where's the rest of me?" yells Mc-Hugh, coming to without his legs and uttering the future title of Reagan's autobiography. *Commonweal* praised Reagan for a "splendid performance," and other reviews were uniformly good. Reagan liked the film too, and in the tradition of ego-laden Hollywood would often show it to house guests after dinner. After Jane Wyman divorced him, she was quoted as saying, "I just couldn't stand to watch that damn *King's Row* one more time."

Reagan never quite fulfilled the acting promise of this period. His career, like so many others, was interrupted by World War II, most of which Reagan spent in Hollywood making training films with the First Motion Picture Unit of the Army Air Corps. Reagan's career couldn't hit its stride after the war, when newer, younger stars were coming along and Hollywood was fighting its own multifront war with television, labor unrest, foreign films, and domestic investigating committees. At the beginning of the war, Reagan had lost out to Humphrey Bogart for a role in a picture that was retitled *Casablanca*. When the war was over he lost his chance to play in another film classic which also starred Bogart, *The Treasure of the Sierra Madre*. Reagan's choice of films, when he had a choice, had never been exceptional and by now his luck was running bad. Given a role in the movie version of the John Van Druten play, *The Voice of the Turtle*, Reagan objected to playing with a new leading lady and asked for June Allyson instead. The actress he objected to was the richly talented Eleanor Parker, subsequently to be nominated for four Oscars. "It took me only one scene with Eleanor to realize that I'd be lucky if I could stay even," Reagan acknowledges in his autobiography.

Reagan's marriage was on the skids along with his movie career. The low point of the career came in 1951, when Reagan played opposite a chimpanzee in *Bedtime for Bonzo*. His marriage had come to an end three years earlier, during Wyman's filming of *Johnny Belinda*, for which she won an Academy Award. Reagan quipped to a gossip columnist that *Johnny Belinda* should be named as correspondent in the divorce action. If Miss Wyman's testimony in the divorce action is to be believed, a better choice would be the Screen Actor's Guild, which increasingly was taking more and more of her husband's time. The picture she painted, both in court and outside of it, was of a bored wife who no longer shared her husband's interests.

Exit Ronald Reagan actor. Enter Reagan, labor negotiator, public spokesman, and future politician. By the early 1950s, although he was still appearing in occasional films, Reagan had in effect established a new career. As leader of the Screen Actors Guild and six times its president, Reagan had become fully embroiled in the economic and cultural issues which shook Hoolywood after the war.

If Main Street represented the climax of American civilization in the 1920s, Hollywood was in this postwar era the undisputed capital of American mass culture. Everything that affected Hollywood was a page one story in Peoria — or in Dixon, where the preferred reading matter was the *Chicago Tribune*. These stories included sensational accusations that the movie industry was honeycombed with Communists, disclosures that a key union was operated by gangsters, the emergence of both television and foreign films as a major competitor and taxation-induced "runaway" of U.S. films to foreign countries. Reagan was in the midst of these battles. During the Red-hunting days, which Hollywood now remembers with embarrassment and some shame, Reagan opposed Communists but also disputed the basic thesis of the House Committee on Un-American Activities in these words: "I do not believe the Communists have ever at any time been able to use the motion picture screen as a sounding board for their philosophy or ideology." At the time of the Congressional investigations, his stand fully pleased neither side. But he emerged from that period as an effective and adroit political leader who had kept his union intact.

Reagan's personal life and political views were now changing. He had described himself as a "near hopeless hemophiliac liberal." But in 1952, four years after his divorce from Wyman, Ronald Reagan married Nancy Davis, adopted daughter of a conservative and wealthy Chicago surgeon Loyal Davis. In 1954, he became the host for "General Electric Theater," a new half-hour television series, with a salary of $125,000 a year and generous expenses. The GE contract, which might be said to have launched Reagan's political career, gave him an opportunity to be seen each week on television and to talk to GE employees all over the country.

While some old Hollywood friends ascribe Reagan's increasing conservatism of this time to Nancy or her father, it is probable that General Electric, and Reagan's growing prosperity, had much to do with Reagan's changing political views.

At the outset, Reagan's message in his speeches to GE employees was patriotic, anti-Communist, pro-Hollywood. Reacting to the general nature of his talk, GE Board Chairman Ralph Cordiner suggested to Reagan that "you work out a philosophy for yourself." Increasingly, that philosophy became probusiness, antigovernment conservatism. It was a philosophy more congenial to the Republican party than to the Democrats, at least in California. But Reagan, like many Americans, found it easier to embrace Republican principles than to abandon the political faith of his family. As a Democrat, Reagan had supported Helen Gahagan Douglas in her U.S. Senate race against Richard Nixon in 1950. By 1952, he was a Democrat for Eisenhower. When Nixon ran for president in 1960, Reagan was still a Democrat but this time supporting Nixon. Two years later, when Reagan was speaking for Nixon during his unsuccessful campaign for governor of California, a woman in the audience asked him if he were a registered Republican. Reagan said he wasn't, but indicated his willingness to join the GOP. The woman, a volunteer registrar, marched down the aisle and signed him up as a Republican on the spot.

By this time, Reagan had become a partisan politician almost without recognizing it. He was becoming an embarrassment to General Electric, which did much business with the government Reagan was consistently denouncing. When Reagan used the Tennessee Valley Authority, a major customer of GE, as an example of government waste, the company asked him to delete the reference. Reagan complied, but there were those at General Electric who now wanted to be rid of Reagan altogether. In 1962, GE suggested that Reagan limit his speeches to touting the company's products. By then, "General Electric Theater" also was in trouble, facing competition from "Bonanza," a show which became one of Reagan's favorites. When Reagan balked at the limitations GE wanted to place on him, the company abruptly cancelled "GE Theater." Reagan never knew whether it was his speeches or "Bonanza" which hurt him most.

However, Reagan was now prepared for a political career. He had shaken hands with 250,000 GE employees during his eight years as company spokesman and made speeches from one end of the country to the other. He had a philosophy, name recognition, and a winning smile. He also had money, and owned valuable ranch land in the Malibu hills. Increasingly active in Republican politics, Reagan in 1964 was named California chairman of the Barry Goldwater presidential campaign. The leaders of that floundering effort, short on money and party unity, decided to put Reagan on national television. The result, wrote David S. Broder after that campaign, was "the most successful national political debut since William Jennings Bryan electrified the 1896 Democratic convention with his 'Cross of Gold' speech."

Reagan's emotional speech on the night of October 27, 1964, stirred millions of Americans, but it was familiar to those who had heard him on the GE circuit. Basically, it was the same speech he had given for eight years and would give for another sixteen until it grudgingly gave way to new material in the 1980 campaign. There was the celebration of economic individualism: "We need true tax reform that will at least make a start toward restoring for our children the American dream that wealth is denied to no one." And, there were statistics: "The Defense Department runs 269 supermarkets. They do a gross business of $730 million a year and lose $150 million." And, there was democratic idealism: "This idea that government was beholden to the people, that it had no other source of power except the sovereign people, is still the newest, most unique idea in the long history of man's relation to man." And, finally, inevitably, there was the influence of Franklin Roosevelt, who first discovered an American "rendezvous with destiny" while accepting the Democratic renomination for president in 1936. Americans have been holding clandestine meetings with destiny ever since, this one from the peroration of the Reagan speech for Goldwater: "You and I have a rendezvous with destiny. We can preserve for our children this the last best hope of man on earth or we can sentence them to take the first step into a thousand years of darkness. If we fail, at least let our children, and our children's children, say of us we justified our brief moment here. We did all that could be done."

Although Reagan didn't know it then — and though he resisted the idea for nearly a year and a half — this speech stands as his opening address in the campaign for the California governorship in 1966. It raised nearly $1 million for the Republican party and its candidates. And it caused wealthy Republican contributors in California, such as auto dealer Holmes Tuttle, industrialist Henry Salvatori, and the late A. C. (Cy) Rubel, chairman of the board of Union Oil Company, to consider Reagan the best hope to wrest the governorship of the nation's most populous state from the Democrats. When an exploratory committee run by his millionaire GOP backers, "The Friends of Ronald Reagan," raised both money and enthusiasm, Reagan agreed to make the race. The rest, as they say, is history.

Reagan's eight years as governor of California also are history — and there is general agreement among the historians that he was at least an adequate governor and perhaps a good one. State Treasurer Jesse Unruh, a Democratic legislative powerhouse at the time Reagan arrived in Sacramento and the man Reagan defeated to win his second term as governor, offered this balanced viewpoint to the *Los Angeles Times* in 1974: "As a governor, I think he has been better than most Democrats would concede and not nearly as good as most Republicans and conservatives might like to think." Bob Moretti, the Democratic speaker with whom Reagan negotiated his historic welfare bill in 1971, wound up liking and respecting his adversary. In the legislative hyperbole of the time Moretti (and Unruh, and most other Democrats) frequently described Reagan as a heartless, know-nothing foe of the poor, higher education, and racial minorities. But in retrospect, Moretti finds Reagan both a reasonable politician and a man of his word, saying of him: "His bark was worse than his bite."

Any serious evaluation of the Reagan governorship collides squarely with Reagan's own exalted view of his accomplishments. As Reagan told the story on the campaign trail in 1980, it was a golden age during the eight years he served as great helmsman of California's ship of state. "Every time we had a surplus, because I don't think government has a right to take one dollar more than government needs, we gave the surpluses back to the people in the form of tax rebates," Reagan would tell his approving audiences. "We gave back over eight years $5.7 billion to the people of California. We stopped the bureaucracy dead in its tracks, the same way I would like to stop it at the national level."

This account omits as much as it relates. What Reagan does not say is that these surpluses, in part, were a result of his own policies. He does not say that he sponsored what was then the largest tax increase in California state history and that state spending and taxes more than doubled during his tenure. Corporation, bank, sales, and personal income taxes all rose sharply during the Reagan years. The annual state budget increased from $4.6 billion to $10.2 billion and the operations portion of the budget, over which the governor has more control, increased from $2.2 billion to $3.5 billion. State taxes per $100 of personal income, a better measurement because it adjusts for population and price changes, went from $6.64 to $7.62.

But a case can be made that, despite these figures, Reagan succeeded in his basic goal of controlling the cost of government. "Reagan was not so much an underachiever as he was an overcommitter," says one-time legislative aide Judson Clark of the Sacramento consulting firm, California Research. "He did some important things, but not as much as he said he would do and not as much as he said he did." Among the things Reagan did do was slow the growth of the state work force, which had increased nearly 50 percent during the eight years of his Democratic predecessor, Edmund G. (Pat) Brown. There are different measurements of work force growth, but the generally accepted one shows a 7 percent increase during the Reagan years at a time when state workforces elsewhere were growing far more rapidly. Reagan cut by 40 percent a capital outlay budget which had increased 200 percent during the Brown years. And if the $4 billion which the state gave back in property tax relief is subtracted from Reagan's budgets, they roughly kept pace with inflation during his two administrations.

Had Reagan accomplished this result with the tax structure he inherited, the result would have been that low-income taxpayers would have shouldered most of the financial burden. The supreme irony of his governorship is that the burden was instead thrust in great part on the corporations and middle-class taxpayers which Reagan had been ritually defending in his speeches to conservative audiences. Under Reagan, in that first tax bill the levy on banks was boosted from 9.5 to 13 percent. The tax on corporations increased 61 percent — from a 5.5 to a 9 percent rate. This happened, in part, because of Reagan's ignorance of the way government actually worked. And it happened, also, because even in his ignorance he proved a masterful and intuitive politician.

This combination of ignorance and intuition worked reasonably well for Reagan as he struggled to understand the intricacies of government. At least it did on most issues. Where it failed him was on the emotional issue of abortion. In 1967, sponsors of liberal abortion legislation had chosen California as the testing ground on which to promote the nation's first liberal abortion law. California at the time, like a majority of other states, permitted abortions only to save the life of the mother. The liberalizing U.S. Supreme Court decision opening the abortion floodgates was yet to come, as was the counterrevolution of the pro-life movement. In those days the leading body of opposition was the Roman Catholic Church, which launched a letter-writing campaign that produced more mail than most legislators have ever seen. Reagan, as he puts it, had never thought much about the issue one way or the other. At one critical press conference, after the bill had advanced through key committees, Reagan showed almost total confusion about the measure's provisions, freely contradicting himself and describing as "loopholes" provisions which sponsors said were the major purpose of the bill. On one side, Reagan was lobbied for the bill by physicians including his father-in-law, Chicago surgeon Loyal Davis. On the other, the church brought its big guns to bear, and Francis Cardinal McIntyre called the governor and urged him to veto the legislation. Reagan finally signed the bill after the author had made some amendments which supposedly made abortions more difficult to obtain. The statistics of what happened after enactment tell another story. In 1967, there were 518 legal abortions in California hospitals. In 1978, the last year for which complete figures are available, there were 171,982 abortions. From 1967 through 1978 there were 1,230,359 abortions performed under the bill signed by Reagan, now the ardent champion of a U.S. constitutional amendment that would impose the restrictions on abortion that were on the books in California when he became governor.

Reagan did better on other issues. He conducted his office with integrity and his governmental appointments, many of them drawn from the business community, were of high quality. So were his judicial appointments, which usually followed the recommendations of the bar. Sometimes this produced a judiciary more independent than Reagan would have liked — as it did when Reagan-appointed Supreme Court Justice Donald Wright tipped the balance in striking down a Reagan-backed capital punishment law.

Occasionally, Reagan approved truly innovative programs, as in authorizing conjugal visits for prisoners with good behavior records. Reagan supported legislation increasing the length of sentences for criminals and more funding for state prisons. Originally, he slashed the funds for state mental hospitals. Then, he restored the funds and gave additional money to community health programs being pioneered in California. State expenditures for mental health doubled during the Reagan administration.

He entered office waging what some called a vendetta against the University of California, scene of a controversial and prophetic "free speech" demonstration. "Obey the rules or get out," thundered Reagan, as he called upon campus authorities to expel "undesirables." Under threat of budget cuts, Reagan tried to force the university to abandon its historic policy of "free tuition" and make students pay more of the costs of higher education. Reagan helped force out University of California administrator Clark Kerr, who had unwisely provoked a vote of confidence, and he did persuade the regents to accept tuition under another name. But the budget-cutting never materialized. Once Reagan had made his point, he was generous to the university. State spending for higher education rose 136 percent during the Reagan years compared to an overall state spending increase of 100 percent and an enrollment growth of 40 percent. Even educators who resented the antiintellectual-ism of Reagan's approach — he had once accused universities of "sub-sidizing intellectual curiosity" — praised the governor for the increased funding. There is disagreement to this day, however, on whether the verbal attacks on the university caused intangible damage which cost the university topflight faculty.

It was the performance of the Reagan administration on environmen-tal issues which proved the greatest surprise. "A tree's a tree — how many do you need to look at," Reagan had said during his campaign for governor. Environmentalists viewed Reagan's election as the coming of the dark ages in a state which always has been in the forefront of the conservationist movement. Reagan fought this impression by choosing William Penn Mott, a nationally known park director, as director of state parks. He picked Norman (Ike) Livermore, a lumberman who also was a Sierra Club member, as director of resources. Together, Livermore and Mott compiled a generally enviable record for the Reagan administra-tion — although it was notably pro-industry on smog control issues. A total of 145,000 acres, including forty-one miles of ocean frontage, were added to an already impressive state park system. Two underwater park preserves were set aside off the Pacific coast. A major bond issue for park development was proposed and the endangered middle fork of the Feather River was preserved.

What some think was Reagan's finest hour as governor came on the issue of the Dos Rios Dam, a proposed 730-foot structure on the middle fork of the Eel River, a steelhead-spawning stream that is one of Califor-nia's few remaining wild rivers. The California water bureaucracy, then considered more powerful than the highway lobby, was enthusiastic about the Dos Rios high dam. When the Army Corps of Engineers joined forces to formally propose Dos Rios under the battlecry of water for populous Southern California, its approval was considered a foregone conclusion. Against an array of big battalions, which included wealthy Reagan con-tributors, were a few Reagan aides (including Livermore, State Finance Director Caspar W. Weinberger, and Reagan's present chief of staff Ed-win Meese) and a few conservationists from Round Valley, which would have been flooded by the impounded waters of Dos Rios. Among these residents were descendants of Indian tribes which had been herded into the valley by army troops late in the nineteenth century. The Indians argued that Round Valley contained gravesites and valley land that was secured by treaty. It was their plea which proved decisive. "We've bro-ken too damn many treaties," Reagan said in turning down the Dos Rios Dam. "We're not going to flood them (the Indians) out."

The major legislative achievement of Reagan's eight years in office was the 1971 Welfare Reform Act. It is one of many bills which looks good on its own and insufficient when matched against the Reagan rhetoric. "When I took office, California was the welfare capital of the nation," Reagan says on the stump. "Sixteen percent of all those receiving welfare in the country were in California. The caseload was increasing 40,000 a month. We turned that 40,000 a month increase into an 8,000 a month decrease. We returned to the taxpayers $2 billion and we increased grants to the truly needy by 43 percent." Most of these figures are exaggerations, or otherwise misleading. The average caseload increase for the two years prior to enactment of the welfare reform measure was 26,000 not 40,000. Reagan's bill did increase the grants for the poorest recipients — which had not been raised a penny during the supposedly liberal regime of Pat Brown — but half of this increase was mandated by federal litigation. The $2 billion which Reagan talks about is a legislative projection which made no allowance for the dropping birth rate or increasing employment in California at this time.

Still, the Welfare Reform Act was good legislation which could be defended as easily in New Deal terms as the ones Reagan used for his conservative audiences. The Urban Institute, a nonprofit Washington research group, called the legislation "a major policy success" in a report issued in 1980. Even taking into account the birth rate, and increasing employment, the institute said that the Reagan program had reduced the welfare rolls by 6 percent under what they otherwise would have been while increasing maximum grants. Frank Levy, the senior research associate who wrote the report, said there were "big symbolic differences in the rhetoric" between what Reagan and various liberals had proposed to improve the welfare system but that the substantive differences were far less than either side was likely to admit. The Reagan program, said Levy, was "reoriented toward fiscal control" but "on balance, more recipients appear to have been helped than hurt." By the time the legislation was passed, there were 1,608,000 persons on the welfare rolls — about one in every eleven Californians. In the next three years the total declined to 1,333,000 — significantly lower but still among the highest in the nation. The Urban Institute study found that the major feature of the control was a simple device requiring each recipient of a welfare check to mail a signed postcard each month certifying income and eligibility. In the face of this rudimentary requirement, welfare fraud seemed to melt away. On the other hand, Reagan's ballyhooed required-work program had little direct effect on the rolls, with only 9,600 persons assigned to jobs during a three-year period.

At ground level, Ronald Reagan is decent, likable, and homespun, used to being the center of attention but reserved to the point of occasional shyness. Unless aroused by some challenge, he is basically a passive person — reacting to Nancy, reacting to staff, reacting to autograph seekers and to questions that are put to him. He seems to like who he is, and the names other men have called him — "Dutch" and "the Gipper" and "the cowboy" — are names of affection and respect. He is considerate of other people. Many who have seen Reagan up close think he is literally considerate to a fault with aides, neither demanding enough of them nor reprimanding them when they do poor work. But he is sensible about some things that other men are not sensible about.

When Nancy Reagan was incensed by an anti-Reagan editorial campaign in the *Sacramento Bee*, Governor Reagan acceded to her request and cancelled the subscription at home. Then he took the paper at the office, confiding that it was a way to have the *Bee* (which he regularly read) and keep Nancy happy at the same time.

Reagan has a genuine sense of humor. When students pressed around his limousine during a college demonstration and yelled, "We are the future," Reagan scrawled a reply on a piece of paper and held it up to the window. "I'll sell my bonds," it said. And when a wire-service reporter of long acquaintance brought him a reissued promotion picture from *Bedtime for Bonzo* showing Reagan and the chimpanzee in bed together, Reagan autographed it with the words, "I'm the one with the watch."

Reagan comes from a milieu where reaction is required. An actor must be prepared, but he awaits the call of others before he can come onto the stage. And the working hours are different, or at least they were in Reagan's day. The phrase "9 to 5 governor" is accurate in a sort of rough-hewn way, but it is not a complete description of Reagan's working habits. As an actor, Reagan might work with great concentration on a film for six weeks or two months and then have a long period of inactivity. He is capable of bursts of very intensive campaigning, as anyone who saw him in New Hampshire in 1980 can attest. But he does not function well working long and hard over an extended period, and he does not want to work that way. "Show me an executive that works long over-time hours and I'll show you a bad executive," Reagan once said. What's more, he really believes this.

Reagan's nature and working habits combine to make him a delegator of authority. Edwin Meese, who served Reagan as chief of staff in Sacramento and then again in the 1980 presidential campaign, once remarked that Reagan was a near-perfect delegator because he gave a grant of authority that was clearly defined. "If you operated within the limits of what he wanted to accomplish, he wouldn't second-guess you," Meese said. "And he was decisive when you brought something to him."

Even those who concede that Reagan delegates well and decides quickly have questions about his basic intelligence. Reagan is, as they say, no rocket scientist. Many find him lacking in imagination. But Reagan consistently has confounded those who have underestimated him. There is a kind of small-town common sense about him that serves him well and shows in moments when it is least expected. And more than most people would suspect, Reagan has an appreciation of his own limitations. "I think any adult man knows his shortcomings and knows his strengths," Reagan has said. "I've never claimed to be the originator of every idea we had in Sacramento, but I do think I have the ability to recognize good ideas. I do think, also, that I set the tone and direction in which we wanted to go. We were fortunate enough in surrounding ourselves with people who shared our beliefs and whose talent was turned in the direction of implementing them." These are not the words of a stupid man. But Reagan's intelligence is functional rather than reflective. He is best under pressure — as at the Nashua debate and again on August 9 in the South Bronx where Reagan turned a disastrously advanced event into a triumph by telling a woman who was screaming at him: "I can't do a damn thing for you if I'm not elected."

Reagan's most unnerving quality is his proclivity for giving verbatim memorized responses he has used repeatedly as if he were saying them for the first time. It is like punching the button of a tape recorder and hearing the coded message, complete with sincere gestures and that "aw shucks" smile. Partly, this may be a learned defense mechanism which permits Reagan to talk safely to reporters and supporters on the campaign trail. But he has done this with friends in private conversations, too, and it leaves some of them wondering whether he has an original thought in his head. Others, more charitably, regard the mind-taped messages as a natural consequence of Reagan's combined acting and speaking career and say he gives memorized answers without realizing that he is doing it.

Perhaps Reagan has simply made too many speeches. There is much to recommend the observation of old foe Hale Champion (Pat Brown's last finance director) that Reagan is "the Reader's Digest of politics." At least well into the 1980 campaign, *Reader's Digest* was certainly Reagan's favorite reading material. "In both cases," wrote Champion in the *Washington Post*, "their statistics and illustrations have a folklore character. They are, if I may use a nonword, factitious. The figures aren't very good, they often don't prove anything and sometimes they are barely tangential to the issue at hand. But they sound great, and they seem to strengthen the message by making it seem more real, even more concrete." These dubious statistics also enable Reagan, in public or private, to tell his audiences what they want to hear. And this desire to please, more than anything else, has been the source of Reagan's trouble in presidential campaigns. Reagan is almost never embarrassed in direct confrontation, where both the physical and the mental juices are flowing. But before a friendly audience he is likely to say almost anything — once calling for a "bloodbath" if necessary to quell student demonstrations, and, in this year's election campaign blandly referring to the Vietnam war as "a noble cause" before a veterans' convention and then four days later questioning the theory of evolution before an audience of fundamentalist ministers.

Reagan's nature and way of doing business make him a natural target for anyone on his staff or in his constituency who wants to foist off a pet proposal on him. Reagan is considerate of others and he wants people to bring ideas to him. While he is pragmatic enough to know that he can't accomplish everything contained in his rhetoric, he nonetheless has real goals and fundamental beliefs.

Watching Reagan struggling to find himself after Noble Cause and Evolution and Taiwan, it occurred to me that he may be more complicated than we have made him out to be. Most of us are. I have been covering Reagan, on and off, since his first campaign for office fourteen years ago, have covered him in office, and have written a book about him. I have seen him on bad days and good, in triumph and defeat. He seems to me a good, if limited, man who has demonstrated that it is possible to govern constructively from a conservative ideological base. And yet there is something about Reagan which remains hidden, never glimpsed in those predictable airplane interviews or in the dreary accounts of how Reagan would use the experience he gained in Sacramento to remake Washington. The something shows occasionally in those "vision of America" endings which drive reporters to the press buses. But it shows even more on those rare occasions when Reagan admits visitors to Rancho del Cielo, the remote fog-shrouded ranch north of Santa Barbara which he has chosen as a haven for himself and his wife Nancy. Watching him tell proudly of how he laid the floors and rebuilt the roof of his understated ranch house and put in the fence around it, watching him saddling horses for the obligatory media ride down the old Western trail, watching him look at Nancy to see if she approved of what he was doing and saying, I thought of the passage in *Death of a Salesman* where the son tells about the porch his father built and says that there is more of Willy Loman in that porch than in all the sales he ever made. I wondered if this were also true of Reagan. He had grown up in Main Street America in the first third of this century believing as his father had told him that the only limits on what he could accomplish were those imposed by his ambition. It is a conceit of our system that anyone can be president and Reagan had taken this idea — this fundamental democratic notion which is close to the wellsprings of our national existence — quite literally. He had become a popular sportscaster, a well-known actor, the leader of his labor union, and twice the governor of the nation's most populous state. Now he was the Republican nominee for president. Because of what he had done, Reagan was Everyman. And because this is America, and it is what America expects of its Everymans, Reagan had not been ruined by this, at least not that I could see. He still liked working with his hands, and he liked to ride. He still hammed it up for his friends, as he must have done in Dixon, and he still needed and desired the public and private approval of those closest to him. But he was not riding off into the sunset, at least not this day. The sun was behind him as he rode down into the television cameras. Ronald Reagan was about to put the democratic ideal to one of its sternest tests. And he had every confidence that he could do it.

THE PRECEDING SELECTIONS have illustrated that increasingly at the national level candidates and their followers give an individualistic cast to party organization. Each candidate has his or her own organization that exists within the broader party. Neither national party committees nor leaders can determine who will run under their party labels.

Political parties have been stronger in the past, especially at local levels. Occupying an important place in party history is the urban party machine, the paradigm of which was the Daley machine in Chicago.

The following selection describes the kinds of people and personalities that controlled the political machine in Chicago, from its powerful leader, Mayor Richard J. Daley, to the men who helped to keep him in office, including precinct workers and captains and city bureaucrats appointed by the mayor to serve the party. Chicago politics clearly revealed a cult of personality in operation. The organization, operations, and policies of the Democratic party in Chicago were a perfect reflection of the personality of Mayor Richard J. Daley.

5 Mike Royko
THE BOSS

KUNSTLER: Mayor Daley, do you hold a position in the Cook County Democratic Committee?

WITNESS: I surely do, and I am very proud of it. I am the leader of my party.

KUNSTLER: What was that?

WITNESS: I surely do, and I am very proud of it. I am the leader of the Democratic party in Cook County.

KUNSTLER: Your honor, I would like to strike from that answer anything about being very proud of it. I only asked whether he had a position in the Cook County Democratic party.

HOFFMAN: I will let the words "I surely do" stand. The words after those may go out and the jury may disregard the expression of the witness that he is very proud of his position.

The Hawk got his nickname because in his younger days he was the outside lookout man at a bookie joint. Then his eyes got weak, and he had to wear thick glasses, so he entered politics as a precinct worker.

He was a hustling precinct worker and brought out the vote, so he was rewarded with a patronage job. The Hawk, who had always loved uniforms but had never worn one, asked his ward committeeman if he could become a member of the county sheriff's police department. They gave him a uniform, badge, and gun, and declared him to be a policeman.

But the Hawk was afraid of firearms, so he asked if he could have a job that didn't require carrying a loaded gun. They put him inside the County Building, supervising the man who operated the freight elevator. He liked the job and did such a good job supervising the man who operated the freight elevator that the Hawk was promoted to sergeant.

When a Republican won the sheriff's office, the Hawk was out of work for one day before he turned up in the office of the county treasurer, wearing the uniform of a treasurer's guard. His new job was to sit at a table near the main entrance, beneath the big sign that said "County Treasurer," and when people came in and asked if they were in the county treasurer's office, the Hawk said that indeed they were. It was a good job, and he did it well, but it wasn't what he wanted because he really wasn't a policeman. Finally his committeeman arranged for him to become a member of the secretary of state's special force of highway inspectors, and he got to wear a uniform that had three colors and gold braid.

The Hawk is a tiny piece of the Machine. He is not necessarily a typical patronage worker, but he is not unusual. With about twenty-five thousand people owing their government job to political activity or influence, nothing is typical or unusual.

The Hawk keeps his job by getting out the Democratic vote in his precinct, paying monthly dues to the ward's coffers, buying and pushing tickets to his ward boss's golf outing and $25-a-plate dinners. His reward is a job that isn't difficult, hours that aren't demanding, and as long as he brings out the vote and the party keeps winning elections, he will remain employed. If he doesn't stay in the job he has, they will find something else for him.

Some precinct captains have had more jobs than they can remember. Take Sam, who worked his first precinct forty-five years ago on the West Side.

"My first job was as a clerk over at the election board. In those days to succeed in politics you sometimes had to bash in a few heads. The Republicans in another ward heard about me and they brought me into one of their precincts where they were having trouble. I was brought in as a heavy, and I took care of the problem, so they got me a job in the state Department of Labor. The job was . . . uh . . . to tell the truth, I didn't do anything. I was a payroller. Then later I went to another ward as a Democratic precinct captain, where they were having a tough election. I did my job and I moved over to a job as a state policeman. Then later I was a city gas meter inspector, and a pipe fitter where they had to get me a union card, and an investigator for the attorney general, and when I retired I was an inspector in the Department of Weights and Measures."

The Hawk and Sam, as precinct captains, are basic parts of the Machine. There are some thirty-five hundred precincts in Chicago, and every one of them has a Democratic captain and most captains have assistant captains. They all have, or can have, jobs in government. The better the captain, the better the job. Many make upwards of fifteen thousand dollars a year as supervisors, inspectors, or minor department heads.

They aren't the lowest ranking members of the Machine. Below them are the people who swing mops in the public buildings, dump bedpans in the County Hospital, dig ditches, and perform other menial work. They don't work precincts regularly, although they help out at election time, but they do have to vote themselves and make sure their families vote, buy the usual tickets to political dinners and in many wards, contribute about 2 percent of their salaries to the ward organization.

Above the precinct captain is that lordly figure the ward committeeman, known in local parlance as "the clout," "the Chinaman," "the guy," and "our beloved leader."

Vito Marzullo is a ward committeeman and an alderman. He was born in Italy and has an elementary school education, but for years when he arrived at political functions, a judge walked a few steps behind him, moving ahead when there was a door to be opened. Marzullo had put him on the bench. His ward, on the near Southwest Side, is a pleasant stew of working class Italians, Poles, Mexicans, and blacks. A short, erect, tough, and likable man, he has had a Republican opponent only once in four elections to the City Council. Marzullo has about four hundred patronage jobs given to him by the Democratic Central Committee to fill. He has more jobs than some ward bosses because he has a stronger ward, with an average turnout of something like 14,500 Democrats to 1,200 Republicans. But he has fewer jobs than some other wards that are even stronger. Marzullo can tick off the jobs he fills:

"I got an assistant state's attorney, and I got an assistant attorney general, I got an electrical inspector at twelve thousand dollars a year, and I got street inspectors and surveyors, and a county highway inspector. I got an administrative assistant to the zoning board and some people in the secretary of state's office. I got fifty-nine precinct captains and they all got assistants, and they all got good jobs. The lawyers I got in jobs don't have to work precincts, but they have to come to my ward office and give free legal advice to the people in the ward."

Service and favors, the staples of the precinct captain and his ward boss. The service may be nothing more than the ordinary municipal functions the citizen is paying taxes for. But there is always the feeling that they could slip if the precinct captain wants them to, that the garbage pickup might not be as good, that the dead tree might not be cut down.

Service and favors. In earlier days, the captain could do much more. The immigrant family looked to him as more than a link with a new and strange government: He was the government. He could tell them how to fill out their papers, how to pay their taxes, how to get a license. He was the welfare agency, with a basket of food and some coal when things got tough, an entree to the crowded charity hospital. He could take care of it when one of the kids got in trouble with the police. Social welfare agencies and better times took away many of his functions, but later there were still the traffic tickets to fix, the real estate tax assessments he might lower. When a downtown office didn't provide service, he was a direct link to government, somebody to cut through the bureaucracy.

In poor parts of the city, he has the added role of a threat. Don't vote, and you might lose your public housing apartment. Don't vote, and you might be cut off welfare. Don't vote, and you might have building inspectors poking around the house.

In the affluent areas, he is, sometimes, merely an errand boy, dropping off a tax bill on the way downtown, buying a vehicle sticker at City Hall, making sure that the streets are cleaned regularly, sounding out public opinion.

The payoff is on election day, when the votes are counted. If he produced, he is safe until the next election. If he didn't, that's it. "He has to go," Marzullo says. "If a company has a man who can't deliver, who can't sell the product, wouldn't he put somebody else in who can?"

Nobody except Chairman Daley knows precisely how many jobs the Machine controls. Some patronage jobs require special skills, so the jobholder doesn't have to do political work. Some are under civil service. And when the Republicans occasionally win a county office, the jobs change hands. There were more patronage jobs under the old Kelly-Nash Machine of the thirties and forties, but civil service reform efforts hurt the Machine. Some of the damage has been undone by Daley, however, who let civil service jobs slip back into patronage by giving tests infrequently or making them so difficult that few can pass, thus making it necessary to hire "temporary" employees, who stay "temporary" for the rest of their lieves. Even civil service employees are subject to political pressures in the form of unwanted transfers, withheld promotions.

On certain special occasions, it is possible to see much of the Machine's patronage army assembled and marching. The annual St. Patrick's Day parade down State Street, with Daley leading the way, is a display of might that knots the stomachs of Republicans. An even more remarkable display of patronage power is seen at the State Fair, when on "Democrat Day" thousands of city workers are loaded into buses, trains, and cars which converge on the fairgrounds outside Springfield. The highlight of the fair is when Daley proudly hoofs down the middle of the grounds' dusty racetrack in ninety-degree heat with thousands of his sweating but devoted workers tramping behind him, wearing old-fashioned straw hats and derbies. The Illinois attorney general's staff of lawyers once thrilled the rustics with a crack manual of arms performance, using Daley placards instead of rifles.

Another reason the size of the patronage army is impossible to measure is that it extends beyond the twenty to twenty-five thousand government jobs. The Machine has jobs at racetracks, public utilities, private industry, and the Chicago Transit Authority, which is the bus and subway system, and will help arrange easy union cards.

Out of the ranks of the patronage workers rise the Marzullos, fifty ward committeemen who, with thirty suburban township committeemen, sit as the Central Committee. For them the reward is more than a comfortable payroll job. If they don't prosper, it is because they are ignoring the advice of their Tammany cousin George Washington Plunkett, who said, "I seen my opportunities and I took 'em." Chicago's ward bosses take 'em, too.

Most of them hold an elective office. Many of the Daley aldermen are ward bosses. Several are county commissioners. Others hold office as county clerk, assessor, or recorder of deeds and a few are congressmen and state legislators. Those who don't hold office are given top jobs running city departments, whether they know anything about the work or not. A ward boss who was given a $28,000-a-year job as head of the city's huge sewer system was asked what his experience was. "About twenty years ago I was a house drain inspector." "Did you ever work in the sewers?" "No, but many a time I lifted a lid to see if they were flowing." "Do you have an engineering background?" "Sort of. I took some independent courses at a school I forget the name of, and in 1932 I was a plumber's helper." His background was adequate: his ward usually carries by fifteen thousand to three thousand votes.

The elective offices and jobs provide the status, identity, and retinue of coat holders and door openers, but financially only the household money. About a third of them are lawyers, and the clients leap at them. Most of the judges came up through the Machine; many are former ward bosses themselves. This doesn't mean cases are always rigged, but one cannot underestimate the power of sentimentality. The political lawyers are greatly in demand for zoning disputes, big real estate ventures, and anything else that brings a company into contact with city agencies. When a New York corporation decided to bid for a lucrative Chicago cable TV franchise, they promptly tried to retain the former head of the city's legal department to represent them.

Those who don't have the advantage of a law degree turn to the old reliable, insurance. To be a success in the insurance field, a ward boss needs only two things: an office with his name on it and somebody in the office who knows how to write policies. All stores and businesses need insurance. Why not force the premium on the friendly ward boss? As Marzullo says, everybody needs favors.

One of the most successful political insurance firms is operated by party ancient Joe Gill. Gill gets a big slice of the city's insurance on public properties, like the Civic Center and O'Hare Airport. There are no negotiations or competitive bidding. The policies are given to him because he is Joe Gill. How many votes does Prudential Life deliver? The city's premiums are about $500,000 a year, giving Gill's firm a yearly profit of as much as $100,000.

Another firm, founded by the late Al Horan, and later operated by his heirs and County Assessor P. J. Cullerton gets $100,000 a year in premiums from the city's park district. Since Cullerton is the man who sets the taxable value of all property in Cook County, it is likely that some big property owners would feel more secure being protected by his insurance.

When the city's sprawling lake front convention hall was built, the insurance business was tossed at the insurance firm founded by George Dunne, a ward boss and County Board president.

Another old-line firm is operated by John D'Arco, the crime syndicate's man in the Central Committee. He represents the First Ward, which includes the Loop, a goldmine of insurable property. D'Arco has never bothered to deny that he is a political appendage of the Mafia, probably because he knows that nobody would believe him. A denial would sound strained in light of his bad habit of being seen with Mafia bosses in public. Besides, the First Ward was controlled by the Mafia long before D'Arco became alderman and ward committeeman.

D'Arco's presence in the Central Committee has sometimes been an embarrassment to Chairman Daley. Despite D'Arco's understandable efforts to be discreet, he can't avoid personal publicity because the FBI is always following the people with whom he associates. When D'Arco announced that he was leaving the City Council because of poor health, while remaining ward committeeman, the FBI leaked the fact that Mafia chief Sam Giancana had ordered him out of the council in a pique over something or other. Giancana could do that, because it is his ward; D'Arco only watches it for him. One of Giancana's relatives has turned up as an aide to a First Ward congressman. Another Giancana relative was elected to the state senate. At Daley's urging, the First Ward organization made an effort to improve its image by running a young banker for alderman. But the banker finally resigned from the council, saying that being the First Ward's alderman was ruining his reputation.

When he is asked about the First Ward, Daley retreats to the democratic position that the people elect D'Arco and their other representatives, and who is he to argue with the people? He has the authority, as party chairman, to strip the First Ward, or any ward, of its patronage, and there are times when he surely must want to do so. Raids on Syndicate gambling houses sometimes turn up city workers, usually sponsored by the First Ward organization. While he has the authority to take away the jobs, it would cause delight in the press and put him in the position of confirming the Mafia's participation in the Machine. He prefers to suffer quietly through the periodic flaps.

The question is often raised whether he actually has the power, in addition to the authority, to politically disable the Mafia. It has been in city government longer than he has, and has graduated its political lackeys to judgeships, the various legislative bodies, and positions throughout government. While it no longer is the controlling force it was in Thompson's administration, or as arrogantly obvious as it was under Kelly-Nash, it remains a part of the Machine, and so long as it doesn't challenge him but is satisfied with its limited share, Daley can live with it, just as he lives with the rascals in Springfield.

Ward bosses are men of ambition, so when they aren't busy with politics or their outside professions, they are on the alert for "deals." At any given moment, a group of them, and their followers, are either planning a deal, hatching a deal, or looking for a deal.

Assessor Cullerton and a circle of his friends have gone in for buying up stretches of exurban land for golf courses, resorts, and the like. Others hold interests in racetracks, which depend on political goodwill for additional racing dates.

The city's dramatic physical redevelopment has been a boon to the political world as well as the private investors. There are so many deals involving ranking members of the Machine that it has been suggested that the city slogan be changed from *Urbs in Horto*, which means "City in a Garden," to *Ubi Est Mea*, which means "Where's mine?"

From where Daley sits, alone atop the Machine, he sees all the parts, and his job is to keep them functioning properly. One part that has been brought into perfect synchronization is organized labor — perhaps the single biggest factor in the unique survival of the big city organization in Chicago. Labor provides Daley with his strongest personal support and contributes great sums to his campaigns. Daley's roots are deep in organized labor. His father was an organizer of his sheet-metal workers' local, and Bridgeport was always a union neighborhood. With politics and the priesthood, union activity was one of the more heavily traveled roads to success. Daley grew up with Steve Bailey, who became head of the Plumbers' Union, and as Daley developed politically, Bailey brought him into contact with other labor leaders.

Thousands of trade union men are employed by local government. Unlike the federal government and many other cities, Chicago always pays the top construction rate, rather than the lower maintenance scale, although most of the work is maintenance. Daley's massive public works projects, gilded with overtime pay in his rush to cut ribbons before elections, are another major source of union jobs.

His policy is that a labor leader be appointed to every policymaking city board or committee. In recent years, it has worked out this way: The head of the Janitors' Union was on the police board, the park board, the Public Buildings Commission, and several others. The head of the Plumbers' Union was on the Board of Health and ran the St. Patrick's Day parade. The head of the Electricians' Union was vice-president of the Board of Education. The Clothing Workers' Union had a man on the library board. The Municipal Employees' Union boss was on the Chicago Housing Authority, which runs the city's public housing projects. The head of the Chicago Federation of Labor and somebody from the Teamsters' Union were helping run the poverty program. And the sons of union officials find the door to City Hall open if they decide on a career in politics.

The third major part of the Machine is money. Once again, only Daley knows how much it has and how it is spent. As party chairman, he controls its treasury. The spending is lavish. Even when running against a listless nobody, Daley may spend a million dollars. The amount used for "precinct money," which is handed out to the precinct captains and used in any way that helps bring out the Democratic vote, can exceed the entire Republican campaign outlay. This can mean paying out a couple of dollars or a couple of chickens to voters in poor neighborhoods, or bottles of cheap wine in the Skid Row areas. Republicans claim that the Democrats will spend as much as $300,000 in precinct money alone for a city election. To retain a crucial office, such as that of county assessor, hundreds of thousands have been spent on billboard advertising alone. Add to that the TV and radio saturation, and the spending for local campaigning exceeds by far the cost-per-vote level of national campaigning.

The money comes from countless sources. From the patronage army, it goes into the ward offices as dues, and part of it is turned over to party headquarters. Every ward leader throws his annual $25-a-head golf days, corned beef dinners, and picnics. The ticket books are thrust at the patronage workers and they either sell them or, as they say, "eat them," bearing the cost themselves.

There are "ward books," with page after page of advertising, sold by precinct workers to local businesses and other favor-seekers. Alerman Marzullo puts out a 350-page ad book every year, at one hundred dollars a page. There are no blank pages in his book. The ward organizations keep what they need to function, and the rest is funneled to party head-quarters.

Contractors may be the biggest of all contributors. Daley's public works program has poured billions into their pockets, and they in turn have given millions back to the party in contributions. Much of it comes from contractors who are favored, despite the seemingly fair system of competitive bidding. In some fields, only a handful of contractors ever bid, and they manage to arrange things so that at the end of the year each has received about the same amount of work and the same profit. A contractor who is not part of this "brotherhood" refrains from bidding on governmental work. If he tries to push his way in by submitting a reasonable bid, which would assure him of being the successful low bidder, he may suddenly find that the unions are unable to supply him with the workers he needs.

Even Republican businessmen contribute money to the Machine, more than they give to Republican candidates. Republicans can't do anything for them, but Daley can.

The Machine's vast resources have made it nearly impossible for Republicans to offer more than a fluttering fight in city elections. Daley, to flaunt his strength and to keep his organization in trim, will crank out four hundred thousand primary voites for himself running unopposed. His opponent will be lucky to get seventy thousand Republicans interested enough to cast a primary vote.

Unlike New York, Los Angeles, and other major cities, Chicago has no independent parties or candidates jumping in to threaten, or at least pull votes away from the leaders. It is no accident. Illinois election laws are stacked against an independent's ever getting his name on a voting machine.

In New York, a regular party candidate needs five thousand signatures on his nominating petitions, and an independent must have seventy-five hundred. With any kind of volunteer organization, an independent can get the names, which is why New York will have half a dozen candidates for mayor.

The requirements are even less demanding in Los Angeles, where a candidate needs a seven-hundred-dollar filing fee and petitions bearing five hundred names. Los Angeles voters have a dozen or so candidates from which to choose.

But Chicago has never, in this century, had more than two candidates for the office of mayor. The state legislature took care of the threat from troublesome independents years ago.

When Daley files his nominating petitions, he needs about thirty-nine hundred names, a figure based on one-half of one percent of his party's vote in the previous election. Daley usually gets so many names that the petitions have to be brought in by truck. Using the same formula his Republican opponent needs about twenty-five hundred signatures, which isn't difficult, even for a Chicago Republican.

But an independent would have to bring in about sixty to seventy thousand signatures. He needs 5 percent of the previous total vote cast. And not just anybody's signature: only legally defined independents, those who have not voted in the recent partisan primaries.

That's why there are only two candidates for mayor and the other offices in Chicago — a Republican and a Democrat. And sometimes there aren't even that many, Mayor Kelly having once handpicked his Republican opponent.

The only alternative for an independent is to run as a write-in candidate, a waste of time.

It has never happened, but if an independent somehow managed to build an organization big and enthusiastic enough to find seventy thousand independent voters who would sign his petition, he would probably need an extra thirty thousand signatures to be sure of getting past the Chicago Election Board, which runs the city's elections and rules on the validity of nominating petitions. Names can be ruled invalid for anything short of failing to dot an "i." An illiterate's "X" might be acceptable on a Machine candidate's petition, but the Election Board is meticulous about those of anybody else.

The board used to be run by a frank old rogue, Sidney Holzman, who summed up its attitude toward the aspirations of independents, Republicans, and other foreigners:

"We throw their petitions up to the ceiling, and those that stick are good."

Despite all these safeguards and its lopsided superiority over local opposition, the Machine never fails to run scared. For this reason, or maybe out of habit, it never misses a chance to steal a certain number of votes and trample all over the voting laws. Most of it goes on in the wards where the voters are lower middle class, black, poor white, or on the bottle. To assure party loyalty, the precinct captains merely accompany the voter into the voting machine. They aren't supposed to be sticking their heads in, but that's the only way they can be sure the person votes Democratic. They get away with it because the election judges, who are citizens hired to supervise each polling place, don't protest. The Democratic election judges don't mind, and the Republican election judges are probably Democrats. The Republicans assign poll watchers to combat fraud but they never have enough people to cover all of the precincts. If they prevented the common practices, imaginative precinct captains would merely turn to others. In some wards, politically obligated doctors sign stacks of blank affidavits, attesting to the illness of people they have never seen, thus permitting the precinct captain to vote the people in their homes as absentee voters for reasons of illness. And several investigations have established that death does not always keep a person's vote from being cast.

The aforementioned Holzman was always philosophical about vote fraud, conceding that it occurred, and even saying that "a good precinct captain will always find a way to steal votes," but asserting: "In city elections, we don't have to steal to win. And in statewide elections, the Republicans are stealing so much downstate, that all we do is balance it out."

Out of this vast amalgam of patronage, money, special interests, restrictive election laws, and organizational discipline emerge a handful of candidates, and they are what it is supposed to be all about.

Most of them come up through the system, as Daley did, beginning as doorbell ringers, working in the jobs their sponsors got for them, pushing the ward book, buying the tickets, doing the favors, holding the coats, opening the doors, putting in the fix, and inching their way up the organizational ladder, waiting for somebody to die and the chance to go to the legislature, into the City Council, and maybe someday something even bigger.

As hard as a party member may try, and as bright and presentable as he may be, he probably won't make it if he isn't from a strong ward with an influential ward boss. A loyal, hard-working City Hall lawyer can become a judge, if his ward brings in the vote and his sponsor pushes him, while in another ward, where the Republicans dominate and the ward boss just hangs on, the City Hall lawyer can only dream of his black robe.

Judge Wexler, Daley's night school classmate, lived with this problem. Wexler had worked feverishly as the city's chief prosecutor of slum cases, dragging landlords into court, reaping publicity for the mayor's administration, while deftly avoiding the toes of slum landlords who had political connections. For years he trotted into Daley's office with his news clippings. But when slate-making time came around, other people got to be judges.

"My ward committeeman was so weak, he couldn't do anything. I used to ask him for a letter to the Central Committee sponsoring me for a judgeship. You have to have a sponsoring letter. And he'd say: 'A letter for you? I want to be a judge myself, and I'm not getting anywhere.' I would have never made it if it hadn't been for Daley and knowing him from night school. He did it for me personally."

Wexler was fortunate. For the others with ambitions, it is either a strong committeeman and advancement, or an obscure job with nothing to put in the scrap book.

Only one other shortcut exists, and it is part of the system of the

Machine: nepotism. A Chicago Rip Van Winkle could awaken to the political news columns and, reading the names, think that time had stood still.

There was Otto Kerner, Cermak's confidante and a federal judge, and he begat Otto Kerner, governor, federal judge, and husband of Cermak's daughter; John Clark, ward boss and assessor, begat William Clark, attorney general and 1968 U.S. Senate candidate; Adlai Stevenson, governor and presidential candidate, begat Adlai Stevenson, U.S. senator; Dan Ryan, ward boss and county board president, begat Dan Ryan, ward boss and county board president; Edward Dunne, mayor, begat Robert Jerome Dunne, judge; John J. Touhy, ward boss and holder of many offices, begat John M. Touhy, Illinois House Speaker; Joe Rostenkowski, ward boss, begat Daniel Rostenkowski, congressman; Arthur Elrod, ward boss and county commissioner, begat Richard Elrod, sheriff; John Toman, ward boss and sheriff, begat Andrew Toman, county coroner; Thomas Keane, ward boss and alderman, begat Thomas Keane, ward boss and alderman; Joe Burke, ward boss and alderman, begat Edward Burke, ward boss and alderman; Paul Sheridan, ward boss and alderman, begat Paul Sheridan, alderman; Theodore Swinarski, ward boss, begat Donald Swinarski, alderman; David Hartigan, alderman, begat Neil Hartigan, ward boss and chief park district attorney; Louis Garippo, ward boss, begat Louis Garippo, judge; Michael Igoe, federal judge, begat Michael Igoe, county board secretary; Daniel McNamara, union leader, begat Daniel McNamara, judge; Thomas Murray, union leader and school board member, begat James Murray, congressman and alderman; Peter Shannon, businessman and friend of Daley, begat Dan Shannon, Park District president; Morgan Murphy, Sr., business executive and friend of Daley, begat Morgan Murphy, Jr., congressman; William Downes, real estate expert and friend of Daley, begat a daughter, who married a young man named David Stahl, who became deputy mayor; James Conlisk, police captain and City Hall favorite, begat James Conlisk, police superintendent; Daniel Coman, ward boss and city forestry chief, begat Daniel Coman, head of the state's attorney's civil division.

They are their brothers' keepers, too.

Alderman Keane keeps his brother on the powerful board of real estate tax appeals; Assessor Cullerton keeps his brother in the city council and his brother-in-law as his chief deputy assessor; Alderman Harry Sain kept his brother as city jail warden when sheriff; and County Board President Dunne keeps his brother as boss of O'Hare and Midway airports, and Congressman John Kluczynski keeps his brother on the state Supreme Court.

Nobody in the Machine is more family conscious than Chairman Daley. Cousin John Daley became a ward committeeman and served several terms in the state legislature, where his remarkable resemblance to the mayor sometimes unnerved his associates. Uncle Martin Daley had a well-paying job in county government that he did so skillfully he seldom had to leave his home. Cousin Richard Curry heads the city's legal department. Daley's four sons are just finishing law school, so their public careers have not yet been launched, but the eldest, Richard, at twenty-seven, was a candidate for delegate from his district to the state constitutional convention. He piled up the biggest vote in the state. The people in Bridgeport recognize talent. And the sons have been judge's clerks while going through school. When one of the mayor's daughters married, Daley promptly found a city executive job for the father of his new son-in-law.

Daley didn't come from a big family but he married into one, and so Eleanor Guilfoyle's parents might well have said that they did not lose a daughter, they gained an employment agency. Mrs. Daley's nephew has been in several key jobs. Her sister's husband became a police captain. A brother is an engineer in the school system. Stories about the number of Guilfoyles, and cousins and in-laws of Guilfoyles, in the patronage army have taken on legendary tones.

There are exceptions to the rules of party apprenticeship and nepotism. A few independent Democrats have been dogged enough to defeat weak Machine candidates in primaries for alderman, or, as happened once in the Daley years, for a seat in Congress. But it is never easy, and the strain leaves most independents so exhausted that most of them eventually embrace the Machine, at least gently, to avoid recurring primary struggles.

In theory, anybody can walk right into party headquarters at slate-making time, go before the ward bosses who make up the committee, and present themselves as prospective candidates. One political hanger-on, a disc jockey, even caught them in a mirthful mood, and when he actually got down on his knees and begged, they let him run for a minor office. But even the slate makers do not kid themselves into thinking they are deciding who the candidates will be. They listen to the applicants, push their favorites, the men from their wards, and wait for Chairman Daley to make up his mind. Some of the men on the slate-making committee have been surprised to find that they themselves were slated to run for offices they hadn't even sought. It is a one-man show, and they know it. This vignette illustrates it:

In 1968, slate makers were putting together their county ticket. They listened to the applicants, talked it over, then Daley and a couple of the party ancients came out of another room with the list.

Daley had decided that the strongest candidate for the crucial office of state's attorney, the county's prosecutor, would be Edward Hanrahan, a former federal prosecutor. It is a "must" office because a Republican would use it to investigate City Hall. Hanrahan was the strongest candidate because his Republican opponent also had an Irish name.

But slating Hanrahan required that the incumbent, John Stamos, who had been appointed to fill a vacancy, be shifted to something else. Stamos, a diligent and skilled young prosecutor, was Greek; Greeks were a small voting bloc, and Stamos was just professional and aloof enough to make some party elders nervous. Daley had decided to let Stamos run for the office of Illinois attorney general, which has prestige but less power and challenge. That completed the ticket.

Their decision made for them, the slate makers filed out of the conference room to go downstairs and meet the news media. As they came out, one of them saw Stamos and said, "Congratulations, John, you're going for attorney general."

"Bullshit," Stamos said, adding, "I won't go for it." Daley reasoned, but Stamos repeated, "Bullshit." And left the hotel.

While the slate makers stood around looking confused, Daley told a secretary to call Frank Lorenz, an obeident party regular who was between elective offices. She got him on the phone and Daley said, "Come on over, Frank, you're the candidate for attorney general."

One of the slate makers later said: "If Lorenz had stepped out to take a piss, he would have missed out, and the next guy Daley thought of would have got it, if he answered his phone. That's the way things are run sometimes, and everybody says we're so goddamn well organized."

A minute or two later, it was all resolved. Normally, Stamos would have been punished. But for party unity and to avoid alienating big Greek financial contributors, he was elevated to the state appellate court.

"You never know what in the hell is going to happen in there," a ward boss said. "He moves us around like a bunch of chess pieces. He knows why he's doing it because he's like a Russian with a ten-year plan, but we never know. I think his idea is to slate people who aren't going to try to rival him or add to someone else's strength. Look at how Cullerton got to be assessor. First he was a nothing alderman. He was a real nothing. But Daley put him in as finance chairman so he could have somebody who wouldn't get out of line. Then he put him in as assessor. Keane wanted assessor for his brother George. George would have loved it. Funny how people love to be assessor, haw! But Daley wasn't about to give Tom Keane the assessor's office, so he looked around and there was faithful Parky Cullerton.

"When he had to pick a chief judge, who were the logical guys? Neil Harrington, but he couldn't give it to Neil because he used to be part of the old South Side faction, and Daley wouldn't trust him. Harold Ward? He is independent, he might tell Daley to go screw himself or something.

"So he gave it to John Boyle, because he knew he'd have Boyle's complete loyalty. Why? Because Boyle had that scandal when he was state's attorney years ago and after that he couldn't get elected dogcatcher. He was a whipped dog, so he was perfect for Daley.

"And there's this thing he has with old people. Jesus, we've reslated people who were so senile they didn't even know what office they were running for. When it gets to that point, you know it has got to be something more than him being soft-hearted. There were some we could have just told them they were being reslated, and they would never have known the difference. He does it because then he doesn't have to worry about them. They'll sit there on the county board or wherever they are and do just what they're told.

"It's one-man rule, absolutely. It used to be that if Kelly got mad at you, there were seven or eight guys you could go to and get it squared. The same thing with Nash, and when Arvey was chairman. But there's only one Daley. You're dead if he doesn't like you. There's no point in going to someone to try to get it squared because they can't, and they won't even try because they're afraid it'll get him mad at them. He's a friend of mine, but he can be a mean prick."

Just how mean, and how subtle, was discovered by Arnold Maremont, a millionaire industrialist and art collector who decided he wanted to go into politics and to start at the top.

Daley does not dislike millionaires. He lets them contribute to the party, serve on advisory boards, take on time-consuming appointments, and help elect Machine Democrats to office.

Maremont had done it all. He contributed money, worked in Governor Kerner's campaign, led a campaign to pass a $150,000,000 bond issue that revitalized the state's mental health program, and pitched in on numerous liberal causes and mental health and welfare programs.

His dream was to be a U.S. senator, and in early 1961 he went to Daley's office and told him that he'd like to run against Senator Everett Dirksen. He made it clear that he wanted to do it properly and not jump into the primary as a maverick. The party's blessing was what he was after.

Daley showed interest, but said he had certain reservations: mainly he wasn't sure if downstate county chairmen would support a Jew. He suggested that Maremont tour the state, talk to the county chairmen, and he indicated strongly that if Maremont made a good showing, he'd be Daley's man.

Maremont pushed aside his business and civic work and spent most of the early summer barnstorming through Illinois. A spunky, brash man, he'd walk into a bar in a tiny southern Illinois town — grits and gravy country — and announce: "My name's Arnold Maremont. I want to run for the Senate and I'm a Jew." People seemed to like him, as he wolfed down chicken and peas dinners at the county meetings, charming little old ladies, and picking up support from the chairmen.

All the while, he sent back regular reports to Daley: They will go for a Jew! Elated, he headed back to Chicago, ready to give Daley his final report and the good news. He got back to town just in time to pick up that day's papers and read that Daley had, indeed, decided to slate a Jewish senatorial candidate: Congressman Sidney Yates, a party regular.

That ended Maremont's political ambitions. Furious, he was convinced that Daley had merely used him to conduct a free one-man survey of downstate Illinois. He wouldn't have even tried had he ever heard Daley explain why he is so dedicated a party man: "The party permits ordinary people to get ahead. Without the party, I couldn't be mayor. The rich guys can get elected on their money, but somebody like me, an ordinary person, needs the party. Without the party, only the rich would be elected to office."

If Daley's one-man rule bothers the men who sit on the Central Committee, they are careful to keep it to themselves. The meetings take on the mood of a religious service, with the committeemen chanting their praise of his leadership. "It has been . . . my pleasure and honor . . . to give him my advice. . . . The greatest mayor . . . in the country . . . the world . . . the history of the world . . ."

Only once in recent years has anybody stood up and talked back, and he was one of the suburban committeemen, generally referred to around party headquarters as "a bunch of meatheads."

The suburban committeeman, Lynn Williams, a wealthy manufacturer and probably the most liberal member of the Central Committee, had been angered by Daley's attacks on liberals after the 1968 Democratic convention. Daley had been making speeches lambasting pseudoliberals, liberal-intellectuals, suburban liberals, suburban liberal-intellectuals, and pseudoliberal-intellectual suburbanites. He had been shouting: "Who in the hell do those people think they are? Who are they to tell us how to run our party?"

Williams, a strong supporter of young Adlai Stevenson, who had angered Daley with an attack on "feudal" politics, stood up, finally, at a Central Committee meeting and delivered a scathing rebuttal to Daley, saying that without liberal participation the party would be nothing but a skeleton, its only goal, power.

As he talked, the committeemen's heads swiveled as if they were watching a tennis game, wonder and fear on their faces. They had never heard such talk, and wondered what Chairman Daley would do. Strike him with lightning. Throw the bum out?

When Williams finished, Daley, in a surprisingly soft voice, said, "I've always been a liberal myself."

Other committeemen joined in his defense, recalling countless liberal acts by Daley. One man shouted at Williams, "Perhaps you didn't know, but this happens to be a very liberal outfit."

The shock of the committeemen at the sound of somebody criticizing Daley didn't surprise Williams. He has said: "Most of them are mediocraties at best, and not very intelligent. The more successful demonstrate cunning. Most are in need of slavery — their own — and they want to follow a strong leader."

In March 1970, the committeemen met for the purpose of reelecting Daley chairman. Alderman Keane nominated him and eighteen other committeemen made lengthy speeches seconding the nomination. One of them recited, "R, you're rare; I, you're important; C, you're courageous; H, you're heavenly; A, you're able; R, you're renowned; D, you're Democratic; J, is for your being a joy to know; D, you're diligent; A, you're adorable; L, you're loyal; E, you're energetic; and Y, you're youthful."

Once again Lynn Williams stood, but not to criticize. He, too, joined in the praise and made one of the seconding speeches. Daley had since slated young Adlai Stevenson III, whom Williams had supported, for the U.S. Senate. Daley and Williams even exchanged handshakes. In a way, Williams seemed to emphasize his own point about the committee's need to follow a strong leader.

MAYOR RICHARD J. DALEY has gone, and with him the machine that dominated Chicago politics for so long. But, as the following postscript to Royko's article reveals, Daley's legacy continued to influence the city's politics long after his death in 1976, as the old-time ward leaders sought to maintain the system against new electoral challenges in the mid-1980s.

6

E. R. Shipp
WILL LOYALTY WIN THE WARD AGAIN?

At the turn of the century, the West Side, where thousands of immigrants worked in factories and lived in tenements while seeking a toehold in the New World, was the site of bitter political battles between the Irish who controlled the Democratic machine and the Italians who outnumbered them.

Now the Twenty-fifth Ward in the West Side, where boarded-up and abandoned factory buildings attest to those industrial jobs of years past, is again the prize. This time it is a battle between the Italians, who gained control from the Irish about fifty years ago, and the Mexicans who outnumber them.

At stake is the post of ward committeeman being vacated by Alderman Vito Marzullo, the last of the old-style ward leaders. It is one of fifty ward committee races to be decided Tuesday. Although committeemen draw no salary, they have been described as the most powerful men in Chicago, the backbone of the Democratic machine that reached its zenith under Mayor Richard J. Daley, the party boss.

The committee races are a key battleground in a continuing struggle between Harold Washington, the city's first black mayor, and Alderman Edward R. Vrdolyak for control of the Cook County Democratic Central Committee. In April the ward committeemen will choose the party chairman, a post that the Mayor is trying to wrest from Mr. Vrdolyak.

Mr. Marzullo, who is eighty-six years old, is retiring as a committeeman after twenty-eight years but staying on as an alderman. Only twice in a political career that has included twenty-three elections has he faced opposition. As he put it: "I never had any trouble until lately." Hispanic residents of the ward have been pressing for a voice in local government.

From *The New York Times*, 19 March 1984. Copyright © 1984 by The New York Times Company. Reprinted by permission.

"Everyone is making so much noise about the Spanish," he said. "Where is their vote? Sure you got Spanish people in my ward, but how many citizens are there? What are they contributing to the country?"

His designated successor is his chief personal aide, Marco Domico, who is seeking reelection to his sixth term as a state representative. Mr. Domico, sixty-six, was chosen, Mr. Marzullo contended, "because he's a man from the organization, not because he's Italian."

But Juan A. Valazquez, a thirty-nine-year-old community activist who is challenging Mr. Domico, sees things differently, saying ward leaders could have chosen a black or Hispanic resident to run for either state representative or committeeman, but had not. This, he said, "proves the point that it's a racist kind of an organization."

"You Don't Groom Us"

"Their excuse is that there is nobody groomed yet," he said. "You don't groom us. We're not dogs or horses."

Mr. Valazquez has been working with other Hispanic activists to register voters and forge an alliance with blacks in the ward. Opinion among political analysts is mixed on Mr. Valazquez's chances against Mr. Domico, but more optimistic people note that last year he ran for alderman against Mr. Marzullo and won 42 percent of the vote.

"People see Mr. Marzullo as an institution more or less," Mr. Valazquez said. "They have asked why don't I wait until he passes away. I tell them he might live to be 106 years old. Does that mean for twenty more years we've got to wait around and be slaves to somebody who really doesn't care about us?"

The power of a committeeman traditionally lay in the hundreds of patronage jobs he controlled over the years. Precinct workers who turned out the vote were hired, and those who did not were demoted or dismissed. At one point Mr. Marzullo directly controlled 400 city jobs.

This power has diminished somewhat, but a committeeman still distributes judgeships and other political offices and influences the delivery of city services in his ward.

Control of Elections

Committeemen also run elections, choosing poll workers and determining polling places. Giving rise to the saying "vote early, vote often," many have sometimes stolen elections, resulting in prison sentences for some. Fifty-seven people, including precinct captains and poll workers, are now under federal indictment for vote fraud stemming from the November 1982 gubernatorial election.

To Chicago's ward bosses, loyalty to the party is the way to success, and a number of black and Hispanic people have followed this route to city jobs.

The time will come when a Hispanic person will become a committeeman, Mr. Domico said, "but it will be a Hispanic from this organization."

In the Twenty-fifth Ward, two-thirds of the 60,000 residents are of Mexican or other Hispanic descent. White ethnic groups, mostly Italian-Americans, are 18 percent of the population, blacks 15 percent.

The Italian-Americans live in the southern end of the ward, in clean, well-kept neighborhoods off main shopping streets. To the north, Hispanic and black residents live in large public housing projects and three-story multifamily homes in rundown neighborhoods dotted with mom-and-pop storefronts selling food, liquor, or cheap furniture on "easy credit terms." Some blocks are in ruins, relics of the riots that followed the assassination of the Reverend Dr. Martin Luther King, Jr. in 1968.

City Services 'Skewed'

"You can literally see where the Italian section ends and the Hispanic and black sections begin — city services are very skewed toward the white areas," said William J. Grimshaw, a professor of political science at Illinois Institute of Technology.

Unemployment has been estimated to be as high as 25 percent among black and Hispanic residents.

"It's all black up here, so what does he care?" said Wilfred Cornell, Jr., a black community activist, referring to Mr. Marzullo. "His attitude is 'Don't bring any black problems to me; take them to Harold. I'm going to take care of my folks and damn the rest.' "

Mr. Marzullo, whose ward activity dates to 1919, says he tries to help all who come to him "like gentlemen and ladies." One time he threw a priest out of his office. As he tells the story, the priest, accompanied by Black Panthers, demanded certain things for the people of his parish, and Mr. Marzullo responded: "Who died and elected you boss? I'm the boss of this ward."

When his health permits, Mr. Marzullo says he spends his days "doing favors and serving the people." He and Mr. Domico attend wakes and weddings, hand out hundreds of free garbage cans, help immigrants become citizens, place residents in jobs, have the ward organization's cadre of lawyers and former judges provide free legal advice, and help the poor in getting public aid.

At a crowded ward rally on a recent snowy night, Harry Kudesh, a businessman and precinct captain, said in an interview, "When it comes to giving $50, $100 to their churches, when it comes to giving them 200 pounds of candy, 400 pounds of candy for Christmas, when it comes to dinners for the poor and elderly at Christmas and Thanksgiving, they know who has been here to help them."

In return for these favors, a vote is expected at election time.[1]

---

[1] Marco Domico won the primary and the general election.

PRESSURE GROUPS
AND LOBBYISTS

Chapter Two

Since the publication of David Truman's classic, *The Governmental Process*, in 1951, many political scientists have become enamored of the "group theory" of politics.[1] Although the origins of group theory date back at least as far as John C. Calhoun, who stated its premises and implications in his posthumously published work, *A Disquisition on Government*, in 1853, real acceptance of the group theory did not come until the twentieth century. There are two essential premises of group theory: (1) individuals function in the political process only through groups; (2) the interaction of political interest groups produces the national interest. Today, group theory is not as widely accepted as it once was. Theodore Lowi, in particular, has led an attack on the group theorists' second assumption.[2] But the idea that politics is essentially a group process, rather than an individual process remains largely unchallenged. The extreme expression of this view treats groups anthropomorphically, that is, as if they are persons. But groups are not mystical entities that can exist apart from the individuals who act as their leaders and members, or from the important intermediaries, such as the Washington lawyers, between pressure groups and government.

Individual character, personality, and style affect the ways in which pressure groups interact with government. The selections in this chapter have been chosen to demonstrate the personal dimension of the group process.

[1] David B. Truman, *The Governmental Process* (New York: Alfred A. Knopf, 1951).
[2] Theodore J. Lowi, *The End of Liberalism,* 2nd ed. (New York: W. W. Norton, 1979).

W ASHINGTON IS THE MAG-net city for political power seekers. It is the Super-bowl of politics, attracting players and spectators from every part of the nation and around the world. Playing the game of Washington politics is a constantly exciting and often rewarding experience.

The Washington political establishment is a closely knit fraternity. Congressmen, bureaucrats, and lobbyists not only know each other but also frequently strive for the same goals. All ambitious members of the political establishment seek to establish their reputations for power. On Capitol Hill, power translates into money for campaign chests, better prospects for reelection, and respect from colleagues. The bureaucrats with a reputation for power have a better chance of withstanding the frequently changing political winds. Lobbyists who can convince their clients that they have power can charge higher fees.

An effective lobbying style maintains the appearance of power. Who the lobbyist is, and what his or her connections may be, are an important part of that appearance. Former members of Congress and their aides often find that lobbying can be an extremely lucrative career, enabling them to stay in Washington and continue to play the game of politics. Former Congressman Dan Kuykendall (R., Tenn.) commented, "A former U.S. Congressman, no matter how capable, is worth more in Washington than any place else — considerably more. Even those members who go to law firms back home end up getting sent back to Washington."[1] The same could be said for former congressional staffers.

The following selection describes the style of a leading Washington lobbyist, Thomas Boggs, Jr., the son of a former congressman and an unsuccessful candidate for Congress himself. Over the years, Boggs has built a reputation for power that enabled him to rise from a $12,000-a-year associate to a $500,000-a-year partner in what has become one of Washington's largest law firms.

7 Albert R. Hunt
THE WASHINGTON POWER BROKERS

Patton, Boggs, and Blow, one of the capital's fastest-growing law firms, is known as a "full-service lobbying firm."

It represents a multitude of conservative clients ranging from the Business Roundtable to right-wing Guatemalan businessmen. Simulta-

[1] *Congressional Quarterly Weekly Report*, December 27, 1980, p. 3643.

neously, the firm's most celebrated partner, Thomas H. Boggs, Jr., is raising campaign funds for some of the most liberal lawmakers in Congress. Over the past fifteen months, the firm has hired two top political operatives of the 1980 presidential campaign: One worked for Ted Kennedy and the other for Ronald Reagan.

"The Boggs firm," one Washington insider says, "looks more like a fusion government than a law firm."

Although some senior partners try to play down this wheeling-and-dealing image, it is these well-advertised political connections that keep clients coming in droves. "You don't hire Patton, Boggs, and Blow because of their legal expertise," says James Mooney, the executive director of the National Cable Television Association. "You hire them because they have good connections with a broad spectrum" of Congress. This reputation attracts such contradictory clients as General Motors Corp., Chrysler Corp., and the Automobile Import Dealers Association.

Although the firm has eighty-two lawyers here, it usually is known as the "Boggs firm." At age forty-one, Tommy Boggs, son of the late Democratic Majority Leader Hale Boggs and Democratic Representative Corrine (Lindy) Boggs of Louisiana, is one of the capital's most powerful lobbyists.

Mr. Boggs makes about $500,000 a year and recently increased his fee to $250 an hour from $225. He is widely credited with playing a major role in congressional approval of the Chrysler bailout bill a few years ago and always seems to be active in special-interest tax legislation, including the tax-leasing provision enacted last year.

There are thousands of lobbyists trying to influence policy in Washington ranging from the proverbial, single-issue "little old ladies in tennis shoes" to well-heeled corporate influence brokers. In addition to law firms, the most successful influence brokers these days include public-relations practitioners, registered agents for foreign governments, and corporate representatives.

Despite the Reagan administration's pledge to reduce regulation and the size of government, the political climate never has seemed better for many of these special-interest pleaders. While some regulatory activities, such as antitrust, may be drying up a bit at some law firms here, any decline is more than offset for many lobbying operations by increased activity in other areas, such as taxes and defense. Money, specifically campaign contributions, is the fuel that generates much of this lobbying prowess. "I won't even take a client now unless he's willing to set up a political action committee and participate in the [campaign-donations] process," Robert McCandless, a lobbyist, says. Although Mr. Boggs and some others won't go that far publicly, a major asset clearly is their ability to funnel funds to politicians from clients and friends.

Tommy Boggs is widely seen as the prototype of the high-powered

Washington lobbyist. The affable, moon-faced, and slightly paunchy Mr. Boggs is very bright, inordinately savvy, and genuinely engaging. He also is cunning, calculating, and seemingly devoid of any real moral compass, driven mainly by money and success.

In short, Tommy Boggs is a nonmalicious, Washington version of TV's J. R. Ewing.

Mr. Boggs uses more soft-sell sophistication than hard-line pressure, and he shows keen awareness of the political process, especially in the House. "Tommy combines an enormous sense of the way things work with an understanding of where power is and where money is in this town," says Representative Thomas Downey of New York, a liberal Democrat on the House Ways and Means Committee and a beneficiary of Mr. Boggs's fund-raising talents.

Mr. Boggs and his firm have their critics, too. "The Boggs firm, in representing legitimate special interests, contributes to the fragmentation of things," says David Cohen, a former president of Common Cause, the self-styled citizens' lobby. "But unlike the big, prestigious law firms of the past, there's no evidence they play much part in helping government put things back together." And Joan Claybrook, who oversees the Ralph Nader operations here, says: "Some attorneys or lobbyists have a reputation of trying to persuade their clients to do the right thing. Nobody ever says that about Tommy Boggs."

Mr. Boggs isn't comfortable talking about what he hopes to contribute to society or about his political philosophy. But criticism doesn't appear to affect the effervescent lobbyist very much. He says, with a big smile, "I really enjoy playing the game."

He certainly works hard for his clients. He is always prowling the corridors of Congress, talking with members and picking up political intelligence. Some weeks he goes to as many as ten political receptions. "I'll go to two a night if one is for a Ways and Means Committee guy and the other is for defense types," he says. But "it's useless to go to two Ways and Means things," he adds.

That constant motion and energy have honed keen instincts for what motivates politicians. A few years ago, he was helping Marathon Oil Co. fight a move to lower duties on some imported specialty steel that competed against a Marathon subsidiary. He first won over liberal Representative Charles Rangel, a Harlem Democrat, with the argument that some of the imports would come from apartheid South Africa. Then he won over a conservative, the late Representative William Ketchum, with the argument that the Marathon subsidiary was based in the congressman's California district. Mr. Boggs still delights in thinking about this left-right coalition.

And he seems omnipresent. When Jimmy Carter was president, a meeting to plot strategy for a "tax reform" bill was held at the White House. Suddenly, Tom Boggs walked into the session. "I almost fell out of my chair," recalls Robert Brandon, a veteran liberal lobbyist on tax measures. Then, Mr. Boggs, others speculate, was able both to talk about his access to the White House and also to advise business clients what the "enemy" was up to.

Mr. Boggs's reputation is probably exaggerated. He does lose sometimes. Last year, his lobbying on behalf of the cable-TV industry was a decided failure in the Senate. And some congressional aides contend that although he gets much of the credit for the Chrysler bailout measures and some tax breaks, most of the real work was done by others.

Nevertheless, as the belief grows that Tom Boggs can make things happen on Capitol Hill, clients come to the firm specifically for his services. William McGowan, the chairman of MCI Communications Corp., recently insisted that Mr. Boggs personally lobby on the company's behalf before MCI would retain the firm. MCI hired the Boggs firm, one communications expert says, not because of any expertise in that area but because "they wanted the biggest rainmaker they could get."

Money Crucial

It's hard to overestimate the importance of money to all this. Mr. Boggs started off with an advantage — he inherited his father's majority leader's campaign fund in 1973 and, with an eye to his own lobbying interests, doled out more than $60,000 over several elections. Now, he gives the maximum legal limit of $25,000 every two years.

More important, however, he funnels much larger amounts of money to strategically situated lawmakers. Six years ago, he advised the American Trial Lawyers Association to start a political action committee as part of its effort to beat federal no-fault insurance legislation. Now, Mr. Boggs and a representative of a Republican lobbyist, William Timmons, advise the lawyers every election on how to dish out some $500,000 from that PAC to congressional candidates.

Mr. Boggs persuaded Chrysler to give to such Democrats as Representative Tony Coelho, the Californian who now heads the House Democratic Campaign Committee. And he gets his clients to contribute regularly to various Democratic party functions. "Some of these clients are getting had," one Capitol Hill insider charges. "They're giving the money, but Tommy is getting the credit."

Network of Lobbyists

Mr. Boggs also has a network of other Washington lobbyists that he calls on. For example, in trying to raise money for Representative Fortney Stark, a liberal Californian on the House Ways and Means Committee, Mr. Boggs is seeking $250 each from a list of three dozen lobbyists. "I hit these guys, and I know they'll come back and hit me up," he notes.

He goes to great lengths to keep this network flowing. Shortly after Tosco Inc., the big oil-shale concern, received a $1.1 billion federal loan guarantee last year, its representatives started getting solicitations to Mr. Boggs's fund raisers and other political activities. A short while later, Patton, Boggs, and Blow started lobbying with Tosco to get its legal business.

When Mr. Boggs deals with a member of Congress legislatively, though, he is the consummate professional. "Tom Boggs never embarrasses me; he never pushes me to vote for something that would be impossible for me to support," Representative Rangel says. But other politicians acknowledge that Mr. Boggs's fund raising gives him special access, and some say they are inclined to give him the benefit of the doubt on some legislative matters.

Family Ties

Mr. Boggs has come a long way since he joined the law firm sixteen years ago. "When Tommy was first around, everybody thought he was just using his family connections," says his law partner, James O'Hara, who then was a Michigan congressman. After his father died in a 1972 plane crash, it was Tommy, on behalf of the family, who gave Tip O'Neill the green light to run for House Democratic majority leader. His mother succeeded his father in Congress. (This year, a sister, Barbara Sigmund, is running for Congress from New Jersey.)

Tommy Boggs himself ran unsuccessfully for a suburban Maryland House seat in 1970 but says electoral politics is out of his system: "I couldn't afford it." His senior partner, James Patton, thinks that the youthful super-lobbyist aspires to be chairman of a major corporation or secretary of defense someday.

Patton, Boggs, and Blow was started twenty years ago by Mr. Patton, a succsssful international lawyer with the city's most established law firm, Covington and Burling. He hired Tom Boggs, "for $10,000 or $12,000 a year," he recalls. The fifty-three-year-old Mr. Patton has directed the firm's enormous growth. A decade ago, the firm had a dozen lawyers; sometime this year, it expects to exceed one hundred attorneys.

Clients number anywhere from four hundred to five hundred, Mr. Patton says, though many are short-term customers. Steady, major clients range from the Mars candy company to Reader's Digest and Northwest Energy Corp. to the state of Louisiana. And yet Patton, Boggs, and Blow (Mr. Boggs became a partner in 1967) isn't considered, among lawyers at least, a top-flight legal firm. Last year, one of its partners left because he wanted to practice substantive tax law instead of always lobbying.

Areas of Expertise

This reputation may be a bit of a bum rap. The firm now has large sections for litigation, international law, administrative practices, and energy. Senior partners say more than 80 percent of their work doesn't involve lobbying.

Still, the political presence of Mr. Boggs and others is ever evident. It is hardly a secret, for instance, that the firm's foreign clients — including retainers of $100,000 a year from the government of Oman and $60,000 from Amigos del Pais, the Guatemalan business group — are based on political connections and not geopolitical expertise. Although the Guatemalan group's chief interest is to spruce up the image here of that country's military dictatorship, Mr. Boggs says he believes that the businessmen are a "moderating influence" and adds that for philosophical reasons his firm wouldn't represent the right-wing government itself.

In keeping with the recent trend in Washington, the firm's lobbying operations have a distinctly bipartisan coloration. The Democratic side is led by Mr. Boggs, former Congressman O'Hara, former Senator William Hathaway of Maine, and Ronald Brown, a former deputy chairman of the Democratic National Committee and a top adviser to Senator Edward M. Kennedy's 1980 presidential campaign.

The Republican Side

The Republican services are no slouches, either. They include Ernest Christian, a top tax official in the Nixon administration; Cliff Massa, a former high official at the National Association of Manufacturers; William Colley, a former American Medical Association lobbyist, and Frank Donatelli, who was hired after the 1980 elections, in which he ran the Midwestern-states campaign for Ronald Reagan.

"This political smorgasbord of lawyers," Mr. Patton argues, "gives our clients the whole spectrum of thinking in this town. . . . It can be very exciting and very stimulating."

It also can be very effective politically. For instance, Representative Barber Conable, the ranking Republican on the House Ways and Means Committee, says he has met Mr. Boggs only "once or twice, and I don't think he has ever been to my office." But asked about Mr. Boggs's partner, Mr. Christian, the New York lawmaker says, "Oh, Ernie is a fine fellow. I talk to him all the time."

Privately, Mr. Boggs also apparently believes that someone with Democratic connections can lobby more effectively for business interests than someone with GOP ties. "Republicans usually vote with you anyway" one corporate lobbyist says. "So Tommy knows he has most of them, and every time he gets a Democrat, particularly a liberal, that's icing on the cake."

Mr. Boggs also sees benefits from the firm's contradictory mix of clients. "With our client list we can build a minicoalition on almost any issue," he declares. A good example, he says, is the controversial taxleasing provision passed by Congress last year. During consideration of the bill, the firm's leverage on Capitol Hill was increased because the firm represented major retailers, which are potential buyers of tax-leasing plans, and Chrysler, a potential seller.

The firm admits that client interests aren't always the same. But it notes that it represents diverse customers on separate issues; Chrysler on the bailout and tax issues, GM on the Clean Air Act, and import-auto dealers on trade legislation. As for the appearance of conflict of interest in some fields, Timothy May, a senior partner, says: "I've wondered about some of this myself, but we've talked to the clients and they don't see it as a problem."

Neither does Mr. Boggs. He enjoys high-powered lobbying and thinks that in time it may bring respectability as well as money and power. "In recruiting, a few years ago, it was a real disadvantage to say you were a firm that lobbied; we hid it," he says. "But now, it's a recruiting asset. The kids love it. They call lobbying public-policy law."

FREDERICK DUTTON DID NOT make Joseph C. Goulden's list of Washington's superlawyers in the early 1970s, although he had already had extensive political experience at the highest levels of government. But as the decade drew to a close, Dutton had become one of the capital's most influential power brokers.[1]

Dutton was a young California lawyer engaged in a modest practice when he began a political column for the *Los Angeles Times* that eventually brought him to the attention of historian Arthur Schlesinger, Jr., who recruited him for Adlai Stevenson's presidential campaign, launching Dutton's political career. He later served as Governor Edmund Brown's chief of staff, a position he left to join the Kennedy administration. He became secretary of the cabinet, and then assistant secretary of state for congressional relations. Arthur Schlesinger recalled in his chronicle of the Kennedy years that in the latter position, "Dutton joined policy sophistication with political skill in running congressional relations."[2]

Dutton soon became part of the inner corps of Kennedy advisers, a trusted aide not only to the president but to his brother Robert. He worked in the presidential campaigns of Robert Kennedy and George McGovern, all of the time sharpening his political acumen and expanding his Washington contacts. He always carefully cultivated the press.

Today, *Washington Post* executive editor Benjamin Bradlee, *New York Times* Washington bureau chief Bill Kovach, and NBC-TV star Roger Mudd attend Dutton's dinner parties, along with the chairman of the Joint Chiefs of Staff and other powerful Washington political figures.[3]

The following selection describes Dutton's Washington style, and how he has become, singlehandedly, a formidable representative of Saudi Arabia.

[1] Joseph C. Goulden discusses what he called the "small and powerful world of the great Washington law firms" in his bestselling book, *The Superlawyers* (New York: Weybright and Talley, p. 171).

[2] Arthur M. Schlesinger, Jr., *A Thousand Days* (Boston: Houghton Mifflin, 1965), p. 445.

[3] Karen Elliott House, "The Power Brokers: A Registered Agent Helps Saudis Fathom and Sway Washington," *The Wall Street Journal*, March 29, 1982, pp. 1, 15.

8

Steven Emerson
DUTTON OF ARABIA

In Washington's political establishment, Frederick G. Dutton appears to be the embodiment of respectability. His civic and government background is stellar, his reputation among journalists impeccable, his political skill remarkable, and his integrity largely unquestioned by supporters and critics alike. Fred Dutton is also the premier foreign agent for the government of Saudi Arabia. And because of his sterling personal qualifications as well as his influence with his clients, Dutton may even be the preeminent and most powerful foreign agent in the country.

Most of the nine hundred foreign lobbyists registered with the Department of Justice are engaged in activities that could be considered routine. They are paid by their foreign clients to secure special immigrant visas, to help change tariff schedules, to arrange press interviews, and even to disseminate tourist information. Rarely do foreign agents become key political spokesmen for other nations; even less frequently do they become architects of other nations' foreign political strategies. Fred Dutton's work on behalf of Saudi Arabia is a major exception.

Dutton's political career began in the 1950s, when he served in the campaigns of Adlai E. Stevenson and then as executive assistant to Governor Edmund G. (Pat) Brown of California. In 1961, after working for the election of John F. Kennedy, Dutton was appointed to be a special assistant to the president. He later moved to the State Department as assistant secretary for congressional relations. As one friend said, this "proved to be his best preparation for his current role. It gave him hundreds of key contacts." He resigned in 1964 and eventually set up his own law firm. The associates were all liberal Kennedy family devotees. One of them was Herb Schmertz, now vice-president of Mobil Oil Corporation. When Schmertz moved to Mobil, he hired Dutton to provide intelligence and analysis of the "general political climate" in Washington. Dutton also suggested to Schmertz that Mobil sponsor the National Town Meetings, lively Washington discussions on domestic and foreign policy issues, which feature journalists and high government officials. Mobil liked the idea, and hired Dutton to run the programs, which, until this year, had been broadcast regularly over National Public Radio. As William Safire discovered last year, because of the Mobil grant, Dutton has also been able "to sprinkle $500 to $1,000 honoraria over hundreds of congressmen and Washington journalists."

Reprinted by permission of *The New Republic*, June 16, 1982. © 1982, The New Republic, Inc.

In 1968 Dutton was one of Robert Kennedy's principal campaign advisers, and was at his side when he was assassinated. In 1972 he became a key aide in George McGovern's bid for the presidency, and has maintained his contacts in the Democratic party ever since. Dutton was also an early and active opponent of the Vietnam war.

In June 1975 Dutton registered as an agent for Saudi Arabia, first for Petromin, the Saudi state oil agency, and later in the year for the embassy itself. When he first signed up with the embassy of Saudi Arabia in November 1975, Dutton noted on his registration statement that he was "being retained for counseling and legal advice, not public information activities, which registrant understands will be the responsibility of others." Yet, in the seven years that Dutton has served as a Saudi agent, he has helped build an image of moderation and legitimacy for the Saudis, which they desperately sought after the ill will they engendered with the 1973 oil embargo. The Saudis have paid him handsomely: over $1.2 million — $400,000 in 1981 alone for him and his wife — including a virtually unlimited expense account.

Dutton says in his registration forms filed at the Department of Justice that his work consists primarily of legal advice and political counsel, not lobbying or public relations. In an interview, Dutton said, "Ninety-nine percent of my time and work, social or otherwise, is interfacing with the Saudis. I generally have avoided going up to the Hill, don't like it, and made clear I don't want that role. And, for example, I saw one senator and no congressman during the AWACS debate. As for a continuing [public relations] program, no."

Dutton has listed no more than five senators and representatives contacted on behalf of his Saudi clients. He has carefully nurtured the image of a lawyer-client relationship with the Saudis. And it is precisely that professional distance, coupled with his long-standing reputation for integrity, that has enabled him to retain his political credibility.

Some of Dutton's former associates were interviewed by Betty Cuniberti for an article that appeared last October in the *Los Angeles Times*. Frank Mankiewicz, president of National Public Radio, who is described by Cuniberti as "a close friend of Dutton from their high school days in California through the Bobby Kennedy and George McGovern campaigns to the present," said, "I assume someone is going to represent the Saudis. I'm glad it's Fred Dutton, because he's an honorable, decent, thoughtful fellow. Better him than some cut-throat lobbyist. I happen personally not to agree with his stand on AWACS. But would I make a moral judgment on Fred Dutton? Surely not."

Over the years Dutton has cultivated friendships with key senators and various former government officials, and with preeminent members of the national media, including, according to a *Wall Street Journal* article by Karen Elliot House, *Washington Post* editor Benjamin Bradlee, *New York Times* Washington bureau chief Bill Kovach, columnist Joseph Kraft, NBC anchorman Roger Mudd, CBS diplomatic correspondent Robert Pierpoint, and Elliot House herself. In addition to scores of other journalists and U.S. officials, they are guests at his frequent brunches and dinners. Even when Saudi policies are not discussed, the Saudis are well served by these social occasions. One senator says, "When I talk with Fred, I simply never have the feeling that I'm dealing with a foreign agent. I never have the suspicion that Fred Dutton could sell out this country's interest." Even members of Congress not friendly toward Saudi Arabia concede that Dutton has worked miracles for the Saudis. One prominent journalist who has been invited to numerous Dutton dinners says, "If Fred Dutton is their man, how bad can they be?" In 1978 the *New York Times* wrote that "Dutton has long been one of Washington's most useful and reliable sources for political reporters." At the *Washington Post*, Dutton is a well-known fixture, and one staffer says wryly that at the *Post's* Monday editorial meetings, it's easy to tell who had brunch with Dutton the day before.

The Fred Dutton who works for the Saudis is generally perceived as an extension of the principled Fred Dutton who long ago became outspoken on a wider range of political matters, from freedom of speech to the Vietnam war. And, in the 1960s, according to friends, associates, and even Dutton himself, he was a strong supporter of Israel — even "uncritically pro-Israel," in Dutton's own words. Many of the people who know Dutton, including members of Congress and the press, view Dutton's contract with the Saudis as almost incidental. His popularity with journalists is sustained by his fund of imaginative ideas.

But during the AWACS debate, Dutton coined the slogan "Reagan or Begin," which reduced the controversy to an issue of national loyalty. And phrased in such terms, it unleashed undercurrents of anti-Semitism. What caused the change in Dutton's views on Israel to such an extent that he became an agent for Saudi Arabia? According to Dutton, it wasn't simply because a generous offer had been made. "The original contract was not that lucrative to begin with. . . . It has grown with time, as the amount of work, or let's say Saudi trust in me, has grown." He says that then-Senator William Fulbright had recommended him to the Saudis in 1973, and that his decision stemmed from a personal connection with Fulbright. "If almost anybody else had come to me and suggested I do it, no. I don't think I would have done it. It was unusual, but interesting. He was chairman of the Foreign Relations Committee, I admired him, he identified the problem, and so I went over there. But I never even thought about the Arab world, the Middle East, other than from a very uncritical pro-Israeli position. I never thought about representing anybody abroad. All my business had been in California and Washington."

Dutton has long insisted on his initial hesitancy to take the Saudi contract in 1975, and friends and associates say that Dutton has also told them of his unwillingness. This reticence has been critical to the avoidance of a crass hired-gun image. The *New York Times* provided the following account on April 2, 1978:

> One day in 1973 Senator William J. Fulbright was discussing the Middle East with Rawleigh Warner, Jr., the chief executive officer of Mobil Corporation, one of Mr. Dutton's clients.
>
> As Mr. Dutton tells the story, the Senator told Mr. Warner that Saudi Arabians "didn't handle themselves well" in Washington and should hire a representative. Mr. Dutton's name cropped up — among others — and Mr. Warner passed Senator Fulbright's advice on to Riyadh.
>
> In 1975 Mr. Dutton was offered a contract by the Saudis, but hesitated. Given the intensely pro-Israeli position of many in the Democratic party, he feared that working for the Saudis might seem the end of his political career, but he took the job anyway.

The real story is somewhat different. Recently obtained secret oil company documents, confidential correspondence, and information from oil company officials reveal that Dutton solicited the Saudi contract as early as 1973, and began assisting Saudi Arabia, directly and indirectly, through the Arabian American Oil Company (Aramco, the oil consortium consisting of Exxon, Mobil, Texaco, and Standard Oil of California) in December of that year through 1974. The new information shows that Aramco hired Dutton because it was being pressured by the Saudis to prove that it was actively supporting the kingdom's political demands. Furthermore, the documents show that as early as 1973 Dutton conceived of an ambitious public relations program, including newspaper advertisements, films, and an "unannounced" public relations operation with fifteen staff people, aimed at turning American public opinion against Israel and more favorably toward the Saudis.

Finally, the new material provides significant insights into how Dutton got the job, the nature of his public relations activities in the United States, and why he has cultivated such close relationships with the *Washington Post* and the national press.

In the spring of 1973 Saudi King Faisal was becoming increasingly bellicose about American Middle East policy. It was clear to oil company officials that the secret political funding operation which Aramco had conducted since 1967 was not going to be enough. American policy was still aligned with Israel; more had to be done. At the same time a bug had been planted in the ears of oil company and Saudi officials by then-

Senator Fulbright, a longtime critic of Israel. He suggested to Rawleigh Warner, chairman of Mobil, that the companies attempt to help upgrade Saudi public relations in the United States.

A search process began in mid-1973 by oil officials for an American adviser for the Saudis — an action taken with concurrence of Saudi officials. The search focused on prominent Washington attorneys. Half a dozen were considered, and by September 1973 Dutton became a finalist.

One former official of Aramco said, "We were interested in this case and in others in getting them an adviser from the U.S. scene who could advise them on whatever subject they wanted — or could direct their efforts of whatever they wanted in the United States. We looked at Dutton, who at that time had no real experience in Middle East but had political experience. He had worked through the Kennedy days and all this sort of thing. We felt he had the kind of a broad expertise on the American scene to offer the Saudis. Up until that point, they looked to Aramco to do it."

According to oil company records, on September 12, 1973, Rawleigh Warner sent a personal appraisal of Dutton to a vice-president of Aramco "as a possible man for the Saudi Arabians." Dutton met Aramco officials in Washington and was told that the Saudis needed an experienced, politically astute, well-connected adviser to help turn American foreign policy toward the Arabs. In one of his meetings, Dutton outlined his plan for a broad public relations operation throughout the United States. Aramco was still evaluating Dutton when he decided to add an extra push. On October 16, 1973 — eight days after the outbreak of the October 1973 war and on the day of a visit to Washington by various Arab envoys bearing the threat of an oil embargo — Dutton wrote a two-page, unsolicited letter to Mike Ameen, then vice-president of Aramco. The letter focused on ways to effect pro-Arab changes in public opinion by use of the media, which Dutton held to be the key to changing American policy. Dutton also warned that Arab threats and warnings about oil cutoffs would only prove counterproductive. Nixon, Dutton added, really wanted a "balanced" policy, but was locked in by public opinion in support of Israel. He wrote:

> I just heard on the morning radio news that a special, high-level delegation of Saudi, Kuwait, and other Arab envoys are coming to Washington today to meet with President Nixon. While that is unquestionably a useful step, I want to urge it is far from enough as a major move even at this juncture — and would seem to misunderstand the overall power system and real decision-making process in this country, especially now.
>
> To the extent the envoys appear to be bearing stern warnings, they only further incite the widespread publicity in the U.S. that the Nixon administration must not give into threats or oil blackmail. Genuinely effective

leverage at least in the U.S. political system must not be a major person but through the public, or key groups, or major news sources. The leverage comes through sympathetic papers, senators, contributors and such.

Dutton went on to say that Aramco should initiate the public relations campaign he had previously suggested, and should solicit help from sympathetic figures in government and the media:

> It must be backed up with the kind of effort we touched on — and quickly. Fulbright and others should be kept briefed; and so should the newsmen here. My own first-hand impression is that the Arabs have far more opportunity in both those sectors than they are beginning to effectively harness. Howard K. Smith on ABC-TV news last evening (nearly twenty million viewers) made a masterful appeal for a more balanced U.S. policy on the Middle East. The Sunday newspapers all contained columns or articles strongly presenting the Arab view. Yet my inquiries of the people writing those (such as Evans and Novak; Smith Hempstone of the *Star-News;* and others) is that they are working out of their own background and digging, not with any real or fresh information. I was at the *Washington Post* again yesterday, and while the paper remains staunchly pro-Israeli in its editorials (as this morning) the working writers there have increasing questions and doubts about the Israeli tilt to U.S. policy. In brief, the opportunity is present for the kind of major effort backing up the diplomacy today suggested above.[1]

In his final paragraph, Dutton reminded Ameen of the need for the special efforts on behalf of Saudi Arabia that cannot be made at the "top" or through regular diplomatic channels. He added, "I do not intend to be implicitly pushing myself to help you in this situation — I am still very much on the sidelines, I realize. But I would think that you might assure there is full understanding of the domestic political, media and particular Congressional aspects and try to bring to bear the necessary steps (the Israelis are massively at work) to assure a balanced policy in this country's own self interest."

In late November Aramco decided to retain Dutton as an adviser. His duties reportedly were to include some of the same services that Aramco had intended for him to provide Saudi Arabia — public relations, political intelligence, and help in planning and arranging visits by Saudi officials to the United States. It was both Dutton's and Aramco's understanding that it was only a matter of time before Saudi Arabia would agree to a formal employment arrangement with Dutton.

On December 7, 1973, Dutton wrote Aramco another remarkable letter. It strongly suggests that Aramco hired Dutton and pushed for his employment by the Saudis because of its need to prove its loyalty to the Saudis. In four pages, Dutton detailed a massive public relations pro-

---

[1] © 1978 by The New York Times Company. Reprinted by permission.

gram that Aramco could take on its own, "responsive to what I assume is a fundamental need to demonstrate to the Saudis that Aramco is taking real steps here to carry forward your and their common interests." Dutton impressed upon Ameen Aramco's self-interest in such a program: "The huge stake that Aramco has there would seem to make that especially important over the next three to six months, with the impending negotiations, oil embargo and underlying struggle looming so large. Not making a genuine effort over the months immediately ahead would seem, in fact, to be readily subject to interpretation by them as that the company is ducking in the really critical clinch." He urged throughout that only programs of a certain type be initiated: those that would result in "press clippings," or that could be "directly verifiable to the Saudis" in other ways. "Sophisticated Saudis like Yamani must be well aware of how much more influential TV has become than newspapers with the White House, Congress, and general public; and showing tapes of films can even make a more indelible impression than thumbing through batches of newspaper stories." Dutton's suggestions included five-minute documentary TV commercials, fifteen-minute radio programs, advertisements in the *New York Times,* and lectures, seminars, and speeches by pro-Saudi Americans at major universities.

Saudi oil minister Sheik Yamani was scheduled to visit the United States in early December of that year, and Dutton provided some assistance to him during the visit. In his talks with Kissinger, Yamani reaffirmed Saudi Arabia's refusal to lift the oil embargo unless the United States acceded to Saudi Arabia's demands that Israel be forced to withdraw immediately from all the occupied territories. At the conclusion of the visit, Dutton delivered a book to Yamani at the Madison Hotel. The book, Dutton wrote in an accompanying note, was "intended as a very small token of appreciation for all you have done on this trip, from those here who believe in an even-handed U.S. policy toward the Middle East. I hope there will be many renewing follow-ups on behalf of that from many sources."

In the course of his work, Dutton also prepared, apparently on his own initiative, a proposed three-page advertisement, to be signed by King Faisal or Sheik Yamani, for publication in the United States. The advertisement, entitled *From Saudi Arabia to America,* defended the Arab view on the Middle East, attacked Israel, and justified the embargo. In the advertisement, Dutton attributed the sole source of Middle East instability to Israel — including its encouragement of Jewish immigration — as the reason for the oil embargo: "The stepped-up recent building of permanent settlements on occupied territories and the international campaign launched for still greater immigration into the area inescapably forewarned for yet further expansionism onto Arab soil and larger injustices if resolute corrective action was not sought."

In a letter dated December 15, 1973, just after Yamani left the U.S., Dutton wrote Aramco chairman Frank Jungers to tell him, "Yamani's trip here was superb, with much good coming of it. But vastly more is needed — and quickly." Dutton then outlined a whirlwind press tour by Prince Saud and Sheik Yamani during their prospective visits to the United States.

Dutton also suggested an increased role for himself in helping to schedule future visits to the United States by Prince Saud and Sheik Yamani.

> Leaving the development of the scheduling for a Saudi visit to the Saudi Embassy in Washington or the State Department will not accomplish what has to be done. None of the Arab embassies here has a feel for these matters; and the State Department is neither sensitive or imaginative enough about the domestic front, as I learned while Assistant Secretary of State under Kennedy and Johnson.

In his concluding paragraph, Dutton expressed his pleasure in meeting Jungers and added:

> And I want to thank you, too, for the opportunity to meet Yamani, who I sensed is about as fascinating an individual as John F. Kennedy, whom I came to think while his Secretary of the Cabinet was about the most interesting political figure (even with his faults) I would ever come to know.

According to correspondence to Dutton from high-ranking Aramco officials, Dutton was to be working under the Saudi official, Kamal Adham, if a contract with the Saudis could be agreed upon. Adham was described by Aramco officials as "special adviser to the King," but, in fact, he was the head of the Saudi secret police. As King Faisal's brother-in-law, Adham also positioned himself to be a middleman for billions of dollars of Western contracts with Saudi Arabia, and he is considered to have been the principal CIA liaison in Saudi Arabia. Adham's nephew, Prince Turki, who has since succeeded Adham as head of Saudi intelligence, was to work with Dutton.

Dutton also conceived of a public relations "operation" for Saudi Arabia to be set up in Washington under the aegis of a high Saudi official, and heavily dependent upon staff personnel from Mobil, SoCal, Texaco, and Exxon. According to an outline, the operation was to " have a low profile" with no announcement made of its creation. "Simply go to work," wrote Dutton. "Set up goals, assignments, small staff. Do through others. Use 'free' outlets to the maximum extent possible." The "staff nucleus" was to consist of a "TV and radio news specialist," "newspaper experts for contact," writers, research assistants, and liaison people with the Senate and House of Representatives. In addition, over ten staff personnel "detailed from the Aramco companies" were to be placed in charge of numerous public relations programs. Senators, representatives, and "major news people" were to be invited to Saudi Arabia. Lucius Battle of the Middle East Institute was to be commissioned to give press interviews throughout the United States. Dutton also suggested setting up college seminars, producing film documentaries, preparing newspaper advertisements, and scheduling Aramco and Saudi officials to speak in the United States and abroad. Targeted groups included the "business community," "blacks," "environmental groups," "peace groups," "individual VIPs," "governors, mayors, and others."

Dutton insisted on being exclusively in charge of the operation and working directly with Kamal Adham and top Aramco officials. Quoting a fee of $1,000 a day for top Washington lawyers, Dutton asked for a $600,000, three-year contract and added, "I will likely be giving thirty days a month for a long time to come, and long evenings." Dutton also added, "I would be burning many bridges to do this — have family obligations." The contract would be subject to cancellation "if Fulbright informally indicates [that I am] not performing or for other grounds." (Incidentally, appraising the adequacy of Dutton's work for the Saudis would have been an interesting role for the chairman of the Senate Foreign Relations Committee to play.) In the final line of the three-page outline, Dutton wrote, *"Start Immediately* — should have started six months ago, or twenty-five years ago" (the year in which Israel was created).

By February 1974, Aramco led Dutton to believe that the Saudis would finally agree to a formal contract. Dutton had met with Adham and Turki several times, in the United States and in Saudi Arabia. He drew up a "Statement of Understanding" with eight clauses enumerating his duties as a "consultant," rates of compensation, method of payment, and expense reimbursement. The contract was to begin on February 15. Dutton stipulated in clause two that he "shall be guided by and report to Sheikh Adham and shall not be assigned to work regularly under a ministry or bureaucracy, nor under other Americans." The contract was to run for three years "because of the almost certainly protracted nature of the problem to be dealt with concerning Saudi Arabian-U.S. ties and because other sources of income and work for me will be affected by my taking this responsibility."

But no contract was signed. At the end of Dutton's visit to the kingdom in early February, where he met with top Saudi officials, Dutton wrote to Jungers expressing his appreciation for making the trip possible. He hoped that "a working relationship with Kamal Adham goes together as it provides striking opportunities for getting at the real problems of these times both here and more broadly."

In a memo sent to Aramco, Dutton detailed a "small vignette" that indicated to him that there was "some dark thinking going on in Washington." On Friday, February 22, 1974, Dutton was scheduled to have a "quick, informal" dinner with Fred Graham and David Halberstam. The oil embargo was still in effect at the time. The three of them dropped by a hotel to see Eric Severeid and Theodore White, whom Dutton had known for a long time. After Dutton mentioned to White that he had recently visited Saudi Arabia, White, in Dutton's words, "immediately assailed me and began a long diatribe of how no little country of 2 million people (he even had his figures wrong) should be able to cause so much trouble to all the industrial nations of the world." White, according to Dutton, continued in his "warped, distorted, incredible diatribe by what is supposed to be a highly intelligent man and certainly an influential one . . . including more with U.S. political leaders (especially Nixon) than the reading public. No argument or moderating could change his attitude. The scene was frankly grotesque. But it is mentioned here because I have run into varying degrees of it with respected political writers at several Washington dinners and several of the younger editorial writers at the *Washington Post*."

By late May 1974, the Saudis had still not signed an agreement with Dutton, despite repeated Aramco requests to Saudi officials. On May 27, Aramco's vice-president, Mike Ameen, promised Dutton that he would finally confront Adham to "get this matter settled once and for all." Why were the Saudis holding up a formal agreement? According to an Aramco official in Saudi Arabia at the time, the delay was due to the "procrastination and deliberations associated with all Saudi endeavors."

While awaiting a formal agreement, Dutton provided services for the Saudis in 1974 for which two high-ranking Aramco officials thought Dutton should be paid. They urged that he submit a bill to the Saudis in May. Even though this arrangement was apparently agreed to by Adham, Ameen advised against it lest the Saudis "misinterpret" the bill. "I feel it best," Ameen wrote Dutton, "that we continue to attempt to have him [Adham] enter into an agreement signed, sealed and delivered."

It was not until December 1975, nearly two years after he began providing relations ideas to Saudi Arabia, that Dutton registered as an agent for its embassy. Dutton has worked hard to convey the image of a lobbyist who is above the level of crass influence peddling or manipulative public relations, and that image has been the key to his credibility with the national media.

When confronted about his earlier unreported work for Saudi Arabia and Aramco, Dutton said that he was not involved in public relations for the Saudis, and "was not made aware of Aramco's dealings with the Saudis" regarding his employment with Saudi Arabia: "I went to work for Aramco in early 1974, as Aramco was trying to assess where it stood in the midst of the oil boycott. I was not paid by the Saudis, but by Aramco, to analyze problems and the changing situation on energy." But as the new information shows, it is difficult to distinguish between Dutton's work for Aramco and his work for the Saudis.

In the end, the issue is not that Dutton solicited a lucrative contract with the Saudis, but that the petrodollar has come to play such an extraordinary role in American society. It can buy more than goods — it can buy influence, prestige, and the services of men like Fred Dutton. And its real target is the foreign policy of the United States.

I F THE ELDERLY HAD A UNION, Florida Congressman Claude Pepper would be its leader and chief Washington lobbyist. Members of Congress must serve their constituents, and serve them well, to get reelected. But that service does not necessarily limit a congressperson's or senator's ability to represent and advocate interests that may transcend his or her electoral constituency. Members of Congress are often highly effective "lobbyists" for special interests. They provide expert advice to other legislators and to the executive branch, testify before congressional committees, raise money through political action committees, and back candidates who support their causes. The position of public trust they occupy gives their advocacy a special boost in the political process.

The following selection describes Claude Pepper as the *national* advocate for the elderly, a role that clearly does not hurt him in his district where 30 percent of the adults are sixty-five years of age or over. But his advocacy goes far beyond what would be required to keep the support of the elderly voters in his district. His cause is time consuming, expensive, and physically draining. The eighty-four-year old Capitol Hill veteran, however, relishes politics and principles, and he continued to champion the causes of the elderly even after he assumed the powerful Rules Committee chairmanship in 1983.

9

John Egerton
CONGRESSMAN CLAUDE PEPPER: COURTLY CHAMPION OF AMERICA'S ELDERLY

If ever a constituency could be expected to belong to a public official, the 25 million Americans age sixty-five and over should belong to Ronald Reagan. At seventy, he is one of them, the oldest person ever to be elected to the White House. Millions of older Americans share the general tenets of his conservative Republican philosophy. He is an attractive and glamorous man, a personification of usefulness and productivity in later years, an inspiration to others his age.

But Mr. Reagan is not without competition for the loyalties of the elderly — and, indirectly, for their votes. One of his most outspoken challengers is a short, combative, and indefatigable elder statesman from Florida, eighty-one-year-old Representative Claude D. Pepper of Miami. A New Deal Democrat and an unwavering liberal from the day he first

From *New York Times Magazine,* Nov. 29, 1981. Copyright © 1981 by The New York Times Company. Reprinted by permission.

gained a seat in the United States Senate in 1936, Pepper is now the oldest member of either house of Congress. He is also chairman of the House Select Committee on Aging, and is widely regarded as the leading Congressional authority on — and advocate of — Federal assistance to the elderly.

When the third decennial White House Conference on Aging begins its four-day meeting in Washington [Nov. 30–Dec. 3, 1981] the 2,200 voting delegates will be primed for a clash between the Reagan and Pepper philosophies, if not a confrontation between the two men themselves. Pepper will not only be a featured speaker but also plans to attend every session of the conference, which has been authorized by Congress to develop recommendations on issues concerning the elderly. But at this writing, it is not yet certain if President Reagan will address the conference, as President Eisenhower did the first one early in January 1961 — when Medicare proposals were developed — and President Nixon did in 1971 — when a collection of bills, mostly dealing with nutrition, were spawned.

Some delegates have charged, as has Pepper, that the administration, through the Republican National Committee, had been attempting to "sabotage" the conference, "stacking the deck" by increasing the voting membership by 200 as a means of blunting criticism against presidential budget cuts affecting the elderly. But these charges have been vehemently denied by Richard S. Schweiker, the Secretary of Health and Human Services, whose department has responsibility for carrying out conference activities. The Republican National Committee has, however, acknowledged that it recently conducted telephone interviews of almost half the delegates during which their views on the President's policies, and other issues, were sought.

Although Ronald Reagan and Claude Pepper have never formally met, their sharply contrasting reputations have preceded them to the conference on aging in the form of high-blown prefight oratory. A highly placed Reagan aide has called Pepper "the perfect embodiment of the Democratic philosophy of big spending that has almost destroyed this nation's economy." Pepper, in turn, has excoriated the President's economic policies as a "multibillion-dollar tax transfer to the rich," a "blueprint for disaster" that will "bring shame to our nation and misery to millions of older Americans."

The White House Conference on Aging is not the only forum in which the Reagan and Pepper philosophies will be joined in battle in the months ahead. Pepper has his Select Committee on Aging as a permanent base which he uses skillfully. Earlier this month, his committee held a conference curtain raiser on pension fraud, and Pepper made a guest appearance before the Senate Labor and Human Resources Committee, as did the venerable eighty-one-year-old actress Helen Hayes, to support additional health-care proposals. Speaker Thomas P. O'Neill has provided Pepper with another forum by designating him to represent House Democrats on the fifteen-member bipartisan Social Security review commission proposed by President Reagan. And, if the Democrats retain control of the House in next year's elections, Pepper will be in line to become chairman of the powerful House Rules Committee and thus will control what legislation goes, or doesn't go, to the floor of the House for a vote.

From opposite ends of the American political spectrum, the President and the Congressman from Florida have become prominent and powerful public figures whose actions are vitally important to all senior citizens. The President has yet to publicly acknowledge his adversary. Pepper says, "I have no ill will against the President, but his has been the most reactionary voice in public life for the past fifteen years. He is an affable man with foolish, dangerous ideas. When the two positions we represent come into conflict, as they inevitably will, it will be an interesting fight, and I look forward to it. In fact, I'll relish it."

Pepper's long-time colleague from Miami, Democratic Representative Dante B. Fascell, says he "can't see Claude losing this battle. He's been around for a long time, and he understands the dynamics of politics, the fine points of positioning and timing. Claude doesn't fall into traps — he might spring a few, but he won't get caught in any. If the President insists on a major overhaul of the Social Security system, I think he'll have to back down. If I were a betting man, I'd put my money on Pepper."

Two weeks after President Reagan's inauguration, the Select Committee on Aging, which can hold hearings but cannot report legislation directly to the floor, presented a briefing for members of the House of Representatives on "the status of the elderly in America." Citing statistics from a variety of government sources, chairman Pepper asserted that 15.7 percent of the elderly — nearly 4 million people — have incomes below the poverty line (pegged at $3,941.00 for single, elderly individuals), that 60 percent would be in those circumstances were it not for Social Security, and that in 1980, more than two-thirds of all senior citizens had incomes of less than $6,000. Medicare, Pepper told his colleagues, is estimated to pay only about 38 percent of the health bills of the elderly, and only "the poorest of the poor" are eligible for Medicaid, with similar limitations applying to various supplemental benefits.

Yet, said Pepper, "There are many voices sounding the call for retreat . . . Social Security, they say . . . must be slashed . . . in order to make it possible to cut the taxes of many . . . who hardly need tax reduction as much as the elderly need the benefits they are receiving."

Far from cutting benefit programs, Pepper advocated "a comprehensive legislative package to improve the state of the elderly in America."

Among its features would be increased minimum benefits for people who have worked all their lives under Social Security but who do not get benefits that would put them above the poverty line; increased private pension coverage to compensate for needs not covered by Social Security and expanded coverage under Medicare. Although he has not spelled out where the money to provide these benefits would come from, Pepper has suggested that most, if not all, of the long-term financial problems of Social Security would be solved if a large portion of the medical expenses now drawn from Social Security funds were to come instead from general tax revenues. He also believes that substantial additional funds would be available if more people were encouraged voluntarily to postpone retirement, thus reducing the number of elderly drawing from the system while increasing the number still putting money into it.

When Pepper's committee invited David A. Stockman, director of the Office of Management and Budget, to testify in April on what impact the budget cuts for fiscal year 1982 would have on the elderly, the budget director presented figures indicating that the total of federal tax dollars in support programs for the elderly would actually rise, from $144 billion in fiscal 1980 to $191 billion in fiscal 1982. Stockman went on to summarize the administration's proposed "economies," including elimination of the minimum monthly benefit under Social Security and a phase-out of certain survivor and death benefits.

In his typical courtly manner, Pepper complimented the "distinguished" and "able" and "honorable" Stockman on how well he had presented his statistics. "As a matter of fact," Pepper added, "if the elderly people had been listening to you they would think you would be conferring a blessing on them by making these cuts." Then the octogenarian committee chairman asked: "Are you able to assure us, Mr. Stockman . . . that [these cuts] comply with the assurance the President gave to the people that his program for budget cutting would not adversely affect the truly needy of the country?"

"I think, in the main, I can give you that assurance," was Stockman's reply.

Pepper was unconvinced. In July, his committee issued a report claiming that the administration's proposals would result in Social Security benefit reductions of $10.65 billion in fiscal 1982 and estimated that over the next few decades expenditures would be cut by 23 percent.

Discussing the matter recently, Pepper said, "They want to make a raid on the Social Security trust funds to finance their own programs and balance the federal budget. I'm going to fight like the devil to prevent that. Congress may need to make some adjustments in benefits and funding, as it has done fourteen times since the Social Security Act was passed. But the trust funds are not going bankrupt, as the administration claims, and we're not going to take away from the American people the little bit of security they have paid for all their working lives."

When the Social Security Act was first passed by Congress in 1936, payroll workers were taxed $20 a year — 1 percent of the first $2,000 of their earnings — to finance the system. As the number of recipients has grown and benefits have been expanded, the cost has risen steadily. In 1982, payroll workers will pay 6.7 percent on the first $32,400 of their earnings, for a maximum Social Security tax of $2,170.80, with their employers paying a matching percentage; self-employed persons will pay 9.35 percent on the first $32,400 of their earnings, for a maximum tax of $3,029.40. Additional increases over the next several years, to be recalculated every year according to a complex formula that includes the cost of living index, have already been mandated by Congress.

Despite rising contributions, however, the three trust funds into which Social Security taxes are paid — the retirement, disability, and health funds — have faced a problem of diminishing reserves in recent years. Opinions differ widely on the causes and possible solutions to the problem. Most experts appear to agree that some relatively simple stopgap measures, such as borrowing from one of the trust funds to shore up another, will provide temporary relief. But the long-term problem is a demographic one: Whereas 3.2 workers now pay into the system for every beneficiary, in another forty years or so, the gradually aging population will have cut that ratio to 2.1, and the trust funds will inevitably be exhausted, some say as soon as the year 2025.

There are, at bottom, only two possible solutions to this long-term problem: increased revenue from higher Social Security taxes, or reductions in the number of recipients or the amount of benefits, or both. Last spring, the Reagan administration proposed thirteen different reductions in benefits or recipients, for an estimated saving of more than $88 billion over the next five years. But only three of these proposals have passed into law — cutting monthly minimum college expense benefits for survivors, burial expenses, and the $122-a-month minimum benefit paid to some three million retired persons. And even before this last measure took effect, strong public opposition has caused Congress to initiate steps to undo it.

Some Democrats — notably J. J. Pickle of Texas, chairman of the House Subcommittee on Social Security — have proposed raising the retirement age of beneficiaries and lowering the automatic cost-of-living increases they receive annually as compromise measures to correct the long-term deficit prospect. But the Democratic leadership contends that such compromises are not necessary, with Claude Pepper adding that "changes of this magnitude would amount to . . . a breach of faith to the elderly."

In the White House, Pepper is seen as a serious impediment to administration hopes of achieving a balanced budget. A White House aide speaks for many of his colleagues when he says of Pepper, "He's got a committee that's stacked with people who won't face the hard choices this country is up against. . . . Everybody admires him enormously for his courage and vitality, but if his view prevails on the funding of entitlement programs for the elderly, the long-term implications are frightening. There's no way this country can afford such enormous expenditures."

Such comments cause Pepper to smile. "I refuse to believe that a country as rich and powerful as ours can't afford to guarantee the basic comfort and security of its older citizens. I know we can do it," he says, "and I intend to be long and loud about it."

In fourteen years as a senator and nineteen as a member of the House — sandwiched around a twelve-year law practice — Claude Pepper has almost always spoken his mind. His Washington career has encompassed the administrations of nine presidents. He was a bell-wether for Franklin Roosevelt, a headache for Harry Truman, a nemesis of Richard Nixon, and a valuable ally of John Kennedy, Lyndon Johnson, and Jimmy Carter. He had been branded a warmonger, a peacenik, a Communist. He has had private audiences with popes and princes and private interviews with such historic figures as Stalin and Churchill during the years he was on the Senate Foreign Relations Committee.

Now he is embarked on a crusade in behalf of a class of citizens to which he himself belongs. "Ageism is as odious as racism and sexism," he says, and with the stamina of a man half his age, he scurries about like an octogenarian Paul Revere, calling people of advanced years to their own defense and demanding that the rest of the population recognize their rights and their worth.

"All his life Pepper has been a partisan," a *Saturday Evening Post* writer said of him in 1946. He has always been tagged as a liberal, too, and that, in itself, is somewhat anomalous, considering his background. Claude Denson Pepper, the oldest of four children in a family of yeomen farmers, was born near Dudleyville, Alabama, in the first year of this century. Both of his grandfathers had fought for the Confederacy. Amid the poverty of their time and place, his parents could be thought of as middle-class — they were small-plot landowners, mainline Baptists, loyal Democrats.

After a brief succession of jobs as a hat blocker, a schoolteacher and a steelworker, Claude Pepper entered the University of Alabama in 1918 and graduated three years later. He went from Alabama to Harvard Law School, after which he taught for a year at the University of Arkansas Law School (J. William Fulbright, later a fellow senator, was one of his students). In 1925, he borrowed $300 to finance a move to Perry, Florida, and a start in a law practice.

By 1929, he had become a member of the Florida Legislature, but lost his bid for reelection in 1930. Moving to Tallahassee, he continued his pursuit of higher office. That same year, he saw "a beautiful girl in a yellow dress" coming out of the governor's office and arranged an introduction to Irene Mildred Webster, of St. Petersburg. Six years later, he married her.

Pepper ran in 1934 against a popular but inactive United States senator, Park Trammell, and lost by just 4,000 votes. Two years later, after the death of Florida's other senator, Duncan U. Fletcher, Pepper was nominated by his party to finish Fletcher's term.

"If you want to know about Claude Pepper," says Jack Ossofsky, executive director of the National Council on Aging, "go back and read his maiden speech in the Senate in 1937. He could give that speech today and it would still be relevant."

In that first speech, the young senator responded with vigorous and expansive rebuttal to the assertion by a colleague that national economic recovery had been achieved and the time had come to cut costly New Deal programs in order to erase the national debt and balance the federal budget.

The new senator from Florida and President Roosevelt quickly established a strong liking for each other. "If I knew anything," Pepper recalls, "I knew the South needed help, and Roosevelt was our only chance to get it." Having arrived in Washington favoring old-age pensions and Federal aid to education, it was a natural progression for Pepper to become an early advocate of Social Security, minimum wage and hour laws, and national health insurance. He became an outspoken defender of Roosevelt's New Deal programs, and, in 1938, his candidacy for a full term in the Senate was of sufficient national interest for him to be pictured on the cover of *Time* magazine above a caption that read: "A Florida fighting cock will be a White House weathervane." He won handily, and, two years later, so did Roosevelt, for the third time.

In 1940, Pepper proposed a national military draft and angry isolationists, reviling him as a traitor and a warmonger, hanged him in effigy on the Capitol grounds. A year later, he almost single-handedly persuaded the Senate to support lend-lease aid to the European allies (columnist Walter Lippmann secretly helped him draft the bill). But somehow his advocacy of social programs and military preparedness, while it provoked controversy among conservatives and isolationists, was not enough to get him into deep trouble at home. He was reelected in 1944, albeit by a mere 10,000 votes.

After the war, Pepper went to Europe, where he met with Churchill,

Eisenhower, and Stalin. He praised the Soviet leader and, because Moscow had been an ally, advocated aid along the lines of the Marshall Plan to the war-torn Soviet Union. He once advocated destroying all atom bombs as the surest way to prevent nuclear war. He was an early backer of Henry Wallace for president in 1948, but when the left-wing former Secretary of Agriculture went the third-party route, Pepper, who has always done his fighting within the party, quickly left him. He became a pleader for Dwight Eisenhower's candidacy as a Democrat and, briefly, an announced candidate himself before coming around to support Harry Truman's nomination. There was more: opposition to the union-regulating Taft-Hartley bill, support for antipoll tax measures, advocacy of laws guaranteeing fair employment practices.

It was all, finally, too much for Pepper's enemies. In 1950, led by the Du Pont empire's Florida boss, Edward Ball, and assisted by such groups and individuals as the American Medical Association, the United States Chamber of Commerce, Joseph P. Kennedy, and Florida's Senator Spessard Holland, the anti-Pepper forces sought and found a candidate to run against him. Their man was a tall, handsome young representative and Pepper protégé named George A. Smathers.

Robert Sherrill, in his book "Gothic Politics in the Deep South," called the Pepper-Smathers race "the most elaborate crusade of political annihilation ever conducted in Southern politics." Smathers won the bruising primary battle by 67,000 votes. He served three terms in the Senate, and since 1969 has been a lawyer and lobbyist in Washington. His remembrance of the 1950 campaign — and of Claude Pepper — has mellowed with time:

"I never said a lot of the stuff about Claude that was attributed to me. I thought Claude was way off track. I felt he was soft on Stalin — he was wrong on a lot of things that gave comfort to the Communists. I said it then, and I still say it. But that was a long time ago, and now, happily, we're friendly when we see each other. He's a remarkable man. There's nobody who can better speak for the aged than Claude. He's the right man in the right place at the right time. He can carry the fight on Social Security, and I'd be happy to see him do it. I think he and President Reagan will have a meeting of the minds."

Pepper remembers the race against Smathers as "a vicious campaign, a smear campaign of innuendo and guilt by association. Richard Nixon started the trend in 1946, the year he and Smathers were elected to the House. Later, that low style of smear tactics personified McCarthyism, but Joe McCarthy didn't invent it — Nixon did, and Smathers refined it."

With a sizable campaign debt and little income, Pepper resumed the practice of law. He opened an office in Tallahassee, then another in

Washington, and a third in Miami, where he eventually took up residence. In spite of his left-wing reputation, he attracted well-heeled clients — Westinghouse, Bethlehem Steel, *Time* magazine. In 1958, he ran for the Senate again, but failed, by 53,000 votes.

Through it all, Pepper remained a loyal and active Democrat, working for Adlai E. Stevenson, John F. Kennedy, and later for Lyndon B. Johnson, Hubert H. Humphrey, George S. McGovern, and Jimmy Carter. In the meantime, the 1960 census gave Dade County and Miami an additional House seat, and Pepper won it in a crowded field in 1982. The district is a mostly Democratic mélange of retirees, white-collar and blue-collar workers, Hispanics, blacks and relocated New Yorkers. It includes parts of Miami Beach, the Cuban and Haitian refugee communities, and the troubled black ghetto of Liberty City.

Pepper has always stayed in close touch with his constituents, and they have rewarded him with nine easy reelection victories. Even in 1972, when Richard Nixon carried Dade County with 59 percent of the vote, Pepper got 63 percent against his own Republican opponent, and in 1980 he beat a Cuban-American Republican by a three-to-one margin. His prospects for victory again in 1982 appear excellent; no opponent has yet materialized, nor, apparently, has he been targeted by any conservative or right-wing groups.

The story of the rise and fall and rise again of Claude Pepper covers so many years that it has a quality of timelessness. Few people now seem to remember how controversial he once was. Democrats and Republicans alike praise his gracious manner, his wit and wisdom, his staying power, his political skill. "He is the quintessence of a good public servant," says Representative Pickle. "He'll always be Lord Chesterfield to us."

Representative Millicent Fenwick of New Jersey, a member of Mr. Pepper's committee on aging, is one Republican who lauds him as "a dear, kindly, gallant gentleman whose concern for the elderly is absolutely genuine. Some feel he goes too far in his zeal," she says, "but none doubt his sincerity, or his influence. Any debate on the future of Social Security in this country has to include him. Others may be more expert on actuarial tables and taxes, but someone has to speak for the heart. Claude speaks for the heart." In a similar vein, Maggie Kuhn, leader of the Gray Panthers, an activist group for the elderly, says Pepper "is not a special pleader for the elderly but an advocate of social justice for the whole society. He sees and serves the larger constituency."

Two freshman House members young enough to be Pepper's grandchildren compliment him from opposite sides of the aisle. Republican John LeBoutillier of New York, at twenty-eight the youngest member now in Congress, says the administration "really blew it last spring when they suggested cuts in Social Security . . . They gave Pepper the ammunition to beat them with, and he has made the most of it." Democrat Ron Wyden of Oregon, age thirty-two, was working in legal and social programs for the elderly when he first met Pepper. "The opportunity to serve with him was a major reason I decided to run for Congress," Wyden says. "He's a bulldog for the elderly, a passionately committed defender."

New York Democrat Mario Biaggi, a House colleague of Pepper's since 1968, praises him as "a man of integrity and principle. In the earlier years of his career, anything less than vocal and vigorous defense of white supremacy was political suicide for a Southern politician, yet he opposed racism."

In Pepper's own recollection of his earlier positions on civil rights issues, he recalls one in particular that he regrets: "In 1938, I filibustered for eleven hours against a bill to make lynching a federal offense. It was the last time I ever opposed a civil rights measure." Nevertheless, twenty years later, in a futile attempt to unseat segregationist Senator Spessard Holland, Pepper struggled uncomfortably to avoid being branded as an integrationist. It was not until he returned to Congress in 1962 that he was able to stake out an unequivocal position on racial issues.

Since his early years in the Senate, Pepper has practiced a style of liberalism that skillfully blends pragmatic and idealistic concerns. He has supported funding proposals for the pure sciences and was instrumental in the creation of the government's cancer-research programs; he has given strong support to Cuban refugees and has regularly denounced the Castro regime; he has sought middle ground on the issues of gun control and abortion; he has voted consistently for the military budgets proposed by the House Armed Services Committee, in the firm belief that the nation can afford guns *and* butter. In general, he is an advocate of government activism as the surest and fairest way to peace and prosperity.

In recent years, he has introduced legislation to abolish mandatory retirement, to help fight crime in housing projects for the elderly, to cut Amtrak fares for senior citizens, to make nutritious meals available to the elderly. His committee on aging has kept up a steady schedule of widely publicized hearings. His newspaper column — "Ask Congressman Pepper" — is circulated to more than 700 papers all over the country.

"We all look to him," says William R. Hutton, executive director of the National Council of Senior Citizens. "He's the focal point of the older American's interests in Congress. Since his wife died, he has lived completely for his job. He's the nearest thing this country has to a national congressman."

Mildred Pepper's death of cancer in 1979 ended what his Florida Congressional colleague Dante Fascell says was "a true love match."

The couple, who were childless, had been virtually inseparable for forty-two years.

After a period of adjustment to his wife's death, Pepper, who stayed on in the modest Washington apartment he and his wife had occupied for ten years, resumed his full schedule. He typically works nine-hour days on Capitol Hill, attends numerous evening functions and returns to Miami almost every weekend to "be available" to his constituents. And, increasingly, he is immersed in the last crusade on his agenda: the welfare of the nation's elderly citizens.

Pepper expects his job to keep him busy indefinitely. "I hate to think I'll have to quit someday," he says. "My goal is to see this century out — and get the next one off to a good start."

Claude Pepper's gray eyes scanned the headlines of his morning paper as he breakfasted in his Miami condominium overlooking Biscayne Bay during a recent weekend visit to his constituency. He tossed down his napkin and chuckled. "Mr. Reagan says the economy is in recession," he announced. "Well, well. I wonder who told him. Mr. Stockman, I guess." The humor was short-lived: "How in the world he could be seventy years old and have so little feeling for the elderly, I'll never know. He seems to have no compassion. He disdains the poor."

At the White House, aides of the President are equally as puzzled, as one of them put it, that "after fifty years of government profligacy, the Claude Peppers of this world still want more. Their idea of serving is simply to spend more money. That's not a solution to this country's problems — it's the primary cause of them."

It seems fitting that two public servants of advanced age should have so much to do with the setting of government policy toward the elderly. They are certainly equal to the challenge, both mentally and physically. Mr. Reagan's health has been one of his great strengths. Mr. Pepper, though he is eleven years older, seems equally fit. For exercise, he plays eighteen holes of golf every week or two, pedals a stationary bicycle in his apartment on rainy weekends, and walks farther and faster than any member of his staff.

On the first Saturday in October, doctors at Walter Reed Hospital in Washington inserted a pacemaker under Pepper's skin. It was, he says, "a preventive maintenance measure to keep my heart strong." Two days later, he was back on the floor of the House to support a bill extending the life of the Voting Rights Act. Then he was off to Florida for a busy week of speeches and public appearances.

"I asked the doctor how long the battery in this thing would last," he remarked later, patting his chest. "He said it was good for about ten years. I told him I'd just take three of them with me now, and come back for more later if I need them."

POLITICS IN WASHINGTON IS often conducted in a social atmosphere. Throughout the town the "power lunch" takes place in restaurants that have achieved a cachet that identifies them as places where the rich and powerful gather to conduct their business. For over a decade, beginning with the Kennedy administration, the political elite met for lunch at the Sans Souci restaurant, a few blocks from the White House. Sans Souci was more a club at lunchtime than a restaurant. It was, like Bernard Baruch's bench in LaFayette Park, a gathering place for political conversation and the discussion of strategies among the powerful. The restaurant's mainstays were humorist Art Buchwald and maitre d'hotel Paul de Lisle. Buchwald could often be seen conducting court from his table, which was strategically located on the side wall where he could observe people coming and going and exchange greetings with his many friends among the powerful. Buchwald wrote, perhaps only half facetiously, that when "people in the Johnson, Nixon, Ford and Carter administrations needed advice they knew where to find me."[1] He continued, "When I held court at the Sans Souci, the inflation rate never rose above 5 percent, people could purchase a decent home for $40,000, banks were begging the public to borrow money at 6 percent, Social Security was safe, and the United States had twice the military might of the Soviet Union."[2]

When the Sans Souci closed its doors to the public, the capital's downtown establishment had to find another watering hole. Many Sans Souci regulars, including Buchwald, went around the corner to the new Maison Blanche, which also became the new in-spot for White House staffers. Washington's superlawyers and their clients continued to frequent Jean Pierre's K Street restaurant, the Palm, Jockey Club, and Jean Louis's at the Watergate.

The host of the power lunch on Capitol Hill is the Monocle, a stone's throw from the three Senate office buildings. It is primarily a Senate scene, although House members and staffers may journey there, usually after work, from their distant location on the other side of the Hill. Senators, staffers, congressmen, an occasional cabinet secretary, print and electronic journalists, and lobbyists mingle to discuss their concerns, interests, and the public weal. The atmosphere is often as raucous as Congress itself, as the following selection illustrates.

[1] Art Buchwald, "Where the Elite Used to Meet," *Washington Post*, September 20, 1981, p. H1.
[2] Ibid.

10 Nicholas von Hoffman
THE WASHINGTON MONOCLE:
SCENE OF THE POWER LUNCH

From below Union Station, New Jersey Avenue runs southeast, dips downward, and then swoops up toward the Capitol grounds. On wet nights the white, illuminated dome rises above the street and hovers with wide, squatting dominance. The men in the backs of the limousines and taxis moving toward it look up to check the cupola above the dome of the Republic. If it, too, is lit, they stare past their drivers' heads, assured, and relax into the cushions or tense up as they tell their radiophones or their companions, "They're in."

The phrase means the national legislature is in session, and when it is a night session, "they" are more prone to get giddy, angry, silly, stubborn, or eccentric. When the light on the cupola is lit deep into the hours of darkness, the Hill is a-scrabble with hundreds of men and women from the limos and the taxis trying to get their way. But legislating is like trench warfare: Hurry up and wait.

The waiting is done in lobbies, in the private offices of the leadership under the Capitol, and in the members' suites in the congressional office buildings. But though a conference room in the Dirksen Building is okay for a meeting, they don't like to wait there. These types need more people, more noise, more jangle and shout.

The late Senator Everett McKinley Dirksen, the Johnson-Nixon-era Republican minority leader for whom that beaux arts pile of marble is named, did his waiting at the Monocle restaurant. The Monocle endures as Washington's premier political bar, not because of the food or the decor, not because this bar is the nearest saloon to the Senate door, but because they run it for workaday politicians.

Other watering places there are, but they're not right for the political life. Over on the House side of Capitol Hill, in the Democratic Club, they have a loudspeaker, as they do at the Monocle, to let a member know when there's a quorum call, but who the hell wants to drink only with Democrats? Besides, women politicians say that after six P.M. the bar at the Democratic Club is unsafe for a female seeking to keep body and reputation intact. The Capitol Hill Club, as the Republicans call their spa, is so dull that Senator Jeremiah Denton, the Alabama Calvinist suspected of wishing that fornication were a capital crime, does his hanging out at the Monocle, amidst trysting adulterers who have as much redeeming virtue as wit, a love of gossip, and the ability to tell a good story can confer.

At Bullfeathers, down First Street from the Capitol Hill Club, they have a jostling bar, where some of the fine physical specimens who make up so much of the Hill staff excite one another. Too much of the musk of the singles bar for the true pol. Not that the customers don't have glands at the Monocle, where for years, they say, a western senator took his lunch between two long-stemmed American beauty roses. The gossip is that his two bud vases were changed every day, but by whom it is not whispered. The senator is serving out the last year of his term, and though he may still lunch at the Monocle, these days he prefers the company of national-security experts. And there was Teddy Risenhoover, from the Will Rogers-Woody Guthrie part of Oklahoma, who got beat for reelection after they said in the campaign that he had a heart-shaped water bed; around the Monocle they say he used to meet girls at the bar and take 'em out back, where he had his van parked, and play 'em X-rated videocassettes. If you don't want people making up nasty stories about you, don't go into politics.

At the American Cafe, up the street from the Monocle, the food is delicious, very alfresco, al dente, alfredo — all the al's — very New York, and so good you can't believe the place is in Washington. Food, however, isn't the food of politics, though the California epigrammatist Jesse Unruh said money was its mother's milk.

They go to the Monocle because Nick, the maître d', sits people at adjacent tables according to affinity and alliance or at distant ones according to the lack thereof. They go to the Monocle because there is a phone at the bar you can use to call your office, if you are known to Robert, the bartender. Otherwise you go upstairs and use a pay phone next to the one where a lobbyist is waltzing somebody at the other end of the line through a list of House members on whose votes he is counting. The difficulty is the ancient one of keeping 'em bought after you buy 'em: "Okay, in New York . . . no, the New York delegation — we got Molinari, Green, and Gilman, but you gotta make sure they stay with us. Stick with 'em."

They go to the Monocle because they make you feel at home if it is your home. When the other phone at the bar, which is for incoming calls only, makes its quiet chime, Nick comes over to your table and tells you that you have a call. He does that if he knows you; if he doesn't know you, you're not in politics — not in Washington anyhow — though you could be big in forestry in Yakima. For you it's paging over the loudspeaker-system, and if you're a big noise from Nogales or Nashville, you'll be pleased they're saying your name in a place packed with pols; you won't know that they are telling the whole company in the barroom and in the restaurant that you are from Texas or Tennessee and you will be returning to your power base shortly.

Nick is a very nuanced guy, to borrow an Alexander Haigism. He keeps tabs on what they are talking about today, who's lovey and who ain't, but some things are out of one's control regardless of how nuanced one may be. Not long ago a group of the most respectable hacks swore by all of whatever is alleged to be sacred to up-market journalists that they and their luncheon guest, Caspar Weinberger, would be out of the private upstairs dining room by one P.M. sharp, don't worry about it, Nick. The Secretary of Defense didn't get to the Monocle until a quarter of, and at the drop of the hour, there was Clarence Long, the chairman of the House Subcommittee on Foreign Operations (aid to El Salvador and such), at the bottom of the stairs with his party, screaming it was his room, he had reserved it. "I'm more important than Weinberger is. I'm an elected official!" Nick shakes his head when he tells that story. "You want to see one nervous Greek?" he asks.

If there are any nervous Greeks around the Monocle, they hide it well. Connie Valanos, propieter, has been catering to politicians since he started the place in Kennedy's time. He knows they are the stars and he is heading up the supporting cast.

In a section of the barroom where the lumber industry has gathered there is a frisson, and not a happy one. "They're calling up the timber bill and McClure's on a plane to Idaho!" "Oh, God!" a man in the crowd says, for the unheard of is being heard. Dugskullery is afoot; someone has maneuvered the amendment onto the floor when the chairman of the committee with jurisdiction over it (Energy and Natural Resources) is not there to play broody hen.

A western multimillionaire from the tall-pine country rises from a table with a politically stricken look on his face. He has something in the bill to protect and no one to do it for him. Connie has him by the elbow, guiding him through the barroom, out the door, and into Connie's Cadillac to run him up First Street to the Capitol and the lobby outside the Senate chamber.

It's not a service that Connie offers all his customers, but most of the lobbyists at the Monocle aren't as jittery as this boy. During a night session some of them may run three separate tabs at the restaurant as they come and go from restaurant to Senate lobby and back.

Behold the true lobbyist in the most authentic of American legislative anterooms, wherein portraits of Clay, Calhoun, Taft, and La Follette look at their latter-day colleagues with wry grimaces of recognition. Near Calhoun the timber barons from the Monocle have reassembled themselves. They have given their cards to Irish, the doorkeeper, who will see they get to a little man with bow legs and sideburns, a veterinarian from Forsyth, Montana, who happens to be a senator. While they wait for their man to come off the floor, the timber lobbyists cluster, staying away from an occasional other senator passing through whom one or the other of them may know. Irish's rule is, No mugging of innocent senators, meaning you wait for the senator you've called off the floor without jumping one who has come into the lobby at the behest of someone else.

The forest-products crowd, as they sometimes call themselves, looks neither crestfallen nor worried. They know they are standing outside the altar room of the god Confusion, in whose temple no question is ever settled, no final vote is ever taken, no decision is ever beyond recall. In case of an adverse stroke tonight, repair to the Monocle, therein to plan the undoing of tonight's damage tomorrow.

All of a sudden there is a rearrangement of people. A woman comes in the corridor whom someone points out as Senator So-and-So's "facilitator," which means she gets him females and speaker's fees. She looks like an ex-nun who left the cloister to go into counseling. From another direction, Biden of Delaware comes off the floor to go into intense huddle with six or eight men and women in frayed cloth coats. Unlike the timber gang from the Monocle, these people look like they really need the money.

It is a moment of legislative pause inside the Senate, for other members are wandering out. Howell Heflin, the great-bodied Alabamian who stoops at the knees and resembles a rambling, shambling question mark, makes his appearance. "How-dee, Judge!" one or another of the members says to him. He answers in tones of warm-worded graciousness; how likable, how charming a relaxed southerner of the broad-faced school can be. Not the tight-assed, Snopesy types, like Jimmy Carter was.

Melcher, the Montana veterinarian, comes into the lobby to stand with the timber people under the crystal swags of the chandelier. The Senate is a time warp; here it is always 1875 and James G. Blaine and the Old Guard are perpetually in power. But Melcher is a goofy little senator whose smile is too wide for his crinkly doll's face. An attractive woman lobbyist with little care for the dignity of her gender once secured his vote by opening the conversation with "Senator, I'm afraid there is something dreadfully wrong with my pussycat."

Back at the Monocle, Robert the barkeeper nods yes to an inquirer. "Yes," he says, "the House is out." And the night is pretty much over. A half an hour later the Senate goes out, as does the light in the cupola above the dome.

The next day, appropriations not passed the night before are the luncheon topic at Jean Louis's at the Watergate, at Jean Pierre's on K Street's restaurant row. Wherever some chap named Jean dishes out sauces in return for getting to handle other people's American Express cards, they order gourmet this and expense account that, talk of dredging canals and bridging them, of dickering with the rules for offshore drilling and whatever else might be in the bill, now some eight hundred pages in length, a document shortly to become the law of the land though no human being has as yet read it or knows all that it might contain.

In these restaurants and, of course, La Maison Blanche, the eating place favored by the most influential persons around the president, the topic is batted around, but not as they do it at the Monocle. Jean Louis's costs more and the food is better, but the people who go there don't get the honk out of politics they do at the Monocle. The restaurants on K Street cater to men who preen in eight-hundred-dollar suits and think politics is only money. Everett McKinley Dirksen of very happy memory, who, legend has it, got reasonably rich having people make discreet drops at some address or other in Pekin, Illinois, would have told them that the best part isn't the money, it's the fun.

They don't have fun on K Street, but when the light went on in the cupola that night, the pile-up of burbly politicians at the Monocle was a giddy, spontaneous combustion of men and women who have a neurologic need to be close and loud in crowded rooms. The big-shouldered blonde who is counsel for the Senate's Indian-Affairs Committee was already seated at her table in the barroom. She comes in many nights, almost always followed by her number-one brave, this guy with black, shoulder-length hair, leather jacket, and jeans.

Alan Dixon, an unknown member of the upper house from Illinois, comes in, his beeper in the outer breast pocket of his suit coat, saying, "We might be here all night." The tone is not weary but anticipatory, like, Goody! The gang's going to have a pajama party over at Jane's!

At the bar a young woman who looks and sounds like Jean Arthur's tough girl pol in *Mr. Smith Goes to Washington* is talking to a fellow House staffer. In this movie she's not playing opposite the young Jimmy Stewart but a nondescript sack of a man with no jaw, who wears a camel's-hair sport coat and wants advice on how to get a second date with some lady. Ms. Tough Girl Pol, having poured several drinks into herself, is off on a voyage of self-importance. "My member votes the way I tell him to," she tells the camel's-hair coat. Down the bar Senator Exon's ag guy is smiling the features off his face and paying court to the unknown person he's drinking with. Pondering the Nebraska senator's staffer for agriculture, somebody remarks, "He's acting like the young Lyndon Johnson. Same smiley eagerness."

Jean Arthur, Jr. is continuing to explain to Camel's-Hair Coat what's what. "My member voted no on the bill. I took a piece of paper and felt-tip pen and wrote no on it. Then I said, 'Tommy [name changed], put on your glasses and read this. . . . ' My boss, my boss, he asks me all the time, *How* would you vote?' " She shakes her head. In the dining room, Connie's son John is at Judge Heflin's table with a bottle of Frangelico, explaining the proper way to mix a drink, when beepers in the members' coats go off all over the place. A quorum call in the House sound like an electronic barnyard at the Monocle.

House members put down their napkins and make for the door while a lobbyist at one table boasts, "I had the Senate greased." At another, representatives from the financial service industry are talking about "the smart card." This is the new credit card with a microprocessor in it that will have encoded its owner's credit history, but apparently the Federal Reserve Board lacks enthusiasm for this small rectangle of plastic progress.

"So what do I say to her tomorrow night?" Camel's-Hair Coat wants to know.

At the hatcheck booth Nick is shaking his head and saying, "What a goddamn day! Senator Lautenberg comes in with fourteen people and wants to have a private place for dinner. I put them in the office and they thought it was wonderful."

"Fresh joke!" is the announcement at a table in the barroom. "Bill Allain [the new governor of Mississippi, elected in a nasty campaign, during which his opponent accused him of being a homosexual] has a new car. It's called a pervertible. The top doesn't go down, but the driver does."

Zorinsky of Nebraska is noted at a table. The senator is best known for wanting to cancel the office subscriptions to The *New York Times* and The *Wall Street Journal* because they seldom have stories about Omaha in them. A few tables away is the people's representative from the Fourth Congressional District of the great state of Oregon. A controversial anti–big business Democrat, Jim Weaver is cherished at the Monocle for the years when he wore the worst-looking toupee in Congress. Of late, though, he has been walking bald in public, to the great disappointment of those who remember the rug with mirthy affection.

The congresspersons are drifting back. Jerry Patterson of Orange County, California, is installed at a table, whence he is shouting to someone, "We're going out now. We just added another billion to it."

"Bridges, bridges, bridges!" a lobbyist in another part of the forest exclaims. "Are we talking Army Corps of Engineers or are we talking dentistry?" That gets a laugh as Patterson tells a story to his dining companions: "So I come running on the floor waving what I think is my voting card but it's my American Express card and some guy says to me, 'What are you trying to do? Charge your vote?' "

Back on the barroom side, two women, one a lobbyist, the other a television producer, are discussing the pencil test for the breast. The robust woman is arguing that if you put the pencil under your breast and it stays there, that "means you're sagging. I could put a Douglas fir under mine." Her companion, who is as thin as a stick, disagrees: "No, I was told if the pencil falls on the floor you're not big enough to need a bra." Then they both laugh and begin chanting. "We must/we must/we must develop our bust."

The word spreading around the Monocle is that the Senate is going out in a few minutes. The crowd has started to thin. The Indian brave from the Senate subcommittee looks at the staff counsel and says, "Goodnight, Candice Bergen."

The last joke of the evening is working its way through the diminishing crowd. Both parties in the Senate and the House have recorded telephone messages you can call up to get the Democratic or Republican line on what's going on. The Democratic message from the House is: "Members should be prepared for a late-night session tomorrow to consider pending legislation, conferences, and other matters in regular order. Cats and dogs may be brought up at any time."

The light in the cupola is extinguished. The Monocle is closed.

THE REVEREND JERRY FALWELL seemed to burst upon the political scene in 1980 leading the disciplined, charging army of the Moral Majority to the polls to elect candidates who supported the fundamentalist Christian positions on a variety of issues. The evangelical community had been politically apathetic, but Falwell and other evangelists exhorted their flocks to join together to make their religious principles a beacon for political leaders at all levels of government. As the 1980 elections approached, Falwell told the four thousand worshipers who packed his Thomas Road Baptist Church in Lynchburg, Virginia, "The moralists in America have had enough. We are joining hands together for the changing, the rejuvenating of a nation."[1]

For Falwell, rejuvenating the nation required the injection of Christian morality, as he defined it, into public policy. The Moral Majority strongly opposed abortion, and supported voluntary prayers in public schools. Falwell and his movement also attacked the the Equal Rights Amendment, homosexuality and gay rights, and pornography, all of which the fundamentalist leaders believe undermine the security, integrity, and central role of the family in society.

As a Southerner, Falwell was well acquainted with the civil rights movement of the 1960s, which had increased the political power of blacks by encouraging them to register and vote. Somewhat belatedly, Falwell took a leaf from the political notebook of Martin Luther King, Jr., and other civil rights leaders when he conducted massive voter registration campaigns among his followers, an estimated 21 million of the faithful.

Outside of his luxurious, church-supported white-columned mansion in Lynchburg, Falwell prefers three-piece polyester suits, but within the grounds of his estate he often works in a bathing suit beside his Olympic-sized pool. Adjacent to the pool is a recording studio where he tapes the "Old-Time Gospel Hour," his Sunday service, which is carried by 681 TV and radio stations.

The Moral Majority, like the New Right, represents a rising conservative tide in American politics. Both the presidential and congressional elections of 1980 appeared to reflect the strength of evangelicals and political conservatives. The Moral Majority joined the New Right in claiming credit for the election of Ronald Reagan and for the defeat of a number of liberal Democratic senators, including Frank Church of Idaho, George McGovern of South Dakota, John Culver of Iowa, and Birch Bayh of Indiana.

The following selection examines the world of Jerry Falwell and other evangelical leaders, describing how they have led the Moral Majority into political combat.

[1]*Newsweek*, September 15, 1980, p. 28.

11 THE REVEREND JERRY FALWELL AND THE TIDE OF BORN AGAIN

The Reverend Jerry Falwell fidgeted impatiently as he waited for a colleague to finish thanking the Lord for his bounty. Finally, the Wednesday evening prayer service almost at an end, Falwell strode to the pulpit to address the well-scrubbed congregation of 3,900 that filled the Thomas Road Baptist Church in Lynchburg, Virginia, a fortnight ago. "Senator [Mike] Gravel of [Alaska] was ousted last night," he told them. "He lost the primary. And that's the beginning." Before the year was out, Falwell intoned, a half dozen more liberal senators would fall: George McGovern of South Dakota and Frank Church of Idaho, John Culver of Iowa and Alan Cranston of California, Birch Bayh of Indiana and Gaylord Nelson of Wisconsin. "The moralists in America have had enough. [We] are joining hands together for the changing, the rejuvenating of a nation."

It was an unconventional litany, to be sure. But such overtly political preaching is an increasingly common—and, to many, worrisome—phenomenon in evangelical churches across the country. Over the last eighteen months a new and potent political force has been taking shape —a "New Christian Right," in the words of theologian Martin E. Marty. Led by religious-TV stars such as Falwell, whose "Old-Time Gospel Hour" reaches an estimated 18 million viewers each week, this movement is attempting to enlist the nation's 30 million to 65 million evangelical Christians in an unabashedly political crusade based on fundamentalist morality. Its ideological bent is distinctly conservative, embracing "profamily" positions against abortion, the Equal Rights Amendment, and gay rights — but also extending to right-wing stands on such secular issues as the strategic arms limitation treaty (which it opposes) and the Kemp-Roth proposal to cut taxes by 30 percent (which it supports). The strategy is more electoral than Biblical. "We want to see more and more politicians in office who believe what we believe," says Charlotte, North Carolina, TV evangelist Jim Bakker.

To that end, politically oriented groups such as Falwell's Moral Majority and the California-based Christian Voice run massive voter-registration and education drives designed to turn traditionally apolitical elements of the evangelical community into a potent force at the polls. They are committed to partisan combat at every level — from campaigns for town council to the 1980 presidential race — throwing imposing organizational and financial resources behind candidates who share their born-again priorities. The movement's leaders maintain that their interest is in principle, not partisan personalities, and they insist that they have no intention of hitching their moral wagon to any secular star. But the main beneficiary of their activism, so far at least, has been the Republican party in general — and GOP presidential nominee Ronald Reagan in particular. "Christians gave Jimmy Carter his razor-thin margin of victory in 1976," says chief strategist Colonel Donner of Christian Voice. "We plan to reverse that in 1980."

Victories: Politics does not come naturally to the evangelical community, which has long held that the road to salvation lies in the Bible — not the ballot box. But many evangelicals have clearly become convinced that their fiercely held conservative values of God, country, and family are threatened by a rising tide of what they call "secular humanism" sweeping through government. "All across the country, Christians are registering to vote like never before," says Gainesville, Florida, minister Gene Keith, who successfully exhorted his flock to take over the local Democratic committee — and who is now a candidate for the state legislature. "We're running for everything from dogcatcher to senator."

And they are winning. In 1978 evangelical activists helped to unseat at least two liberal U.S. senators (Dick Clark of Iowa and Thomas McIntyre of New Hampshire) and elect one governor (Fob James of Alabama). Since then they have helped to block passage of the ERA in fifteen states, disrupt the White House Conference on the Family, impede the most recent Congressional effort at criminal-code reform and force both the Federal Communications Commission and the Internal Revenue Service to back down on challenges to religious organizations. This year their candidates have scored upset victories in primaries for the Senate and House in Alaska, Iowa, and Alabama — and though they lost the fight to keep George Bush off the Republican ticket, they did manage to shape large sections of the GOP platform.

The movement's rapid growth and early success worries not only its political opponents, but many mainstream theologians as well. "Its leaders are profoundly immature," says Richard John Neuhaus, a Lutheran pastor and member of the board of the influential *Worldview* magazine. "They don't really understand the ethical and philosophical traditions of democracy or how to bring about change in a pluralistic society." Even some evangelists themselves are uneasy about the new movement's often strident partisanship and its creative use of scripture to justify the most secular of political positions. "God isn't a right-winger or a left-winger," argues preacher Pat Robertson, president of the Christian Broadcasting Network and host of "The 700 Club," a popular daily religious program. "The evangelists stand in danger of being used and manipulated." In judging political performance on the basis of Biblically derived standards, others contend, the movement is in danger of crossing the constitutionally drawn line between church and state. "They are violating Article Six of the Constitution, which says there must not be any religious test for holding office," says Rabbi Marc Tanenbaum of the American Jewish Committee.

'Buzzards': Predictably defensive, evangelical politicians charge that such criticisms are themselves political sour grapes from liberal opponents. "Nobody's ever accused the National Council of Churches of mixing religion and politics," Falwell says. "But when ol' Jerry gets into it, that's violating separation of church and state. The problem isn't violating anything. The problem is that we don't agree with those buzzards — and that we outnumber them." Perhaps — although there is a real question whether leaders like Falwell really do represent a huge and potentially monolithic political bloc. According to a new Gallup pool, evangelical Christians are as politically divided as most Americans (see Table). Though as a group they are somewhat more conservative than the nation as a whole, the majority of the registered voters among them nonetheless identify themselves as Democrats, and they favor Jimmy Carter by a wide margin over Ronald Reagan. What's more, a majority (53 percent) support ERA, and only 41 percent favor the extreme position of banning abortion entirely.

Still, there is no mistaking the enormous potential of evangelical politics. The movement's basic raw material is the vast number of fundamentalist Americans who do not normally vote — Christian Voice's Donner estimates it as 25 million — and whose attitudes, as a result, are not reflected in Gallup's findings. So far this year, the movement claims to have registered some 2 million new voters from the ranks of the born again — and, says Falwell, the total should reach 4 million by Election Day. Even if those figures are inflated, born-again politics could well play a decisive role in this year's presidential race. "The significance of the fundamentalist vote is not numbers but geography," says Reagan campaign aide Roger Stone. Close elections, he notes, tend to be won or lost in the heartland states of Ohio, Illinois, and Michigan — all of which boast growing evangelical communities. "Some of the southern counties in Ohio are as fundamentalist as the Deep South," Stone says. "The return of the fundamentalist vote [to the GOP] will allow Reagan to carry Ohio and, conceivably, the country."

The movement's political gurus are prone to play down their immediate prospects. "Anybody who thinks this group is going to contribute to a political revolution this election is going to be disappointed," says Paul Weyrich, who runs a highly regarded "training school" in Washington for conservative candidates as well as a clearinghouse operation for thirty or so evangelical and secular pro-family groups. But as the strategists see it, the longer-term future is bright. "The basic problem, only now being overcome, is to get people involved," says Howard Phillips, organizer of a right-wing lobbying group called The Conservative Caucus. "Once that is done, this movement will be formidable."

The effort began in earnest less than three years ago, spurred in part by disappointment with the first born-again candidate, Jimmy Carter. "It was a tremendous letdown, if not a betrayal, to have Carter stumping for the ERA, for not stopping federally paid abortions, for advocating homosexual rights," says Donner. The original movers and shakers were mainly political pros, not preachers. The core group consisted of Phillips and Weyrich (who were old comrades-in-arms from the political wars), Robert Billings (a failed GOP Congressional candidate from Indiana who had attended Weyrich's candidate-training school) and Ed McAteer, a veteran marketing man for the Colgate-Palmolive Co. who had come to know hundreds of evangelical preachers around the country. In January of last year they persuaded Falwell to set up a political organization — which Weyrich suggested calling "Moral Majority" and which Billings was assigned to direct. Falwell's backing was crucial; the financial and logistical resources that he commanded were immense.

Allies: There were other allies as well. McAteer had set up a nonpartisan, interdenominational group called the Religious Roundtable. It had just fifty-six members, but among them were most of the major television preachers as an impressive list of New Right politicians. Funded mainly by what McAteer describes as "some gifts from businessmen," it sponsored rallies, seminars, and training sessions aimed at increasing the political sophistication of evangelists. Meanwhile, Weyrich had begun holding informal get-togethers for evangelical and pro-family activists every other Thursday in his Washington offices on Library Court, behind the Library of Congress. The Library Court group, as it came to be known, now coordinates strategy for the entire movement.

Another politically potent evangelical group had arisen on the West Coast. Called Christian Voice, it sidestepped IRS strictures on political lobbying by setting up a political action committee (PAC) called the Christian Voice Moral Government Fund. Unlike the other born-again political organizations, Christian Voice has no compunctions about endorsing specific candidates for office. "We make judgments based on principles," says Gary Jarmin, executive director of the Moral Government Fund. "When you go into a voting booth, you pull a lever for a name, not a principle." Last February it set up another group — called Christians for Reagan.

Agenda: Working together in an informal but very real alliance, these organizations are trying to mobilize a conservative evangelical electorate. The concerns of born-again politics are defined by Falwell's "agenda for the '80s" — a pro-family, pro-life, pro-morality platform that, in a triumph of political packaging, turns out to be considerably more "anti" than "pro." Among other things, Moral Majority — and its evangelical allies — are against abortion, ERA, gay rights, sex education, drugs, pornography, SALT II, the Department of Education, and defense cuts. They are for free enterprise, a balanced budget, voluntary prayer in the public schools, and a secure Israel.

Using Falwell as its main drawing card, Moral Majority has been holding rallies around the country to spread the word and develop a truly national base. The work is already beginning to pay dividends as a cadre of budding evangelical politicos takes root. Reverend Keith of Gainesville, Florida, is typical — a total neophyte when Moral Majority suggested he attend the weeklong "Campaign Training Conference" run by Weyrich in Washington last November. When he returned to his pulpit at the Southside Baptist Church he persuaded his congregation to run for seats on the local county Democratic committee. Ultimately, they swept forty-two of the fifty-three seats they went after.

Falwell says he is not "candidate oriented." Still, he has managed to lend a hand in several campaigns. At a recent Moral Majority rally in Des Moines, for example, he made a point of praising Senate candidate Representative Charles Grassley as a "dear friend of ours and a fine Christian." And in Birmingham, Alabama, a fortnight ago, Falwell noted pointedly that Moral Majority's local bête noire, Reresentative John Buchanan, had "unfortunately" voted to extend the time limit for passage of the ERA. Buchanan lost in last week's GOP primary.

Falwell's political sermonizing doesn't always work out so well. Several months ago he told a Moral Majority rally in Alaska a completely fabricated story about an actual meeting he and other evangelists had with President Carter in the White House last February. According to Falwell's first account, he had boldly asked the President why he had "known practicing homosexuals" on his staff — to which Carter supposedly replied that it was because he considered himself "President of all the American people." When the story got back to the White House, angry Carter aides released a transcript of the meeting — which showed that there never had been any such exchange. "I shouldn't have said it," Falwell conceded recently. "Obviously it was a reckless statement."

Questions: Such gaffes don't really worry him. "There are only two things a preacher just can't afford to be accused of," he says. "One of them is sexual impropriety . . . the other is messing with the church funds." Falwell's reputation as a family man is impeccable. But the Securities and Exchange Commission once raised questions about his ministry's finances (box) — and there are indications that Moral Majority, ostensibly independent, has received favored treatment from Falwell's lucrative religious enterprises Although contributions have been flowing into Moral Majority lately at the rate of $400,000 a month, the organization has been strapped for cash all year. It has been consistently bailed out by the "Old-Time Gospel Hour," which has allowed Moral Majority to run up debts to it for months — apparently free of any interest charges.

By far the most controversial of the evangelical political groups is the unabashedly partisan Christian Voice. Earlier this year it raised hackles by rating all the members of Congress on how they voted on what it described as "fourteen key moral issues" — ranging from prayer in the schools to the security of Taiwan. On the basis of the ratings, it issued a "hit list" of thirty-six senators and congressmen, each of whom it accused of having a poor "moral voting record." Though lobbying groups do this sort of thing all the time, Christian Voice's ratings drew heavy fire. For one thing, four ordained clergymen in Congress received among the lowest marks — while Representative Richard Kelly, one of the

How Far Right?

Despite the conservative message of many evangelical political leaders, a new Gallup poll [found] President [Carter] ahead among born-again Christians registered to vote; they [were] not very far to the right except on abortion and prayer.

If the presidential elections were being held today, which candidate would you vote for?

	Carter	Reagan	Anderson
Evangelicals	52%	31%	6%
All Voters	39%	38%	13%

Which category best describes your own political position?

	Left of center	Middle of the road	Right of center
Evangelicals	20%	31%	37%
All Voters	22%	37%	31%

How They Differ on Issues

	Evangelicals	All Voters
Favor death penalty for persons convicted of murder	51%	52%
Favor government programs to deal with social problems	54%	53%
Favor increased spending for defense	78%	70%
Favor banning all abortions	41%	31%
Favor requiring prayer in public schools	81%	59%

Abscam bribery defendants, was given a perfect, 100 percent rating. For another, the group's equation of Christian morality with political conservatism outraged preachers and pols alike. Even Senator Jesse Helms, the influential conservative who agrees wholeheartedly with Christian Voice's politics, found the rating system questionable. "I could never take the position that anyone who disagreed with me was less a Christian," he says. "Hubert Humphrey and I didn't agree 90 percent of the time. Does that mean he was more immoral?"

Flood: Unfazed by the criticism, Christain Voice is now gearing up for a massive effort in behalf of Ronald Reagan, including plans to flood the Midwest and the South with 5 million pieces of pro-Reagan literature between now and the election. "The South is reputed to be Jimmy Carter's base," says strategist Donner, "but remember, it's the Bible belt. Our message that Ronald Reagan is *the* Christian candidate of 1980 may sufficiently weaken Carter in the one solid base he still has."

The Reagan campaign takes such analyses seriously, and has been assiduously wooing the evangelicals all year —in the process, hiring Billings away from Moral Majority to become Reagan's liaison with the born-again community. The courtship began in earnest at the GOP convention, to which both Falwell and his Liberty Baptist College choir were invited. Perhaps more important, Falwell and his fellow evangelical politicians got a good crack at shaping the Republican platform.

"Out of the Closet": Reagan further solidified his hold on the evangelical pols by being the only major presidential candidate to appear at the Religious Roundtable's National Affairs Briefing, a revival meeting cum political rally held in Dallas three weeks ago. More than 15,000 of the faithful turned out for two days of speechmaking and organizing. "It's time for God's people to come out of the closet and the churches — and change America," thundered James Robison, the fire-and-brimstone Ft. Worth evangelist whose weekly TV show is syndicated to 100 stations. Said Reagan: "I know you can't endorse *me.* But . . . I want you to know that I endorse *you.*"

Not everyone there shared Reagan's enthusiasm. Preacher Pat Robertson, for one, argues that "active partisan politics" is the wrong path for true evangelicals. "There's a better way," he says: "Fasting and praying . . . appealing, in essence, to a higher power." That feeling is shared by many in the evangelical community who are uneasy over the fact that, as the Reverend Jimmy Allen of Ft. Worth puts it, what is supposed to be "a nonpartisan movement for Jesus . . . always seems to turn into a Republican rally." A sincere concern for traditional values clearly motivates many in the movement, but critics point to an apparent lack of concern for minorities and the poor. "There are more than 300

verses in the Bible on the commitment to the poor, to justice and righ-
teousness, but they are silent on that," complains the Reverend Tom
Skinner, a born-again black activist.

What seems to trouble such critics the most is the movement's inex-
orable reduction of religious and moral values into crude political options. "I would hate for evangelical Christianity to become a spiritual
version of the National Rifle Association," says Dr. David Hubbard of
the Fuller Theological Seminary, who worries about the possible exploi-
tation of politically naïve evangelicals. And whatever it does to evangelicals themselves, the effect on the rest of society could be devastating.
"If in order to be faithful you have to support a certain stand regarding
Russia, what's the next step?" asks the Reverend Theodore Edquist of
the First Congregational Church of Boise, Idaho. "It strikes at the very
heart of the whole notion of religious pluralism and religious and political freedom."

"Mad as Hell": The movement's leaders insist that such worries are wildly
overblown. "We're not religious fanatics who have in mind a Khomeini-
type religious crusade to take over the government," says Falwell. "We
support the separation of church and state . . . we want influence, not
control." For the activist liberal theologians who have been in politics
for years — fighting for poverty programs, urban aid, and an end to the
Vietnam war — that argument is hard to dispute. "This is a populist
reaction of resentment," says *Worldview*'s Neuhaus. "These are very ordinary Americans and they are mad as hell. It's arrogant and self-
defeating for those of us whom they are mad at to pretend they will just
go away."

The challenge of the New Christian Right may stir more activism among
liberals. But attention will have to be paid to born-again sensibilities.
"No group on a crusade is willing to moderate its demands until it feels
secure of its place, until it feels recognized as a power to be dealt with,"
says Neuhaus, adding that many of the liberals who propound the separation of church and state have gone beyond that to the separation of
moral judgment from public policy. "They are the ones who have driven
us into this current dilemma by trying to purge American life of religion
and values — by creating a 'naked public square' where anything goes."
What is clear on both the philosophical level — and in the rough-and-
tumble arena of politics — is that the Falwells of the nation and their
increasingly militant and devoted flock are a phenomenon that can no
longer be dismissed or ignored.

A $1 Million Habit

In his dark three-piece polyester suits, the Reverend Jerry Falwell always looks dressed for church. He has to. As chief pastor, executive officer, and full-time salesman for his own evangelical empire, Falwell is rarely out of the pulpit. Like a prophet seeking honor in — and for — his own country, Brother Jerry has moved beyond his Lynchburg, Virginia congregation to seize vocal leadership of the emerging Christian right, constantly pouring forth a torrent of Biblical rhetoric on behalf of his own conservative vision of a moral America.

To those who know him best, Falwell is a cool, tireless organizer and past master at riding evangelism's new electronic circuit. In a whirl of nineteen-hour days, he darts from board meetings to televised prayer services, jets from political rallies to church conferences, gulps down a dozen cups of coffee daily and rarely misquotes a Bible verse or a financial statistic. His hometown church claims 17,000 members — more than a quarter of Lynchburg's population — but his real constituency is an estimated 21 million faithful who listen to his broadcast sermons every week and support his pyramid of enterprises. Falwell's Sunday service, the "Old-Time Gospel Hour," is carried by 681 TV and radio stations. The yield from this and other fund-raising operations ($1 million each week) supports what is, in effect, Falwell's own Christian denomination — including a children's academy, a Bible institute, a correspondence school, a seminary and Library Baptist College, an as yet unaccredited campus with nearly 3,000 undergraduates (and a former major-league pitcher as baseball coach). To this complex, Falwell last year added Moral Majority, Inc., a political-action organization aimed at unseating politicians who reject his recipe for a righteous republic.

Lapel Pins: Falwell's multifaceted ministry depends on a variety of marketing techniques. Once true believers send in for such premiums as Old Glory lapel pins, their names are added to his massive computerized mailing list. Regular donors (average weekly gift: $12) become Falwell's "faith partners" and are subject to regular computerized pleas for more. In terms of what he calls his "gross ministry," Falwell says he is "neck and neck with Oral Roberts." And by 1981, he predicts, Falwell ministries will lead the evangelical pack.

A driving need to succeed is as much a part of Falwell's pulpit power as his business acumen and folksy fundamentalism. Young Jerry's family was a brawling bunch; his father killed one of Jerry's uncles in a family feud and later died from alcoholism. But Falwell excelled in the classroom and on his high-school football team. He was prevented from delivering the valedictory address only after auditors discovered that he and other athletes had eaten free for a year on bogus lunch tickets. Jerry didn't get religion until a wintry Sunday in 1952 when he went to church in search of girls and found both Jesus and a pretty organist named Macel Pate. In 1956, after dominating the student body at a Bible college in Missouri, Jerry returned to Lynchburg to found his own independent Baptist church, in an abandoned popbottling factory, and continued courting Macel — whom he later married. Six months later he aired his first religious show on local television.

At times his knack for fund raising has caused problems for Falwell's empire. Seven years ago the Securities and Exchange Commission sued his Thomas Road Baptist Church for issuing allegedly fraudulent bonds; after an acrimonious trial Falwell agreed to institute more rigorous financial discipline. And some questions still shadow his financial operations. Falwell says, for example, that he spends only 17½ cents to raise every dollar he takes in, but some former financial employees and advisers insist the actual figure is three to four times higher — well above the norm for most charitable causes. Others criticize Falwell's borrowing from Peter to pay Paul — specifically borrowing up to $1 million from the college (with approval of the school's board) to pay his TV expenses.

'Their Way Out': Falwell also makes periodic pitches for money to support specific causes such as the Cambodian refugees in Thailand. There is no way for donors to know how much money such appeals bring in — or where it all goes. Says the Reverend David Brown, who served as controller for the "Gospel Hour" last year: "Jerry would say in his promotional literature that the money raised would be used for a project *and* for other operating costs of the ministry. That last phrase in fine print was their way out." "There's only one problem with a ministry like Jerry's," adds a prominent Lynchburg banker. "He can't stop raising money; if he does, it all falls apart."

There is no evidence that Falwell has ever siphoned off any money for himself. Still, at forty-seven, he lives in comfort. His home (which is owned by a wealthy follower) is a twelve-room Southern mansion complete with portico, swimming pool, and verdant lawns — all protected by a high wall and a Bible-quoting guard. Although his salary is only $42,500, Falwell enjoys the perquisites of many big-time entrepreneurs: His ministry affords him an expense account, free life insurance, and a private jet that enables him (and often one of his three children) to take in diversions such as World Series games while traveling on "church business." Falwell is hardly embarrassed by these worldly appurtenances. Material wealth, he says, "is God's way of blessing people who put him first."

THE MEDIA AND POLITICAL CONSULTANTS

Chapter Three

The First Amendment's guarantee of freedom of the press both reflects and protects the political power of an institution that has always played an important role in the nation's politics. The publishers and pamphleteers of eighteenth-century America considered freedom of the press a natural liberty, and acted accordingly. Their criticisms of British and colonial authorities helped to plant the revolutionary seed in the minds of the colonists. Colonial governors were aware of the dangers of a free press, and sought unsuccessfully to control it by requiring government licenses for printing. Moreover, the authorities did not hesitate to bring charges of seditious libel against journalists who criticized the government.

The freedom of the press that was won in the eighteenth century created an environment in which political journalists could and did flourish. Reporters could build successful careers by covering politics at state or national levels, although Washington inevitably became the mecca for the political press.

By the time of the New Deal, the Washington press had become a firmly entrenched establishment force in the nation's capital. Jonathan Daniels, an experienced Washington hand who had served as President Franklin D. Roosevelt's press secretary, commented, "It would be difficult to find a body of men who more clearly represent Washington than the gentlemen of the press who report it. There are notions, carefully cultivated, that they are in Washington but not of it, and that they stand in scrutiny but also in separation. Actually, of course, they are probably more representative of the good and the bad on the Capital scene than any other body of bureaucrats. As they stay in Washington, which most of them hope to do, they are at least as remote from the country as the administrators are."[1]

The media is a powerful political force at all levels of the govern-

---

[1]Jonathan Daniels, *Frontier on the Potomac* (New York: Macmillan, 1946), p. 159

ment. A century before the advent of radio and television, Tocqueville pointed out that the diversity and power of the press is a major characteristic of democracy, and particularly of a government such as that of the United States, which contains so many political subdivisions. "The extraordinary subdivision of administrative power," remarked Tocqueville, "has much more to do with the enormous number of American newspapers than the great political freedom of the country and the absolute liberty of the press."[2] Newspapers, concluded Tocqueville, can persuade large numbers of citizens to unite for a common cause. Moreover, "The more equal the conditions of men become and the less strong men individually are, the more easily they give way to the current of the multitude and the more difficult it is for them to adhere by themselves to an opinion which the multitude discard. . . . The power of the newspaper press must therefore increase as the social conditions of men become more equal."[3]

The press has always attempted to create, in Tocqueville's terms, associations of citizens to back causes and candidates. The press attempts to be the kingmaker for many of the ten thousand or more elected offices throughout the nation.

The growth of the electronic media, radio and television, added a new dimension to the traditional political role played by the press. While newspaper publishers and correspondents are free to express their political views, supporting whatever candidates they choose, the electronic media are in an entirely different position. The airwaves used by the electronic media to communicate information are technically "owned" by the public. The government licenses broadcasting stations for a three-year period, after which it reviews the licensee's conduct in relation to statutory and administrative standards to determine whether or not the license is to be renewed.[4] One of the regulatory standards governing broadcasting requires impartiality in the expression of political views. When a station editorializes it must give "equal time" for the presentation of opposing opinions. Broadcasters, unlike publishers, do not often endorse political candidates.

While broadcasting is supposed to be politically neutral, it is inevitably drawn into partisan politics. All news and public affairs programs have a slant, which indirectly shapes citizen attitudes on important is-

---

[2] Alexis de Tocqueville, *Democracy in America*, Vol. 2 (New York: Vintage Books, 1954), p. 121. Tocqueville's volumes were first published in 1835.

[3] Ibid., p. 122.

[4] In fact, almost all license renewals are automatic, making the licensees virtually permanent owners of their stations.

sues. Statements about public policy are often made simply by the choice of subjects to be covered. The White House, which is so frequently the focus of media attention, complains constantly that it is not being treated fairly. Republicans attack the "Eastern liberal establishment" press, while Democrats always echo President Harry S Truman's lament: "I was sure that the American people would agree with me if they had all the facts. I knew, however, that the Republican-controlled press and radio would be against me, and my only remaining hope of communicating with the people was to get the message to the people in a personal way."[5]

However much politicians may criticize the media, they increasingly depend upon it to project their personalities and communicate their views to the electorate. Political consulting has become a major industry.[6] By 1952, 45 percent of households owned television sets, and not surprisingly, that year marked the advent of political television in a big way in presidential campaigns.[7] General Eisenhower, portrayed as the simple and sincere man from Abilene, easily won over the sometimes acerbic but always witty Adlai Stevenson of Illinois. The Stevenson campaign spent only $77,000 on television, compared to a Republican expenditure of $1.5 million on its media campaign. The use of media consultants and the expenditure of large sums of money for public relations has been considered *de rigueur* for almost all political campaigns, presidential, congressional, and at the state level, as television has become the principal political medium. Media consultants are the new political gurus.

The vignettes in this chapter reveal the character and the style of two powerful political consultants on opposite sides of the ideological spectrum and the way in which one presidential press secretary attempted to manage the news during a national crisis.

[5] Harry S Truman, *Memoirs*, Vol. 2 (Garden City, N.Y.: Doubleday, 1956), p. 175.
[6] See Larry J. Sabato, *The Rise of Political Consultants* (New York: Basic Books, 1981).
[7] Ibid., p. 113.

COLORADO SENATOR GARY Hart's strong bid for the presidential nomination of the Democratic party in 1984 surprised many political observers, who thought Walter Mondale and his organization were invincible. But the political cognoscenti underestimated both Hart, and perhaps more importantly, his pollster and political consultant Patrick Caddell.

Consultants and pollsters have become a permanent part of the political scene. No creditable candidate can do without expert advice as he or she attempts to assess public attitudes, raise money, and deal with the complex world of the media. The ever-growing consultant corps adds a new dimension to the traditional political world of politicians, parties, and elections.

The professional political consultant as a hired gun first appeared in California in the 1930s. A Sacramento newsman and press agent, Clem Whitaker, joined forces with public relations specialist Leone Smith Baxter, establishing a San Francisco consulting firm that for over two decades boasted a 90 percent success rate in seventy-five major campaigns.[1] Imitators followed Whitaker and Baxter's lead, as established advertising firms undertook political consulting. The professional consultant corps itself did not grow significantly until the 1960s and 1970s.[2]

By the 1980s, all candidates would agree that, with respect to political consultants, they would not leave home without one. Although many consultants are hired guns, a number have their own political identification and do not work for candidates who do not conform to their ideological views. Richard Viguerie, for example, the direct-mail specialist, is a New Right leader who would not think of working for liberal candidates. (See selection 13.) By contrast, Patrick Caddell is strongly identified with the Democratic party, where he works for liberal and middle-of-the-road candidates. Caddell, like many of his colleagues, puts candidates through a screening process. He seeks "real patriots in the sense of really caring about the country. If I were to apply one single criterion, it would be whether the individual really gives a good damn about what happens to the United States. Large numbers of politicians, frankly, could care less as long as they stay in office."[3]

Caddell believes that his polling and consulting services must be used to support not only viable candidates, but those who will make, in his opinion, an important contribution once elected. "Today there is a crisis of public confidence," he says, "not merely in specific officeholders, but in the functioning of government itself; not merely in bad policies, but in the entire process of policymaking.

[1] Larry J. Sabato, *The Rise of Political Consultants* (New York: Basic Books, 1981), pp. 11–12.

[2] Ibid., p. 13.

[3] Ibid., p. 31.

It is a crisis of confidence in the political process and the future of the nation."[4]

Caddell is one of many political consultants who have injected their own personalities and values into the political process, helping to determine the kinds of candidates that run and even the policies they work for once elected. Consultants are becoming an important political elite in their own right.

Caddell's search often leads him to offbeat antiestablishment candidates. The following selection portrays how he "found" Gary Hart, and the role he played in Hart's campaign for the Democratic presidential nomination in 1984.

12 Ralph Whitehead
FOR WHOM CADDELL POLLS

For much of 1983 the wunderkind of American electoral strategy roamed the corridors of the Democratic party, searching for a presidential candidate who could expose the House of Mondale as a house of cards. Bumpers and Biden and even Markey turned him down before he was finally welcomed into the Hart campaign, then struggling for survival. The invitation was not without significance: Patrick Caddell has been the winning pollster for every Democratic nominee since 1972. He is the backroom general who can plot campaigns six moves in advance, the political psychologist who plots voters along the axes of the American psyche. His uncanny knack is for turning raw survey numbers into abstract insights, and insights into usable tactics. In a word, he's good.

He is also abrasive. Once an *enfant terrible*, he has ripened with the seasons into a full-blown prima donna. He plays a maddeningly high hand with his candidates and their campaign staffs. Charming and engaging at first meeting, he has turned scores of admirers into detractors. A falling out with partners at Cambridge Survey Research a few years ago led to a bitter fight that is still going through the courts. Caddell and Walter Mondale saw the world very differently during their years at the Carter White House and some wonder how much of Caddell's 1984 posture is vendetta.

Opinion on Caddell splits sharply. For some he is the Merlin of the highly volatile electorate of the eighties and must be heeded by all who

[4]Ibid., p. 74.

From *Boston Observer*, Vol. 3, no. 4, April 1984. Copyright 1984, The Boston Observer Company. Reprinted by permission.

would draw the sword from the stone. To his critics he is a bomb thrower, a nihilist, a manipulator, a man who sets fires in the electorate just to watch them burn. He can tear down the establishment, the incumbent, the front runner, but what, ask his critics, can he build? They wonder whether Caddell was responsible for inflicting Jimmy Carter on the American people and whether he is about to do it again with Gary Hart.

Over the years, I've worked with Caddell and I've worked against him. And, for all his faults, I think he's on to something fundamental: a realignment with the Democratic party.

Pat Caddell is what naturalists call an edge species. These rare strains of plant life flourish on nature's edges, where the forest meets the tundra or the ocean washes the land. They eventually die if they move off these narrow margins, but their life on the edge gives rise to newer and hardier forms of life that *do* survive far from the margin. The edge species is one of nature's innovators.

Caddell sits at the edge of our political landscape. On one side looms the rocky face of the political establishment: the White House, the Congress, the special-interest lobbies, and the grand old men of the Democratic party. Caddell has sniffed the establishment's brandy, savored its food, diverted its women, taken lots of its money, sampled the townhouses, the private jets, and the celebrity. He has scaled these heights but hasn't taken root there.

On the other side sprawl the fields of the American electorate, which Caddell has laboriously surveyed. Through the force of his imagination and the magic of probability theory, he can run those green-and-white printouts through his fingertips and divine the fears and hopes of millions. What he has found is a deep undercurrent of distrust of establishment institutions that touches, even unites, voters on the left and right. He finds in these fields fertile soil for a candidate who can plant the seeds of hope and idealism, a candidate who gives voice to their suspicions that establishment politics are a "consensus of cynicism . . . that has lost faith in the American people — lost faith in their ability to discern carefully or choose wisely, lost faith in their enduring commitment to idealism and compassion, and lost faith in their strength of character to respond to hard truths or call for shared sacrifice."

The enduring picture of Caddell is that of the outsider. He was the Irish Catholic kid from Massachusetts who grew up on the edge of cracker culture in the Protestant Florida panhandle. As an undergraduate at Harvard, he had one foot in the campus and the other in his own commercial polling firm. He thrives today on underdog or insurgent candidacies: New York's Mario Cuomo and Chicago's Harold Washington were recent clients.

"Pat came to me as a junior tutorial student in the fall of 1970," recalls Josiah Lee Auspitz, then a graduate student in government at Harvard.

"He wanted to do a paper on the Wallace vote." As a third-party insurgent in the fall of 1968, George Wallace had reached double digits; the Nixon forces had set these third-party voters as their prime target by the fall of 1970. Caddell, even at the outset of Nixon's campaign, understood that it would fail. He had surveyed these people in Florida and felt that he knew them. "He told me that Wallace voters aren't racist, they're frustrated and they're antiestablishment," Auspitz recalls. Caddell was on to something, and the 1970 returns showed it. The Republicans didn't get the southern gains they sought, and the successful candidates in the South, such as Jimmy Carter of Georgia, shared one quality: They were relatively new faces with strong convictions.

For most of his junior and senior years, Caddell studied these voters. Auspitz helped him to look past the numbers and into the depths of the southern culture, especially its religious heritage. "He was doing finely tuned studies of how Baptists and Methodists differed in their histories and views of the world," says Auspitz. Up North, Caddell paid particular attention to pockets of Wallace strength in industrial cities like Manchester, New Hampshire, and in liberal states such as Wisconsin. It is no coincidence that in 1972 McGovern confounded the expectations of the political establishment in New Hampshire and broke the race open in Wisconsin. His young pollster was Pat Caddell.

If you're a seasoned Massachusetts voter, you've probably got some of Caddell's furniture in your cognitive attic. If you were fed up with traditional Democrats and Yankee Republicans and felt that Mike Dukakis should be governor, then you and Caddell have met somewhere in the printouts, for he was feeding your purifying impulses back to you through his advice to the 1974 Dukakis campaign. If you regard Kevin White as cold and aloof and crooked, a loner in love with himself in the baronial vastness of the Parkman House, then you qualify as a collector — Caddell positioned Joseph Timilty on this score in his 1975 campaign for mayor. Similar themes were writ large, of course, for the 1976 Carter campaign.

Caddell's trade secret is a simple one. Most voters regard politics now as a craft specialty practiced somewhere far from the cultural and economic rhythms of their own lives. A Caddell campaign tries to connect a candidate with those rhythms. And the rhythms he senses in the electorate this year reveal a profound anxiety over the future: "We tried Carter and that didn't work. We tried Reagan and it isn't working. What next? Who next?" Enter Gary Hart.

The official Caddell literature, so to speak, consists chiefly of three long papers.

The first, written just after the Carter victory, warns the president that he takes office in the wake of "the breakdown of party and the failure of ideology," following a campaign that provided no mandate on policy. Caddell's recommendation is for a continuing campaign marked by inaugural strolls, town meetings, and fireside chats. The idea was to build support for policies by keeping public attention positively focused on antiestablishment themes — keep tapping into those rhythms. A parenthetical note from the memo is often quoted by Caddell's critics: "The old cliché about mistaking style for substance usually works the reverse in politics. Too many good people have been defeated because they tried to substitute substance for style; they forgot to give the public the kind of visible signals that it needs to understand what is happening."

Caddell's second paper lives in infamy as the "malaise memo." I have never read it although it has been described to me briefly by its author and others. It was the basis for Carter's week-long retreat to Camp David and his speech upon his return. Its premise: We've got a problem that takes two forms. One is literal — long lines, shrinking supplies, rising prices. The other is symbolic and psychic — our national spirit is running on empty. By solving the energy crisis we can rescue our economy and restore our morale.

The trouble was that while Caddell's themes were compelling, the energy proposals themselves were strictly business-as-usual. Big Government and Big Business would move in a Big Way, but there were few roles for the ordinary citizen. The problem articulated by Carter was rooted in the culture and the economy but the proposed solutions fell to the policy specialists in Washington. Caddell has a one-sentence explanation for this contradiction: "Mondale controlled the policy."

It is not surprising, then, that Caddell's third major paper, "Caddell '83," takes direct aim at Mondale and stresses innovative, populist policies to advance antiestablishment themes. Its 150 pages contain a campaign strategy in search of a candidate, but it holds many other things besides: a diatribe against interest groups, a shrewd critique of the Democratic party's delegate selection rules, a pastiche of speech drafts, a compendium of applause lines, a withering view of the Mondale campaign, an indictment of Reagan and a credible blueprint for beating him, a portrait of the surging activism and importance of minorities and younger white voters. Written in October 1983, it contains a step-by-step strategy of how the Mondale juggernaut could be stopped and how an insurgency candidate might capture the momentum and "rekindle the dry tinder of idealism." Read today, in full view of the Hart phenomenon, it can only be described as remarkably foresighted.

Caddell wrote his memo to prompt a left-of-center, antiestablishment candidate into the presidential race because none of the announced Democratic candidates fit Caddell's bill, *including Gary Hart*. By Caddell's analysis, Hart's was *for* new ideas and *against* interest-group politics, but his candidacy had not been infused with sufficient populist zeal to get the voters stirred up or give an edge to his themes. Nonetheless, at the outset of 1984, with the filing deadline for the New Hampshire primary having passed, Caddell's effort to bring a fresh face into the Democratic field had failed. Hart called Caddell and asked for some help. Although they approached each other warily, they each realized then that the other was the only game left in town.

In the ensuing months, Caddell provided a script for the story line that Gary Hart had created. Hart had long before declared himself the candidate opposed to old formulations and solutions. But it was Caddell who prodded Hart to root his appeal in the cultural and social rhythms of his own experience and appeal more directly to a generation whose political attitudes were shaped by the peace movement, the civil rights movement, the woman's movement, the environmental movement. Simply put, it was that appeal which brought Hart enough caucus votes in Iowa to establish him as *the* alternative to Walter Mondale. And as Caddell and others had predicted, the House of Mondale began to crumble.

Pat Caddell is trying to define the two faces of the Democratic party for the 1980s. Michael Barone has divided the party into Traditional Democrats and Trend Democrats. Bob Squier, a political consultant, has divided it into an institutional wing and a problem-solving wing. Caddell doesn't draw his formulations so crisply, nor does he highlight them with opposing phrases. But let me try to do it for him: We have Hardware Democrats and Software Democrats.

The Hardware Democrats are elitist. This isn't because some of them are graduates of Choate, but because they view the world as being run chiefly by institutionally-backed elites. Consider, for a moment, national security. Walter Mondale has the Trilateral Commission and the Council of Foreign Relations just as Chernenko has the Politburo. Until recently, the terms of the nuclear arms race were based on this elitism. Nuclear policy is driven by superpower strategy and this strategy requires strategic secrets. If there are secrets, then there are a few people who are in on the secrets. Thus the Soviet elite sustains the American, and vice versa. Main-frame talks to main-frame.

Software Democrats are populist. This isn't because they all grew up behind mules in South Dakota, but because they've grown up distrusting the establishment and trusting their own experience. They are working through the freeze movement to democratize our policies for preventing nuclear war by overturning the notion of the nuclear secret. They believe that the critical piece of evidence in the nuclear debate is our own anxiety. Our nightmares are our software.

The Hardware Democrats are bureaucratic. This isn't because their souls are cut from red tape, but because they fear the future as a time of vast uncertainty. Bureaucracies create certainty — not always the certainties we'd like, but certainties. Bureaucracies slow down the rate of change; bureaucrats are the peasants of postindustrial society. Through bureaucracy, tomorrow is daily cast into the mold of yesterday. You can't beat the bureaucratic machinery unless you come up with a superior method for creating certainty.

The Software Democrats are idealistic. They have confidence in the energy of ideas and values. For them, these qualities do create a sense of certainty. They can look at the blueprint and visualize the house (bureaucrats look at blueprints and visualize change orders and cost overruns). If we change our ideas, Software Democrats believe, we change realities.

The Hardware Democrats take what sociologists call an ascriptive view of our status and role: We are pretty much what others say we are. The world creates roles and defines us by bringing us into them. To fight for justice and change is to add to the supply of these existing roles: more entitlement lines, more affirmative action slots, more union jobs. This is our social and economic infrastructure. The Hardware Democrats have built it.

The Software Democrats believe we define ourselves. It isn't enough to add to the supply of exisiting roles; we've got to equip people to create all kinds of new and distinctive roles. The infrastructure doesn't define women or gays or blacks or browns. They define themselves, control their own history, and choose their own fate. Hardware Dems value status because it is the means for gaining security; Software Dems value equity as the means. A union card is status, but a college education is equity: It is mobile, it can be improved upon, and it's usually pretty liquid.

Caddell believes the electoral weight of the party now favors the Software Dems. Here's how he puts it in his 1983 memo:

> Presidential elections are always forays into the future — historically, socially, psychologically, and although inextricably linked to the past, their sustenance is future hope, future aspirations, future acts; they are the future while it happens. Conventional wisdom is always, at best, a consensus about the past, shaped against the rocks and stones of past events, past prejudices, past experiences as they are analyzed from hindsight. In politics, there is no real present, only an "apparent present" . . . squeezed between the grinding wheels of past and future.

More than anything else, "Caddell '83" is a ghost story. The shades of two men can be felt on every page and their voices heard in every paragraph. They are Robert Kennedy and Martin Luther King, Jr. The promise they brought to America's public life is clearly what drives the best in Pat Caddell.

Had these men survived, they might have formed an alliance for the 1968 election. Wiretaps aside, they had a relationship of several years' standing. Surely the tides of the year would have drawn them together. For civil rights. For peace. For a shift from guns to butter, hardware to software. For new sense of national purpose.

The passions stirred by the promise of 1968 later moved in at least two directions following their assassinations. They fell into the channels of older institutions such as the NAACP and the Urban League, the activist churches, and the industrial unions such as the UAW. Or they kept some of the volatility and scattered in the wind, into the Wallace movement (and hence Caddell's original interest in it), the antiwar movement, the precursors of the New Right, perhaps even today's freeze movement. Caddell chose to turn his eyes off the beaten path and watch for the crackling of heat lightning.

Obviously, the ghosts of 1968 animate the Democratic field of 1984. The heir to Hubert Humphrey. The aide to Martin Luther King. The aide to Bobby Kennedy. For better or worse, Caddell has been writing the 1984 script for a long time. All he did last October was put it down on paper.

POLITICAL CONSULTING IS A growth industry that is becoming more and more profitable as the costs and skills required to campaign in the modern technological age increase. Consultant fees, commissions, and expenses account for approximately 20 percent of campaign costs.[1] Consultants charge fees ranging from $10,000 to $100,000 to handle electoral campaigns. In addition, they bill candidates for their expenses and collect commissions that may range up to 33 percent on the costs of media advertising.

In many cases, the names of consultants have become as prominent as the candidates they advise. California consultant Stuart Spencer gained widespread publicity after successfully managing Ronald Reagan's gubernatorial campaign in 1966. He was a leading Reagan consultant in 1980. David Garth was credited with making Ed Koch mayor of New York, and winning reelection for incumbent New Jersey governor Brendan Byrne in 1977 against long odds. Gerald Rafshoon, who handled Jimmy Carter's publicity in 1976, gained national prominence after the election of the former Georgia governor. Consultants who become stars are often masters of the electronic media, using their creative talents to mold the television images of their candidates favorably and place opponents in an unfavorable light. Most would agree with Patrick Cad-

dell that "too many good people have been defeated because they tried to substitute substance for style."[2]

While the Stuart Spencers, David Garths, and Patrick Caddells of the political consultant corps gain the most notoriety, the direct-mail consultants have taught candidates how to use the mundane facilities of the post office to raise money — the lifeblood of the political process. Some consultants see direct mail as an essential communications channel to build political constituencies.

Richard Viguerie, the subject of the following selection, is the undisputed master of the direct-mail consultants. Viguerie is the force behind the National Conservative Political Action Committee (NCPAC), which spends millions of dollars to support conservative candidates. NCPAC claimed credit for the defeat of a number of liberal Democratic senators in 1980, including George McGovern of South Dakota, whose direct-mail techniques in the 1972 presidential campaign so impressed Viguerie that he later copied them. McGovern's direct-mail consultants had amassed a 600,000 member list of potential contributors by the time the South Dakotan declared his presidential candidacy in 1971. The list yielded over $12 million for the McGovern campaign.[3]

Viguerie has used the most advanced computer technology to target conservatives for fund raising and

[1] Larry J. Sabato, *The Rise of Political Consultants* (New York: Basic Books, 1981), p. 52.
[2] Ibid., p. 144.
[3] Ibid., p. 231.

votes. His skills have helped conservatives to outdistance their liberal opponents by a wide margin in the race for money. Viguerie also uses direct mail to convey his passion for the conservative cause. His character and style are portrayed in the following selection.

13 Sidney Blumenthal
RICHARD VIGUERIE:
THE POSTMASTER GENERAL OF THE RIGHT

Just as Hollywood producers once found starlets sipping sodas at Schwab's Drugstore, the New Right now discovers candidates at meetings in motel function rooms called to protest issues like the Panama Canal Treaty or Salt II. The rise to power of U.S. Senator Gordon Humphrey (R., N.H.) is a case in point. Humphrey, a thirty-eight-year-old commercial airline pilot, got his start when he was invited to a gathering against the canal treaty. Nine people showed up, and Humphrey volunteered to serve as chairman of a "Keep Our Canal" rally. This time, five hundred people attended. From that group, Humphrey built up the Conservative Caucus in New Hampshire to fifteen hundred members, providing a network of support for his candidacy. When Humphrey won the GOP nomination, the New Right summoned its considerable resources. Huge sums of money were raised, enough to buy into the Boston television market, which blankets southern New Hampshire, and to hire expensive political consultants. The result: Humphrey unseated the popular sixteen-year Democratic incumbent, Thomas McIntyre.

Was Humphrey's victory a lucky accident? Not quite. His name originally surfaced on the mailing list of political entrepreneur and generalissimo of the New Right, Richard A. Viguerie. "Things don't happen by accident," he says. "They're planned. They're organized. We don't have a notebook with the whole thing carefully mapped out, although that's not a bad idea. But we have plans."

Forty-six-year-old Viguerie has become a very powerful man in a short span of time. He's the publisher of a flotilla of publications ranging from the mass circulation *Conservative Digest* to the insider's newsletter *New Right Report*. Several political action committees are run by his associ-

From *The Permanent Campaign: Inside the World of Elite Political Operatives* by Sidney Blumenthal. Copyright © 1980 by Sidney Blumenthal. Reprinted by permission of Beacon Press.

ates, providing modern consulting methods to specially selected candidates. Several U.S. senators owe their seats to Viguerie in some way. Senator Jesse Helms (R., N.C.) was dubbed the Six-Million-Dollar man last year when he ran for reelection, a reference to the amount Viguerie raised for him as a result of direct-mail solicitations. (Viguerie, incidentally, keeps a hefty chunk of the loot; in some cases more than 75 percent of what he raises goes to him and his subsidiaries.)

Viguerie's IBM tape decks and high-speed printers work twenty-four hours a day, with time off only on Christmas, Thanksgiving, and Easter. In the vault of his computer room, to which entry is permitted only by a security guard, is his treasure of 11 million names on tape. This is the core of the New Right.

Viguerie is ready for the presidential election year, another milestone, he hopes, in the progress of the New Right. At first, Viguerie's candidate was Congressman Philip Crane of Illinois. In the eleven months after his announcement in August 1978, Crane raised $2,490,276 in funds through direct mail. But he paid out $1,191,847 to five companies of which Viguerie is an owner, officer, or director. Crane disagreed with Viguerie about the direct-mail strategy. He wanted to resolicit those on the "house list." Viguerie wanted to keep "prospecting" for new supporters. Eventually, Crane and Viguerie had a falling out.

Meanwhile, Viguerie approached another presidential contender, John Connally. "He was interested and we got married," says Viguerie. "Connally and I agree on 75 percent of the issues. And he has the best chance of beating Ted Kennedy." This factor is paramount to Viguerie. He is terror stricken by the thought of a Kennedy presidency. He believes Kennedy will attempt to put the New Right out of business by promulgating campaign contribution reforms and by political use of the Justice Department. If Kennedy is the candidate for the Democrats, Viguerie sees the election as a life-and-death struggle.

"It's a sign of our strength that there is no candidate in the Republican party who is going to run a left of center campaign for president," says Viguerie. "I think the new vitality of the conservative movement definitely is responsible for that. This will be the first time in our lifetime that no one who is a serious candidate will appeal to that liberal perspective. Slowly but surely we're moving the political balance much more to the center. Not to the right. But things are definitely moving our way. We've got some momentum."

One of his confederates, Massachusetts conservative Howard Phillips, believes that Viguerie's mailing lists are at the base of the New Right's sudden influence. It was Phillips's Conservative Caucus that "discovered" Gordon Humphrey in New Hampshire, courtesy of Viguerie's computerized lists. "They're indispensable," he says. "Without assembling that body of names we couldn't have achieved anything. As

Jesse Unruh said, money is the mother's milk of politics. Unless you have money you don't have anything. Without the magic of direct mail, conservatives would be relegated to part-time activity. There would have been no fight over the Panama Canal Treaty unless there was a New Right. We helped defeat instant voter registration. If the New Right wasn't involved, the two parties would take the same position and there would be no debate."

Viguerie is the High Tech Lenin of the New Right. He didn't come to the right through disillusionment or defeat. He isn't brooding or starkly resentful. He's relaxed in his corner office, surrounded by paintings of famous golf courses. His head is a gleaming sculpted dome with a few strands of hair brushed across it. He's at ease with himself, not threatened by conversations with journalists. On the contrary, he welcomes these exchanges. He's animated, yet completely self-possessed. He's eager to state his position. He wants challenges. Interviews are exercises, preparatory drills, jogs in anticipation of the long-distance run. He bubbles with optimism.

"If I had been in a lot of the foxholes a lot of the conservatives have been in for thirty years and been shot and shelled and just torn apart and suffered all the defeats and have a what-the-hell attitude . . ." Viguerie shrugs and plows on. "That's just not the attitude of the new conservatives. We believe we will win and prevail. There isn't a Communist leader in the world worth his salt who doesn't feel that Communism isn't the wave of the future. They just believe that they are the stuff of history. There's not a leader I now of in the Free World who believes freedom is the wave of the future. That's what we have going for the conservatives now: The conservatives believe that they will govern America. They see themselves as winners in life. They are totally convinced that they have the ability to govern and that they *will* govern in the foreseeable future. There's an electricity, an excitement that wasn't here six years ago."

Viguerie is a fundamentalist in his political beliefs. What sets him off from mossbacks of previous generations is his sophistication. He knows that without a contemporary approach his ideas would remain ethereal, unconnected to real politics. He wants to win. He's reaching for power. He knows how to work the levers and his intentions are clear. All of this makes him an original American political type, unlike the old rightists who were nurtured on failure and developed what the late historian Richard Hofstadter termed "the paranoid style in American politics."

Richard Viguerie is a modernist. He may not accept the precepts of the New Deal, but he abides the canons of advertising as if they were eternal verities. He's pragmatic in his use of technique. He wants to use what works. Viguerie has been willing to learn from sources other than fellow rightists. He is an apt pupil of George McGovern, the New Left, and the AFL-CIO, all Satan incarnate to old rightists. But Viguerie is confident that he can truck with the devil without being marked. He emerges stronger in his convictions and surer in how to realize them.

"We've taken close to 100 percent of the left's tactics," he confesses unashamedly. "What we're doing is what they did. We have been thirty years late in realizing how the left did it. We're into making a list of all the things they do and doing the same things." The methods he's adopted are simply common organizing techniques, at least common to the labor movement, the peace movement, and the civil rights movement.

On Viguerie's desk, when I paid him a visit, was a thick book containing copies of the direct-mail solicitations from the 1972 McGovern for president campaign, which Viguerie holds in high professional esteem. "I'm studying it," he says. "I'm trying to build a movement. I don't know if you've heard that word much. Among us conservatives that's a word that's used constantly. The movement." Hearing him speak in the shorthand of the left is eerie. The word *movement* resonates oddly when Viguerie uses it. But the right, after all, has momentum. It is in movement. It is a choice, not an echo.

Viguerie's achievement is considerable. He has forged a distinctive New Right, moving it beyond its narrow complaints, melding it into a movement. Previously, the right embraced a politics of nostalgia for a past that never existed; the right expected and needed defeat because defeat certified its opinions. Its politics were concerned with loss of status in a rapidly changing world. Viguerie has helped the right transcend status politics to become a brand of interest-group politics, a far more efficacious approach. The New Right often seems to be a collection of motley single-issue groups, very particularized, dependent on the old anxieties. But within the new structures the right is able to have much more of an effect. Viguerie has wedded the substance of status politics to the form of interest-group politics. It's a real advance for the right, a signal change in its methodology. Viguerie has pushed the right into the modern era, educating conservatives in the craft of marketing and advertising, essential instruments of American politics. The New Right is much more dangerous because of his pedagogy.

"Years and years ago, I decided that I wanted to do something in a major way to help the conservative movement," he says. "There were different routes I could have gone." He ticks off the names of influential conservative writers. "Bill Buckley, Bill Rusher, Russell Kirk. I could have gone that route. I probably wouldn't have amounted to a hill of beans. That wasn't my nature. I didn't have the educational background for that. What we didn't have, what we had zero people doing, was having someone take the ideas, the writings, the books and market them to the masses. A new cause came along, a new candidate, we didn't really have someone who understood how to market them on a national scale.

So I set out for myself to become the best marketer I could be. I wanted to communicate wiht the masses, to market ideas. And I did that. It may not have occurred to other conservatives. It's not an easy thing to do. It requires certain skills. I had to train myself, to teach myself. I've been doing it a long time, but I've got a long way to go yet. I went to college to learn one profession and then I had to learn a different one. Not a lot of people are willing to do that, put in those kind of hours. I majored in political science at the University of Houston. I went to law school for about a year and a half. I always, always, always, wanted to be a politician. I didn't understand *how* I was going to do it. I just knew I *was* going to do it."

An optimistic rightist like Viguerie had to have been born and raised on the cusp of the Sun Belt. Richard Viguerie is a sunny new-wave reactionary. He is idea and act, free of cobwebs. He was born in Golden Acres, Texas, a town outside Houston. His father was a middle-level petrochemical executive, his mother a practical nurse. "My parents were the silent majority out there," he recalls. "Their instincts were conservative. We don't disagree on hardly anything philosophical. But there wasn't a situation where I can remember discussing politics in the evening at dinner. It's something I picked up on my own. My philosophy wasn't counter to my parents, but they weren't very political."

When he was very young, perhaps seven, he became enthralled with American Indians. He was very shy and small for his age, even as a teenager. Although he had never actually seen an authentic Indian he was obsessed with their plight. Movies, which mainly portrayed Indians as ignoble savages, perked his interest. He immersed himself in books on the subject. At some point he linked victims of Communism with Indians. The Communists were the white men. The American way of life — entrepreneurial capitalism — was imperiled. It could be wiped out like the Indians. America was the underdog. Communists were closing in. For a boy in Texas, the end of the frontier was vivid.

In college Viguerie had two heroes — "the two Macs" he calls them — General Douglas MacArthur and Senator Joseph McCarthy. When the Army-McCarthy hearings were broadcast Viguerie was riveted to the radio. These hearings, more than anything else, led to McCarthy's demise. During them, McCarthy's penchant for character assassination and coarse tactics was revealed unadorned on nationwide television. As McCarthy went down, Viguerie, listening attentively in his dormitory room, rooted for him. "Here was a man fighting Communism," he says. "So I became a fighter."

His start in politics wasn't auspicious, a typically undistinguished beginning running the Houston headquarters of Senator John Tower. The following year he moved up the ladder to become the first executive secretary of the Young Americans for Freedom, William F. Buckley's finishing school for future conservative leaders. As part of his job Viguerie was supposed to raise money for the organization. He did not like asking rich people for contributions directly. He decided to write them letters, and his first direct mailings worked. Soon he made the plunge into business. With a $300 investment he rented a one-room office on Capitol Hill in 1965; today he grosses over $15 million a year, a conservative estimate. He was like an oil wildcatter, an independent driller in politics. He sank his lines and hoped for a gusher. It was just a trickle to begin with. Direct mail, while part of an overall political consulting media package, wasn't regarded by most operatives as lucrative enough to base a firm on. It was fine as a supplement to television, but in itself it was patently inadequate. Viguerie kept at it.

Then came three big breaks. The first of these was the 1972 McGovern campaign for the presidency, which demonstrated conclusively the power of direct mail. McGovern's campaign was a sterling example of a faultless direct-mail operation. "George McGovern," explains Viguerie, "ran over the Henry Jacksons and the Hubert Humphreys of the world because he understood the new technology. He was a creature of direct mail. McGovern was thinking direct mail from the beginning." The reason McGovern was thinking direct mail was because he had to. He didn't have the backing of the regular Democrats, the AFL-CIO, the urban machines, or the ethnic groups. In early polls his standing with Democrats wavered between 2 and 3 percent. He had no wealthy supporters. His candidacy seemed particularly farfetched then. He desperately needed a means to nourish his campaign in its lean phase, at least until it could take off. McGovern contacted Morris Dees, the most successful political direct-mail operator in the country. Dees, a liberal Southerner, built the biggest direct-mail company outside New York and Chicago, sold it, and, when McGovern contacted him, was devoting his time to public interest law and civil rights. (Dees had begun his career as a student at the University of Alabama selling birthday cakes to students' parents.) Dees calculated that the right pitch would enable the McGovern campaign to carry itself through its nascent stages. He wrote a letter asking recipients to contribute ten dollars a month to the McGovern for President Club. A coupon book for making payments was enclosed; those who signed up were sent an "insider's" newsletter and monthly reminders to pay their "dues." By early 1972 monthly income from the scheme totaled about $100,000. "The club idea proves that Alexis de Tocqueville was right when he observed almost 150 years ago that America was a nation of joiners," Dees declared. Viguerie took notice of Dee's scheme. In his own work, Viguerie began to write fund-raising appeals with participatory gimmicks, asking recipients to send in an enclosed poll or an odd dollar contribution for a specific purpose. He was catching on.

His next leap forward was provided by Arthur Bremer. When George Wallace's putative assassin incapacitated the Alabama governor in 1972, Wallace's 1976 presidential campaign was cast into doubt. Wallace had little personal control over the political efforts on his behalf. The collection of money, which would determine if there would even be another run, was farmed out to Richard Viguerie, whom Morris Dees suggested as ideologically compatible. In eighteen months Viguerie raised $2 million and spent as much in the effort. Eventually he garnered $6.9 million for Wallace. Viguerie was Wallace's life-support system, sustaining him for one final campaign.

Wallace's campaign was the real making of Viguerie and the New Right, for it provided a list of 600,000 names, sifted from a larger list of contributors, that was as good as gold. While Viguerie did a lot for Wallace, Wallace was a godsend for Viguerie. His campaign gave Viguerie free-and-clear proprietary rights to the hardcore of the New Right. Unintentionally and indirectly, however, it also contributed to the rise of Jimmy Carter, whose 1976 primary victories over Wallace in Southern states made him the leading candidate, acceptable to blacks and liberals.

The third and perhaps most important boon for Viguerie was Watergate. Besides the removal of Richard Nixon from the Oval Office, the most tangible result of Watergate was a campaign reform act passed by Congress that limited contributions to $1000. Supposedly, this would inhibit arm twisting of corporate executives by presidential hopefuls, democratize the political process by making parties less dependent on major contributors, and involve more citizens who would feel that their small gifts carried weight. It didn't exactly work out that way. The principal beneficiary of this reform, enacted mainly at the behest of liberal Democrats, was Richard Viguerie.

It was a bonanza for him. With his Wallace list he could sell his services to appropriately reactionary candidates to help them reach the small contributors they now urgently needed. Through a series of campaigns Viguerie piggybacked his list, gathering more and more names, prospecting for the best ones to add to his computer tapes. The list expanded geometrically. The Wallace campaign itself depended upon these small givers. Watergate made his jackpot seem almost inevitable.

Suddenly, Viguerie was in the big time. But he continued to see everything through an ideological lens. He considered his fortuitous elevation to a position of influence to be more than a simple political victory: it was a triumph of modern marketing. "The left has missed a lot of things," he advises. "They think of direct mail as fund raising. They miss the whole boat if they think that. *It is a form of advertising*. It is not an evil conspiratorial thing. It is just a fact of life, which I haven't found anybody to deny, that the major media of this country has a left-of-center perspective. The conservatives can't get their message around this blockade, except through direct mail. It's a way for conservatives to by-pass the monopoly the left has on the media. It's a way of mobilizing our people; it's a way of communicating with our people; it identifies our people; and it marshals our people. It's self-liquidating and it pays for itself. It's a form of advertising, part of the marketing strategy. *It's advertising.*"

Viguerie began his thrust for leadership of the New Right in 1974, when Gerald Ford nominated Nelson Rockefeller to serve as his vice-president. This appointment was the final affront to the New Right. Viguerie moved into action to attempt to block the selection. He tele-phoned more than a dozen conservative movers and shakers and invited them to his office to formulate tactics. The meeting was a disappoint-ment. "The conservative leaders of America in that room didn't know how to go from point A to point Z," recalls Viguerie. "I saw very dra-matically that nobody knew how to organize."

It was then that Viguerie started to develop his theory of leadership, a conception of a counterrevolutionary vanguard that would take com-mand of the right by giving it direction. "There is a lot of planning and communication within the conservative movement that didn't exist half a dozen years ago," says Viguerie. "It's basically happening because of a dozen or so key leaders who are moving in a very bold, dramatic, decisive way. Of all the problems the conservative movement has had over the years it has been lack of leadership that's hurt the most. We've had people who were well known, who were very articulate, who could write very well, could speak, had charisma. Naturally everyone would think that's a leader. But there's a difference between a spokesman and a leader. We've had our spokesmen and now we have our leaders."

Viguerie's desire to form a vanguard is derived from his sense of his-tory. He believes that history is the story of great men, that personalities are the driving force of events. The masses to him are inconsequential compared to their leaders. "This country is here today," he explains, "because of a few dozen people. Maybe twelve. It wasn't the million that demanded the freedom from England. Take away a Washington, a Franklin, where would you be? The same with the conservative move-ment today. Take away that dozen and you've got problems."

This somewhat imperious attitude, however, generates extraordinary passion in Viguerie. The day I spent with him he was up at four in the morning to write a fund-raising appeal. He reserves his most fervent evangelism for his copywriting. His true pulpit is in an envelope. "I feel," he says, "that when I have spent five or six hours writing a letter, I am the audience. I am the person I am writing to. When I am finished I am physically wrung out. I am exhausted because I put myself in there emotionally. I am in my copy. I feel for the people, for the cause. It's very emotional. A lot of my clients don't like the copy because they say it sounds too cornball, too conversational, it's not dignified. But people respond to emotionalism. The successful and effective speakers are emotional."

His feelings aren't wasted. There's more to these solicitations than just a visceral release for Viguerie. Direct mail is part of a grand strategy. It fits in with his theory of the counterrevolutionary vanguard; he believes that a vanguard without a movement is simply a sect. Viguerie doesn't just tender advice to candidates and single-issue groups for a fee. He is building a movement that will support a certain kind of candidate. He is working from the bottom up to create a constituency to back his politics. In the language of the left, he's base building.

Direct mail is not Viguerie's only organizational tool, however. He has created a political conglomerate with satellites spinning around the direct-mail operation. Viguerie keeps extending his frontier with a sense of surety; he believes in political manifest destiny. Political action committees (PACs) expedite his missions. They spend millions: In 1972 congressional races, established conservative groups dropped a mere $250,000; but in 1976, with Viguerie geared up, conservative groups raised close to $5.6 million. Viguerie's PACs differ from the corporate PACs in that they're much more ideological. They're also more organizationally minded. Corporate PACs just give their money to candidates they feel best represent their interests. Viguerie wants more than that from his PACs. He wants commitment; he wants more movement activists. So his PACs are designed to train politicians. One of his PACs, the National Conservative Political Action Committee (NCPAC), which helped elect fifty-five New Rightists to office in 1978, prefers to give candidates material services rather than outright grants of money. NCPAC will provide politicians with an ensemble of modern techniques — polling, media advice, and campaign management training. When U.S. Senator Frank Church of Idaho felt threatened by NCPAC support of an opponent in the 1980 race for his Senate seat, he reacted by raising the issue of a Soviet brigade in Cuba in connection with passage of the SALT II treaty. Church was running scared, and thus was influenced by Viguerie's cohorts on this very important matter.

Another of the Viguerie sponsored PACs, the Committee for the Survival of a Free Congress (CSFC) selects the candidates it wants to elect and then runs them through a training seminar. In 1978, CSFC helped elect twenty-six congressmen and five U.S. senators. The key to the success of this PAC is a precinct organization plan, which is presented as a revelation. It calls for an organization of precinct workers to be assigned voter turnout goals and to be supervised by area chairmen. The average twelve-year-old in Chicago could devise a more complicated scheme. But to the New Right this approach is novel.

The group that best reflects the comprehensive Viguerie viewpoint —

combining the vanguard with the base, the single-issue campaigns with political races — is the Conservative Caucus. Headed by Howard Phillips, it is located in a rabbit's warren of offices occupied by other New Right groups above Papa Gino's on Tremont Street in Boston. (The offices are rent-free since the owner of Papa Gino's is a New Rightist and on the executive board of the Conservative Caucus: Ideology to go.) Phillips is burly and forceful. Viguerie attests to his political acumen. "Howie's one of the six key people," he confides. In 1978, Phillips ran as a Democrat for the Senate nomination, which struck most Bay State Democrats as ludicrous. Phillips, after all, is a former official of the Nixon administration. But his move indicated the drift of New Right strategy. What happened to his particular candidacy is relatively unimportant. What was meant by it is far more significant.

Phillips's ideas reflect his experience. He doesn't engage in idle theorizing. Obviously, he has a strong impact on Viguerie and the rest of the New Right. He carries weight. "In 1968 I was a conservative Republican," he says. "In 1979 I'm a conservative period." He received his education at the hands of Richard Nixon. When Phillips was a student government leader at Harvard in 1960, he was a fervent Nixon backer. Nixon was his hero. Now he sadly admits, "I'm without heroes." To New Rightists, Nixon is the great betrayer. Democratic presidents simply carried out the tasks they set out for themselves; they were liberals. But Nixon promised something new, fulfillment of the conservative dream, an evolutionary antireformism, unraveling the liberal program. They feel he had power in his grasp, but never used it. He shattered their expectations, which were probably somewhat naive to begin with. Nixon was far too centrist for the far right. "He damaged everthing I hold dear," says Phillips. "He was the most liberal president in American history, except for Gerald Ford. He's a fundamentally weak man who groveled for Establishment recognition. He just wanted to look good in the history books, have the *New York Times* say nice things about him. At the same time, he hated them. He didn't have the courage of his intestines. I owe him a great deal because I got an education in his administration. My real education is that even presidents are flawed."

In 1974, Phillips formed a group called CREEP II, Conservatives for the Removal of the President. He was afraid that Nixon would make concessions to the Russians as he tried to fend off the Watergate inquiry. After Nixon's abdication, Phillips blueprinted plans for the Conservative Caucus. "I went to Viguerie," he says. "And we sent out material in the mail. Had it not been for Viguerie we couldn't have made much progress. Direct mail has done more than give us money. It gives us a way to get to our people."

Once outside the Nixon administration Phillips explored political options. Perhaps he learned the most from the left. "People in the conservative movement today aren't conventionally ambitious. It's the same

way on the left," he says. "A lot of conservatives have read Saul Alin-
sky. I read all the liberal publications including the *Progressive*, the *Nation*, *Working Papers*. If something works, we're for doing it. In terms of
the Caucus, the strategy comes out of trial and error. We need a grass-
roots organization and we're developing a system for doing it broadly."

Phillips's Conservative Caucus can take credit for Gordon Humphrey's victory in New Hampshire. Less directly, the New Right has
influenced other elections, mainly by creating a favorable conservative
climate. "The greatly expanded base of conservative strength permitted
Democratic primary upsets," the *New Right Report*, Viguerie's newsletter, gloated. "And the best news is this: This is not a temporary trend.
This coalition will be bigger and stronger in 1980."

The New Right strategy calls for support of conservatives, whether
they're Republican or Democrat. Before the 1976 election, William Rusher,
publisher of the conservative *National Review*, argued, in a book entitled
The Making of the New Majority Party, for a conservative party to replace
the Republicans. For a while, New Rightists embraced the Rusher thesis. Now they've jettisoned it. They're for building coalitions across party
lines that maintain ideological consistency. Much of this tack derives
from Phillips's experience. "My experience in the Nixon administration
persuaded me that parties are less important than I had thought. It doesn't
matter which party succeeds. Principles matter."

Viguerie's empire will be at the eye of the coming political storm. Yet
he is being criticized by old-style conservative Republicans for his business practices. From three of his PACs, for example, his companies clear
83 percent of the total take. Certainly, he makes piles of money. But it
seems out of character for these conservatives to attack a political rival
for his entrepreneurial zeal. Isn't that what they're fighting for? Viguerie
is an exemplar of economic individualism. He embodies the Ayn Rand
ideal, suggested in the title of one of her books, *The Virtue of Selfishness*.

There's more than a touch of Horatio Alger to Richard Viguerie. He's
driven to self-improvement, up at four in the morning. But Viguerie
isn't a conventional go-getter. He believes that free will is tied to post-
mortem punishment. "I believe in reincarnation," he asserts. He doesn't
know who or what he was in the past, but he's doing his best not to
wind up another species next time: if you don't do the right thing you
might become a cockroach. Viguerie is hammering himself into line out
of fear of metamorphosis. Strangely, he sees this as a liberating concept.
"After I began to understand reincarnation," he says, "the idea that we
are all responsible for ourselves, that things don't happen to us acciden-
tally, it was exciting. You reap what you sow. Sometimes you're going
to reap it in this life, sometimes in the next life. Life is a learning experience. There's a law out there. You violate the law, you're going to be
punished. You stick your hand in an electric socket, it's going to hurt.
Life is not luck, it's not chance. It's a question of choice. Anything that

I do that's not Christ-like I'm going to have to pay for it. This time or the next time. Doggone it, I want to get it right this time."

His mysticism suffuses his politics with confidence. Viguerie's religion gives him a sense of divine direction. More, his religiosity is a justification for his practicality. He feels free to pursue his career, certain that it meets with heavenly approval. He is in control of his life and his machines.

He doesn't fear his computers. "Technology is neutral," he says. "It's just a tool." For him, science is the servant of ideology. Although Viguerie maintains a sure hand on his IBM machines he still reveals doubt about the effect of the new technology on politics generally: "It's seldom that you will find older, established candidates that will be interested in using direct mail. Things you don't understand you don't feel comfortable with. When I'm sixty years old, I may not be any different than they are. It's fear of the unknown. You feel comfortable with what you've done for twenty or thirty years successfully. Why do it a different way? Why change? But there are people doing it a different way and they're running over the older politicians. It's possible to get elected today with the computers and the direct mail and the telephones and not really know how to govern. You can use these techniques to win the nomination and the election, but not know how to govern. That's right, you become a permanent compaigner. Take old Lyndon Johnson. He had all kinds of problems, but he knew how to govern. He knew how to make the bureaucracy work. He knew how to run things and administer things. He wasn't out of place in the Oval Office. The old politicians might understand how to govern better than a lot of the new ones. The new ones are relying on technology that is basically being applied by others. The old ones don't know how to campaign and the new ones don't know how to govern. There might be something to that."

Does this mean that he worries about the depth of commitment of some of the New Right candidates who owe so much to him? He expresses no such feelings. He's upbeat, 1980 promises to be a good year, and after that things look even better. "We're definitely going against the anti-ideological grain," he says. "And we're succeeding." He believes the left is beginning to retreat before his advancing legions. He thinks he can set the order of battle. "If the AFL-CIO wasn't worried about my direct mail, they wouldn't stay up nights worrying about me," he says. "It's a defensive posture by basically older people who don't know how to stop it. You can't stop it. Ask the French how defense works. It doesn't."

"Offense picks the terrain," I suggest.

"Exactly," Viguerie replies. "That's good," he muses. "I'll have to use that."

SUCCESSFUL POLITICAL CAN-didates learn to deal with the media from the day they run for office until they retire. The grist of the reporter's mill is information, and sometimes misinformation. Reporters follow political candidates like hawks stalking their prey, hoping that in one fell swoop they will be able to capture information that will command a front-page headline or a spot on the nightly television news. At least that is the view of the press held by many politicians.

The focus of the most intense press attention is, understandably, presidential politics, both running and governing.

Before Richard Nixon boarded over the indoor White House swimming pool to make a press-briefing room, presidential aides going to their offices in the West Wing walked through a press lounge. There, one White House aide told the author, the "piranha" eagerly waited to devour White House staffers. In the paranoiac atmosphere that so frequently pervades politics, the press is always the enemy unless it is controlled. Every president in the modern era, from Franklin D. Roosevelt to Ronald Reagan, has attempted to manage the news. William Safire defines managed news as "information generated and distributed by the government in such a way as to give government interest priority over candor."[1]

The media are, to use the phrase of Douglass Cater, the fourth branch of the government.[2] The press, which now includes the electronic as well as the print media, has appointed itself guardian of the public interest. Although many members of the press have a cozy relationship with public officials, upon whom they depend for valuable information, the theory of the press that is taught in journalism schools requires reporters to distance themselves personally from the subjects of their stories. The adversary relationship between investigative reporters and the government enables a reporter to ferret out the facts no matter how unpleasant they may be.

While the Washington press includes reporters like Bob Woodward and Carl Bernstein, whose investigations of the Nixon White House's coverup of the break-in at the Democratic National Headquarters in the Watergate office complex led to impeachment proceedings against the president and his resignation, they are exceptions and not the rule. Understandably, the seductive Washington environment, in which power and status mean everything, has co-opted many reporters. The press has become part of the Washington establishment because it has learned to play the game of power politics itself. The Gridiron Club, an old and exclusive organization of newspaper people, symbolizes the press elite. Annually it invites members of the political establishment to join it in a fun-filled session of humor and satire. The spirit

---

[1] William Safire, *Safire's Politcal Dictionary* (New York: Random House, 1978), p. 397.
[2] Douglass Cater, *The Fourth Branch of the Government* (Boston: Houghton Mifflin, 1959).

of camaraderie that prevails at such a gathering can best be appreciated by those on the inside. President and Mrs. Reagan were the highlights of the club's meeting in 1982, as the First Lady skillfully performed a skit that satirized the prevailing press view of her activities.

The Gridiron Club may roast politicians, but its members recognize that the press and the politicians are in the same broader club of the politically powerful. Washington reporters recognize that to be at the top of the newspaper profession they must have access to the top of the political world. The linkage between success and power often softens the adversary stance of the press.

Washington's political centers of power recognize that the press is an important fourth branch of the government. Presidents, members of Congress, and even Supreme Court justices know that managing the news will buttress their power and may even be a key to survival. Presidents, especially during their first few years in office, feel besieged by a press that they consider hostile and unfair. Even before he became president, John F. Kennedy went out of his way to warn an aide about the press, "Always remember that their interests and ours ultimately conflict."[3]

Kennedy cultivated political reporters, and his good press relations not only helped him to win the presidential election in 1960 but also buttressed his presidency. Richard Nixon blamed his 1960 defeat on an unfair press, an attitude that was intensified after he lost his race for the California governorship in 1962. Nixon understandably put managing the news at the top of his agenda when he became president.

ALL PRESIDENTS WOULD LIKE to manage the news, which, in the view of Jimmy Carter's press secretary Jody Powell in the following selection, gives the White House the right to lie when national security is at stake.

14 Jody Powell
THE RIGHT TO LIE

Since the day the first reporter asked the first tough question of a government official, there has been an ongoing debate about whether government has the right to lie.

The debate took on its present form one day in 1963, when then Pentagon spokesman Arthur Sylvester, for reasons known only to himself,

[3] William Safire, *Safire's Political Dictionary*, p. 397.

responded to the question officially and honestly. "Yes," he said, "under certain circumstances I think government does have the right to lie."

The resulting furor has made every sitting press secretary and senior government official leery of the question from that day since. Like all my predecessors, I was always careful not to give a direct response. It was one of those questions for which you prepare and keep on file a standard evasion.

But Sylvester, of course, was right. In certain circumstancee, government has not only the right but a positive obligation to lie. For me, that right-obligation flows directly from two other principles:

First, that government has a legitimate right to secrecy in certain matters because the welfare of the nation requires it. In other cases, individuals, even public figures, have a certain right to privacy because common decency demands it.

Secondly, the press has a right to print what it knows within very broad limits, without prior restraint, because the survival of democratic government depends on it.

Those two principles are often in conflict. Fortunately, the confrontation is not usually irreconcilable. Questions can be evaded. Answers can be devised that may mislead, but do not directly misrepresent. A "no comment" can sometimes be used without its being taken as a confirmation. Or the reporter can be sworn to secrecy himself and told why it is that certain information would be terribly damaging if published.

That is usually the case, but not always. Occasionally, the conflict is so sharp and the matter involved so important that there is no way to slide off the point. There is simply no answer that is both true and responsible. In such cases, the only decent thing to do is to lie and, I would argue, to make it the most convincing lie you can devise.

In my four years in the White House, I was only faced with that type of situation twice.

The first involved a question from a so-called reporter who was noted for trading in gossip and personal scandal, and who worked for a publication that had an even worse reputation in that regard.

The question involved the personal life of a colleague and that of his family. To have responded with what I believed to be the truth would have resulted in great pain and embarrassment for a number of perfectly innocent people. Beyond that, I could see no reason why the matter should be of public interest.

I had little doubt that an evasion or "no comment" would be taken as more than adequate confirmation by this particular writer, and no doubt whatsoever that there was no hope of successfully appealing to a sense of compassion and fair play. So I lied.

I did not just deny the allegation, but went to some trouble to construct a convincing argument as to what I suspected to be the case. Apparently, it worked, probably because others who were asked responded in much the same way I did. In any case, the story never appeared in print anywhere that I know of.

I have absolutely no regrets for what I did, and can say without hesitation that I would do the same thing again if similar circumstances arose. Quite simply, it seems to me that to the extent journalism insists upon the right to probe into matters that can destroy families and ruin careers, but which in no way involve a breach of public trust, it must also grant the right to those who become targets to defend themselves by the only means available.

Moreover, there will inevitably be a disputed area between journalists and public figures over what is, and what is not, a legitimate matter of public interest. In some cases, the answer may not be clear, even to the most unbiased observer, except in retrospect. And it hardly needs to be said that a *post hoc* decision that a personal matter should have remained private is of absolutely no benefit to those who have been hurt by its publication.

The other situation in which I believed, and still believe, that I had an obligation to lie occurred in April of 1980.

Following the collapse of the first of two attempts to negotiate an agreement with the Iranian government to secure the release of our hostages, because those nominally in positions of authority either could not or would not live up to their promises, the President began to look more seriously at a military rescue operation.

He had given orders for work to begin on such an option as soon as the hostages were seized. At that time, there seemed to be no feasible way to go about it with a decent chance of success. In the intervening months, as the Pentagon studied, planned, and trained, and as we learned more about the situation in the embassy compound through intelligence operations and the news media, the chances for a successful attempt began to increase.

Although I knew the work was being done, I knew nothing about its specifics, and indeed did not want to know, until March 22, 1980. In a meeting at Camp David to review our options following the disintegration of the first agreement, Secretary of Defense Brown and Joint Chiefs of Staff Chairman General David Jones presented a full briefing on their plans for a rescue operation.

It was impressive, both because of the work that had gone into it and the intelligence that we had managed to gather, and because the detailed consideration of such an option inevitably has a powerfully sobering effect on anyone with a say in whether or not it will be implemented.

Still, no one seemed to feel that this was the correct choice at the time. There were some questions raised about whether some aspects of what was necessarily a complex plan could not be simplified. More important in the decision not to go ahead then was the willingness, although reluctant, to give diplomacy one last chance. No one doubted that there would be American casualties, even in a successful operation. One Israeli soldier and three hostages had been killed at Entebbe, and the problem that faced our planners, and would face the strike force, were many times more difficult than anything the Israelis had confronted. There had also been messages from our intermediaries, and indirectly from Iranian officials, almost begging for a chance to put the negotiated agreement back on track.

Even though no one argued that day that we should choose the rescue option, I left the meeting feeling that we were heading down a road that would soon bring us to that choice unless the Iranians suddenly came to their senses. Despite my agreement with the decision to try the diplomatic approach again, I had to admit to myself that the odds seemed to be against the Iranians' implementing the agreement they had already reneged on once.

On the morning of April 11, shortly after that second diplomatic effort had indeed collapsed, the President called me into his office a few minutes before the regular Friday morning foreign-policy breakfast was to begin. During most of the administration, I had not attended these breakfasts on a regular basis. When the President felt that the agenda required my presence, he would let me know. Occasionally, I would ask to be included if I had a point I wanted to raise, or if I felt the need to listen to the discussion on a particular topic.

Once the hostage crisis began, however, I asked to attend on a regular basis, so that I could keep abreast of the latest thinking by the decision makers, as well as the often fast-breaking events. The President readily agreed. So I was somewhat surprised that morning when he said that he wanted to talk to me about whether I should attend the breakfast.

Then he explained that one of the topics, not included on the written agenda, was the rescue mission. I could tell, or thought I could, by his tone of voice and expression that this had now become a serious option for him.

Was this something I would rather not know about? the President asked. Would it make my job easier if down the road I could honestly claim to have had no knowledge of this option?

I replied that I had given some thought to the matter since the Camp David session. It seemed to me that if he decided to go ahead with the rescue option, we would need an aggressive effort to protect its secrecy. That might involve purposely misleading or even lying to the press. If it did, I was the person to do it. And if I did it, I wanted to have the information necessary to make my effort successful. Since I was also being asked about the Iran crisis almost every day, I said, there was the chance that I might inadvertently compromise the mission unless I knew exactly what activities were the most sensitive.

The President said he had expected that would be my response, and he agreed with it, but he had wanted to hear it from me.

Then he added with a hint of a smile, "If you have to lie to the press, I may have to fire you when this is all over, you know. I'm not sure I can have a press secretary who won't tell the truth to the press."

"That," I said, "would be doing me a real favor."

"And an even bigger one for the country," said the President with what I hoped was a smile, as he turned to walk to the Cabinet room, where his foreign policy team was waiting.

The briefing, on which I took no notes, was much the same as the earlier session at Camp David. Maps and charts were positioned on an easel and occasionally spread on the table for closer examination. The questions and suggestions from three weeks earlier had been taken into account, and the military planners had come up with a few new wrinkles on their own.

By the time it was over, I sensed that the men around the table, including the President, were leaning strongly toward ordering the plan to be implemented. The comments that followed confirmed my hunch. I added my endorsement, and emphasized again my feeling that we would need to give some thought to cover stories and an aggressive effort to protect the secrecy of the mission if the President decided to go ahead.

The only partial demurral come from Deputy Secretary of State Warren Christopher. Although he was inclined to recommend that the President order the mission, as he made clear later, he did not know how Secretary of State Vance (who was taking a brief and well-earned vacation) would react and did not feel that he should express a personal opinion.

The President said he was tentatively inclined to proceed with the mission, but would defer a final decision until he had discussed it with Vance.

As we got up to leave the room, I found myself standing next to Harold Brown. "Mr. Secretary," I said, "the President is going to go with this thing, I can sense it. If we can bring our people out of there, it will do more good for this country than anything that has happened in twenty years."

"Yes," said Brown, "and if we fail, that will be the end of the Carter presidency."

"But we really don't have much choice, do we?"

The Secretary shook his head no as we walked out the door.

A moment later, Helen Thomas, of UPI, walked around the corner from the press room on the way to my office.

"Big meeting, huh?" she called down the short corridor. "You guys decide to nuke 'em?"

Brown and I both nodded yes, and I offered to let Helen and her colleagues know in plenty of time to be on the scene when the warheads struck.

If she only knew, I thought.

In fact, one of the problems we faced, once the President made his final decision four days later, was the number of press people in Tehran. As part of his objections, Cyrus Vance had warned that the Iranians might seize some of the several hundred Americans still in Tehran, thus leaving us with more hostages to worry about, even if the mission was a success. A fair number of this group were journalists.

I told the President that I saw no way for us to make the reporters come home, short of telling the news organizations what was about to happen, and that was clearly out of the question. Still, he felt an obligation to try. The President's first inclination was to order them home. I argued against this. There was no way to enforce the order, and I suspected that the attempt would so enrage the news executives that they would insist on keeping people there who might have been planning to come back anyway.

"Some of them are so ornery that they might just send an extra correspondent over to prove they can do it," I said.

In the end, we decided to use the increasingly volatile situation in Iran as an excuse to try to get journalists and other Americans to come home.

At a news conference on April 17, the President announced that he was prohibiting all financial transactions between Iranians and Americans and barring all imports from Iran. Then he stated that "to protect American citizens," he was banning all travel to Iran.

These steps, he said, would "not *now* be used to interfere with the right of the press to gather news.

"However," he continued, speaking slowly and precisely, "it is my responsibility and my obligation, given the situation in Iran, to call on American journalists and newsgathering organizations to minimize, as severely as possible, their presence and their activities in Iran."

As we had feared, the only effect was to provoke angry calls, particularly from the networks. After listening to Washington bureau chiefs and presidents of news divisions berate us for trying to repeal the First Amendment and stifle news coverage for political ends, I finally lost my temper with Sandy Socolow of CBS.

"Look Sandy," I said, "the President told you what he thinks you ought to do, and I have nothing to add to it. I warned him that you people would get on a high horse, but he wanted to do it anyway. I personally don't give a good goddamn what you people do. If I had my way, I'd ask the fucking Ayatollah to keep fifty reporters and give us our diplomats back. Then you people who have all the answers could figure out how to get them out."

As soon as I hung up the phone, I regretted having lost my temper. Not because I feared that I had hurt Socolow's feelings — he is not an overly sensitive fellow — but because I was worried that my angry response might have implied that something dramatic was about to happen. I had come that close to saying that he would have to accept the consequences for what happened if he ignored the President's warning, but had caught myself in time. I vowed to keep my temper in check, at least until this operation was complete.

The President's statement of April 17, in addition to being a futile attempt to get Americans out of Tehran, also fit into our cover story. By announcing additional sanctions, he implied that there would be a period of time during which we would wait and see if they would work before any other actions were taken. I, and others who knew what was actually afoot, strengthened this impression with background briefings.

We also suggested that if we were forced to consider any sort of military option, it would be something like a blockade or mining of harbors. This was the cover story we had devised for the military movements necessary to prepare for the rescue mission. On several occasions I speculated with reporters off the record about the relative merits of a blockade as opposed to mining.

We had, in fact, ruled out both of these options. They were unlikely to force the Iranians to yield, and once attempted would have to be followed up by an escalation of military force if no response was forthcoming. We would thus be starting down a road the end of which no one could see. We also believed that once any sort of military move was made, the Iranians as part of any general reaction might tighten security around the embassy, which we knew to be extremely lax, or disperse the hostages, thus denying us the rescue option.

The problems associated with the blockade were much the same as those associated with bombing power stations or other valuable targets in Iran — ideas that were being advanced by several columnists and commentators. I had suggested to the President earlier that what he ought to do was "bomb the hell out of every dam and power station in Iran. Let the Ayatollah shoot two hostages and call on the Russians for help, then turn the whole thing over to Agronsky and Company to handle."

His response is not printable.

By the week of April 20 it was becoming clear that our cover story was working too well. All the talk about mining and blockades was making some people nervous and everyone curious. That presented a problem. We did not want anyone, even on the White House staff, snooping around in an effort to find out what was going on. They just might stumble on something. In addition, once the staff begins to talk a great deal about anything, it is only a short time before the press gets interested, too.

But this also presented us with an opportunity to reinforce our cover story. On Tuesday, April 22, little more than forty-eight hours before the Delta Team would enter Iranian air space, Hamilton called a staff meeting to address the concerns that were buzzing about the staff. He assured them all that we had no plans, at the moment, for mining or blockading. When asked about a rescue mission, he lied.

As soon as I heard what had taken place, I began to prepare for a press call. It came less than ninety minutes after the meeting ended. Jack Nelson, bureau chief of the *Los Angeles Times*, wanted to talk to me about something he had heard from a "pretty interesting staff meeting you people had this morning." I said I had not been there but would check with Hamilton.

I then called Hamilton to tell him what I was about to do. I hated to do it to Nelson, who was one of the more decent journalists that I had gotten to know since coming to Washington, and one who would become a good friend once the administration was over. But I did not feel that I had any choice. I knew what he wanted to talk about. It was an opportunity to reinforce the web of deception we had constructed to protect the rescue mission.

When I called Nelson back, he said he had heard that some staffers had expressed concern that we were about to take some action that might "involve us in a war." I confirmed this report and repeated Hamilton's assurances that we were planning no military action whatsoever, and certainly nothing like a rescue mission.

Later that day, Nelson came by my office to continue our discussion. Toward the end of that conversation, he asked, "You people really aren't thinking about doing anything drastic like launching a rescue mission, are you?"

This was the moment of truth, or, more accurately, of deception. Up to this point, I had only repeated false statements made by others, an admittedly fine distinction, but a distinction nevertheless. Now I was faced with a direct question. With a swallow that I hoped was not noticeable, I began to recite all the reasons why a rescue operation would not make any sense. They were familiar because they were exactly the ones that it had taken four months to figure out how to overcome.

"If and when we are forced to move militarily, I suspect it will be something like a blockade," I said, "but that decision is a step or two down the road."

I made a mental note to be sure to call Jack and apologize once the operation was completed, hoping he would understand.

The result was a story in the *Los Angeles Times* reporting Hamilton's assurances to the staff that no military action was in the offing, and that a rescue operation was still considered to be impractical.

When I read it the next day, I remember hoping that some Iranian student at Berkeley had enough loyalty to the Ayatollah to phone it in to Tehran.

Two days later the hostage rescue attempt ended in disaster. Nelson, to his credit, seemed to understand what I had done, even though he could not explicitly condone it. Most other reporters reacted in similar fashion when the story of my deception came out. A few even stopped by to say privately that they would have done the same thing in my position. A few others were quoted, anonymously, as saying that I had destroyed my credibility and ought to resign.

The issue quickly faded as we dealt with the spectacle of Iranian leaders boasting over the bodies of American servicemen, the tortured but eventually successful efforts to secure their return, and the ceremonies honoring their courage and dedication to duty.

There were a few attempts to exploit the situation for political purposes: Stories were planted with reporters that the mission had been discovered by the Soviets and a call from Brezhnev had brought about the cancellation, and that the military commanders had wanted to go ahead after the loss of three helicopters but the President had lost his nerve and ordered them to turn back. These attempts at disinformation were largely unsuccessful. Later, as we shall see, those responsible for these efforts were able to find journalists whose indifference or incompetence made them useful political tools.

In October of 1983, . . . controversy flared again between the White House and the press over the relative rights and responsibilities of the two institutions. The occasion was the American invasion of Grenada, and there were several reasonably separate issues involved.

The first was the same one that I had dealt with three and a half years prior: the right of government to lie. On the afternoon before American forces landed in Grenada, CBS White House correspondent Bill Plante learned from a reliable source that an invasion would take place at sunrise the next morning. He checked with the White House Press Office and got a flat denial."Preposterous," said spokesman Larry Speakes. Other reporters got the same response from other government officials.

The decision by the Reagan administration to deceive journalists rather than risk the possibility that the invasion plans would be disclosed seemed to me to be eminently defensible.

When I asked Plante later what he would have done if the White House had confirmed the invasion plans, his response was "I don't know; we would have tried to find some way to use what we knew without endangering the operation."

That in itself would seem to confirm the wisdom of the White House judgment. You cannot expect government to leave such questions in the hands of the fourth estate. The consequences of an error are too severe.

Moreover, given the extent of eavesdropping capabilities in Washington, it would be an unacceptable risk to have Mr. Plante and others at CBS chatting at some length over open telephone lines about how they would use the information. By the time their decision was made it most likely would be moot.

Some journalists were willing to agree privately that this situation was one of those in which there was no other choice but to lie. Most, however, were unwilling to endorse publicly the idea that lying could be condoned under any circumstances, feeling that government does enough lying as it is without any encouragement from them.

They make the very valid point that once you step away from the categorical, there is no easily discernible place to draw the line.

Still the essential dilemma remains. What about those situations where an evasion simply will not work, where a "no comment" is almost certain to be taken as a confirmation? If, at the same time, the information to be protected is of sufficient importance, if lives are at stake for example, a lie becomes in my estimation the lesser evil of the choices available. It is ludicrous to argue that soldiers may be sent off to fight and die, but a spokesman may not, under any circumstances, be asked to lie to make sure that the casualties are fewer and not in vain.

Churchill made the point with his usual flair in 1943. "In wartime," he said, "truth is so precious that she should be attended by a bodyguard of lies."

Unfortunately, once one steps onto the slippery slope of relativism, firm footing cannot be established, even on the basis of "wartime" or "lives at stake." There are other dilemmas that can and do arise, where calculated deception might be appropriate.

Although I never faced it personally, the protection of an important intelligence source or method, even in peacetime, might be one.

And what about the protection of an important diplomatic initiative? I almost faced such a situation at Camp David when reports of bad blood between Sadat and Begin arose and when there were leaks about Sadat's threat to break off the talks. . . . I was able to deal with those problems without telling a bald-faced lie, but that was mostly a matter of luck.

In the midst of the Grenada controversy, a columnist revealed that the premature publication by Jack Anderson of a story about Henry Kissinger's secret diplomatic initiatives had damaged, although not fatally, the movement toward normalization of relations with China. That initiative became arguably the most significant strategic event since the Second World War. Would lying have been appropriate in an effort to keep it on track?

In the early months of the Carter administration the *Washington Post* published accounts of secret payments through the CIA to King Hussein of Jordan. The story appeared on the day that Secretary of State Vance arrived in Amman to discuss a Middle East peace initiative with Hussein. Needless to say, the result was a less than positive environment for the talks.

In that case, we had chosen to be candid with the *Post* and appeal to their sense of responsibility. From our point of view the effort was a failure. Although we had not asked them not to publish the story, feeling that such a request would be futile, we had requested a delay. When it came out at the most unfortunate of all possible times, we felt the *Post* was guilty of bad faith. The *Post* maintained that the timing was a result of a misunderstanding.

In any case, the question remains. In our judgment the *Post* had enough information to go with the story whatever we said. But what if we had concluded that it was possible to kill the story with a lie, would we have been justified in doing so?

To take another step down the slope, what degree of deception would be acceptable from a Justice Department official trying to protect the rights of an innocent person whose name had cropped up in an investigation?

Or what about a spokesman at Treasury attempting to avoid the premature disclosure of information on a financial decision that could lead to severe damage to innocent parties and great profits for those in a position to take advantage of the leak?

The problem becomes, as noted above, where precisely to draw the line. There is no convenient place. About the best one can do is to argue that it must be drawn very tightly, for practical as well as moral considerations. Distinctions may be difficult at the margins, but we can all tell the difference between mountains and molehills. If government does have the right to lie in certain situations, that right is as precious as the truth it attends. It must not be squandered on matters of less than overriding importance.

Which brings us to another issue in the Grenada controversy. Many correspondents said that the exchange between Speakes and CBS was not the cause but the catalyst for their outrage. They charged that the administration had repeatedly lied to them on matters that were in no way vital to national security or the protection of lives. They listed examples that ranged from the dates of resignations to travel plans to attempts to square the facts with some off-the-cuff presidential remark.

They also pointed to a history of efforts to curtail the flow of information from the screening of calls to White House officials from reporters by the communications and press offices to proposals for the review of anything written by thousands of government officials after they leave office. (At this writing, Congress has wisely blocked this last absurdity, but the administration has vowed not to give up.)

That attitude was not unanimous, but it was clearly shared by a large number of White House correspondents. And that is a dangerous set of circumstances for the administration and potentially for the nation. The danger for the administration is that it will find itself lacking credibility across the board, that no explanation will be accepted at face value and every action will be subject to the most unflattering interpretation.

For the nation, the danger lies in the fact that an administration that is generally believed to be dishonest will not command the respect necessary to protect legitimate secrets. There are many cases in which truths less vital than the timing and objective of military operations are protected by successful appeals to reporters not to publish. The full and exact reasons for such requests cannot always be disclosed, because they too may be quite sensitive. Needless to say, such appeals — which amount to a request to "trust me" — can only be effective in a climate of mutual trust.

To the extent that this climate was placed in jeopardy following the Grenada controversy, the problem was not primarily a conflict over government's right to lie about issues of ultimate importance, but a perceived pattern of deception solely for the sake of convenience — of lies designed to protect and promote nothing more precious than someone's political backside.

Even during the Grenada operation, there were lies from the government that were difficult to justify by any reasonable standard. Claims that coverage was curtailed, after the invasion had begun, because of concern for the safety of reporters were poppycock. Even experienced spokesmen had a hard time making that argument with a straight face.

Similarly, attempts to blame the decision to restrict coverage on "military commanders" were deceptive and cowardly and dangerous. There is no doubt that many uniformed military officers hold the press in less than great esteem or that the restricted coverage was completely in line with their preferences. But that is not the point. Such decisions are always subject to White House review. And they were repeatedly brought to the attention of White House officials. If the preferences of the military commanders were honored, it was because the President and his men agreed with them.

This refusal to accept responsibility for one's own actions was dangerous in this case because it served to exacerbate tensions between the military and the fourth estate, to heighten mutual distrust on both sides. These tensions are already high enough and that problem is going to be with us for the indefinite future. Already it works against responsible and accurate reporting of national security issues. It also promotes an unreasoning distrust of all things military in our society. There is, in my view, no excuse for an administration's hiding behind the armed forces simply to avoid facing ticklish questions.

A related issue has to do with how much the White House press secretary should be told in situations such as this. It very quickly became clear in this particular case that the press secretary and the press office had been kept in the dark until the invasion was under way. Mr. Speakes and his people were not intentionally lying themselves when they denied the reports from Plante and other newsmen; they were merely passing on what they had been told by members of the National Security Council staff.

This quickly became a bone of contention within the White House. Mr. Speakes and his people were none too happy about the way they had been treated. One deputy resigned as a result. However, more senior White House officials declared themselves well pleased with the procedure and stated that they would handle things the same way if similar situations arose in the future.

Mr. Speakes made it clear that if a lie was required and he was to be sent out to tell it, he wanted to know what was at stake. And he was exactly right. Keeping the press secretary in the dark can create serious problems.

First, it inevitably erodes the press secretary's effectiveness. It costs him in prestige and status, factors that may mean more than they should in Washington, but still cannot be ignored. The press secretary's job is tough enough as it is; he deserves every break his colleagues can give him. Putting the guy whose business is information in a position that makes him appear to be uninformed, out of touch, and not trusted makes no sense over the long haul.

Beyond that, if a secret is worth lying about to protect, it makes sense to come up with the most effective lie possible. Most sensitive operations are accompanied by a cover story, designed to provide an innocent explanation for bits and pieces that might leak out. Since the first group of people that such a story must convince is the press, having the press secretary involved in designing the story is not a bad idea. He more than anyone else is likely to know what will be convincing and what will not.

Furthermore, the use of the story, if it ever becomes necessary, is likely to be more effective if the person who puts it out knows exactly what he is trying to do. Dealing with the press, particularly in ticklish situations, is very much an art. You cannot treat the press secretary like a robot and then expect him to perform like an artist.

Another danger in keeping the press secretary uninformed comes from the way in which a press office operates. When a new question arises or an issue looks like it is going to get hot, the press office begins to function very much like a news organization. Deputy and assistant and deputy assistant press secretaries immediately get to work calling all over the government to try to find out what is really going on and where it may lead.

As information is gathered, it is often passed on to the reporter who has made the query in bits and pieces as part of a continuing exchange of information and ideas. Needless to say, if there is something highly sensitive that has to be protected, the press secretary needs to know about it. Otherwise, this process could stumble into and lead to the uncovering of information that should be kept secret.

In matters large and small, keeping the press secretary in the dark is risky business. If he cannot be trusted with sensitive information, he should be replaced. Failing that, he ought to be given the information he needs to do his job effectively.

Having said all that, however, I suspect that the most important lesson from this episode is to be found in the fact that the press was a clear loser in its fight with the administration over Grenada. It lost in the court in which such matters will eventually be decided — the court of public opinion. In the immediate aftermath of Grenada it was sometimes difficult to tell which the American people enjoyed more, seeing the President kick hell out of the Cubans or the press.

And the reasons the fourth estate lost were to a large extent its own fault.

The strength of the public reaction in favor of the administration's policy of denying access to the press was a shock to many Washington journalists. The more thoughtful were concerned as well as surprised.

It is true that the press is particularly vulnerable among our major institutions because it is so often the bearer of sad tidings, the forum for criticism of ideas, individuals, and institutions that Americans hold dear. It is also true, as journalists are fond of pointing out, that their job is not to win popularity contests. But the vocal and sometimes vicious public reaction against the press in the wake of Grenada was more than just some sort of "shoot the messenger" syndrome.

In part it sprang from the way the fourth estate handled the terrorist bombing of our marine headquarters in Beirut, which occurred just prior to the Grenada operation. The behavior of some news organizations was not the sort that would inspire public confidence in their judgment or self-restraint.

There was, for example, the repugnant spectacle of CBS camped ghoulishly at the home of parents awaiting word on the fate of their marine son in Beirut. And they hit the jackpot. The boy was dead. So they got to film the arrival of the casualty officer and the chaplain bringing the tragic news to the parents.

The tragic scene, for which every standard of good taste and decency demanded privacy, was then offered up to satisfy the voyeurism of the worst segments of the American television audience and the demands for the higher ratings that are believed, with some justification, to come with sensationalism.

Nor was this sort of gross insensitivity confined to television. A few days after the Beirut bombing, readers of the *Washington Post* were treated to the incredibly insensitive comments of a *Newsweek* executive describing at some length what a wonderful thing the tragedy was for his magazine:

"We are exhilarated by this. It's the sort of thing *Newsweek* does best — react to a big story in a big way. We'll be pulling out all the stops. . . . one hell of a story . . . pursuing a variety of angles . . . expect a lot of competition, it's the biggest story of the year."

If the tasteless coverage of the Beirut tragedy was a factor in the public's reaction to Grenada, it was by no means the whole of it. The attitudes reflected did not develop over a few days or weeks.

If the government has in this and other instances been guilty of excess in the exercise of what I believe to be its legitimate right to mislead and even deceive on matters of vital import, the fourth estate has also been guilty of excess in its cavalier insistence on the right to do as it pleases with little regard for good judgment, good taste, or the consequences of its actions — and the American people know it.

One consequence of the information explosion has been that more and more Americans have had the opportunity to see news coverage of incidents they knew something about. And they have come away disillusioned, and sometimes angry, because of the wide gap that too often existed between what they knew to be the case and what was reported.

And if they were foolish enough to try to set the record straight by appealing for a correction, they also ran head on into that determination never to admit a mistake, much less do anything about it.

The public's reaction to Grenada ought to be a danger signal for journalism. The question . . . is how the fourth estate will react. The greatest danger is that the reaction will be defensive, a renewed determination to pretend that nothing is wrong except the short-sightedness and lack of sophistication of the American public.

THE
PRESIDENCY

Chapter
Four

The administrations of Lyndon B. Johnson and Richard M. Nixon changed the perspective of many Americans about the presidency. In spite of the bitter partisanship that always precedes presidential elections, the office of the presidency had before Lyndon B. Johnson always been treated with great reverence, which often led to reverence for the man who occupied the White House. This is not to suggest by any means that presidents had always been extolled for their virtues and placed on a kingly throne, for anyone familiar with American history knows that there have always been bitter personal attacks on presidents by a wide assortment of critics. And these presidential critics were not above calling their prey "mentally unbalanced." Nevertheless, most presidential biographies concentrated on the heroic and not the neurotic qualities of their subjects. An eloquent illustration of this was Carl Sandburg's biographical volumes on Abraham Lincoln. All the resources of the poet were directed toward enshrining President Lincoln in the Temple of the Gods. Contrasting Carl Sandburg's biography of Abraham Lincoln with more recent works on presidents by such authors as James David Barber or Doris Kearns, not to mention Bob Woodward and Carl Bernstein, reveals the major differences between past and present approaches to assessing presidents.[1]

Although the administration of Lyndon B. Johnson seemed entirely rational to his supporters, other persons, particularly critics of the Vietnam war, believed the president to have relentlessly, single-mindedly, and more importantly *irrationally* embarked on a highly destructive policy. David Halberstam began an extensive study of the history of the war in order to determine how the United States became involved. His bestselling book, *The Best and the Brightest*, published in 1972, emphasized the role of personalities, not so much of the president himself as of his top level advisers, in making the critical decisions

---

[1] See James David Barber, *The Presidential Character* (Englewood Cliffs, N.J.: Prentice-Hall, 1972); Doris Kearns, *Lyndon Johnson and the American Dream* (New York: Harper & Row, 1976); Bob Woodward and Carl Bernstein, *The Final Days* (New York: Simon & Schuster, 1976).

committing the country to the war.[2] In the same year, political scientist James David Barber published his ground-breaking book, *The Presidential Character*, in which he made personality profiles of a variety of presidents in order to determine the effect of presidential character on performance. With the publication of Barber's book, psychopolitics came of age.

James Barber attempted a complex classification of different character types, and came to the conclusion that the best presidents were what he termed "active-positive." The active-positive president is achievement-oriented and productive, and has well-defined goals. He is rational, "using his brain to move his feet." Above all, he is flexible; he can change his goals and methods as he perceives reasons for altering his course of action. He has a sense of humor about the world and, more importantly, about himself. John F. Kennedy was, according to Barber, an ideal active-positive president.

Perhaps even more significant than the active-positive presidents are the "active-negative" presidents. These are the presidents that may do irreparable damage, according to Barber. They have a compulsive need to work because of personal problems and a misguided "Puritan ethic." They are ambitious and power hungry but lack goals beyond that of rising to power. They tend to be politically amoral, as was Richard Nixon, but may take on false and misleading goals, such as making the world safe for democracy, as did Woodrow Wilson. The great energy of the active-negative type is frequently directed in irrational ways, and once set in a course of action the active-negative president tends to become very rigid, especially in the face of opposition and criticisms from the outside. Because of personal insecurity, the active-negative president surrounds himself with yes-men in order to fortify him in confrontation with the hostile world outside. Barber's portraits of various active-negative presidents, including Richard Nixon, when taken in conjunction with the portrait of President Nixon in Bob Woodward's and Carl Bernstein's *Final Days*, is truly frightening. Because of the enormous power that presidents possess, it is especially important to examine their characters and styles, which set the tone of presidential administrations.

The selections in this chapter illustrate various dimensions of presidential personality, and what is frequently overlooked, the way in which the personalities and styles of the president's staff can influence the political process.

[2] David Halberstam, *The Best and the Brightest* (New York: Random House, 1972).

DURING HIS FIRST TERM, Ronald Reagan was clearly a positive president, although whether or not he was, in James David Barber's terms, active or passive can be debated. Before the 1980 presidential election Barber had characterized Reagan as passive-positive. He predicted that "his would be a rhetorical presidency. Reagan's style is centered on speech making. He has been a speechmaker ever since, as a young college freshman, he made a dramatic speech that won great support on the campus. He can move and act to capture an audience."[1]

Barber typed Reagan as a passive-positive personality because he "has always been a kind of booster, an optimist, a conveyer of hopefulness. He is passive in the sense that he has a long record of saving his energy, of not working too hard. He was a nine-to-five governor, and as a campaigner he takes it pretty easy. The danger is that people with this kind of personality give in to pressure too quickly."[2] However, concluded Barber, the time might be right for a Reagan presidency because the country "is in need of a rest. . . . In that environment, Reagan might prove somewhat of a unifying figure, conveying a folksiness that's less electric and dramatic than what we've been through. His presidency might be a kind of Eisenhower second term, where the danger is drift and inaction but the plus is a kind of healing and recovery."[3]

Reagan's personality and style won him public affection during his first term, even with some groups that did not approve of his policies. The following selection portrays his positive personality and upbeat presidency, which, combined with his mastery of the media, made him seem electorally invincible.

15 Steven R. Weisman
RONALD REAGAN'S MAGICAL STYLE

Americans like him. Amid the whir and clank of machinery at a Ford Motor Company assembly plant in Claycomo, Missouri, a few weeks ago, even the men wearing "Mondale" baseball caps joined in cheering Ronald Reagan. In New York City, he told Jewish leaders some things they didn't want to hear about Israel. Then he grinned and wished his audience a joyful Pesach, and they responded with appreciative laughter and applause.

[1] *U.S. News and World Report*, October 27, 1980, p. 30.
[2] Ibid.
[3] Ibid.

From *The New York Times Magazine*, 29 April 1984. Copyright © 1984 by The New York Times Company. Reprinted by permission.

When a president runs for reelection, conventional wisdom holds that he runs on his record. Across the country, voters are surely sizing up Mr. Reagan's performance on the economy and foreign policy. But presidents must also strike a personal chord and they must embody the dreams and values of the nation. "You cannot be a successful president unless you can project a vision about the purpose of America," says Thomas E. Cronin, a leading scholar of the presidency. And it is becoming clear that this year, to a degree unmatched in modern times, the public is being swayed by these intangibles. One of the most astonishing features of Mr. Reagan's political success is that, whether or not they agree with him and his policies, Americans *like* him.

As a candidate, President Reagan still benefits from the public's yearning for a take-charge leader after the succession of national traumas from Watergate to the Iran hostages. His political fortunes have been helped by the expanding economy and by the vitriolic Democratic primary campaign. Yet the White House's own political experts say that Mr. Reagan's greatest political asset is his ability to project himself as a man of conviction, genial self-confidence, optimism, and old-fashioned values. It has enabled the President to weather countless political storms largely unscathed.

He has committed untold public bloopers and been caught in dozens of factual mistakes and misrepresentations. He has presided over the worst recession since the Great Depression. The abortive mission in Beirut cost 265 American lives, and there has been a sharp escalation in United States military involvement in Central America. An extraordinary number of Mr. Reagan's political appointees have come under fire, with many forced to resign, because of ethical or legal conflicts. Yet he is The Man in the Teflon Suit; nothing sticks to him.

Millions of voters do approve of Mr. Reagan's conservative policies, and millions more don't concern themselves about policy issues. That is to be expected. What is extraordinary is the President's support from another quarter. Opinion polls show that he wins substantial allegiance among those very people who worry about his record-breaking deficits, who fear that his actions could lead to war, and who believe that his economic program has clobbered the poor.

Says Fred I. Greenstein, professor of politics at Princeton University: "He is more successful than any recent president in establishing space between himself and his policies."

Clearly, the creation of that space has been a major goal of the administration. Richard B. Wirthlin, the Reagan campaign polltaker, puts it in terms of a "social contract" between the president and the public —"the giving of a stewardship to a president based upon trust, confidence, and congruence with a system of beliefs, rather than a congruence with a set of articulated policies." Mr. Reagan's unmatched skills as a communicator of basic values have been applied to achieving that end.

It remains to be seen, of course, whether Mr. Reagan's magic will prevail in this election year. A series of foreign-policy setbacks might well tarnish his public image. He suffered a stunning defeat earlier this month when the Republican-controlled Senate overwhelmingly repudiated CIA participation in the mining of Nicaraguan ports. A major disaster in Central America might turn the race around. And his popularity could be damaged if the economy sours.

Yet it seems evident that, given the success of his strategy to date, the political marketing of Mr. Reagan's personal qualities may change the nature of the 1984 campaign. To a degree unknown in recent elections, the challenger will have to meet the incumbent's personality head on, matching his style and countering his overarching message with one of his own.

The Reagan approach may also have a more lasting effect. He has fashioned a new chemistry of image, message, and personality — a presidential persona — that could change the boundaries of the American presidency itself.

In his book *Why Not the Best?* Jimmy Carter quotes a line from Reinhold Niebuhr that summarizes the former President's view of the world and of his trade: "The sad duty of politics is to establish justice in a sinful world."

Americans in this century have tended to elect presidents who represented change rather than continuity. John F. Kennedy's youth and vigor were an antidote to the era of Dwight D. Eisenhower. Jimmy Carter, like Mr. Reagan, based his appeal on his persona, offering the nation integrity in the aftermath of Watergate. But the contrasts between Mr. Carter and his successor are particularly illuminating.

Mr. Carter bore the burdens of office like a cross. He identified personally with his administration's traumas, and told Americans that there were no simple answers. The apotheosis of his martyr presidency came with his refusal to set out on the campaign trail in 1980 because of the Iran hostage crisis. Clinging to the Rose Garden, he succeeded in turning the White House into a kind of prison.

He also regarded the mastery of the details of his job as crucial to his leadership. During the Middle East summit meeting at Camp David, he got down on hands and knees to study maps of the Sinai. He read volumes of Russian history before meeting with Leonid I. Brezhnev, the Soviet leader. He sought to educate Americans to nuances. Discerning a "crisis of confidence" over energy shortages, he consulted leading intellectuals on their view of the national malaise. He called on Americans to accept limits on future growth.

On every count, Ronald Reagan's approach to the presidency is dramatically different. Mr. Reagan positively enjoys the job, keeps his distance from crises, ignores details both as Chief Executive and Chief

Communicator. No matter how grave things look, his attitude is invariably upbeat and reassuring.

Some of the differences were inevitable, given the nature of the two men. More significantly, Mr. Reagan and his aides perceived the style of the Carter administration as wrong-headed and doomed to fail. They had altogether new and different ideas about how to present the president to his people.

Every administration for a generation has spent substantial time and energy seeking to make optimum use of television and the print media in the president's behalf. But as the candidate of the minority party and a president whose legislative plans represented a dramatic break with the past, Mr. Reagan had a special need. And because of the long history of presidents driven from office or defeated for reelection, White House aides were also determined to use the media to strengthen the institution of the presidency itself.

To an unprecedented extent, Mr. Reagan and his staff have made television a major organizing principle of his presidency. His day is planned around opportunities for television coverage. Every effort is made to assure a constant flow of positive visual images and symbols from the White House.

In 1982, as unemployment soared and the President was accused of lacking compassion for those out of work, Mr. Reagan avoided appearing in public and before the television camera in black tie. Instead, he showed up for events concerned with unemployed teenagers, dock workers and others being trained for new jobs. When disaster strikes a community, Mr. Reagan doesn't stop at sending relief funds — he makes a detour, as he did to flooded-out Louisiana last year, to be photographed stacking sandbags. When a presidential journey overseas is in the works, producers from the television networks accompany White House aides on the advance trips. The two groups jointly figure out the best photo angles of the President — staring into the demilitarized zone from South Korea, gazing grimly across the Berlin Wall. Plans for the President's trip to China were similarly television tailored.

This administration's exceptional ability to manipulate the media is impressive. One means of assuring that the cameras stay on the President, for example, is a White House policy that has Mr. Reagan himself making important announcements on television. For details and analysis, the news media are handed over to Treasury Secretary Donald T. Regan, Defense Secretary Caspar W. Weinberger or other top aides — but under ground rules whereby that may not be identified in news accounts. As a result, the only person who can be shown on the 7 o'clock news's coverage of such announcements is the President himself, offering broad, positive precepts.

Another goal is to keep Mr. Reagan's image as far from bad news and negative discussion as possible. Sometimes the President disappears altogether. The momentous announcement of the withdrawal of the Marines from Lebanon was made in a written statement distributed late in the day, minutes after Mr. Reagan had left for his ranch in California. There were no senior officials immediately available to the press to explain why the withdrawal was ordered.

The White House communications staff is nothing if not imaginative. Last year, former Interior Secretary James G. Watt stirred up a hornet's nest of rock-and-roll lovers after he ousted the Beach Boys from their July 4 concert on the Mall. Mr. Watt was summoned to the White House and handed a large plaster foot that had a bullet hole in it, a brilliant device for making light of the incident. Later, it was learned that David R. Gergen, director of communications at the time, had commissioned the making of the foot weeks before, with the thought that it would come in handy if someone in the Administration happened to make a gaffe.

A sense of timing showed up on a more serious topic last December when the White House learned that the Pentagon was about to release a report criticizing the administration for alleged failures in the massacre of marines in Beirut. White House officials preempted the negative impact of the report by leaking Mr. Reagan's reaction to the charges the day before the report was made public.

The mastery of media techniques has been placed in the service of a president with a remarkable approach to political discourse.

According to Aristotle, the art of persuasion requires more than logic and argument. One of a speaker's most important tasks, he wrote, is to understand the psychology, the "ethos," of his audience. Instead of lecturing his audiences about limits, President Reagan offers good news. There is no limit, he says, to what the nation can accomplish. He talks of heroes on the battlefield and tells Americans that if they work hard, pay taxes, and seek a better life for their children, they are heroes, too. It is a message — known among his advisers in the 1980 campaign as the "can-do-America" theme — aimed at a public that has felt the nation floundering through years of economic and foreign-policy crises. It is particularly potent in its appeal to blue-collar ethnic Roman Catholics in the Northeast and Middle West and to fundamentalist Christian groups in the South.

Mr. Reagan keeps his message simple. Campaign aides speak of a hierarchy of public feelings: A voter has an "opinion" about money for a new B-1 bomber and an "attitude" toward increasing military spending, but he regards the defense of freedom as a "value." As much as possible, Mr. Reagan seeks to appeal to "values." And as his aides say, for all his ability as a performer, his appeal would not work except for the fact that he is a true believer.

"He operates on a separate plane from the rest of us," says a senior

Republican in Congress. "We may find him flawed because he doesn't know the details and can't analyze them. But he can have a simple dialogue with the voters. It's raw personality. Jimmy Carter agreed with you, and you didn't like it. This guy can disagree and you think he's great."

As much as possible, the President tries to prevent his message from being undermined by the details of political issues. For example, he seeks often to transform a debate over the effects of his programs into a broader issue of his personal compassion. Asked at news conferences about his civil-rights record, the President speaks less of his policies than of how he campaigned as a radio sports announcer to integrate baseball. His parents, he says, wouldn't allow him to see "The Birth of a Nation" because it was a racist film. Accused of being indifferent to the hardships suffered by the unemployed, he tells of the pain he felt when his father lost his job on Christmas Eve during the Great Depression.

Sometimes, the President transcends the details of an issue by focusing on a single element with all the force of his persuasive powers. In 1982 and 1983, Europe was roiled by protests over American plans to place new missiles on that continent. Rather than devote his time to the intricacies of his arms-control policies, the President addressed the issue generally. With utmost sincerity, he spoke of his commitment in principle to arms control, and of his fervent wish that nuclear weapons could one day be banished from the face of the earth. The speeches helped ease European fears, clearing the way for the missiles to be installed on schedule.

Mr. Reagan has used a similar approach — ignoring the elements of an issue to concentrate on general principles — in talking about the Middle East. "How many people follow the ups and downs in Lebanon closely?" asks a top Reagan adviser. "It's probably less than 20 percent. But how many people understand that his attempt to establish peace was the major objective? You're getting closer to 50 percent."

If positive communication with the mass of the public is the goal, Mr. Reagan seems to achieve it. He seems to know intuitively how to communicate on the right plane for his larger audience, even when doing so involves skirting over the nitty-gritty of an issue.

In political terms, the President thus enjoys remarkable freedom from attack on the frequent occasions when his statements are at variance with the record. Even the press is less inclined than it once was to pay much attention to such statements.

Mr. Reagan claims that the government is spending more on those in need than ever before. But he fails to note that inflation has eroded the value of most such government programs: Food stamps, for instance, buy less food today than they did a few years ago. Moreover, he has made many poor people ineligible for federal aid.

In defending his domestic programs, Mr. Reagan typically makes two claims. He leaves the clear impression with his audiences that there have been no outright budget cuts in major programs, and that where cuts have occurred the poorest families have not been affected. In fact, the funds budgeted this year for the Environmental Protection Agency, job programs, aid to families with dependent children, social-services block grants for the poor, and aid to elementary and secondary schools are less today than in the 1981 fiscal year, even without including the negative effects of inflation. And according to the nonpartisan Congressional Budget Office, about 40 percent of the reduction in benefit payments has fallen on families making less than $10,000 a year.

The President's willingness to stretch the facts takes a variety of forms. In 1982, he portrayed his program of tax increases as a corrective measure to eliminate loopholes and "ornaments" others had hung on his 1981 tax cut. In fact, Mr. Reagan had placed those ornaments himself to corral enough votes to get the legislation passed.

After seeking to weaken key enforcement provisions of the Voting Rights Act, he finally signed the strengthened version demanded by Congress. Then he announced: "This legislation proves our unbending commitment to voting rights."

More often than not, such presidential comments attract scant public attention. Even when they are reported in the print media and on television, they apparently have little negative effect on Mr. Reagan's public image. The voters seem to have come to recognize that the President is absolutely sincere in his statements. What might be construed as deviousness in another politician is accepted in his case as a simple mistake or a mistaken simplification or nitpicking on the part of the press. Moreover, there is evidence that the public is willing to draw a distinction between Mr. Reagan and his personal beliefs, on the one hand, and his government policies, on the other. According to a mid-March Gallup Poll, 55 percent of Americans approve of Mr. Reagan's performance in office. Yet several other polls show that they give his policies in Lebanon and Central America substantially lower ratings.

Though much is made today of Mr. Reagan's years as a film actor, in fact he was not as well known on the movie screen as he was on television. As Christopher J. Matthews, a top aide to the Speaker of the House, Thomas P. O'Neill Jr., has pointed out, it was not until Mr. Reagan took over as host of the General Electric Theater that he became the proverbial household word. He was known throughout the nation as a genial host who was not a GE official, but a kind of mediator between the company and the audience.

In Mr. Matthews's view, Mr. Reagan has found a similar spot for himself as president. He is, says Mr. Matthews, "not in government" but "at some unique point — previously uncharted — between us and government." He presents himself as independent of whatever problems may be vexing the nation — a kind of genial host to the whole country.

At press conferences, Mr. Matthews notes, the President consults a seating chart that helps him to call on reporters by their first names as though he were the host of a friendly get-together rather than an adversarial press conference. Delivering the state of the union message, he introduces heroes in the audience — Lenny Skutnik, who saved a man from drowning in the icy Potomac River, or Stephen Trujillo, an Army sergeant who performed bravely in Grenada. He uses radio and television addresses to salute such developments as the efforts to combat drunk driving or to arrange for organ transplants.

As the nation's host, Mr. Reagan can fully exercise his profound skills as a communicator. His charming manner and his oratorical gifts are seen and heard to best advantage. (His greatest gift is for narrative: The strongest speeches, such as the one last September after the downing of a South Korean airliner, or the one in October after the invasion of Grenada and the truck bombing in Beirut, were masterpieces of storytelling.)

But the President's public stance apart from his government has another, more significant advantage. It removes him from the firing line, softening public anger toward him personally over unpopular or mistaken policies. In 1982, he addressed rallies on Capitol Hill, denouncing the members of Congress as though he were just another citizen with a bill of grievances. In fact, incongruous as it may seem, Mr. Reagan — four years after being elected Chief Executive — continues to blame many of his problems on those he calls "the people in Washington."

Strategy and technique help explain President Reagan's ability to make himself liked by Americans, but his efforts to project himself come easily. Backstage, by all accounts, Mr. Reagan is the same person he is out front.

To be sure, there are certain anomalies about the President's public image. For many voters, he embodies an old-time America of tightly knit families, small-town neighborhoods, and God-fearing values. Yet he came of age in show business, became the first divorced man to serve as president, has had an often-troubled relationship with his children, rarely goes to church, and, though he has publicly praised the notion of tithing, doesn't personally come close.

On most counts, though, Mr. Reagan is much the way he presents himself. Dwight Eisenhower had some of Mr. Reagan's public qualities — the infectious smile, the mangled syntax, the relaxed working habits — but Mr. Eisenhower struck many of those who knew him privately as a crafty operator and a demanding boss. Close associates of

Mr. Reagan describe him as "guileless" and an "undemanding" person to work for.

Mr. Reagan's old-school, noblesse-oblige quality also shows up even with his staff. On a sweltering afternoon in the Oval Office in 1981, for example, a close aide suggested that the President might want to remove his jacket; after all, the two men were alone. Mr. Reagan was shocked at the suggestion.

Mr. Reagan extends myriad courtesies to his staff, autographing pictures for them, remembering their birthdays, and greeting their families in the Oval Office. He goes out of his way to assure adversaries that he does not hold grudges or take their criticism personally. He seems to recognize that graciousness is the best policy politically, as well.

In 1982, while on his way to Bogota, Mr. Reagan learned that President Belisario Betancur of Colombia was going to denounce him in a speech. Mr. Reagan's aides debated what action to take until he finally announced, "We're going to smother him with kindness." Mr. Betancur's tongue lashing took place as expected, but the relationship between the two men flourished. Before seeing Mr. Reagan off at the airport, the Colombian President commented with some amazement: "You are such a friendly man."

More recently, White House aides were divided over how much hospitality to show the Reverend Jesse Jackson and the downed Air Force pilot he brought back from Syria. Mr. Reagan cut short the debate by saying: "The only way we can lose is if we're not gracious."

When Mr. Reagan was seventeen years old, he wrote a poem for his high-school yearbook in Dixon, Illinois, containing the following passage:

> I wonder what it's all about, and why
> We suffer so, when little things go wrong?
> We make our life a struggle,
> When life should be a song.

That upbeat message is still part of the President's personality. "He is an absolutely unstoppable optimist," says one Administration official. Throughout the 1982–83 recession, for example, Mr. Reagan saw each new economic development as a sign that prosperity was on its way back. During a hopeless moment in the negotiations to prevent a war over the Falkland Islands, Mr. Reagan counseled aides in the Situation Room not to despair. The United States, he said brightly, could be "the envy of the world" if it could broker a solution.

Like the President's graciousness, his optimism is a useful quality in building support for his programs. All presidents come to recognize that persuasion is their principal task, and Mr. Reagan is typical in that regard. White House aides estimate that he spends 80 percent of his time selling his programs and only 20 percent of his time actually shaping them. Optimism is the hallmark and chief technique of a successful salesman.

But congressional critics charge that the President's optimism keeps him from giving policy problems the rigorous analysis they deserve. Repeatedly, for example, Mr. Reagan has rejected the pessimistic warnings of key economic advisers of what might happen if the federal deficit is not reduced drastically.

And while the situation in Lebanon deteriorated, the President continued to tell congressional visitors that prospects were good for a settlement. Speaker O'Neill, for one, said later that he felt deceived. Some senior administration advisers now admit, in fact, that Mr. Reagan's optimism may have prevented him from seeing that events were undermining his original assumptions in sending American troops to Beirut.

The picture of the President's decision-making process, as painted by his aides, makes for a sharp contrast with what is known of most of his predecessors.

For one thing, Mr. Reagan enjoys the job. He never complains about the loneliness of making difficult decisions that has for generations been a staple of presidential leadership. Typically, Mr. Reagan puts in an eight-hour day, does homework in the evening, and takes the trouble to master material for meetings and trips.

But a vacation is a vacation: Last February, he was on his way to his ranch in Santa Barbara when — in the course of a few days — the Lebanese government virtually collapsed, his decision to withdraw the Marines from Beirut produced an uproar, and Yuri V. Andropov suddenly died in Moscow. Mr. Reagan refused to interrupt his holiday to return to Washington. His personal inclination fit with his aides' aversion to having the President seen as a super crisis manager — another break with the attitudes of previous Administrations. "If he had come back and held a bunch of meetings," a White House official explained, "the public might have developed unrealistic expectations about what could be accomplished."

The distaste for details is a trademark. In his memoirs, Jimmy Carter offers an incredulous description of the briefing he gave Mr. Reagan on the hostage crisis just before his inauguration; Mr. Reagan took no notes. Nor does President Reagan have much of a memory for details. In 1982, he toasted the people of Bolivia when he was in Brazil. During a recent meeting, he referred to his administrator of the Environmental Protection Agency, William D. Ruckelshaus, as "Don." (Later it became clear he had mistaken him for Donald H. Rumsfeld, the Middle East negotiator.) In front of reporters at his ranch, he called his own dog by the wrong name.

If Mr. Reagan receives a sheaf of papers with a short covering memorandum, he generally reads the memorandum. On the eve of the Williamsburg economic summit conference last year, he set aside his stack of carefully prepared briefing documents to watch "The Sound of Music" on television and never got back to the papers.

To refresh his memory on the points he wants to raise, the President uses cue cards in meetings with foreign leaders and others. Although some call the cards a distraction, Mr. Reagan seems not at all embarrassed.

An aide recalled that at a White House session last year, the President sat down at the cabinet table with a group of educators. Their spokesman confessed that he was quaking with nervousness; would the President mind if he read from his notes? Mr. Reagan told him not to worry. With a grin, he held up his own cue cards.

More serious problems arise, however, from the fact that the President rarely puts aside significant amounts of time to look into subjects he knows little about. He doesn't devour books, engage in intellectual argument, or seek out information from unofficial sources. If he is seated at dinner with a stranger who might be an expert on a topic Mr. Reagan knows little about, the President prefers to banter about sports or show business. In general, he relies more on what he hears and observes than what he reads. He is not one to reach out for ideas. "The possibility that you can teach him is not there very much," says a former foreign-policy adviser. "You get the feeling that his mind is pretty much made up."

The President's approach can lead to significant confusion. He astounded associates recently with an admission: Not until last fall, he said, did he realize that the Soviet Union has 70 percent of its strategic nuclear warheads placed on its land-based missiles, whereas the United States has only 20 percent of its strategic warheads on such missiles. Not until then did he realize why his original proposal for Russian cuts in land-based missiles, without similar American concessions, had been perceived as one-sided. The failure to master such basics has prevented him from resolving philosophical divisions in his administration over arms control.

A top White House official likens a policy session with Mr. Reagan to a meeting between a client and his lawyers: He focuses less on minutiae than on the extent to which a proposal is consistent with his personal guidelines. Before asking the President to make a decision, his aides try to achieve a consensus among themselves, but, like any client, he sometimes rejects even unanimous advice. Mr. Reagan took that tack when he dismissed the striking air traffic controllers in 1981 and when he refused to entertain the idea of tax increases in early 1982.

Close aides concluded long ago that it is often useless to try to persuade Mr. Reagan to support something he cannot believe in. In fact, as his aides recognize, his success in communicating an idea to the public is in part a function of his genuine emotional commitment to that idea. "So many politicians tire of that stump speech," says an adviser. "Reagan is willing to repeat it again and again because he believes every word of it." A Republican ally in Congress adds: "If he gets an idea firmly fixed in his head, he uses it forever."

Sometimes, though, the President's aides feel that he must be made to see the light on a particular issue. Then they may try to administer what they call "reality therapy." It usually takes the form of a visit by congressional leaders who agree with White House aides that the time has come to urge Mr. Reagan to be more flexible.

White House aides avoid appealing directly to the President on political grounds. "You argue from weakness if you go in there and tell him, 'If you don't do this, you're going to suffer a loss in your job approval rating,'" says James A. Baker III, the White House chief of staff. But Mr. Baker and others admit that they cannot ignore their mandate to help win legislative approval for Administration programs, or to strengthen Mr. Reagan's political standing. If the political stakes are high enough, they find a way to get his cooperation.

Their time-tested technique is to persuade the President that he is not reversing course even if that is precisely what they want him to do. Mr. Reagan truly does not believe that he changed policies significantly when he accepted a tax increase in late 1982, or when he dropped his efforts to delay construction of a natural-gas pipeline from Siberia to Europe, or when he decided to withdraw American troops from Lebanon.

White House aides say that Mr. Reagan is a genius at boiling abstractions down to concerete concepts that the public will understand. Often, his staff may look over the draft of a speech he has been working on and point out that a statement is incorrect. "How can we state it so that it is correct?" he will reply and prod his aides to find the down-to-earth facts and images to support his notions. He seizes on any bit of information that comes to him if it reinforces something he already believes.

Mr. Reagan, himself, skims the leading newspapers each day in search of telling anecdotes. He also seeks them in letters he receives and in articles in such publications as *Human Events*, the ultraconservative magazine. The stories tend to be about people who use food stamps to buy vodka or who falsify papers in order to obtain disability payments.

Mr. Gergen, the former communications director, calls them "parables," arguing that the public cares little about their authenticity. But press attention has forced the White House to "scrub" the stories for accuracy before Mr. Reagan uses them. "I always think that if we can get through a press conference without some disaster, it's a success," says a senior White House official.

More problematical are what the President's aides refer to as "notions." These include his debatable statements that the Great Society caused poverty to increase in the 1960s or that the United States actually decreased military spending in the 1970s. Asked recently why the President says things that are untrue, a long-time adviser laughed and said: "I don't know. He's been doing it for years."

The role of Mr. Reagan's staff is much debated in Washington. Some fear that his refusal to become involved in the intricacies of policymaking leaves him vulnerable to manipulation. Moderates claim, for example, that the President was persuaded to approve a crackdown on "leaks" to the press last fall without realizing that it called for lie-detector tests for his cabinet and staff.

Other critics charge that the White House staff is not activist enough, that they are cowed by Mr. Reagan's strong positions on some issues. Despite briefings from budget experts, Mr. Reagan resists accepting the idea that his programs to cut tax revenues and increase military costs have widened the federal deficit. His aides no longer push the point. One comments: "He doesn't like to be crowded or pushed hard by one individual."

The result of the staff's wary attitude toward Mr. Reagan is that, for all his geniality and attentiveness, he is not close personally to anyone. He tends to regard his closest aides at the White House as retainers or surrogate sons, but not as cronies.

Their manner toward him, in return, is highly deferential and respectful. Even Mr. Reagan's closest advisers find him to be basically remote, operating on a different plane and by his own lights — distanced from them. By all accounts, it is so rare for Mr. Reagan to confide in them, to share his darkest concerns or inner turmoils, that there is some doubt among his staff that he is troubled by any. Not until he was ready actually to announce his decision, for example, did Mr. Reagan tell even the members of his inner circle explicitly that he had indeed decided to run for reelection. Mr. Reagan is known to be similarly circumspect with his long-time friends in California. The only person with whom Mr. Reagan is known to share his inner feelings is his wife, Nancy.

Backstage at the White House, much as in his public persona, there is a wall of his own making between the affable president and his audience. The nation's host is a solitary man.

Long before the age of television, political experts complained about the electorate's limited attention span. In 1925, Walter Lippmann observed: "The public will arrive in the middle of the third act and will leave before the last curtain, having stayed just long enough perhaps to decide who is the hero and who the villain of the piece."

No modern president has exploited that tendency more effectively than Mr. Reagan. His performance inevitably raises questions about his prospects for reelection and the larger legacy he will have left as president.

The Democratic candidates hope to defeat Mr. Reagan by capitalizing on voter concerns about world tensions, fears that inflation, or unemployment may resurface or worries that Mr. Reagan will cut Social Security, Medicare, and other domestic programs.

And it remains to be seen how long the President's popularity would hold in the face of a barrage of policy reverses. The outer limits of his magic touch have yet to be tested. In the 1982 recession, for example, Mr. Reagan's approval rating dropped substantially. If there were a major increase in inflation or unemployment before election day, that rating might very well fall again.

Moreover, there is no way to be certain how the public will react to such events as the rebuke Mr. Reagan received April 10 when the Senate voted eighty-four to twelve for a resolution opposing American support of the mining of harbors in Nicaragua. Among those voting against him were the majority leader, Howard H. Baker, Jr., and forty-one other Republicans.

It was one of the worst setbacks Mr. Reagan has experienced in his relations with Congress, and one of the most serious rejections of a presidential policy since the Vietnam War. Administration officials state that the mining has ceased, and the future of all covert assistance to rebels in Nicaragua is now in doubt. But Mr. Reagan has a record of being able to carry his case to the public, bringing enough pressure on Congress to salvage much of what he seemed to have lost and preserving his popularity.

In January, when Congress returned after the holiday recess, Republican Congressional leaders informed Mr. Reagan that his policy of maintaining American troops in Lebanon had lost most of its support in Congress. The President withdrew the troops and his policy was widely described as a debacle. But his approval rating among the voters has been steadily rising ever since.

The President's astonishing political success to date suggests that the Democrats will have to do more than base their challenge on a catalogue of issues. They will have to run against the nation's host. Even now, Mr. Reagan's reelection strategists are planning some daunting presidential extravaganzas. Mr. Reagan plans to open such national celebrations as the World's Fair in New Orleans and the Olympic Games in Los Angeles. After returning from China, he will be off for a summit meeting in London and ceremonial stops in France and his ancestral home in Ireland.

Presidential pageantry gives all incumbents an advantage. But Democrats have a special problem because of Mr. Reagan's skills. Should they question his work habits and misstatements? The voters may continue to feel that these are simply unimportant. More likely, the Democrats will have to meet Mr. Reagan on his own terms, raising the political debate to a choice between two visions. Senator Gary Hart would be under more pressure to define his ideas. Former Vice-President Walter F. Mondale would be under more pressure to give his ideas fresh urgency and drama. Any Democrat will have to find a way to convince the voters that he, like Mr. Reagan, is speaking from his heart.

What impact will Mr. Reagan's performance have on the presidency itself? It seems hard now to remember the days when much of official Washington patronized him as an amiable amateur. He ended up transforming the conventional definition of the job.

In part, he has avoided some traditional pitfalls. He has not allowed himself to be unduly awed by the trappings of power — he has not taken the obsessive personal interest of his predecessors in assigning seats at state dinners or aboard Air Force One or in deciding who can use the White House tennis court.

"The main problem with power is that the person who uses it has trouble holding onto his identity," says John P. Sears, who managed Mr. Reagan's campaign in 1980 before being dismissed the day of the New Hampshire primary: "I think Reagan really does believe he's just a temporary custodian. This is where his training as an actor comes into play. An actor realizes that he's out front, and that he might get credit if the movie is a hit or blame if it's a bomb. But he knows there are people behind him who are working to pull the whole thing off."

That perspective might well be emulated by future presidents, whatever their background. They may also be tempted to learn from Mr. Reagan's political success. By concentrating on general themes and by projecting an upbeat spirit he has minimized the political damage that comes with running a government. By formulating a compelling vision of national purpose and by breathing it into every act and statement, he has forced critics and would-be challengers to debate the issues on his terms. He has shown that it is not enough for a president in the modern age to have such a vision; he must also be willing to spend most of his time selling it — persuading, cajoling, and communicating.

Mr. Reagan may also have altered the experts' perception of the qualities required for the presidency. "We better take another look at the nature of the job," says Mr. Sears. "We've had an awful lot of intelligent people in the White House who have done a poor job at it. Sometimes intelligence in a president can lead to confusion of purpose. Simplicity, on the other hand, has its merits."

And its dangers. Some of the President's closest aides, in fact, are concerned that Mr. Reagan is too insulated. "His instincts are the right ones, but that doesn't mean they shouldn't be tested against reality," says a senior White House official. What's more, Mr. Reagan's aloof managerial style has left an enormous amount of power to be fought over by his staff and led to considerable confusion in arriving at the final decision.

But there are larger questions posed by Mr. Reagan's first term in office: How far should a president try to separate himself from the political consequences of his policies? Is it enough for a president to speak to the yearnings of an age if he fails to confront the electorate with complex, difficult choices? In November, the voters may provide some answers.

AMONG THE IMMEDIATE RE-
wards of public office are
power and prestige, not prosperity. Often elected officials and political appointees in the executive
branch make financial sacrifices to
serve. Many congressmen, for example, are lawyers who can earn far more
in the private sector than they do on
Capitol Hill. Once they leave Congress, however, members and staff
alike can boost their incomes greatly
by becoming lobbyists. In addition,
congressional retirees take with them
generous pensions as well as the
money remaining in their campaign
chests, which in some cases may
amount to several million dollars from
political action committee and individual contributions.

Former presidents, with the help of
a government stipend, do the best financially among retired politicians.

Under the Former Presidents Act,
passed in 1958, they receive a $70,000-
a-year pension. They also retain many
of their former perks, including Secret Service protection, office expenses, and staff salaries that amount
to hundreds of thousands of dollars.
Even more lucrative for former presidents may be book royalties for their
memoirs, and the numerous speaking
engagements and public appearances
they make for substantial fees.

Although not supported by the
government, former vice-presidents
can do extremely well for themselves
as the following selection illustrates.
Former Vice-President Walter Mondale was able not only to set himself
up financially after leaving office, but
used the money and free time at his
disposal to mount his 1984 campaign
for the Democratic presidential nomination.

16 Charles R. Babcock
THE REWARDS OF LOSING: MONDALE OUT OF OFFICE

On January 28, 1981, eight days after leaving the vice-presidency, Walter
F. Mondale met with representatives of a nonprofit Chicago group who
wanted his help starting a national campaign to publicize family issues.
Mondale, a supporter of aid to disadvantaged families all his political
life, agreed to work with the charity.

He also was entering the private job market after twenty years of
public service. When an official of the group, Family Focus Inc., called
Mondale aide James A. Johnson — who is now the Mondale presidential campaign manager — to work out the details of a consulting arrangement, he was told the former vice-president's fee would be $50,000

From *The Washington Post National Weekly Edition*, 21 November 1983. © 1983
The Washington Post. Reprinted by permission.

a year, preferably paid in advance. A check was sent to Mondale three weeks later, on February 19.

That payment was one of the first of more than $1 million that Mondale reports earning in 1981 and 1982: $430,000 from corporate director and consulting fees; nearly $300,000 from part-time legal work; more than $224,000 in speaking fees, and $56,000 in government pensions.

At the same time, he was considered the front runner for the 1984 Democratic presidential nomination and was perhaps the chief figure in the party after the Democrats lost the White House and control of the Senate in 1980.

In the two years before he officially announced his candidacy, he spent about half his time on the road, making at least 250 political appearances in thirty-nine states.

Mondale is not the first government official to convert his name and experience to big money after leaving government service. Some, such as former vice-president Nixon and former governor Ronald Reagan, also pursued private business affairs while seeking their party's presidential nomination.

Between 1961 and 1968, Nixon was a lawyer who traveled the globe for clients such as Pepsi Cola while campaigning hard for GOP candidates and collecting political IOUs.

Reagan did the same after stepping down as governor of California and losing the 1976 Republican presidential nomination to Gerald R. Ford. A highly paid speaker and columnist, he set up a political action committee (PAC) to raise money to finance his political travels.

Mondale seems to be following the same rough blueprint, including the formation of a PAC and joining a law firm, the Washington office of Winston and Strawn.

Unlike some of his Democratic rivals, Senators John Glenn (Ohio), Gary Hart (Colo.), Alan Cranston (Calif.) and Ernest F. Hollings (S.C.), Mondale didn't have a public office as a platform from which to be heard and to draw resources. So he and his closest aides, Johnson and Michael S. Berman, created a platform, a sophisticated Mondale conglomerate to give him high visibility, staff, money, and the foundation to launch his campaign formally, which he did last February 21.

Mondale's schedule shows that he could combine business and political appearances on one trip. November 17 and 18, 1982, in Chicago, he had dinner at the Winston and Strawn offices, was paid $7,000 for a speech to a Blue Cross/Blue Shield symposium, held one reception for his PAC, attended another for Adlai E. Stevenson III, Democratic candidate for governor, and spoke for no fee to the Anti-Defamation League of B'nai B'rith.

Johnson said Mondale's first decision after the 1980 election was a "working presumption" that he would run for president in 1984. "That would be one of the things that would guide him as he decided what kind of personal and business relationships he should develop," Johnson said.

Mondale's daughter, Eleanor, was quoted recently as saying her father told the family of his plans the day after the 1980 election, when he and President Carter lost their bid for a second term. The former vice-president says he was able to separate his business and political roles.

"I have been punctiliously careful to separate the two," he said in a forty-five-minute interview. . . . "I had to make a living and I did." His aides set up an accounting system to allocate the costs of his political and business affairs.

"I wanted it that way," Mondale said. "That is also the law. You can't have private funds paying for political activities."

It appears that Mondale and his advisers were diligent in obeying the election finance laws. But at times the distinction between his private and public roles seemed to blur.

Many of his business relationships, for example, were arranged by men who support his presidential ambitions and didn't require specific commitments of time from him in return for their money.

"I didn't reach a relationship with them [clients] based on time," Mondale said. "I did it based on the market value of the quality of my advice, counsel, experience, background and an agreement with them with which we were both satisfied." His advice, he said, often was on international economic or political problems.

Mondale made his 1981 and 1982 tax returns and travel schedule available to the *Washington Post*. He and most of his clients declined, however, to say exactly what he did or how much time he spent working for the $730,000 in legal, consulting, and director fees he reported as income for the years 1981 and 1982. The remaining $280,000 came from speaking fees and pensions.

He said the question of his time commitment for his various fees is irrelevant. "I don't agree with the concept," he said when asked how much time he gave to Winston and Strawn. "In other words, that was not the basis on which I came to he firm. I am satisfied. They are satisfied. I don't have a time card."

In the one case where a client talked openly, Family Focus officials said he spent little time with them, and they voiced some unhappiness with the result.

Mondale's major effort for Family Focus in 1981 was visiting private foundations in what turned out to be an unsuccessful attempt to obtain grants for the national publicity campaign. The group also paid more than $50,000 to Johnson's consulting firm, Public Strategies Inc., that year to help prepare proposals to the foundations.

The five foundation presidents Mondale visited said they didn't know

Mondale was being paid. Some said they thought he had volunteered because of his past interest in family causes as United States senator from Minnesota and as vice-president.

Although the foundation effort failed, Family Focus paid Mondale another $50,000 the next year, 1982. During that second year, Family Focus officials said, Mondale's time with the group was limited to a half-hour tour of a teen-age parents' center, while he was on a political campaign swing in Chicago, and a separate appearance at a meeting of an advisory group he helped organize.

Irving B. Harris and Bernard Weissbourd, two wealthy Chicago businessmen, donated $200,000 to Family Focus during the two years and earmarked the money for the national publicity program. Harris said he suggested hiring Mondale.

The two men also support Mondale's presidential candidacy; they and their families have contributed more than $44,000 to Mondale's political action committee and presidential campaign since 1981.

Harris and Weissbourd said the $150,000 that went to Mondale and Johnson from their tax-deductible donations was unrelated to their support for Mondale's candidacy.

Mondale said he was surprised that some foundation presidents thought he had volunteered his services to Family Focus. "I would have had a different impression than that," he said.

"I don't think there's anybody in the country that's worked harder on the practical problems of developing public policies to support families and children than I have," he said. "I think my credentials are there for all to see. I think it's entirely consistent with the interests of that foundation to have used my service, quite apart from any possible interest in the presidential race. I'd say the same thing about the other relationships."

"About the only way I could absolve myself from that . . . is to join some order and live off food stamps somewhere or something," Mondale said.

Family Focus chairman Harris said he thinks now that the Mondale-Johnson money "stands out as a large fee that was wasted, if you will" because the foundation effort failed.

In all, Mondale combined several different roles in what Johnson has called "Mondale Inc." They included:

Former vice-president. He received about $150,000 in transition funds to close down his office.

Professor. Mondale gave about twenty lectures at the University of Minnesota and two private colleges in the Minneapolis area without pay. The university did pay $35,000 to J. Frederick Martin and Eric H. Vaughn for research on his teaching assignments. The two men also were speech writers for Mondale's political action committee, but Mondale said their time was monitored to ensure that the university didn't pay for their political work.

Lawyer. Mondale collects $150,000 a year as a part-time lawyer in the Washington office of Winston and Strawn, a major Chicago law firm. Mondale serves "of counsel," which allows him freedom for speaking and consulting work, he said, and doesn't identify him with all the firm's clients, as a partnership contract would. He is provided with an aide, a secretary, and use of a car.

Speaker. Mondale was paid more than $224,000 for thirty speeches arranged through a New York agency, according to his disclosure statement. The most lucrative were overseas, where the fee was $20,000 or $25,000 per appearance, plus expenses. The agency took a 30 percent commission. In this country, Mondale's fee was usually $10,000 or $15,000.

Presumed presidential candidate. Mondale was careful not to declare his candidacy officially until early this year. "I did everything consistent with the law, which is that I was not a candidate," he said of his PAC-paid travels. "I was helping congressional candidates. It was for that purpose, and I was very careful both never to say anything different and believe anything different."

Through June 1983, his PAC, called the Committee for the Future of America, raised and spent nearly $2.5 million. It reports spending some $263,000 — less than 11 percent — in contributions and in-kind services to Democratic candidates. Before the 1980 campaign, Reagan's similar political action committee gave about 13 percent of its money to candidates.

Most of the $2.5 million Mondale raised went for operating costs, including a staff of consultants, many of whom now work for his presidential campaign committee.

About $1 million was spent on direct mail, which developed a list of 23,000 Mondale supporters. That list couldn't be donated to the presidential campaign committee because it was worth more than $5,000, which is the limit on gifts. So it was sold to a list broker for $23,000 and is rented by the Mondale presidential campaign committee for less than $1,200.

In many of his political speeches Mondale has attacked the role of special-interest money and PACs. Records of his PAC show it accepted more than $200,000 in PAC donations, including more than $50,000 after his presidential campaign said it wouldn't accept any such money. Johnson said that pledge applied only to the presidential campaign committee, not to the Mondale PAC.

Corporate director and consultant. In addition to the $100,000 he received from nonprofit Family Focus, Mondale received the following from corporate relationships: Control Data Corp., a Minneapolis company, $134,000; Columbia Pictures Industries Inc., where longtime Mondale friend and supporter Herbert A. Allen was chairman, $103,000; Allen & Co. Inc., headed by Allen, $50,000; and Northwest Energy Co., whose president, John G. McMillian, is another Mondale contributor, $43,750.

Some people said that at times they weren't sure which Walter Mondale they were seeing. Orville G. Brim, Jr., president of the Fund for Child Development in New York, one of the foundations Mondale visited for Family Focus in 1981, doubted Mondale was there as a paid consultant.

"No one there was getting paid," he said. "When you work in this field you get a lot of volunteer work. Paying for it would be something new."

Richard Lyman, president of the Rockefeller Foundation, said that he, too, had thought Mondale was volunteering his services. Phoebe Cottingham, Rockefeller's assistant director for social sciences, said of Mondale's fee: "That's certainly way out of line for that kind of work." Consultants in the field usually charge $200 to $300 a day, she said.

At times, too, Mondale's paid speeches had the potential for other benefits. He was paid $70,000 for nine speeches to United Jewish Appeal and Israel Bond dinners, for instance, while giving pro-Israel speeches to audiences of potential contributors and backers.

Ellen Bayer, head of the speakers' bureau for the United Jewish Appeal Federation of Greater New York, said both Mondale and her group benefited from two speeches that cost a total of $20,000.

"We get a draw, a name that lends prestige to the event," she said. "And of course it doesn't hurt any politician." Bayer said her nonprofit group has a policy against hiring active candidates to speak.

"Of course that's a very fine line anymore, when some people are running four years ahead of time," she added. "By implication he was a candidate, not officially, of course."

A spokesman for another Jewish organization, the Anti-Defamation League of B'nai B'rith, which didn't pay Mondale for three speeches, said simply: "With us obviously he was wearing his candidate hat. He was after the Jewish vote."

Not all his listeners were satisfied. Joel W. Greenberg, who helped plan a dinner for Israel bonds in Chicago March 18, 1982, said he refused to pay Mondale's expenses and asked for return of part of the $15,000 his group paid.

"For a seventeen-minute talk I thought we deserved a refund," Greenberg said, adding that he didn't get the refund and the Israel Bonds office in New York paid the $600 expense bill.

Mondale also was able to mesh his roles as statesman and lawyer. On a trip to Peking in 1981, Mondale joined a law firm client, Beatrice Foods Corp., in meetings setting up a business venture with the Chinese. Beatrice paid his expenses. During the trip Mondale met with China's leader, Deng Xiaoping.

Douglas Stanard, vice-president and director of corporate relations for Beatrice, said Mondale played a big role in getting the agreement.

"Mr. Mondale, obviously, as a former vice-president, as viewed differently than other members of the law firm," Stanard said. "There's a certain element of trust. When you bring someone like that to the bargaining table it just adds something."

Richard Holbrooke, a former assistant secretary of state for the Far East, accompanied Mondale on the trip. He said, "It would have been absolutely inappropriate and bizarre if the host government didn't want to have private and serious talks with him." He said the Chinese were interested because of courtesy and because Mondale was a person whose "political future may still lie ahead of him."

Holbrooke, who is vice-president of Public Strategies Inc., the firm headed by Mondale's aide, Johnson, likened Mondale's trip to ones Nixon made in the 1960s as a lawyer for Pepsi Cola. "Some people laughed and called him a Pepsi salesman," Holbrooke said. "Most of the foreign governments didn't. They received him, and those that didn't regretted it later."

Holbrooke said half of his own expenses on the trip were paid by Beatrice, and half by other clients. He said Beatrice hired Public Strategies, which rents space from Mondale's law firm, "through the Winston and Strawn landlord connection. It all fits together."

On the same trip, Mondale combined visits with government leaders in South Korea and Japan with a visit to a Control Data plant in Seoul and to a Columbia Pictures distributor in Tokyo. He was a board member and consultant to both companies at the time.

Mondale joined the board of Control Data, the Minneapolis computer company, soon after he left office. It was the only arrangement based on time, according to Berman. Control Data paid Mondale $2,000 a day for general consulting, in addition to his director's fees and $2,000 a month for unspecified legal consulting.

Mondale became a director and consultant to Columbia on Allen's recommendation. Berman, a longtime Mondale aide and his financial adviser, is a Columbia lobbyist here. Allen contributed $10,000 to Mondale's PAC and has also contributed to and sponsored a fund raiser for Mondale's presidential campaign.

When Coca-Cola took over Columbia in the spring of 1982, Mondale switched over to the payroll of Allen's investment banking firm at $50,000 for the last nine months of the year.

Allen said, "I can't and won't give you any specifics. We're not a publicly traded company. We don't have any stockholders. But it had nothing to do with government operations or influence peddling, anything like that."

When Mondale left the vice-presidency at age fifty-three, he had a net worth of about $225,000, including a house in the affluent Cleveland Park section of Washington. His tax returns show that nearly 40 percent of the $1 million earned in 1981 and 1982 went to pay federal and local taxes. Some of the rest was used to fix up the house, $50,000 went as a down payment on a $210,000 second home in an exclusive Minneapolis suburb, and $40,000 was put into a trust fund, according to Berman.

"Theoretically they could have lived on less because they had lived on less for a helluva long time," Berman said. "But this was an opportunity to make a little stronger income, and he took advantage of that opportunity."

Since he officially declared his candidacy, Mondale has stopped accepting paid lecture dates and resigned most of his business posts. "He hasn't got time," Berman explained. Mondale still is receiving a $150,000 annual salary from the law firm and his $2,000-a-month retainer for legal consulting for Control Data, Berman said.

The job Mondale is interested in now is a full-time one. It pays $200,000 a year, plus expenses, and provides living quarters at 1600 Pennsylvania Avenue NW.

"There's probably nobody in public life that's been more careful about his private affairs than mine," Mondale said. . . . "When I become president, as I plan to be, I will be totally free to serve the public interest and will do so. That's the test."

THE WORLD OF THE WHITE House staffer is unique. In the rarefied atmosphere of the West Wing of the White House the president's press secretary, national security adviser, top personal assistants and troubleshooters, and other staffers who are particularly close to the president work near the Oval Office. Occupying physical space that is near the president is of enormous symbolic significance, being generally taken to reflect a close relationship with the president himself. Not all of the White House staff works in the West Wing; many occupy offices in the old and new executive office buildings, which are respectively adjacent to and directly across Pennsylvania Avenue from the White House. The formal office of the vice-president is in the old executive office building with a view directly overlooking the West Wing. President Carter moved Vice-President Walter Mondale into an office in the West Wing to symbolize a close presidential–vice-presidential relationship (the former vice-president's office is occasionally used for ceremonial functions and stands ready to receive vice-presidents in the future).

The White House staff is a relatively new institution; President Roosevelt created it in 1939 as part of his reorganization plan establishing the executive office of the president. The White House staff, however, did not come into its own as an independent force until much later. While it always included powerful and influential persons, its original purpose was best expressed by Harry Truman: "The Presidency is so tremendous that it is necessary for a President to delegate authority. To be able to do so safely, however, he must have around him people who can be trusted not to arrogate authority to themselves."[1] Truman continued, "Eventually I succeeded in surrounding myself with assistants and associates who would not overstep the bounds of that delegated authority, and they were people I could trust. This is policy on the highest level: it is the operation of the government by the Chief Executive under the laws. That is what it amounts to, and when that ceases to be, chaos exists."[2]

President John F. Kennedy put together a dynamic and forceful staff that was later inherited by Lyndon B. Johnson and described as "the best and the brightest" by journalist David Halberstam.[3] Halberstam argued persuasively that major White House decisions escalating the Vietnam war during the Johnson administration could be traced directly to powerful White House staffers such as Walt Rostow, McGeorge Bundy, and Robert McNamara (who later changed from hawk to dove and resigned his position as secretary of defense to become president of the World Bank).

It was during the Nixon years that the White House staff, controlled by H. R. (Bob) Haldeman and John Ehr-

---

[1] Harry S Truman, *Memoirs: Volume 1, Year of Decisions* (Garden City, New York: Doubleday, 1955), p. 228.

[2] Ibid.

[3] David Halberstam, *The Best and the Brightest* (New York: Random House, 1972).

lichman, arrogantly wielded power around Washington in the name of the president. The Nixon White House staff was dubbed the "Palace Guard," because of its reputation for preventing direct access to the president by cabinet officers and other top officials. Like Truman, Nixon recognized the need to delegate power, but unlike Truman, he did not recognize the critical importance of retaining absolute control over his own staff. Many of the acute embarrassments to the White House that occurred during the Nixon administration, including possibly the Watergate break-in itself, might have been avoided had the president been less optimistic about the system of broad delegation of powers that he established in the White House.

Regardless of who is president, the tendency of those on the White House staff is to aggrandize their personal power. White House staffers continually seek to be in the good graces of the president, which not only may involve backroom intrigue among different individuals and groups of staf-

fers, but also tends to mute honest criticism of the president if he embarks on what an ambitious staffer feels to be the wrong course of action. In the following selection George Reedy, a longtime associate of Lyndon B. Johnson, both on Capitol Hill and in the White House, provides a succinct personal account of the way in which the institution of the presidency affects staffers. Reedy was Lyndon Johnson's press secretary in 1964–1965, after which he returned to private life, only to be summoned back to the White House in 1968 as a special adviser to the president on domestic matters. When Johnson was in the Senate, Reedy served with him at various times, both as a staffer on the committees Johnson chaired and as a member of the senator's personal staff. Reedy's thesis is that the atmosphere of the White House tends to breed "blind ambition," to borrow John Dean's phrase (see Selection 18), on the part of staffers, even though their personalities might not have revealed this trait before they entered the White House.

17 George E. Reedy
THE WHITE HOUSE STAFF: A PERSONAL ACCOUNT

The most frequently asked question of any former presidential assistant is whether he misses the White House. My answer is a heartfelt no!

It is an institution which can be regarded with a far higher degree of approbation from the outside — where reverence softens the harsh lines

From George E. Reedy, *The Twilight of the Presidency*, pp. xii–xvii. Copyright © 1970 by George Reedy. All rights reserved. Reprinted by permission of Harry N. Abrams, Inc.

of reality — than from the inside. Like any impressionistic painting, it improves with distance. . . . The factor that I have missed in most of the works on the presidency I have read is the impact of the institution on individuals. The literature on the subject seems to assume that the White House somehow molds the man and his assistants into finer forms and that the major problem of government is to assure channels through which these forms will have full expression. It is virtually taken for granted that the proper objective of a study of our chief executive is to identify those inhibiting factors which frustrate his efforts to resolve national problems and to devise mechanisms which will remove those frustrations. This is a type of study which should be continued on a priority basis. The frustrations are many and could be catastrophic.

But the analysis is inadequate. It ignores the fundamental reality of society, which is that institutions are manned by individual human beings and that government — regardless of the managerial flow charts produced by the behavioral scientists — is still a question of decisions that are made by people. The basic question is not whether we have devised structures with inadequate authority for the decision-making process. The question is whether the structures have created an environment in which men cannot function in any kind of a decent and humane relationship to the people whom they are supposed to lead. I am afraid — and on this point I am a pessimist — that we have devised that kind of a system.

To explain this, I must start with a highly personal reaction. The trouble with the White House — for anyone who is a part of it — is that when he picks up a telephone and tells people to do something, they usually do it. They may sabotage the project, after they have hung up the phone. They may stall, hoping that "the old son of a bitch" will forget about it. They may respond with an avalanche of statistics and briefing papers in which the original purpose will be lost and life will continue as before. But the heel click at the other end of the wire will be audible and the response — however invalid — will be prompt. There will be no delay in assurance, however protracted may be performance.

This is an unhealthy environment for men and women whose essential business is to deal with people in large numbers. It is soothing to the ego, but it fosters illusions about humanity. It comforts the weary assistant who may have gone round the clock in his search for a solution to an insoluble problem, but it paves the way for massive disillusionment. And for the very young, the process is demoralizing. It creates a picture of the world which is ill adapted to that which they will face once the days of glory come to an end. There should be a flat rule that no one be permitted to enter the gates of the White House until he is at least forty and has suffered major disappointments in life.

My own heart is back in the Senate, where I spent so many years of my adult life either as a newspaperman or a staff assistant. This is not because the people at the other end of Pennsylvania Avenue are any better in terms of character, wisdom, or goals. It is simply that their egos must face daily clashes with similarly strong egos who stand on a par and who do not feel any sense of subordination. In the Senate, no course stands the remotest chance of adoption unless a minimum of fifty-one egotistical men are persuaded of its wisdom, and in some cases the minimum is sixty-seven. These are preconditions under which even the most neurotic of personalities must make some obeisance to reality.

The inner life of the White House is essentially the life of the barnyard, as set forth so graphically in the study of the pecking order among chickens which every freshman sociology student must read. It is a question of who has the right to peck whom and who must submit to being pecked. There are only two important differences. The first is that the pecking order is determined by the individual strength and forcefulness of each chicken, whereas in the White House it depends upon the relationship to the barnyard keeper. The second is that no one outside the barnyard glorifies the chickens and expects them to order the affairs of mankind. They are destined for the frying pan and that is that.

The White House does not provide an atmosphere in which idealism and devotion can flourish. Below the president is a mass of intrigue, posturing, strutting, cringing, and pious "commitment" to irrelevant windbaggery. It is designed as the perfect setting for the conspiracy of mediocrity — that all too frequently successful collection of the untalented, the unpassionate, and the insincere seeking to convince the public that it is brilliant, compassionate, and dedicated.

There are, of course, men who seethe inwardly over this affront to human dignity — most of whom either go smash or leave quietly, their muscles set rigidly to contain an indescribable agony. There are, of course, the warm and relaxed permanent White House staff members, secure in their mastery of the essential housekeeping machinery of the mansion and watching with wry amusement and some sympathy the frenetic efforts to shine forth boldly of those who have only four years out of all eternity to grab the brass ring. But the men of outrage are few and for some reason avoid each other after they slip out the side door. There are experiences which should not be shared. A reunion would lead only to a collective shriek.

It is not that the people who compose the menage are any worse than any other collection of human beings. It is rather that the White House is an ideal cloak for intrigue, pomposity, and ambition. No nation of free men should ever permit itself to be governed from a hallowed shrine where the meanest lust for power can be sanctified and the dullest wit greeted with reverential awe. Government should be vulgar, sweaty, plebeian, operating in an environment where a fool can be called a fool and the motivations of ideological pimpery duly observed and noted. In a democracy, meanness, dullness, and corruption are entitled to representation because they are part of the human spirit; they are not entitled to protection from the harsh and rude challenges that such qualities must face in the real world.

It is not enough to say that the White House need not be like this if it is occupied by another set of personalities. It is not enough to point out that I may subconsciously be exaggerating the conditions which I describe in overreacting to the reverence that has characterized most studies of the presidency. The fact remains that the institution provides camouflage for all that is petty and nasty in human beings, and enables a clown or a knave to pose as Galahad and be treated with deference.

Is my reaction purely personal disappointment or shaped by service in a specific White House in a specific administration? Obviously, no man can be truly objective about an experience so central to his life and so vital to all his goals and his aspirations. All I can say is that I am fully aware of the treacherous nature of one's sensory mechanisms in surveying the immediately surrounding universe. I have taken this factor into account and tried to allow for it in every possible way. . . . I believe that what I am saying is more than the conclusion of one man in a unique set of circumstances.

The thirty years I have spent in Washington have been punctuated with a number of telltale incidents. I have observed, for example, that former White House assistants are reticent about their experiences. When pressed for a description they invariably resort to words like "richly rewarding" and "fulfilling" — the clichés that men always use when they wish to conceal, rather than to convey, thought. And their congratulations to newly appointed assistants begin always with perfunctory "best wishes" and then shift to heartfelt friendly tips on how to survive. Only once have I felt a genuine flash of fire. It came from one of the top "assistants with a passion for anonymity" of the Roosevelt days. I described to him White House life as I saw it and his response — which was passionate — was: "Don't worry! That's the way it has always been and that's the way it will always be!"

I have a feeling that Camelot was not a very happy place. Even the gentle language of Malory does not fully cloak hints of intrigue, corruption, and distrust — reaching as high as Guinevere. And the "Table Round" seems better adapted to boozing in a vain effort to drown disappointment than to knightly discourse on chivalrous deeds and weighty matters of state.

In fact, Malory makes virtually no effort to describe Camelot as a seat of government. King Arthur was presumably beloved by his subjects because he was wise and valiant. But how did he handle roadbuilding, public charity, or the administration of justice? Such questions had to wait several hundred years for the advent of Mark Twain, whose entirely fictitious (and wholly irreverent) account was probably much closer to the reality than that produced by the original sources.

It is this aspect that gives cause for concern. The psychological ease of those who reside in Camelot does not matter except to the individuals themselves. But the type of government that Camelot produces affects every individual and, ultimately, can determine the character of the society in which we all must live.

It is my highly pessimistic view that Camelot will no longer suffice — however effective it may have been in the past. As a rallying point for men who would beat off dragons and ogres, it was superb. As a device to lead us through the stresses of modern life, it is wholly inadequate. And one of the few historical principles in which I still retain faith is that an inadequate government will either fall or resort to repression.

There is no reason to believe that the United States is exempt from the forces of history. We have no special writ from the Almighty which will substitute for normal human wisdom. There is no evidence that such wisdom is being applied effectively to the overwhelming problems that beset us nor is there any light on the horizon. And while it may seem premature at this point, we may well be witnessing the first lengthening of the shadows that will become the twilight of the presidency.

ALTHOUGH THE NIXON WHITE House was anything but ordinary, the feelings of John Dean when he first approached the southwest gate of the White House to put in his first day on the job were in many respects typical of new White House staffers. From the very beginning Dean's chief desires were to enter the inner circle of the president, and to acquire both the symbols and the realities of power. Dean entered the White House with a sense of awe; he left it with bitterness less than three years later, after being fired by President Nixon. Dean could not imagine on that first day at the White House the quagmire in which he would eventually find himself. Everyone in politics has ambition, and many have "blind ambition." It was the latter that led Dean to become part of the Watergate coverup conspiracy, a blind ambition that was characteristic of the Nixon White House during the Watergate era.

18 John Dean
MY FIRST DAY
AT THE WHITE HOUSE

I arrived early for my first day on the new job, July 27, 1970, and drove to the southwest gate of the White House grounds. A guard found my name on his clipboard and instructed me to park in one of the visitors' spaces, since my permanent spot had not yet been assigned. Bud Krogh pulled in a few spaces away. He waved a greeting at me and hurried off, mumbling like the Mad Hatter that he was late. He would see me later, he called. It was not yet eight in the morning. *Late,* I thought. I had been worried about getting there too early. No one had told me when the work day started.

I'd barely got acquainted with my new office in the Executive Office Building when Bud called in, "Hey, John, have you had a chance to take a real look around yet?"

"No, I haven't."

He seemed pleased. "Let me take you on a tour and show you some of the places no one sees." There was a look of mischief on his face.

Bud Krogh — Egil Krogh, Jr. — was a long-time friend of John Ehrlichman and his family in Seattle. After spending much of his childhood in the Ehrlichman home, he had joined Ehrlichman's law firm and then followed Ehrlichman to the White House as his assistant. Such intimate sponsorship from Ehrlichman gave Bud a head start in the White House, and he made the most of it. Despite his youth, he was already known in the administration for his quick grasp of complex issues and his forceful presence. Even when he was largely ignorant of the subject matter, he was sharp enough to dominate meetings and win the participants' respect. Already he was the White House man in charge of relations with the District of Columbia government, with responsibilities ranging from reviewing its budget to overseeing its response to the massive antiwar demonstrations of the early Nixon years. He was also in charge of the White House effort to combat heroin and other dangerous drugs, a subject of great concern to the President. Later he would be selected to run the highly secret Plumbers' Unit that was to stop up leaks, and still later he would go to jail for his activities there.

Bud Krogh was someone I considered a friend. We took off toward the basement of the Executive Office Building like the Hardy Boys. Hidden in the depths we found the telephone switchboard headquarters, and behind it a massive equipment room filled with transformers, generators and electrical circuitry. Bud introduced me to the chief operator, who seemed pleased by our visit. "This equipment we have, Mr. Dean, could handle a whole city the size of Hagerstown, Maryland," she said proudly. I wondered why she picked Hagerstown, of all places, but her domain was certainly impressive, as were the skills of the women who worked as operators. They could locate anyone, just as they had found me for Larry Higby when Haldeman wanted me to fly to San Clemente. (Only once did I abuse this skill, when I asked one of the operators to track down a woman I had met who would not give me her unlisted telephone number.) Bud and I lingered briefly and then pressed on to the basement of the White House's West Wing and the Situation Room.

The Situation Room, I had heard, was where Henry Kissinger took his dates to impress them. It operated twenty-four hours a day to keep the President aware of what was happening throughout the world, Bud explained. I pictured this nerve center as a gleaming room packed with uniformed admirals and generals seated at long computer consoles, surrounded by lesser-ranking aides and walls of incomprehensible charts and maps. Wrong. The room was dreary and overcrowded, jammed with cluttered desks and staffed by a few young military men wearing out-of-date civilian clothes and a secretary checking the antique-looking teletypes. Even the windowless wood-paneled conference room, designed to prevent eavesdropping, was boring. This vital communications post was far less imposing than the switchboard rooms, and I decided that Kissinger must have something more than the Situation Room to impress the ladies.

Outside the "Sit Room" we peeked into a large storage area beside the mess, where workmen were building an executive dining room for senior staff and cabinet officers, which would resemble a private men's grill at a posh country club. We walked on, peering into the White House barbershop, the limousine drivers' waiting room, the photographer's office, the vault safe for sensitive presidential papers, and a Secret Service command post.

We went upstairs to the first floor of the West Wing, where the President's Oval Office is located. Bud was amazed that I had never seen it. As we approached, he pointed out a small monitoring device that kept constant track of the President's whereabouts. It indicated that the President was in his hideaway office at the Executive Office Building next door. An Executive Protective Service officer was posted near the monitor. A thick velvet rope guarded the door to the Oval Office, which was standing open. Bud, never shy, asked the officer to remove the rope so that we could take a closer look. He obeyed reluctantly, with the request that we step *just* inside.

"This is The Man's office," said Bud. "What do you think?"

"Not bad, not bad at all. In fact, it's damn impressive." I could feel the importance of the office as I took it all in. My attention was caught by the conspicuous rug and the huge desk. The oval rug was deep blue, with a ring of gold stars and a huge gold eagle in the middle, a replica of the president's seal of office. It struck me as surprisingly flashly for Richard Nixon, who had such strong feelings about appearing dignified and presidential. He would not, despite the advice of his television experts, wear a blue shirt. Blue shirts weren't presidential, he said, and he didn't care if his white shirts made his dark features appear harsher on television; white shirts were presidential. His blue-and-gold rug, like the short-lived Bavarian-guard uniforms he commissioned for the White House, was in odd contrast to all that.

His desk was enormous and had allegedly been used by Woodrow Wilson. Two presidents, maybe four, could have worked at it without disturbing each other. There was a story about the desk around the White House. The President liked to sit with his feet on it, and his heels had scarred the top. Once, when he was out of the country, someone noticed the damaged mahogany surface and sent the desk out to be refinished. When he returned, Nixon noticed that his heel marks had been removed. "Dammit, I didn't order that," he snapped. "I want to leave *my* mark on this place just like other presidents."

We moved on to the East Wing, with Bud pointing out places of interest along the way — the doctor's office, the chief butler's office, the Map Room, the Lincoln Library, the kitchen, the secret tunnel. We stopped briefly at the door of the secret tunnel, which ran from the basement of the White House to the Treasury Department a block away. Bud said the Secret Service had contingency plans for bringing troops through the tunnel if a hostile demonstration ever got out of hand. But the only trooper to use the tunnel was Chief Justice Warren Burger. On the day his Supreme Court nomination was announced, the tunnel enabled him to enter the White House unnoticed by the press.

Down we went to the East Wing basement, until halted by a large steel door posted "Restricted Area." Bud ignored the sign, and I followed him through a room of furnaces, low-hanging pipes and huge valves to a second steel door with a small window. He rang the doorbell, and a face appeared that recognized him. The door opened and Bud stated his purpose: "I want to show Mr. Dean, the new counsel to the President, the area we use as a command post during demonstrations."

We walked through a corridor maze until we came to a small suite of rooms. "This," Bud announced, "is the President's bomb shelter." I looked around. Ventilated air. Stored supplies. Beds. An appropriately presidential desk flanked by flags. And a conference room with three built-in television sets, plus radio equipment and telephones everywhere. It *looked* like a President's bomb shelter.

Bud said Ehrlichman found this an ideal command post for monitoring demonstrations, which puzzled me. It was remote, to say the least, and totally out of touch with what would be occurring on the streets. I conjured an image of "Field Marshal Ehrlichman," whose interest in demonstrations Haldeman once likened to that of a firehouse Dalmatian at a blaze. I knew I wouldn't use the shelter for monitoring demonstrations, although Haldeman had told me that that would be one of my responsibilities. The only time I ever returned there was for a secret screening of *Tricia's Wedding,* a pornographic movie portraying Tricia Nixon's wedding to Edward Cox, in drag. Haldeman wanted the movie killed, so a very small group of White House officials watched the cavorting transvestites in order to weight the case for suppression. Official action proved unnecessary; the film died a natural death.

As Bud and I went past the offices of the White House staff members, I noticed furniture and files being moved. The White House, far more than any other government office, was in a state of perpetual internal flux. Offices were constantly exchanged and altered. One day I visited the President's congressional-liaison man, Bryce N. Harlow, in his first-floor West Wing office (which later belonged to Clark MacGregor and then to William E. Timmons) and found a team of workmen busy constructing a new wall where a door had once been. Bryce explained he had been forced to give up his private bathroom because the stairwell from the basement to the second floor was being made smaller so that Henry Kissinger's office could be expanded. "In a way, I'm glad to know the place I used to shit will be Henry's office," he said with a wry smile. "That tells me who's who around here." Harlow was perhaps the only man in the White House who did not care about losing space; he was planning to leave anyway.

Everyone jockeyed for a position close to the President's ear, and even an unseasoned observer could sense minute changes in status. Success and failure could be seen in the size, décor, and location of offices. Anyone who moved to a smaller office was on the way down. If a carpenter, cabinetmaker, or wallpaper hanger was busy in someone's office, this was a sure sign he was on the rise. Every day, workmen crawled over the White House complex like ants. Movers busied themselves with the continuous shuffling of furniture from one office to another as people moved in, up, down, or out. We learned to read office changes as an index of the internal bureaucratic power struggles. The expense was irrelevant to Haldeman. "For Christ's sake," he once retorted when we discussed whether we should reveal such expenses, "this place is a national monument, and I can't help it if the last three presidents let it go to hell." Actually, the costs had less to do with the fitness of the White House than with the need of its occupants to see tangible evidence of their prestige.

Our tour ended and it was time to go back to my "temporary" EOB office and work. By all White House standards my office was shabby. The walls needed painting and the furniture looked like military discards. I was across and down the hall from Special Counsel Charles W. Colson, whose growing staff had lovely views of the White House and its tree-filled south lawn from their freshly decorated offices. From my window I could gaze on an interior asphalt courtyard filled with delivery trucks and parked cars plus the rear ends of air conditioners in other office windows.

I spoke with Larry Higby about this situation, which I felt did not befit a man with my title. "Larry, I don't want to sound like a complainer, but I'm embarrassed to invite anyone to my office for a meeting, it's such a dump. Also it's sometimes hard to concentrate, listening to the urinals flush all day, since you've got me right beside the men's room."

"It's only temporary," he said. He agreed to have the walls painted and some decent furnishings delivered, but added a teaser: "Bob hasn't decided where he wants to put you yet." Then he dangled "possibilities" before me — nice big offices of people Haldeman might move out in order to move me in. I did not have to be told what was happening. I was being tested and my performance would determine what I would get. I was at the bottom of the ladder, and instinctively I began to climb.

For a thousand days I would serve as counsel to the President. I soon learned that to make my way upward, into a position of confidence and influence, I had to travel downward through factional power plays, corruption, and finally outright crimes. Although I would be rewarded for diligence, true advancement would come from doing those things which built a common bond of trust — or guilt — between me and my superiors. In the Nixon White House, these upward and downward paths diverged, yet joined, like prongs of a tuning fork pitched to a note of expediency. Slowly, steadily, I would climb toward the moral abyss of the President's inner circle until I finally fell in it, thinking I had made it to the top just as I began to realize I had actually touched bottom.

F EW PRESIDENTIAL ADMINIS-
trations have been free of scandal. While presidents themselves are not often implicated, one
or more presidential aides invariably
get themselves into trouble because
of conduct that the press and other
outside critics perceive to be an abuse
of their position and power. Even the
most minor indiscretions are grist for
the political mill, as investigative reporters seek to cash in on their scoops,
and political opponents strive for as-
cendancy.

Presidents largely determine the
ethical tone of their administrations.
Although most presidents have ad-
hered to the highest ethical standards
and have expected their aides to do
likewise, at least one major scandal has
accompanied most modern presidencies. Presidential style and personality
determine to a considerable extent the
way in which the White House con-
fronts and deals with the reality of
scandal. Whether or not presidents
stand by their accused aides often depends upon White House politics, an
important part of which is the president's need for loyal and trusted advisers. A president faces the most difficult dilemma when the subject of a
scandal is a long-time associate who
has remained loyal to him throughout
his political career.

The following selection depicts the
different styles of modern presidents
from Franklin D. Roosevelt to Ronald
Reagan in dealing with their staffs and
cabinet members. The character of the
president, and his relationship with his
aides and top administration officials
can go a long way in determining
whether or not scandal will arise in the
first place, and if it does what the outcome will be.

19 David Wise
WHY THE PRESIDENT'S MEN STUMBLE

Almost unnoticed by official Washington, the Republican National
Committee recently hired Richard V. Allen as its foreign policy and national security adviser. Allen, the former assistant to the president for
national security affairs, remains a consultant to the presidential advisory board on foreign intelligence. He is also a "distinguished fellow" of
the Heritage Foundation, a conservative research institution with close
ties to the Reagan administration.

For all of these august titles, Allen, at forty-six, is now a man on the
periphery of power. He was forced out last January in the first scandal
of the Reagan White House, a $1,000 "misunderstanding" that arose

From the *New York Times Magazine,* 18 July 1982. © 1982 by The New York Times
Company. Reprinted by permission.

when three visiting Japanese tried to hand the cash to Nancy Reagan after an interview Allen helped to arrange.

While the reasons that presidential advisers get into trouble vary widely, they may involve lack of judgment (often the case), outright larceny (rare), and past activities that come to light after an official reaches the White House (fairly frequent).

Ironically, in Richard Allen's departure was sown the seeds of the stunning resignation of Alexander M. Haig, Jr. as secretary of state six months later. Haig got rid of a rival when Allen left, but as part of the shuffle, the power of the president's national security adviser was restored to its traditional level. Allen had reported to presidential counselor Edwin Meese III. Allen's successor, William P. Clark, Jr., a former Haig aide, reports directly to President Reagan. And, by most accounts, Clark's growing power was a key factor in Haig's decision to quit.

Other members of President Reagan's inner circle have recently been the focus of embarrassing allegations:

A federal special prosecutor found "insufficient credible evidence" to indict Secretary of Labor Raymond J. Donovan or to link him to organized-crime figures. A key witness in the inquiry was found murdered in a car trunk in lower Manhattan, leaving an untidy loose end to the affair that is still under investigation by the Justice Department and the Federal Bureau of Investigation. President Reagan has declared that he would "stick with" Mr. Donovan, but for how long is a matter of much conjecture.

Attorney General William French Smith, perhaps with one eye on a Supreme Court seat, decided to give back a $50,000 "severance payment" from a California company and to limit his tax deductions on two controversial drilling deals to the cash he actually invested.

Joseph W. Canzeri, who was supposed to be a presidential trouble-shooter, himself got into trouble when it was disclosed that he had bought a town house with $400,000 borrowed from Laurance S. Rockefeller and Donald M. Koll, a California developer, neither of whom seemed to require any immediate interest payments. Canzeri, who was a deputy assistant to the president, also submitted expense claims for the same trips to both the federal government and the Republican National Committee. (The Justice Department later absolved Canzeri on both counts, and he reimbursed the government for his trips.) When the storm broke, Canzeri, an old political hand who had worked for Nelson A. Rockefeller for seventeen years, knew what to do and resigned instantly.

Few modern presidents have been immune from staff troubles. Scandals, conflict-of-interest, and ethics cases involving White House aides have occurred with remarkable frequency since World War II. Of the eight postwar presidents, only John F. Kennedy and Gerald R. Ford, neither of whom served full terms, escaped major scandal among their closest advisers.

Why does it happen? Why do men at the pinnacle of power, presumably chosen because of their sure-footed political skills, regularly commit errors of judgment that embarrass the presidents they serve? Errors that at a minimum cause damaging publicity, or at worst lead to resignation, dismissal, or even prison.

On a quiet Saturday afternoon, James A. Baker III, chief of staff to President Reagan, and possibly the second most powerful man in America, sits in his large corner office in the White House, talking very softly and with surprising directness about the Richard Allen episode, and the dilemma such cases pose for a president.

As scandals go, the affair was somewhat unusual. Allen had, after all, been cleared of any misconduct by both the Justice Department and an internal White House investigation. Why, then, was he forced to walk the plank? Because the president or Mrs. Reagan had been embarrassed? Because he performed poorly on the National Security Council? Because he scrapped too much with Al Haig?

"I'd have to say it was probably a combination of those factors," Baker replies. But most important was "the political damage to the president. And the likelihood that the damage would continue well into the future."

"The president," continues Baker, "feels very strongly that you have to bend over backward to be fair. A career, a man's life, and reputation hangs in the balance. He also believes that you don't toss somebody over when he's being investigated. A president is really put to a choice of tossing somebody over the side and being inherently unfair, or taking the political damage that will result from not doing anything."

"It became clear to me that it wasn't going to subside," Baker says. "And the good of the president, and the good of the presidency, has to prevail whether someone's done something wrong or not."

In examining why the president's men fall from grace, one could, of course, begin with ethical or moral lapses by presidents themselves. Warren G. Harding experienced the joy of sex in the White House coat closet. Dwight D. Eisenhower accepted many thousands of dollars worth of equipment, livestock, and trees as gifts for his farm in Gettysburg, Pennsylvania. John F. Kennedy apparently shared the favors of a woman with a Mafia figure who was trying to assassinate Fidel Castro for the Central Intelligence Agency. Richard Nixon was an unindicted co-conspirator who accepted a presidential pardon from his successor, Gerald Ford, for all federal crimes that he had "committed or may have committed" during Watergate. And President and Mrs. Reagan have been criticized for the more than $30,000 in gifts they have accepted since coming to the White House.

These cases — along with Spiro T. Agnew's alleged acceptance of more than $100,000 in bribes from Maryland contractors while governor and vice-president, which forced him to resign as vice-president — are fascinating, but they do not necessarily shed a great deal of light on the problem.

However, from extensive conversations with present White House aides, former presidential advisers — including some who were central figures in scandals — leading presidential scholars and present and former Washington correspondents, a fairly cohesive set of possible answers does emerge. Five factors recurred most often in the discussions: the tendency of power to cloud judgment, the effect of professional and personal backgrounds, the confusion created by a double standard of morality in government and in the private sector, the level of scrutiny focused on the White House, and the example set by the president himself.

"You sit next to the Sun King," says Jack Valenti, a former aide to President Lyndon B. Johnson," and you bask in his rays, and you have those three magic words, 'the president wants.' And all of a sudden you have power unimagined by you before you sat in that job. And if you don't watch out, you begin to believe that it is your splendid intellect, your charm, and your insights into the human condition that give you all this power. You can go to the highest reaches of this government and abroad and cause an otherwise strong man to blink. That really has an effect on you."

"And even people who would like to discipline themselves are sometimes caught off guard," Valenti adds. "The arrogance sinks deeper into their veins than they think possible. What it does after a while is breed a kind of insularity that keeps you from being subject to the same fits of insecurity that most human beings have. Because you very seldom are ever turned down. You are lionized in Washington. There are stories in *Newsweek* and *Time* about how important you are. I'm telling you, this is like mainlining heroin. And while you are exercising it, it is so blinding and dazzling that you forget, literally forget, that it is borrowed and transitory power."

Joseph A. Califano, Jr., another former Johnson aide, remembers the day that work was completed on LBJ's first legislative program in 1965. The president told his cabinet that he could not personally coordinate every single issue. "And I'm just sitting there against the wall in the cabinet room, and Johnson says that Joe Califano's going to do this and when he speaks, that's my voice you hear. You know, that's fairly heady for a thirty-four-year-old kid from Brooklyn."

Johnson's former press secretary, George E. Reedy, has compared the executive mansion to a monarch's court. "After a while," he says, "it's very easy to get the impression that the whole world should revolve around you." Reedy, now a professor of journalism at Marquette University in Milwaukee, adds: "It's only derivative power, but that doesn't matter. Anyone that you call in the entire executive branch of the government is just going to be as respectful and subservient; it's incredible."

Joseph Laitin, who survived in the White House and in other senior government public affairs posts during six administrations, agrees that "a chemical change seems to come over you in that place, from the president on down to the messenger boy. A driver told me once that during the Eisenhower administration, one of the secretaries at the White House had to stay late, so she sent an Army sergeant in a White House car out to her house in the suburbs to turn on the lights so her cat wouldn't be lonely."

The privileges that go with a job in the White House add to the sense of power. Dom Bonafede, chief political correspondent for the *National Journal*, stresses the euphoric effect of the perquisites. "They have a car and chauffeur, if they're high enough up; the use of a swimming pool, and a tennis court, the presidential box at the Kennedy Center. They have their own mess, where they're served by Filipino stewards. They can requisition priceless paintings from government art galleries. They can even order furniture made for their office — they have their own cabinetmakers. After a while they think they're invulnerable, untouchable."

Typically, White House aides are young, and often have no administrative experience to prepare them for the vast responsibility they are suddenly called on to exercise. More often than not, they come straight from the campaign trail to the executive mansion. And the skills that may elect a president are not necessarily the same ones needed to run the government.

"The thing about the White House," emphasizes Robert J. Donovan, author of books about Presidents Truman, Eisenhower, and Kennedy, "is that every four or eight years you bring in a raft of amateurs to run the country. Can you imagine if IBM did that?"

In the Nixon White House, for example, John D. Ehrlichman had been a Seattle zoning lawyer, H. R. Haldeman had been an advertising man, and Ronald Ziegler, also a former ad man, had once been a tour guide on the Jungle Cruise boat at Disneyland.

Professor Thomas E. Cronin of Colorado College, a perceptive student of the American presidency, suggests that the kinds of people who go into public life and make it to the White House may also have a bearing on the problem. "You have to be a risk taker. You have to have a lot of ambition. Usually, you have to be someone with fund-raising experience. And it's very difficult to separate fund raising from bribery. There's a very thin line." Cronin, a Democratic candidate for Congress in Colorado this year, also points out that "people involved in campaigns deal with the brutal realities, the sleazier aspects of our system. Often, people in politics have low pay and high expenses. And the temptations are high at the White House."

There is, too, the double standard of morality. "If we were to get a true norm of behavior of people similarly situated in the private sector," says Nelson W. Polsby, professor of political science at the University of California at Berkeley, "we would not view the political behavior of White House assistants as so deviant from that of people in other segments of society."

Robert Donovan agrees. "Look at the whole history of the human race," he says. "There has always been corruption. Corruption in business dwarfs corruption in government. Every year, white-collar crime runs into hundreds of millions of dollars. Take local zoning — my God. If you except something like Watergate, the White House may be quite clean."

Another veteran Washington journalist, James Deakin, who reported on numerous scandals as the longtime White House correspondent of the *St. Louis Post-Dispatch,* says: "You run into particular trouble with the businessmen. They've been running corporations, so it's inevitable that an awful lot of them come here and try to run the government like a business."

If a double standard of morality is applied in the case of public officials, who may be pilloried for behavior that would not seem out of place on Main Street or in the corporate suite, that is perhaps as it should be. Voters expect public officials to shed their private standards of morality when they enter the White House.

The intense level of press scrutiny under which presidential advisers operate may be another hazard. If a mid-level official in the Agriculture Department is wined and dined by a lobbyist in one of Washington's plush K Street restaurants, hardly anyone will notice, or care. But if Ed Meese goes for a moonlight sail on a lobbyist's yacht, it may well be noticed, and reported.

Although there has been more emphasis on "investigative reporting" since Watergate, the fact is that investigative reporting has been around much longer than the use of that term. It was, after all, a reporter, Paul Y. Anderson of the *St. Louis Post-Dispatch,* who helped to force the reopening, after five years, of the Teapot Dome case, which sent a former cabinet member, Interior Secretary Albert B. Fall, to jail, and won Anderson a Pulitzer Prize.

Despite the Watergate scandal, we may not be living in a particularly corrupt political era. The nineteenth century — with its robber barons, the Crédit Mobilier financial thievery, the Whiskey Ring liquor tax frauds, and the other scandals of the Grant administration — was not a time of overwhelming ethical purity. But in the climate of post-Watergate morality, there may be an increased sensitivity to scandal on the part of the press and the public. There are more people peering in the fishbowl. And, to some extent, the game has new rules. The Ethics in Government Act of 1978, for example, requires senior government officials to make annual financial disclosure statements. Another provision of the same law provides for the appointment of a special prosecutor, or at least a preliminary investigation at the drop of an allegation.

Above all else, the president sets the tone. A Lyndon Johnson who, whatever his own flaws, rides herd tightly on his staff, may have less trouble than a Harry Truman, whose fierce loyalty and benign attitude toward his aides may be unappreciated by the electorate.

"The White House staff is what the president wants it to be," declares John Ehrlichman, counselor to President Nixon. "The Nixon White House was destroyed because Richard Nixon involved himself in Watergate."

Ehrlichman says he has no knowledge of whether Nixon knew about the break-in at the Democratic National Committee headquarters beforehand. But another former senior Nixon aide, who prefers to remain anonymous, says he has little doubt about it: "No way would anybody ever think of doing anything at all, even feeding King Timahoe, without checking with the president."

Alexander P. Butterfield, the presidential aide who revealed the existence of the Watergate tapes, testified that Nixon concerned himself with whether or not salad should be served at state dinners and "whether or not the Secret Service would salute during 'The Star-Spangled Banner,' and sing." "The president was 100 percent in charge," Butterfield concluded.

One obvious reason why White House staff scandals are, by and large, a postwar phenomenon is that prior to the administration of Franklin D. Roosevelt the White House staff, in the sense that it operates today, simply did not exist.

George Washington had exactly one staff assistant, his nephew, Lawrence Lewis, whose salary he paid out of his own pocket. After Washington, other presidents had only one or two secretaries, usually relatives, also paid from personal funds. Not until Andrew Jackson moved into the White House was a government clerk assigned to assist the president.

By the beginning of the twentieth century, the White House payroll had begun to expand, but the staffs were still mostly clerks, file managers, and secretaries. With the coming of Franklin Roosevelt's New Deal, the picture changed measurably. "The president needs help," a study committee headed by Louis Brownlow, a public administration expert, wrote in 1937. And these White House aides, the report said in a phrase that was to become famous, should have "a passion for anonymity."

Two years later, FDR established the Executive Office of the President (EOP), an umbrella agency that today includes such key presidential units as the National Security Council and the Office of Management and Budget. Within the Executive Office is the smaller White House Office, also established in 1939. This is the group of men and women, mostly housed on the three floors of the West Wing, that is usually referred to as "the White House staff." Under Ronald Reagan, the EOP has 1,520 employees and an annual budget of $91,624,000. Of this total, the White House staff numbers 314 and costs $19,652,000 a year.

No major staff scandals surfaced under FDR, who kept everyone on a very tight leash. One of Roosevelt's brain trusters, the Washington attorney James H. Rowe, Jr., recalls: "Once, FDR saw my name in the paper, in a story saying I'd been at a cocktail party. 'If I see your name in the paper much more,' he told me, 'you'll need a new job.' "

Rowe, who was twenty-eight when he went to work in the White House in 1938, thinks youth had something to do with the New Deal's relative purity. "They were mostly young, idealistic people and they didn't know how to steal. People weren't interested in money. I don't even remember being offered anything."

"Another reason," Rowe says, "was Harold Ickes's goons. They were all over the place," toiling for Ickes in his dual capacity as Interior Security and Public Works Administrator. "Once, a top lawyer for Ickes found that his mail had been opened by Ickes's security men. It was a dividend check from AT&T. The lawyer was outraged, but Ickes said, 'Well, we wanted to know why you were getting mail from big corporations'!"

"There were three Democratic national committeemen who came here and opened up law practices," Rowe recalls. "Roosevelt announced publicly one day that they'd all resigned from the national committee. They hadn't! But then two of them did. FDR watched that sort of thing, but there wasn't much of it."

FDR's staff had at least one blot on its record, however. It centered on Louis McHenry Howe, the gnomelike former newspaperman who served as Roosevelt's secretary. Frank Freidel, author of a multivolume biography of Roosevelt, recalled "the Civilian Conservation Corps' 'mess kit' scandal early in the New Deal. Howe had arranged with some old friend of Roosevelt's — not a very savory character — to sell 200,000 mess kits to the CCC boys at a very high price. But there wasn't a nickel in it for Howe.''

Gifts to White House aides — sometimes linked to official favors by the recipients, sometimes not — have frequently figured in the troubles that have caused scandal in the president's house. Perhaps the quintessential gift taker was President Truman's jovial, poker-playing friend and aide, Major General Harry H. Vaughan, who indelibly stamped the word "crony" on the history of the Truman administration.

"Vaughan and Truman met as young lieutenants during World War I," says Robert Donovan. "Vaughan was not in any sense a corrupt man. But the White House was not the place for him. He was used to doing favors for people when Truman was vice-president, and he carried that mentality over into the White House."

"Vaughan got in trouble," says Donovan, "because a friend visiting the White House overheard him talking on the telephone about Mrs. Truman's problems with food spoilage out in Independence. Next thing you know, seven freezers were being shipped. Vaughan got one, for the White House Mess, and so did Mrs. Truman." Vaughan kept a freezer for himself and the rest went to other Truman administration officials.

Professor Richard E. Neustadt of Harvard University, who worked for a time in the Truman White House as a budget aide and later as a special assistant, may be the only eminent scholar of the presidency to have actually eaten a meal prepared from Harry Vaughan's freezer: "Early in the Truman administration, they organized a little lunchroom for the staff down in the basement of the West Wing. Vaughan talked some messenger at the White House into serving as chef. They had a crummy old stove and used to serve terrible meals. Vaughan went around scrounging free, cast-off equipment for the galley. Somebody gave him a freezer. After that — great scandal."

To the Republicans, at least, the freezers became the symbol of the Truman administration, along with the $8,540 royal pastel mink coat that a Washington lawyer, Colonel Joseph Rosenbaum, bestowed upon a White House stenographer, Lauretta Young, whose husband, an influence peddler, specialized in obtaining loans for businessmen from the Reconstruction Finance Corporation.

Gifts were also the undoing of Harry Truman's appointments secretary, Matthew J. Connelly, who served six months in a federal prison after accepting a $3,600 oil royalty, a topcoat, and two suits from the lawyer representing a St. Louis shoe manufacturer, for whom Connelly intervened in a tax case. In all, nine Truman administration officials served prison sentences.

"The Truman scandals were serious," says Robert Donovan, "but not even Truman's worst enemies ever connected him with any of the scandals. After all these years, one is confident Truman was an honest politician. He never had any money."

Dwight Eisenhower promised to clean up "the mess in Washington." But during his first presidential campaign, the "Nixon Fund" story broke, revealing that a group of California businessmen had contributed $18,235 to pay Nixon's political expenses as a senator. Nixon went on national television and delivered his celebrated "Checkers" speech, declaring: "Pat doesn't have a mink coat. But she does have a respectable Republican cloth coat."

None of the string of scandals that ensued in the Eisenhower administration reached directly into the White House until Sherman Adams, the president's chief of staff, got into trouble. Adams, a former governor of New Hampshire, was generally portrayed as a man of granitelike integrity, the last person who would be mixed up with a wheeler-dealer textile manufacturer like Bernard Goldfine. So the shock was even greater when it was revealed that he had accepted a $700 vicuña coat from Goldfine and intervened on his behalf with two federal regulatory agencies who were after Goldfine for, among other sins, mislabeling his wool (Goldfine's vicuña contained nylon). Although Adams had accepted more than $6,000 in gifts and hospitality from Goldfine, it was the coat that remained fixed in the public's mind.

In testimony before the House subcommittee investigating the case, Adams conceded that he could have acted "a little more prudently." The next day, Eisenhower defended his staff chief and declared, "I need him." Harry Vaughan graciously offered Adams the use of his freezer in which to store the vicuña coat over the warm summer months. Adams hung on until fall, but when the Republicans lost the Senate and gubernatorial elections and two of three House seats in Maine that September, Adams had to go.

John F. Kennedy's White House was, more or less, scandal-free, although Frank D. Reeves, a special assistant to the president, was forced to resign when it was disclosed that he had been billed by the District of Columbia for $741.90, in delinquent taxes.

According to Meyer Feldman, a Washington attorney who handled highly sensitive economic matters as an assistant to President Kennedy, a very big contributor to the Kennedy campaign complained incessantly about the extended antitrust investigation of his company by the Justice Department under Robert Kennedy. Feldman finally arranged a face-to-face meeting with the president. At the conclusion of the campaign contributor's argument, Feldman says, President Kennedy looked at the man and said, 'Mr. ———, there's one thing wrong with this administration. We don't have an attorney general we can fix.' "

Despite Lyndon Johnson's reputation as a wheeler-dealer, and his involvement with Robert G. (Bobby) Baker — who went to prison for crimes committed while a Senate aide to LBJ — the Johnson White House was considered generally free of scandal except for the Walter Jenkins case. Last October, however, an article in the *Atlantic* charged that Johnson, as a congressman and vice-president, accepted "envelopes stuffed with cash," which he used to help the campaigns of other politicians, and as president handled business affairs that were supposed to be in a blind trust. When the author of the article, Robert Caro, was criticized for not documenting his charges, he said he would do so in the first volume of a book about Johnson to be published in a year's time.

Jack Valenti thinks he knows why the Johnson administration fared as well as it did: "Johnson bullied, humiliated, harassed his assistants, saying, 'You never ran for sheriff and all these people are courting you. By God, they want you — Valenti, Moyers, Califano — because they think you've got my ear. You think it's because they like you? They don't give a ——— about you, but they damn sure give a ——— about what you can do through me, so by God, you'd better be careful.'

"Nobody in the Johnson White House could ever make an appointment for anyone at Treasury, Defense, or the Justice Department. He used to say, 'Remember Matt Connelly, remember Matt Connelly. One day you'll make an appointment over in Defense and the ——— will turn out to be a fraud and you'll be up before some Senate committee answering questions, and you won't be able to answer them right and they'll put you in jail. By God, I'm not going to have it, and I'm going to fire your ——— or anybody else's that ever violates that rule.' As a result, we were frightened to death of something like that."

LBJ's dire warnings apparently worked. The one exception was Walter Jenkins, who was arrested on a morals charge at a YMCA one block from the White House in the midst of the 1964 presidential campaign. Valenti was in New York with Johnson at the Walforf Astoria when press secretary George Reedy called with the doleful news. "The president was very stony-faced," recalls Valenti. "He said, 'George, get Walter's resignation immediately.' Now, you have to understand, this man was like a brother to Johnson; he'd been with him for twenty-five years. But he did not hesitate. Because he was going to protect the presidency."

The trouble that Jenkins, married and the father of six children, got into was, of course, of a different nature from the conflict-of-interest or corruption cases that felled other White House aides.

There is an epilogue to that story that is not generally known. Johnson, Valenti says, "never saw Walter while he was president, after that. But the minute he got out of the White House he resumed his long friendship with Jenkins."

Under Richard Nixon, who found it necessary to proclaim that he was not a crook, the White House became involved in a continuing scandal that ultimately consumed and destroyed his presidency. There were enemies lists, wiretaps, break-ins and buggings, as well as obstruction of justice, perjury, political spying, forgery, and other high and low crimes and misdemeanors. These were the men, Senator Lowell P. Weicker, Jr. said at the start of the Senate Watergate hearings, "who almost stole America." An astonishing ten top White House aides marched off to jail before it was over: H. R. Haldeman, John D. Ehrlichman, Charles W. Colson, John W. Dean III, E. Howard Hunt, Jr., G. Gordon Liddy, Dwight L. Chapin, Egil Krogh, Jr., Jeb Stuart Magruder, and Herbert L. Porter. And Richard Nixon became the first American president forced to resign his office in utter disgrace.

Gerald Ford's staff was not around long enough to get into much trouble, and its members were presumably a bit cautious, in the wake of Watergate. But trouble was not long in coming to Jimmy Carter's White House. The tangled and dubious banking practices of his close friend and budget director, Bert Lance, were making headlines by the summer of 1977. Most of Lance's questionable activities had taken place before he joined the administration, but by defending Lance instead of dismissing him outright, Carter compounded his difficulties. Lance did not resign until that September.

The embarrassments continued. Three months after Lance left, guests at a dinner party attended by Egyptian Ambassador Ashraf Ghorbal and his wife reported that presidential assistant Hamilton Jordan had peered down Mrs. Ghorbal's cleavage and remarked that he had always wanted to "see the pyramids." Jordan denied the allegation, but soon afterward the columnist Rudy Maxa wrote in the *Washington Post Magazine* that Jordan had spit Amaretto and cream down the front of a young woman's blouse at a Washington singles bar, a report that led the House Minority Leader, Representative Robert H. Michel, Republican of Illinois, to comment that the Carter administration had "gone from great expectations to great expectorations." The Carter White House put out thirty-three pages of documents in an effort to refute the story.

Then Dr. Peter G. Bourne, Carter's principal adviser on drugs and narcotics, had to quit because he wrote a false name on a drug prescription for his assistant, Ellen J. Metsky. And special prosecutors found insufficient evidence to act on separate allegations that Jordan and Tim Kraft, another White House aide, had used cocaine, which both denied. The cases took place against an obbligato of murky charges about the financial operations of the Carter family peanut warehouse and, of course, "Billy gate," which involved $220,000 in "loans" to the president's brother, Billy, from the government of Libya.

Which brings us back up to President Reagan and Richard Allen. In an interview with this writer, Allen charged that "the real reasons" he was forced out were "to eliminate my views" on foreign policy. He said that he and Alexander Haig had "important and enduring policy differences, reflecting on the one hand one fellow's determination to uphold the mandate on which the president of the United States was elected, versus having that mandate supplanted."

Allen admits to "human error" in handling the $1,000 that the Japanese visitors attempted to give to Mrs. Reagan. Allen says he "intercepted" the money and told a secretary to turn it over to "appropriate officials" but that she forgot. "I suppose, with 20/20 hindsight, you could have given it back." But he didn't, and he was out. And, like a character in a Kafka novel, he was never really sure what the charges against him were.

In fairness to Allen, almost no one in the White House, even now, fully understands the complex, overlapping laws and regulations governing acceptance, or handling, of gifts. In general, small gifts are all right and large ones are not, but how big is small? Things were easier in the old days when there were no size limits. Calvin Coolidge accepted a hippopotamus from Liberia.

"If you want to get along, go along," House Speaker Sam Rayburn was fond of saying. It is perhaps in the nature of politics for the players to go along, to engage in a wide variety of favors, back scratching, and mutual aid and admiration. In politics, a "contract" refers not to a written agreement but to an understanding to use one's influence to help a political friend; both sides know that the favor may have to be returned sometime. It is easy enough for political operators to carry that attitude into the White House where it could cause them major difficulties.

No doubt, there are other reasons why presidential appointees continue to get into trouble. Perhaps one is the national appetite for scandal. Both press and public seem to relish the fall from grace of a high official. This is particularly true in the nation's capital: Washington loves a victim.

Americans, observes Professor Cronin, are proud of their country but "hate government and politicians; always have. I think Americans yearn for flaws in politicians. So when scandals break, they say, 'There, that's just what I expected.' There's a great distrust of politicians. It's one of the reasons we designed a system of checks and balances. If men were angels, we would need no government."

THE
CONGRESS

Chapter Five

Congress is a fascinating amalgam of individual characters, personalities, and styles, which help to shape the institution. Personality is particularly important as it affects congressional leadership, both of party leaders and of committee chairmen. Different personality types in positions of power within Congress develop contrasting styles that influence the way Congress operates. For example, the Senate under the majority leadership of Lyndon B. Johnson operated very differently than it did under Mike Mansfield. Johnson's active-negative character was evident in the Senate as in the White House. His personality compelled him to seek control over the Senate, which he managed through knowledge of the strengths, weaknesses, and needs of his colleagues, skill in manipulation of institutional procedures, and an extraordinary ability to persuade others. Each senator became a challenge to Johnson, who sought personal loyalty above all else. The aggressive and dominating style of Lyndon Johnson as majority leader of the Senate was similar to, but much more flamboyant than that of his mentor, House Speaker Sam Rayburn, and it stemmed from different personal needs.

In sharp contrast to Johnson's style as majority leader was the style of Mike Mansfield, who was elected majority leader in January 1961, and served until his retirement at the end of the Ninety-fourth Congress in 1976. Mansfield's style was, to say the least, more muted than Johnson's. He treated each senator with great respect and as an equal. No attempt at a personal cult of leadership was evident during Mansfield's tenure. Johnson was highly effective as a personal leader, whereas Mansfield's effectiveness was as a team player. The contrasting personalities of Johnson and Mansield go a long way toward explaining differences in Senate operation during their periods of leadership. Under Mansfield, senators were far freer to pursue their own legislative interests without fear of retaliation if they happened to disagree with the majority leader. Mansfield's style became the model for his successor, Robert Byrd. Howard Baker too led by consensus, not by command, in a Senate that would no longer tolerate LJB's system of unilateral control.

Personality is as important in the House as in the Senate in determining who runs for positions of party leadership, and what their styles of leadership will be. Sam Rayburn, Speaker of the House for seventeen years, enforced discipline in the House. Like Lyndon Johnson in the Senate, Sam Rayburn knew every member of the House, their constituencies, and their needs and aspirations. He was able to use this information to consolidate his power as Speaker. Again like Johnson, Rayburn operated on a highly personal basis in the House. The House was his constituency, as the Senate was Johnson's, and he did not hesitate to involve Republicans as well as Democrats in his decisions as Speaker. The election of John McCormack as Speaker of the House in 1962 brought about profound changes, primarily because of the contrasting personalities of Rayburn and McCormack. Robert L. Peabody says:

> Peaceful succession brings on more incremental change, but the impact of such *different personalities* as Rayburn and McCormack on the Office of the Speaker was considerable. McCormack's style was both more institutional and partisan than Rayburn's. He called more meetings to discuss legislative strategy and involved the Majority Leader and Whip to a much greater extent than Rayburn did. . . .
>
> The telephone was one of McCormack's most effective weapons — "I'd call the Devil if I thought it would do any good." In contrast, Rayburn operated on a more independent and personal basis. He preferred the intimacy and informality of after-the-session gatherings of the "Board of Education." The Whip organization was used less frequently and Rayburn almost never called a party caucus beyond the opening meeting.[1]

Both Rayburn and McCormack, although differing in their personalities and styles, provided effective leadership to the House. Carl Albert, of Oklahoma, became Speaker in 1971, and his personality and style were criticized as weak and ineffective. Peabody points out that "One reason he easily advanced to the Speakership was summed up in a widely affirmed statement — 'Nobody's mad at Carl.' "[2] Being a "nice guy" is usually a reflection of inability to make hard decisions that inevitably antagonize others.

After an extensive analysis of congressional leadership, Peabody concluded:

---

[1] Robert L. Peabody, *Leadership in Congress* (Boston: Little, Brown, 1976), p. 309. Italics added.

[2] Ibid., p. 155.

Of the twenty variables highlighted in this analysis, the most pervasive and continuing influence upon leadership's selection for party office has been exerted by the personality and skill of the candidate and, especially, of the incumbent. Every leader in Congress, as in other organizations, brings to office a unique set of characteristics: age, ambition, education, health, personal skills, prior political and professional experience — in sum, a personality. Not only does this personality affect the opportunities he may have to obtain a leadership position, they also, in part, influence the extent to which he can maintain office and perhaps even alter the scope and potential of a given party position. A leader's personality, his strengths and liabilities, also is the single most important variable that affects his ability to withstand or succumb to a challenge.[3]

Personality is also a factor in the selection of committees and in the functioning of committee chairmen. The Senate Government Operations Committee (renamed the Governmental Affairs Committee in 1977), under the chairmanship of Senator Joseph McCarthy from 1953 until 1955 operated very differently than it has at any other time. The personality and the style of Senator McCarthy were responsible for this difference. The Senate Foreign Relations Committee under the chairmanship of Senator J. William Fulbright from 1959 until his defeat in 1974 was quite different than it became in 1975 under the chairmanship of Senator John Sparkman of Alabama.

South Carolina Republican Strom Thurmond runs the Senate Judiciary Committee in an entirely different way than did his predecessor, Massachusetts Senator Edward Kennedy.

Weak chairmen, strong chairmen, chairmen who seek the limelight, and those who use chairmanships for "grand-standing," all have contrasting personalities and styles. The committee system is an important institution of Congress, and the way it functions largely depends on the personalities of committee members. Committees are used to advance the goals of their chairmen and key members, who are attempting to gain power and status within and without Congress. Thus the legislative work of committees is often undertaken as much to serve personal ambition as to respond to constituents' needs; legislators may use the committee hearing and investigation process for personal aggrandizement, as well as for legislation.

Beyond Capitol Hill personality is also a key factor in determining the way in which representatives and senators relate to their constituents. Personal choice and preferences determine the amount and kinds of electoral responsibilities that will be delegated to staff, how much

[3] Ibid., p. 498.

time a candidate will spend in his or her district, the nature of constituent contacts — whether in large or small groups, or one-on-one — and what type of media will be emphasized. Political campaigning always reflects the character and style of the candidate.

N EW JERSEY SENATOR BILL Bradley has the right stuff. He was a basketball star at Princeton and a member of the United States Olympic team, and after graduation in 1955, a Rhodes Scholar for two years. He then joined the New York Knicks, becoming their star player from 1967 to 1977. As a professional athlete, he refused commercial endorsements and wrote a probing book about his professional basketball career.

Always fascinated with politics, Bradley decided to change careers in 1977 and aimed his sights at no less than a seat in the United States Senate. The popular Republican Senator Clifford Case had occupied the seat for twenty-four years, winning by large majorities. But the liberal Case, as he grew older, devoted an increasing amount of time to his Washington career and gradually lost touch with his Republican constituents, who were

becoming more and more conservative. Happily for Bradley, Case lost the Republican primary election in 1978 to Jeffrey Bell, a conservative who had adopted supply-side economics, which became the cornerstone of Ronald Reagan's economic program. Bradley's celebrity status combined with a highly effective electioneering style to give him a decisive win over Bell of 56 to 43 percent.

Bradley's victory launched his Washington career, but he knew, as do all freshmen senators and representatives, that he could not rest on his laurels. To guarantee electoral success in the future he would have to develop and maintain an effective "homestyle."[1] Homestyle refers to "presentation of self" — the way in which members of Congress personally relate to their constituents. Senator Bill Bradley has developed an open and effective homestyle, which is portrayed in the following selection.

20 John McPhee
SENATOR BILL BRADLEY: OPEN MAN

Nine P.M. on the boardwalk at Seaside Heights, New Jersey. Against the black sky, lights revolve on wheels and whirling rides. Half a block west, off the edge of the glow, New Jersey's senior United States senator is coaching two college-age sisters, each of whom holds a placard saying "MEET SENATOR BRADLEY."

[1]Richard F. Fenno, Jr., *Homestyle* (Boston: Little Brown & Co., 1978). Fenno uses the term homestyle in reference to members of the House, but it can be applied with equal validity to the Senate as well.

"You go out in front about twenty yards, stay apart, and funnel them in," he says, and the three step into the light.

"Hey, Bill!"

"Hey, big Bill!"

"Keep it up, Senator. You're doing a good job."

The device is as effective as it is simple. The girls are creating a V in the human river, and it is working like an eel trap.

"Man, you are tall! You looked small when you played for the Knicks."

"I *was* small when I played for the Knicks."

He weighs two hundred and five pounds, up zero from his weight in college. Which is not to imply a continuum. A year ago, his jowls were competing with the gross national product.

"Good job, Bill."

"Good to see you around, Senator."

"You've lost weight."

"I've lost about thirty pounds."

Senator Bradley has an athlete's contempt for exercise. He runs for office. To get rid of the thirty pounds, he developed the habit of eating lightly. He will work a twelve-hour day on half a sandwich and a cup of soup. Leaning forward as he walks — characteristically creating the impression that he is about to charge — he makes his way, shaking hands, from Shorty's Shish Kebab to Meat Ball City and on into the purview of the Arcade Skeeball. His haircut is fresh — a dark, rising wave in front, reliefmapping a bold headland flanked by a large bay. He wears a blue-and-white striped shirt with a button-down collar. His tie is brown and has small gold New Jerseys all over it like sea horses. His equine midriff is no bigger than it was when he played for the Knicks.

"Nice to meet you, Senator."

"Thank you. Where are you from?"

"Westfield. I go to Westfield High School. I had to write an essay about a fascinating American person, and I wrote about you."

"Did you get an A?"

"B-plus."

Generally speaking, middle-aged people in the crowd address him as Bill. Younger people call him Senator. Still younger people call him Bill. Nearly everyone is from New Jersey. Two out of three mention basketball.

A woman shakes his hand, turns to her several children, and says, "This is the next president. Remember what I said."

The next president reaches for another hand, in front of Sand Tropez. "Hello. Anything on your mind tonight?"

"Get teachers more money."

"Hello. How are you? Anything on your mind tonight?"

"What's going to happen in the Philippines?"

"There may be some changes; I don't know. I've long thought that we should move our bases to the Marianas, and not be beholden to a dictator."

"Senator Bradley! What a surprise! I just got a letter from you."

"Bill, Tom Berry. You may remember the name."

"Senator, my father met you the other night in the rest room at the Holiday Inn."

"Give me your autograph, please, like a good fella, Bill."

"Hey, I'm glad to meet you, Senator, but you gotta do something about the Philadelphia wage tax."

"Senator, the new auto-insurance rates are killing me. I've never had an accident and I pay nine hundred dollars a year for two cars."

"Senator, how do you feel about skateboards? Do you think skateboards should be allowed on the boardwalk?"

The question has arisen from a gentleman in short shorts who has recently become eligible to vote. Bradley is attentive to his arguments, which begin with the fact that he has invested forty dollars in the skateboard he holds in his hands. In this long day — in which the senator has covered nearly three hundred miles — officials, editors, and miscellaneous citizens have sought his views on toxic waste, the telephone company, public transportation in southern New Jersey, Medicare, Social Security, internal revenue, nuclear safety, a nuclear freeze, the MX missile, violence in Sri Lanka, New York sewage, the Strategic Petroleum Reserve, the qualifications of schoolteachers, federal aid to education, bilingual education, the Reagan way with women and blacks, the Middle East, Central America, health care for senior citizens, the deregulation of natural gas, food waste, and the fingerprinting of bus drivers, and now, at nine-thirty in the evening, this shirtless citizen before him has raised the only issue for which he has not been prepared: skateboards on the boardwalk. He does not evade the question. Placing a hand on the kid's shoulder, he says, "Sure."

The senator got up at seven in Denville, in Morris County, where he long ago hung his carpetbag, having been born and raised in Missouri, educated at Princeton and Oxford, and employed ten years in New York. (The carpetbag is not a mere figure of speech. It is a handsome and capacious carpetbag, full of New Jersey mementos, and it hangs by the front door.) After kissing his wife and six-year-old daughter, he took off in his car, heading south, remarking en route that this would be a varied day, for it would contain what he called structural settings, a constituent setting, a town meeting, and a walking town meeting.

Structural settings turned out to be newspapers, where he sat in small groups with circles of writers and editors, listened to their interests, and told them his own. "They tend not to be aware of what I'm absorbed with in Washington, so I visit them and tell them," he said as he approached Vineland, the agricultural epicenter of Cumberland County, below the Mason-Dixon Line. In Cumberland County, unemployment is at an exceptional level, the concerns of farming are uppermost in people's minds, and one could expect the conversation to dwell right there. In the offices of the Vineland *Times Journal*, he had scarcely sat down when, sure enough, Marvin Smith, editor of the editorial page, asked him what he thought might happen in the immediate future in Lebanon. This touched off a complex dialogue on foreign policy, during which Bradley said that he knew of no satisfactory answer to the question "Why are twelve hundred U.S. Marines functioning as city policemen in Beirut?" He suggested that American troops were too readily dispatched — "almost haphazardly, by reflex action" — to many foreign places, including, most emphatically, Central America, where the recent arrival of a force of twenty thousand to do "war exercises" in Honduras, some of them close to the Nicaraguan border, might "invite a wider involvement there."

Smith said, "Are we ever going to see your 14 percent tax?"

Bradley said he was hoping for 1985, with a preliminary resolution in 1984. To write a fair and simplified federal tax code has become one of his principal goals as a senator. In five years on the Finance Committee, he has seen three major tax bills go through Congress, and there have been six in the past ten years — each adding loopholes, and collectively raising the value of all loopholes to nearly three hundred billion dollars, in a tax code no less unfair than unintelligible. "Anyone might reasonably ask what is going on here," he said, and this is what he meant to try to do: For about four-fifths of all taxpayers, Bradley would lower the income-tax rate to 14 percent. For higher incomes, the percentage would rise to thirty. A family of four would pay no tax on an income below eleven thousand two hundred dollars. Corporate taxes would be reduced to a basic rate of 30 percent. "There's no free lunch," he observed. "You've got to give up loopholes to get lower rates." His fair-tax bill would close many dozens of loopholes, from the tax immunity of people working abroad to oil-depletion allowances to the rapid amortization of pollution-control equipment. Certain deductions would remain in effect, such as medical expenses, local property taxes, home-mortgage interest, charitable contributions, private retirement funds.

Someone said, "Isn't that a bit of a compromise with the idea of the tax?"

"I'm a political realist," said Bradley. "I'm not an academic. I didn't want to devise a perfect tax system. I wanted to devise one that would work." Numbers have been run that seem to show that "the fair tax would raise the same amount of revenue as current law." Meanwhile, equal incomes would be paying roughly equal taxes, and that was the point. Not only would the system be fairer but a lower tax rate would encourage more people to obey the law, to pay the nation its due, and thus would retrieve resources from the so-called underground economy.

Would the new law combat unemployment?

"I don't view the tax code as a creator of jobs. I view the tax code as a hurdle the private sector has to get over. The idea is to make that hurdle as low as possible. It is in the general interest to have a lower tax rate with fewer loopholes."

The subject changed to education and Bradley's assessment of the amount of federal aid. "Increased funding is needed from all levels of government for all levels of education," he said. "Let me just tell you, we need maximum investment in education, and that includes more than the kindergarten through twelfth grade we had when we were growing up. To adjust to the age of high technology, retraining schools are required for people of all ages." Earlier in the year, he had written an amendment to stop the cutting of federal aid to education, and it had passed the Senate eighty to twelve. He had written another amendment that restored a billion dollars. "The fact of the matter is" — he said now in Vineland — "computers cost more than slide rules."

Through time, Bradley has acquired some touches of the accents of New Jersey, where new cars are filled with un-let-it and one hears the shortest "a"s known to diction.

"When are you running again, Senator?"

"I run again in 1984. Tell me who my opponent is going to be."

"I don't see any sacrificial lambs around," said Marvin Smith.

Scarcely five years ago, when Bradley was a would-be candidate, people in New Jersey were saying that he was a nice guy but politics was for the politician — the adroit, experienced pro. Today, anyone who might oppose him is seen as a bleating creature on a slab.

"Would you accept the nomination for vice-president?"

"No."

"As time goes by, is basketball mentioned less? Is it going away?"

"In part, yes. In part, no. I had a great ten years in basketball. It was rewarding in various ways — and has been, frankly, in this job."

"When you were playing basketball, did you take muscle-building drugs?" an editor asked.

"Obviously not," muttered the low voice of a fly on the wall.

Now, more than an hour since the senator had arrived, Marvin Smith — gray haired and matter of fact — had a final subject he wanted to explore. "The casinos of Atlantic City have become a new economic force in New Jersey," he said. "They could turn their economic clout into political clout. Does this bother you?"

Bradley said, "Is there an assumption in your question?"

Smith said, "It's a harsh-type industry. In it, there is not much concern for human . . ."

"I think I know what you are driving at," said Bradley. "This is what the Casino Control Commission is all about."

"Would you take a campaign contribution from a casino?"

"No."

The senator departed, saying, "When you have questions, call whenever you like. You can always find me, even though I don't have an eight-hundred number."

Senior senators tend to have licence plates that say "U.S. SENATE 1." Bradley's plates say "881 KUW." The car is an old Olds, with two rock-impact craters in its windshield. The car appears to have been mugged. Bradley's Knickerbocker teammates used to say that Bradley was the person in New York least likely to be mugged, because his manner of rumply dress suggested that he had been mugged just moments before. There is no telephone in the car. He is a senator, not an architect. To make his phone calls, he stops at diners, where he leans over pay telephones that come up to his hips.

After crossing the Delaware River on the Benjamin Franklin Bridge, he sat in a circle with the editorial board of the *Philadelphia Inquirer*, the most influential newspaper in southern New Jersey. The *Inquirer* likes Bradley and he likes the *Inquirer*. Around the piled sandwiches, there was atmosphere of teammates sitting in front of their lockers. Guthman, Wilson, Nichols, Boasberg, Joyce . . . The big front line was there in depth. Middle East, march on Washington, underground economy, carrot on a stick — the subject moved around through foreign affairs and taxes and alighted on President Reagan and his suavity with blacks and women. Bradley said, "My theory is — if you want to hear my theory — he's going from bad to worse. In areas like these, you either have the touch or you don't, as any of us who have lived with strong-willed women will attest. Reagan has gone to too great a length to protect his racist right front, which is a part of his coalition. He has mobilized blacks. He has mobilized women. They are more than enough to defeat him. Thanks to Reagan, a Democrat can now go to resources that not only will elect him but will enable him to run the country."

Meanwhile, what would Bradley be doing after Congress reconvened?

He said he would try to fill up the federal Strategic Petroleum Reserve, and would introduce an amendment to that end. "It's a dull issue, because at the moment there's a gasoline glut and no one is remembering the crises," he said. "The reserve stockpile is supposed to be seven hundred and fifty million barrels, and it's not half of that."

Asked about the Middle East, he said, "The center of the story there is not Lebanon but the Iran-Iraq War. A hundred thousand are already dead. Remember, we lost fifty-eight thousand in the entire Vietnam War."

An editor said, "The Iran-Iraq War is not on television. It doesn't exist."

At the end of a discussion of federal aid to education, Bradley turned his palms upward and said, "Computers cost more than slide rules."

In an office at the *Burlington County Times*, journal of record of the state's largest county (Pine Barrens, Fort Dix, Delaware River communities), an editor wearing tinted glasses, a pink shirt, and a white tie with a pearl stickpin said the paper was concerned about a new twelve-dollar fee the Federal Bureau of Investigation was charging for fingerprint checks. Fifty thousand people in the state had not been processed, and in New Jersey such a number could be expected to include some thirty-five hundred felons.

"Budgetary," said Bradley, manifesting minimal interest.

The editor, whose name was Joseph Molmer, said the paper was also preparing a piece on food waste, having learned that McDonald's and Burger King throw out anything cooked that is not sold within ten minutes. While thrift is not Bradley's middle name, it could be. He sat up attentively, and turned the cuff of one sleeve from the forearm to the elbow. Molmer asked for national figures to set the context of the story, and Bradley said his staff would help. Food waste had not been a preoccupying issue for him, but he would like to know more about the subject.

Toxic waste, on the other hand, was much on Bradley's mind, New Jersey being the national leader in creeping carcinogens and leaching acids. He said that measures he had already introduced would extend the federal cleanup Superfund from 1985 to 1990, thus doubling the resources, and would also change the policy of the Environmental Protection Agency from "Negotiate first and clean up second" to "Clean up first and negotiate second." He went on, "There are two ways to deal with toxic waste. One, take it away. Two, contain it. Taking it away is represented as a capital cost. Containing it is, for the most part, 'operations and maintenance.' The federal government pays 90 percent of capital cost and nothing for operations and maintenance. We need a ninety-ten split on both. Sometimes it is better to contain wastes than to take them from one place to another. We have to stop pushing pollution around."

Is he for or against tuition tax credits?

"For."

Will the public-school system suffer?

"No. It is doing a good job now and it will continue to do a good job," he said, waxing on into a synopsis of federal aid to education, which he concluded by saying, "Computers cost more than slide rules."

After the subject shifted to nursing homes, Bradley spoke at some length about the successes and failures of Medicare, the structure of the program, and his belief that Medicare coverage should be extended to pay for home-health aids, physiotherapists, and the like, who visit people in their homes. He said that he and Senator Bob Packwood, of Oregon, had introduced a home-health-care bill. Their calculations indicated that home service could be "delivered cheaper than a hospital bed and would be more humane." The plan would be tried out in four states — "one of which would be New Jersey, naturally, because I'm a New Jersey senator."

In his office in Turnersville, on the Black Horse Pike, he kept an appointment with the South Jersey RAGE. Some time ago, the state's Department of Transportation announced plans to restore a decrepit railway line and run several trains a day from Philadelphia to Atlantic City. The service was promoted as an enhancement of public transportation in southern New Jersey, but one did not require a degree in regional planning to discern that the purpose of the program was to siphon something like a million people a year out of the Amtrak corridor and into Atlantic City's casinos. Senator Bradley, like New Jersey's governor, Thomas Kean, had said he could support this project only if the route were to be used as a multistop service for commuters employed in one city or the other. Meanwhile, citizens whose suburban homes pressed close to the quiet roadbed — joined by anticasino factions and issue-sniffing politicians — had formed South Jersey RAGE: Residents Against the Gamblers' Express.

Eight of them now faced Senator Bradley — five women, three men, including a Baptist minister, the assistant administrator of Pennsauken, the mayor of Haddonfield.

The senator addressed a television crew, saying, "A commuter rail service could enhance the quality of life in south Jersey."

"The whole idea is to zip people to Atlantic City," said Robyn Selvin, of South Jersey RAGE. "Four trains a day. Four trains do not a commuter line make. And there is only one planned stop." The trains were going to be traveling at seventy-nine miles an hour and whistling and thundering at eighty-eight decibels for twelve seconds before each grade crossing — figures yielding a combined total of eight miles of screaming decibels. Evelyn McGill, of Merchantville, said her property was ten feet from the rails, and she remembered years ago sitting many a night in her yard and watching the old Nelly Bly coming up from Atlantic City; and one night, at forty-five miles an hour, Nelly Bly jumped the curving rails. "Imagine what would happen at seventy-nine," she said, and she spread before Senator Bradley an athology of wreckage: "AMTRAK TRAIN DERAILS, INJURING 51 IN ILLINOIS," a picture of an Amcoach hanging off an overpass in Connecticut, a picture of train cars in Colorado piled up like bacon. "That would be in my kitchen," she told him — not to mention the gamblers lying in the peonies, the creosote splinters in the Sunday ham.

Bob Cummings, the administrator from Pennsauken, said, "This is not an opposition against gambling. The line, though, is nothing but a working shuttle for gamblers." An Atlantic City casino had volunteered to build a twelve-million-dollar terminal for the new trains. The State of New Jersey would be subsidizing the new service at the rate of five dollars per travelling gambler. "The casinos took in over a billion dollars last year. We fail to see that this is an industry that needs help."

Possibly someone failed to see that the state was making money, too — that casinos are meant to be to New Jersey what the Alaska Pipeline is to Alaska. Bradley told RAGE that he was impressed with its presentation.

After a ninety-mile drive to the northeast, the Senator arrived in Lavallette, a town on a barrier beach. En route through the dinner hour, he sipped Dunkin' Donuts' soup. A meeting room in the Lavallette First Aid Squad Building was filled to the walls, body temperature: toddlers chattering in strollers, a receiver erupting on a policeman's hip ("Lavallette police . . . Get rid of that phone . . . You've already been advised . . ."), and every age group represented, with a preponderance of seniors. Gradually, in the course of the day, Bradley's sleeves, fold by fold, had made their way to his upper biceps, and now — with a microphone in one hand and waving the other as he used to when he was the open man — he caught an hour's questions in reeling juxtaposition.

From a wheelchair, a man held up a cassette recorder, light glowing red, and asked a two-part question about the MX missile and the incineration of garbage.

Of the MX, Bradley said, "It is an unnecessary system. It is offensive. It is a first-strike weapons system."

A young Puerto Rican who said that he had come to the mainland years ago and been shunted into a public school for retarded children asked if the Senator was disposed to support bilingual education.

"I am for giving bilingual education a full role if it is used as a bridge to full participation in an English-speaking culture," he answered.

A white-haired man said, "I would like to ask your opinion of the breakup of the telephone company, which I think is a very heinous thing. What can we do to stop these egomaniacs from destroying the finest telephone system in the world?"

"I'm a friend of the telephone company," said Bradley. "I lean toward your analysis. But maybe the horse is out of the barn, and cannot be brought back in."

Despite the heat and humidity, arms were flying to attract his attention.

"We in Holiday City . . ."

"I've seen scows dump garbage within a stone's throw of . . ."

"I am a young American citizen concerned with building a military apparatus creating a backlash of resentment around the world. Please tell us how you would vote on these three matters. One: The nuclear-freeze resolution. Two: Aid to El Salvador. Three: The Martin Luther King holiday."

Bradley answered, "One, yes. Two, probably — at some level. Three, yes. I'm a co-sponsor of the bill."

Social Security, Medicare . . . His replies were short and economical, and included a two-minute summary of "the arcane subject of the pricing of natural gas."

Why not import natural gas from Russia, someone said — matching the Russians' purchases of grain.

"I don't want to put the fox in charge of the chicken coop," said Bradley.

Social Security: "I've held conferences on the subject all over the state, and at first I thought that seniors would just say, 'Decrease our tax and keep our COLAS.' But the conferences taught me that senior citizens sympathize with the financial plight of the younger generation and are willing to share the crisis costs."

And now, on the boardwalk in Seaside, 10 P.M., he says goodbye to the citizen with the skateboard and moves along through another half mile of crowd.

"Hey, Bill!"

"There's Dollar Bill!"

Whether for a town meeting or a college conference on a specific subject or a walking town meeting ("You go where the people are"), he will be up at seven in the morning to do this sort of thing all day tomorrow, and the next day and the next, and a day or two a week in New Jersey while the Senate is in session. On sheer fatigue and vegetable soup, he sways a little and his eyes are glazed.

In front of the Seaside Coin Castle, he is asked to explain American participation in the International Monetary Fund. He is asked to shoot a basket (declined). He is asked "to keep the Commies on the other side of the ocean."

"Hey, big Bill!"

"You gotta do something about the Knicks, Bill."

A two-year-old child coming toward him in a stroller is wearing camouflage-cloth battle dress from hat to foot and is carrying a plastic automatic weapon. The man pushing him runs forward, takes Bradley's elbow, and pulls him toward the child, saying, "Senator, you've got to shake hands with this man." The Senator lifts a tiny hand from the rifle, gives a squeeze, and moves on.

"Nice to meet you, Bill."

"Nice to meet you, Senator."

"What job bills before Congress do you support?"

"You were a big help to my daughter in getting her boyfriend over from Scotland."

"Senator Bradley, you helped me get Social Security for the disabled."

"Keep it up, Senator."

"Stay in there, Bill."

"Are you the best foul shooter in the Senate?"

"I'm the *only* foul shooter in the Senate."

A N OLD SAYING IS THAT POL-
itics makes strange bedfellows. That the adage is not always true is illustrated by the extraordinarily successful personal and
political union of Kansas Senator Robert Dole and his wife, Elizabeth Hanford Dole, who became Ronald Reagan's secretary of transportation.

A North Carolinian, Elizabeth Dole
graduated from Duke University and
went on to the Harvard Law School,
where one of her male colleagues told
her in all seriousness that she should
relinquish her place to a male student
who would have the opportunity to do
something with his life! Bemused and
chagrined, Elizabeth Hanford went on
to earn not only a law degree, but also
a graduate degree in education at
Harvard.

Before she married Robert Dole in
1975, Elizabeth Hanford had made her
mark on the Washington political
scene. She was a White House aide to
President Lyndon B. Johnson's consumer affairs adviser, Betty Furness,
who described her as "just dandy."
Her North Carolinian charm and wit,
combined with intelligence and energy, had a bipartisan appeal. President Nixon appointed her to a special
commission on consumer interests, on
which she served from 1968 to 1971,
then becoming deputy director of the
White House Office of Consumer Affairs. Nixon nominated her in 1973 to
serve on the Federal Trade Commission, a position she held until 1979
when she resigned to help in her hus-

band's unsuccessful bid for the Republican presidential nomination.

After Robert Dole dropped out of
the presidential race, his wife toured
the country for Reagan. During the
Reagan transition she chaired a task
force on human services, and became
assistant to the president for public liaison. She quickly and effectively mobilized support for the President's
programs. Anne Wexler, who had held
the post under the Carter administration, was impressed with Dole's work.
Before you could blink, she said,
"there were a series of groups in to
meet the President. They got everybody on record in favor of the economic program and locked in early."[1]
Describing her job to an eclectic group
of Washington lobbyists, Dole said,
"We're in the same business, communication, coalition building, outreach."[2]

President Reagan named Elizabeth
Dole to become his secretary of transportation in 1983, making her the first
woman in his administration to head
a cabinet department. As expected, her
confirmation hearings before the
Senate committee resembled more a
gathering of old friends than an adversary proceeding. Robert Dole, one
of four senators who introduced her,
said, to the committee's laughter, "I
regret I have but one wife to give for
my country, my country's infrastructure. TV dinners are a small price to
pay."[3] Committee chairman Robert
Packwood (R., Ore.), set the tone for
the hearings as he commented, "I can

[1] *Congressional Quarterly Weekly Report,* June 6, 1981, p. 976.
[2] Ibid., p. 975.
[3] *Congressional Quarterly Weekly Report,* January 29, 1983, p. 196.

240

vouch for her ability and integrity."[4] Asked about possible conflicts of interest because of her husband's position, Elizabeth Dole responded that their marriage would not undermine the separation of powers between the executive and legislative branches. She would not tell confidential information to her husband. "It's a matter of professional integrity," she said, "all information is not exchanged."[5]

As Elizabeth Dole's career was reaching ever-new heights in the executive branch, Robert Dole's power and prestige continued to increase on Capitol Hill. As chairman of the Senate Finance Committee, he combined knowledge and expertise with skillful political maneuvering to make a strong imprint on public policy. Once viewed skeptically as Gerald Ford's hatchet man, when he was his running mate in 1976, Dole emerged during the Reagan presidency as a statesman and national political figure. Many Republican party regulars consider Dole a likely presidential candidate in 1988.

The following selection describes how the secretary and the senator balance their marriage with the demanding world of politics in which they find themselves.

21 Douglas B. Feaver
THE SECRETARY AND THE SENATOR

When Transportation Secretary Elizabeth Hanford Dole proposed last summer to cut traffic at every congressman's favorite airport, Washington National, the $28 billion appropriations bill for the entire Transportation Department became a hostage on Capitol Hill.

"I figured she'd strike out," says Republican Senator Robert J. Dole of Kansas, her husband and chairman of the Senate Finance Committee. He volunteered that assessment at dinner. She took umbrage.

"It was just an offhand comment by one Bob Dole," she remarks. "It was kind of like a challenge . . . I've got a little note pad and pencil by my bed, and I scribble all these things down. So my strategy evolved while he was sleeping away next to me. 'I'll do this and this. I'll show him.' "

The troops were marshalled; the appropriation saved. The plan to reduce traffic at National Airport is alive if unresolved. A strikeout? "No. She got about a single on it," the senator says.

[4] Ibid.
[5] Ibid., p. 196.

From *The Washington Post National Weekly Edition*, 2 April 1984. ©1984 The Washington Post. Reprinted by permission.

"That shows who's the smarter politician," remarks Republican Senator Mark Andrews of North Dakota, a Dole family friend who is also chairman of the Senate Appropriations subcommittee on transportation.

Elizabeth Dole may or may not be the smarter politician, but there is no question that she is half of one of the more fascinating acts in the capital: the powerful senator and the able cabinet secretary, the successful two-career marriage. It is an aggregation of public power under one roof, one that creates ambiguous situations not often seen in Washington.

The senator is politically committed to modifying the tax on heavy trucks. The transportation secretary testifies in favor of an administration position that can be compromised to fit the senator's.

The transportation secretary makes a political appearance for Senator Ted Stevens of Alaska. Campaign America, the senator's political action committee (PAC), contributes to Stevens's campaign, as it does to the campaigns of many Republicans.

A number of transportation interests contribute to the senator's PAC, a normal thing for the chairman of the Senate's tax-writing body. Do their contributions reflect their knowledge that he also happens to be married to the transportation secretary?

There is no way to tell, and no evidence of anything improper. But Federal Election Commission records show that eighteen firms or persons readily identifiable with transportation companies contributed a total of $22,300 to Senator Dole's PAC in 1983, a pittance for a PAC that took in $846,700.

Together and apart, the Doles are building an impressive list of political IOUs; there is nothing more entertaining than the Bob and Elizabeth show.

"She gets two to three times as many invitations to speak as [former transportation secretary] Drew Lewis did, because she gets them not only from the transportation groups but also the women's groups and people who think it would be nice to get Bob and Elizabeth together," says Ralph Stanley, who is head of the Urban Mass Transportation Administration and who was previously on the personal staffs of Lewis and Dole.

Both Doles are clearly aware of the potential for conflicts of interest. Both say they pay little attention to the other's activities.

"Right now," Elizabeth Dole says, "he's got a couple of major things up there [in the Senate] and I'm learning more about it from your newspaper than I am from him. . . . He doesn't know what I'm doing on Conrail; I don't know what he's doing on some of the intricacies of his issues. . . ."

"It is a legitimate question," Senator Dole says. "I would say we just don't discuss a lot of that. She'll take some work home with her and get tied up on it; if you get home at 8 o'clock, 8:30, the last thing I want to do is get right into business. Get that Lean Cuinsine out and eat it."

Of the two Doles, she appears to have the more difficult balancing act. At one time or another in the same day, she is:

The eighth U.S. secretary of transportation.
An effective Reagan administration fire extinguisher for smoldering gender-gap issues.
The helpful spouse of the politically ambitious senior senator from Kansas.
A potential political candidate in her own right.

There have been a few joint appearances with Senator Dole, including a tour of Topeka, Atchison, and Wichita on Kansas Day last summer. She accompanied Senator Dole in February to a Los Angeles fund raiser for Campaign America and several Republican incumbents and candidates. But she did not speak and was not introduced.

The secretary of transportation is not subject to the Hatch Act's prohibition on government employees participating in partisan politics. The department's ethics officer, Rosalind Knapp, says Secretary Dole was briefed on ethics questions, as all incoming secretaries are briefed.

"She is subject to the same conflict rules with respect to what Senator Dole does as she is with respect to anybody else," Knapp says. "She should avoid fund-raising events that are focused on [transportation] interests with which she would have a conflict, but that does not preclude events" attended by a few transportation personalities.

Last June, she made a political swing through the Northwest that included appearances on behalf of Oregon Senator Mark O. Hatfield in Portland and Washington Senator Slade Gorton in Seattle. Then she was joined by Senator Dole for a visit and vacation with Senator Stevens that included a tour of the federally owned Alaska Railroad, which DOT is selling to the state. Her Christmas card was a picturesque photograph of the smiling Doles waving from the back of an Alaskan railroad passenger car bearing the DOT seal.

About the same time, Senator Dole's Campaign America PAC handed out contributions to a number of Republicans seeking election, including $5,000 for Stevens. "I give money to all my potential opponents," Dole says, referring to the fact that he and Stevens are among those seeking to replace Senator Howard H. Baker, Jr. of Tennessee as majority leader.

The Doles and Baker showed up in New Hampshire recently to campaign for President Reagan. Secretary Dole attacked Democratic presidential candidate Walter F. Mondale. Senators Dole and Baker — both presidential prospects for 1988 — defended Republicanism. Bob Dole dropped one-liners, such as: "Howard and I came along to keep an eye on Elizabeth and see if she's running for president."

She has been seriously suggested as a future vice-presidential nominee. What do you think of a Bush-Dole ticket, Senator Dole tells crowds he was asked by a reporter. "I said I just don't think I'd have any interest," Dole says he replied. "That's a good thing," said the reporter, according to Dole. "We didn't have you in mind."

Did he see a situation, Dole was asked, where he and his wife might have conflicting political ambitions? "I think that's a possibility," he says. "I think she's hotter property than I am right now."

The Senate Finance Committee has direct responsibility for only a few transportation-related matters, including "user fee" taxes to support federal trust funds for highways and airport development. "I'm in charge of loopholes; she's in charge of potholes," Senator Dole says.

There is only one occasion when the Doles seem to have joined forces to attack a problem. The Transportation Department has made no secret of its desire to eliminate the United States Railway Association, a small federal agency set up to oversee Conrail. The USRA's mission is almost complete now that Conrail makes money, all bankruptcy questions have been settled, and the railroad is ready for sale to the private sector.

But Congress, especially the House, wants to keep the USRA's experts around to monitor the sale. Last July, during debate on the Transportation Department's appropriations bill, Senator Dole rose on the floor to call the USRA "a quasi-governmental body whose useful life has long expired, in my opinion."

Asked about that, Secretary Dole said, "You're never going to believe me, but it was independent. It really was. We didn't talk about it."

She was sworn in as transportation secretary February 7, 1983, after serving as Reagan's assistant for public liaison, where she was often isolated from decisionmaking. People who know her give two reasons for that: She was a woman in a male-dominated White House, and she was Senator Dole's wife, which made some staffers nervous when it came time, for example, to talk about strategy in dealing with the Senate Finance Committee on tax issues.

For a variety of reasons, it took months for Dole to get her key subcabinet positions filled after she became transportation secretary. Her strongest aide, Deputy Secretary James H. Burnley IV, was widely perceived within the transportation community as the one really running things.

Burnley, a North Carolinian like Secretary Dole, has taken great pains to shoot down that notion. "We have a very clear understanding about who's in charge around here," he said. "She is."

The early reviews are being revised, because it is clear that Dole has made the Transportation Department her own and redefined issues along lines that interest her.

There is no shortage of issues: whether to mandate auto airbags; how to guarantee consumer protection for air passengers when the Civil Aeronautics Board dies next January 1; how to manage burgeoning air traffic without constraining the deregulated airlines; how to allocate sparse funds among many competing new mass transit systems, and how to denationalize Conrail and keep Congress smiling.

There are also major and minor controversies about further deregulation of trains, planes, boats, and buses; management of the mammoth highway and bridge project fund; port development; truck and waterway taxes; what to do about drunken railroad engineers; airline safety; Coast Guard drug interdiction; even the commercialization of space.

It takes time to master those subjects, particularly for someone who wants to know all the details before she opens her mouth. "We send in paper, it comes out with questions; we send in more paper, it comes out with more questions," one member of her staff explains.

There has been some grumbling, never for attribution, among congressional aides that the Transportation Department runs on automatic pilot while Secretary Dole studies details. As for members of Congress, nobody is going to fire at her, on or off the record.

Republican Senator John C. Danforth of Missouri, a member of the Finance Committee and chairman of the Commerce Committee's surface transportation subcommittee, has worked hard over the past two years to move a truck safety bill. Safety is Secretary Dole's first priority, she says over and over. The day Danforth held hearings on truck safety, he had to settle for Burnley as the Transportation Department witness.

Secretary Dole was busy later that day testifying on truck taxes in front of Senator Dole, over at the Finance Committee, in a hearing that was widely covered by the media and watched closely by the trucking lobby.

"Elizabeth Dole is such a strong person and such an effective person herself, I really don't think of her as Mrs. Bob Dole," Danforth says.

House Democrats also praise her performance. Representative William Lehman of Florida, chairman of the House Appropriations subcommittee on transportation, calls Secretary Dole "a voice of reason and moderation in an administration that can often become extreme."

The two major Senate panels that handle transportation issues have nine members who also are members of Senator Dole's Finance Committee. Three of them are chairmen of significant transportation committees or subcommittees. Republican Senator Nancy Landon Kassebaum of Kansas, a friend of both Doles, is chairman of the Commerce Committee's aviation subcommittee.

The Transportation Department's new federal railroad administrator, John Riley, was chief legislative assistant to Republican Senator David F. Durenberger of Minnesota. Its new assistant secretary for governmental affairs is Charles G. Hardin, who was chief transportation staffer for Andrews' transportation appropriations subcommittee. One of Secretary Dole's new special assistants is Rebecca C. Gernhardt, who was Senator Stevens's chief of staff.

Secretary Dole is a member of the club. "She's a Senate wife; I'm a cabinet spouse," Senator Dole says.

The Transportation Department's proposed fiscal 1985 budget was clearly a victory for Dole. Mass transit and aviation spending rose, and the number of safety inspectors, cut earlier in the Reagan administration, was increased.

Before Dole arrived, Drew Lewis had managed the air traffic controllers' strike with skill, had turned the administration around on the need for new gasoline and trucking taxes to support highway and transit improvements and had won a number of lesser skirmishes. But Lewis ignored automobile safety issues, which are subject to regulation by the department's National Highway Traffic Safety Administration (NHTSA).

Under Lewis, NHTSA abandoned a Carter administration rule requiring installation of airbags or other so-called passive restraints in new cars. The Supreme Court subsequently ruled that NHTSA had given insufficient grounds for abandoning the rule and remanded it to NHTSA. Dole reopened the case, promising a decision by April 12. That date will slip into late April, she says, but not by much.

Whatever she proposes will have to pass White House muster. "I will make a recommendation to the president based on what the record shows," she says. Her personal view is that airbags are effective; she has had one installed in her DOT car.

Consumer advocate Ralph Nader attaches cataclysmic importance to the airbag question. That decision, he says, "will either confirm the impression that Elizabeth Dole is not willing to stand up for victims against power or it will make Elizabeth Dole the most courageous cabinet secretary in the Reagan administration."

Neither Dole nor the White House supports federal laws raising the drinking age to twenty-one. They believe that the states should do it themselves. She said on NBC's "Meet the Press" recently that if states pass a law, "I think there's more of an effort for enforcement and it's more effective."

When Dole is asked what she is doing about auto safety, she talks about new regulations and about using "the bully pulpit" to support getting drunk drivers off the street or to advocate seatbelt use, an effort started during Lewis's tenure as a substitute for requiring airbags.

She persuaded the Office of Management and Budget to approve a requirement that new autos have brake lights mounted on the top center of the trunk — a proved reducer of rear-end collisions. That idea had been kicking around NHTSA for at least seven years.

NHTSA under Dole has been more active in pursuing defects in new cars than it was under Lewis, though there is a belief on Capitol Hill that more needs to be done. Democratic Representative Timothy E. Wirth of Colorado, chairman of a House Energy and Commerce subcommittee, wrote Dole recently that NHTSA's "track record over the last three years is extremely disappointing and poses grave dangers for the driving public."

Dole responded that "the number of defect investigative actions is up significantly over the last six months. Moreover, NHTSA influenced the recall of 70 percent of the vehicles recalled in 1983 — the highest level since 1971." She also noted that the Justice Department, at her department's urging, sued General Motors for X-car defects and that Transportation has budgeted more highway money for safety improvements.

"Part of the good statistics we've had on safety have to be due to this kind of thing," Dole says, referring to the fact that the highway death toll of 43,028 in 1983 was the lowest in twenty years and that there were fewer highway fatalities over the Christmas holiday than at any time since 1946.

Dole has also shaken up the Federal Aviation Administration after a flurry of disturbing air safety incidents indicated that FAA inspectors were overworked or underdirected. In addition to authorizing more inspectors, Dole ordered a systemwide investigation of airline safety.

She and Senator Dole have worked at avoiding obvious conflicts. When several small Kansas cities were interested in being the site for a new, centralized FAA flight service station, Wichita got it. The others will lose existing stations.

Normally, the senior senator from Kansas would just phone the transportation secretary and tell her of his great concern. In this case, he could mention it at dinner. "I didn't lobby her on the flight service station," Senator Dole says. Pause. "I lobbied Burnley. I just called him and said, 'Now Jim, are sure you made the right choice?' "

LYNDON B. JOHNSON, A MEMber of the Senate freshman class of 1948, was majority leader from 1955 until 1960, when he was elected vice-president. His experience in Washington predated his Senate career; he had been a congressional staff member in 1931 and at the age of twenty-eight had defeated seven other candidates in a special election to fill the seat of the tenth Texas congressional district left vacant by the death of the incumbent representative.

Johnson was a consummate politician from the very beginning of his stay in Washington. He embraced the New Deal, and became a favorite of President Franklin D. Roosevelt; he even supported the president's ill-fated court-packing plan, which was opposed by many of Roosevelt's Washington supporters.[1]

While still a congressman, Johnson ran and was defeated in a special election for a Senate post vacated by the death of incumbent Senator Morris Sheppard in 1941. Johnson continued to serve in the House (with a brief leave in 1942 to serve as a naval reserve officer) until, with John Connally as his campaign manager, he defeated arch-conservative Governor Coke Stevenson in the Democratic primary in 1948 by 87 votes out of almost a million cast. Since there was essentially no Republican opposition in Texas at that time, the election in the Democratic primary was tantamount to victory in the general election held in November.

When Johnson became majority leader the "Johnson era" began in the Senate. The "Johnson system" of power reflected his personality and style: He unhesitatingly rewarded his friends, from whom he demanded loyalty, and punished his enemies. His formal powers as majority leader were minimal. His chairmanship of the Democratic Steering Committee, for example, did not automatically guarantee him personal control over Democratic committee assignments. But Johnson exerted such control. He developed an informal network of power, and a dazzling style that came to be known as "the treatment."

[1] In 1937 Roosevelt recommended legislation to Congress under which he would be given authority to appoint one new Supreme Court justice for each justice over seventy years old. At the time there were six septuagenarian justices, so that Roosevelt could easily have "packed" the court with his own appointments.

22

Roland Evans and Robert Novak
THE JOHNSON SYSTEM

To build his Network, Johnson stretched the meager power resources of the majority leader to the outer limit. The mightiest of these was his influence over committee assignments. Still, it was not comparable to the absolute power enjoyed by Nelson Aldrich, a half century before. As chairman of the Democratic Steering Committee, Johnson steadily widened the breach in rigid seniority rules, working delicately with a surgical scalpel, not a stick of dynamite.

In January 1955, his ally and adviser, Clinton Anderson, pressed his claim for an overdue assignment on either Foreign Relations or Finance. Each committee had one vacancy. But former Vice-President Alben Barkley, who had just returned to the Senate as a "freshman" from Kentucky in the 1954 elections, asked for the Finance Committee — a request that could scarcely be denied. A further complication was the still unresolved problem of Wayne Morse, the Oregon maverick who had bolted the Republican party in the 1952 campaign and, after two years in the political wilderness as an "Independent," now joined the Democratic caucus in 1955. Morse's decision was vital to Johnson. It provided him with the narrow one-vote margin he needed to cross the bridge, incalculably important in terms of power, from Minority Leader to Majority Leader. Thus, it was incumbent upon Johnson to give Morse a good committee assignment, and Morse wanted Foreign Relations.

Johnson duly explained these facts of life to Anderson, who agreed not to insist (as he well could have) on either Finance or Foreign Relations. But Johnson remembered his old friend's personal loyalty and, on a 1956 speaking engagement in New Mexico, he publicly — and unexpectedly — promised that Clint Anderson would become the next chairman of the Joint Atomic Energy Committee. That post, because of New Mexico's Los Alamos atomic installation, would solidly enhance Anderson's prestige. To make good his promise, Johnson was required to jump Anderson over none other than Richard Russell, who outranked Anderson on the joint committee.

The Foreign Relations maneuvers temporarily drew the sharp-tongued Morse to Johnson, in sharp contrast to a year earlier. In January 1954, Morse had told an ADA Roosevelt Day Dinner in Texas: "Johnson has the most reactionary record in the Senate. Look at his voting record. If he should ever have a liberal idea, he would have a brain hemor-

From *Lyndon B. Johnson: The Exercise of Power* by Roland Evans and Robert Novak. Copyright © 1966 by Rowland Evans and Robert Novak. Reprinted by arrangement with The New American Library, Inc., New York, N.Y.

rhage. . . ."[1] But a little more than a year later, ensconced on the Foreign Relations Committee, Morse gently confided to the Senate: "During the past year, I have been the beneficiary of one kindness after another from Lyndon Johnson. I consider him not only a great statesman but a good man."

And as chairman of the Joint Atomic Energy Committee, Anderson was even more pleased than he would have been on Foreign Relations. The only grumbling over Johnson's ingenious shuffling came from Russell, who had not agreed in advance to step aside for Anderson. But the grumbling was private and soft, not public and bitter. Lyndon Johnson could count on Dick Russell not to make a public fuss about such matters.

Two years later, Anderson was the center of far more devious committee maneuvers by Johnson. After the presidential election of 1956, Estes Kefauver of Tennessee and John F. Kennedy of Massachusetts, who had competed on the national convention floor at Chicago for the vice-presidential nomination the previous summer, were competing again — this time for a single vacancy on Foreign Relations. Johnson, who had backed Kennedy against Kefauver at Chicago, was not trying to bring Kennedy closer to his orbit. He was determined to have the vacancy go to Kennedy over Johnson's old foe, Kefauver. But how to get around Kefauver's four-year seniority bulge over Kennedy? In December 1956, long before Congress convened, Johnson telephoned Anderson with a most curious question: "How are you getting along with your campaign for the Foreign Relations Committee?"

Anderson was puzzled. Could Johnson have forgotten that his "campaign" had ended two years earlier? But Johnson persisted.

"This may be your chance," he said.

Before Anderson could reply that he had his hands full as chairman of Atomic Energy, Johnson rushed on.

"You have seniority now over Jack Kennedy," Johnson explained. "But if you don't claim it, Estes Kefauver may get there first."

Johnson's ploy suddenly came through to Anderson. Both Anderson and Kefauver were members of the Class of '48 and therefore had equal seniority. If they both applied for the one vacancy on the Foreign Relations Committee, Johnson could throw up his hands in the Steering Committee, declare a standoff — and give the vacancy to Kennedy. Anderson went along with this neat strategy, and Kennedy was given the seat, just as Johnson wanted.

Johnson's use of power to influence committee assignments cut both ways. "Good" liberals, such as Humphrey, could be prematurely boosted

---

[1] Johnson retaliated in kind: "Texas doesn't need any outsiders to come in and tell them [sic] how to vote. I don't think Texas will pay any more attention to him than the Senate does." In those early days of his leadership, Johnson was far more ready to engage fellow senators in a war of words than he would be later.

into the Foreign Relations Committee, and a "bad" liberal, such as Ke-fauver, could be made to cool his heels for years. A "bad" liberal such as Paul Douglas could be barred from the Finance Committee for eight long years, while five fellow members of the Class of '48 (Kerr, Long, Frear, Anderson, and Johnson himself) and one from the Class of '50 (Smathers) were finding places there.[2] Senators who dared to function too far outside the Johnson Network waited long to get inside the prestige committees.

In these clandestine committee maneuvers, Johnson seldom exposed his hand. But in the routine committee shifts, he enjoyed wringing out the last drop of credit. One evening in early January 1955, shortly after the committee assignments for the Eighty-fifth Congress had been settled and announced, Johnson invited a couple of friends into his majority leader's office in the corner of the Capitol for a political bull session over Scotch and sodas. Nothing relaxed him more than these feet-up, hair-down chats. They invariably lasted well into the night and they invariably ended in long, often hilarious LBJ monologues, full of ribald yarns and racy mimicry.

Suddenly, he interrupted himself. "My God," he said, "I forgot to call Senator Stennis and congratulate him." Stennis had been valuable to Johnson a month earlier in the McCarthy censure fight, and now had just landed a coveted seat on the Appropriations Committee — thanks to Lyndon Johnson. Johnson reached over, cradled the phone between his shoulder and chin, and dialed.

Mrs. Stennis answered the phone, and the conversation commenced. "Ma'm, this is Lyndon Johnson, is your husband there? . . . He isn't? . . . Well, I must tell you, Ma'm, how proud I am of your husband and how proud the Senate is, and you tell him that when he gets home. The Senate paid him a great honor today. The Senate elected your husband to the Appropriations Committee. That's one of the most powerful committees in the Senate and a great honor for your husband. I'm so proud of John. He's a great American. And I know you're proud of him, too. He's one of my finest Senators. . . ." Accompanying this monologue were nods and winks in the direction of Johnson's fascinated audience.

Johnson went on to tell Mrs. Stennis how the Steering Committee had selected her husband unanimously for the Appropriations spot and how the full Senate had unanimously concurred, but implicitly he was belaboring the obvious — that it wasn't the Steering Committee or the full Senate that really was responsible. It was LBJ.

---

[2] This extraordinary treatment of Douglas also reflected Johnson's desire to keep the Finance Commiteee free of Northern liberals opposing special tax advantages for the oil and gas industry. But if Douglas had been a "good" liberal in the Humphrey mold, Johnson could have shaved a point, since the Finance Committee was already so stacked in favor of the oil and gas industry.

Johnson quietly commandeered other bits and pieces of Senate patronage that previous majority leaders ignored. To cement his budding alliance with Senator Margaret Chase Smith, for instance, he arranged for a special staff member of the Senate Armed Services Committee to be appointed by her and to be responsible to her alone, even though she was a Republican on the Democratic-controlled committee, and only fourth-ranking Republican at that.

Although in the past, office space for senators, a source of sometimes intense competition, had been distributed by strict seniority as a routine housekeeping chore of the Senate's sergeant-at-arms, Johnson quickly perceived its value as a weapon of influence and fitted it into his growing system of rewards and punishments. When Paul Douglas lost that top-floor Capitol office to Johnson in 1955, the Senate took notice. It was a dramatic sign of the consequences of a lack of rapport with the majority leader. Johnson skillfully exploited the gleaming New Senate Office Building in 1958, with its spanking new suites, as an inducement for help on the floor. Senator Mike Monroney of Oklahoma, sometimes troublesome for Johnson, was brought into line on one bill with the award of a handsome corner suite that Johnson knew Monroney coveted.

Johnson also kept his ears open to discover which senator — or senator's wife — was really anxious to go on which senatorial junket abroad. At a cocktail party early in 1957, Johnson was chatting with the wife of Frank Church, the young, newly elected liberal Democrat from Idaho. Mrs. Church innocently revealed that she had always wanted to see South America. Knowing that Frank Church might become a valuable addition to the Johnson Network, the majority leader saw to it that he was named to the very next delegation of senators to visit South America.

Even before that, however, Frank Church had reason to be grateful to Lyndon Johnson. Bitterly opposed by the Idaho Power Company and other private-power interests because of his public-power stand, Church was hard-pressed for funds in his 1956 campaign for the Senate. He sent an S.O.S. to the Senate Democratic Campaign Committee in Washington. Senator Smathers, chairman of the campaign committee, was dubious about pouring money into what seemed a hopeless cause in a small mountain state. But Johnson and Bobby Baker argued Church's cause, and their wishes prevailed.

De facto control of the campaign committee's funds was one of Johnson's least obvious but most effective tools in building his Network. He controlled the distribution of committee funds through both its chairman — first Earle Clements and later George Smathers — and through its secretary, Bobby Baker. More often than not, the requests for campaign funds were routinely made to Baker, and the money was physically distributed by him. Johnson further tightened his control when Clements was named the committee's executive director after his Senate defeat in 1956. Johnson got the most out of the committee's limited funds (at the time a mere four hundred thousand dollars) by shrewdly distributing them where they would do the most work. In the small mountain states like Idaho, a ten-thousand-dollar contribution could change the course of an election. But in New York or Pennsylvania, ten thousand dollars was the merest drop in the bucket. Johnson and Baker tried to reduce contributions to Democrats in the industrial Northeast to the minimum. Since senators seldom bite the hand that finances them, these westerners were naturally drawn into the Johnson Network, while the Eastern liberals tended to remain outside.

But this ingenious stretching of the majority leader's limited stock of patronage could not by itself explain the brilliant success of the Johnson Network. The extra, indeed the dominant, ingredient was Johnson's overwhelming personality, reflected in what came to be known as "The Treatment."

The Treatment could last ten minutes or four hours. It came, enveloping its target, at the LBJ Ranch swimming pool, in one of LBJ's offices, in the Senate cloakroom, on the floor of the Senate itself — wherever Johnson might find a fellow senator within his reach. Its tone could be supplication, accusation, cajolery, exuberance, scorn, tears, complaint, the hint of threat. It was all of these together. It ran the gamut of human emotions. Its velocity was breathtaking, and it was all in one direction. Interjections from the target were rare. Johnson anticipated them before they could be spoken. He moved in close, his face a scant millimeter from his target, his eyes widening and narrowing, his eyebrows rising and falling. From his pockets poured clippings, memos, statistics. Mimicry, humor, and the genius of analogy made The Treatment an almost hypnotic experience and rendered the target stunned and helpless.

In 1957, when Johnson was courting the non-Senate Eastern liberal establishment, he summoned historian and liberal theoretician Arthur Schlesinger, Jr., down from his classroom at Harvard. Wary at the prospect of his first prolonged meeting with Johnson (whom he suspected of disdaining the liberal cause), Schlesinger had in his mind a long list of questions to ask Johnson. Never known for shyness, Schlesinger was nevertheless on his guard when he entered Johnson's Capitol office and sat in front of the great man's desk.

The Treatment began immediately: a brilliant, capsule characterization of every Democratic senator: his strengths and failings, where he fit into the political spectrum; how far he could be pushed, how far pulled; his hates, his loves. And who (he asked Schlesinger) must oversee all these prima donnas, put them to work, knit them together, know when to tickle this one's vanity, inquire of that one's health, remember this one's five o'clock nip of Scotch, that one's nagging wife? Who must find the hidden legislative path between the South and the North, the public power men and the private power men, the farmers' men and the unions'

men, the bomber boys, and the peace lovers, the eggheads and the fat-
heads? Nobody but Lyndon Johnson.

Imagine a football team (Johnson hurried on) and I'm the coach, and
I'm also the quarterback, I have to call the signals, and I have to center
the ball. run the ball, pass the ball. I'm the blocker (he rose out of his
chair and threw an imaginary block). I'm the tackler (he crouched and
tackled). I'm the passer (he heaved a mighty pass). I have to catch the
pass (he reached and caught the pass).

Schlesinger was sitting on the edge of his chair, both fascinated and
amused. Here was a view of the Senate he had never seen before.

Johnson next ticked off all the bills he had passed that year, how he'd
gotten Dick Russell on this one, Bob Kerr on that one, Hubert Humphrey on another. He reached into his desk drawer and out came the
voting record of New Jersey's Clifford Case, a liberal Republican. You
liberals, he told Schlesinger, are always talking about my record. You
wouldn't question Cliff Case's record, would you? And he ran down the
list and compared it to his voting record. Whatever Johnson had on those
two lists, he came out with a record more liberal than Case's.

Johnson had anticipated and answered all of Schlesinger's questions.
The leader rolled on, reiterating a theme common to The Treatment of
that time. He'd had his heart attack, he said, and he knew he'd never
be president. He wasn't made for the presidency. If only the good Lord
would just give him enough time to do a few more things in the Senate.
Then he'd go back to Texas. That's where he belonged.

Breathless now, ninety minutes later, Schlesinger said good-by and
groped his way out of Johnson's office. Eight years later, he was to record his impressions. Johnson had been "a good deal more attractive,
more subtle, and more formidable than I expected." And, he might have
added, vastly more entertaining.

The Treatment was designed for a single target or, at most, an audience of three or four. In large groups, what was witty sounded crude,
what was expansive became arrogant. It was inevitable, then, that when
Johnson allowed The Treatment to dominate his "press conferences" a
sour note entered his relations with the press. Reporters en masse didn't
like being on the receiving end of The Treatment. Johnson's failure to
understand that annoyed the press, which in turn made Johnson increasingly wary and suspicious. Unable to tame the press as he tamed
so many senators, he foolishly took offense at routine questions, and
was quick to find a double meaning in the most innocent point raised
by a reporter. Although Senate reporters and Washington's top columnists were captivated in their *private* sessions with Johnson in his office or
at the LBJ Ranch, his press conferences were fiascoes. They simply could
not be harnessed to The Treatment. . . .

EDWARD F. KENNEDY AND ROBert C. Byrd have fundamentally different personalities, which have shaped their respective Senate careers. Each, like most of his colleagues, has sought power and status on Capitol Hill. But the route to power each has selected reflects a different background, character, and style. Kennedy is a star and has embraced an individualistic style; through the astute use of the committees he chairs he has sought to put the Kennedy imprint upon legislation, investigations, and committee reports. Kennedy's style represents the "new Senate," in which individual senators are more independent of their colleagues. They seek power not so much through the traditional emphasis upon collegial cooperation, but by gaining personal recognition among colleagues for hard work on committees, specialized knowledge, and legislative accomplishments. There remains an important collegial aspect to these efforts, but in the modern Senate an increasing number of members tend to focus on the separate worlds of their committees more than upon the collective demands of the institution.

Robert Byrd, in contrast to Kennedy, adopted a collegial style of operation; he sought positions of leadership in the Senate body rather than emphasizing his individual power through committees. Because of his service to fellow senators, Byrd was elected majority whip and majority leader. His personality is more muted than that of Kennedy, his style less flamboyant and aggressive. As the following selection makes clear, each has made an important contribution to the Senate.

23 Laurence Leamer
ROBERT BYRD AND EDWARD KENNEDY: TWO STORIES OF THE SENATE

The Capitol is the greatest public building in America. Visitors can sit in the House and Senate galleries, climb the broad staircases, roam the marble halls, and ride the elevators. They can go almost anywhere they choose. Yet hidden within the Capitol are offices and nooks and gathering places that are private. On the House side of the Capitol, down a back staircase from the House floor, stands an unmarked door. Behind the door is a dark room shrouded in drapes, with an old desk and a few chairs casually arranged. Here Speaker Sam Rayburn's "Board of Education" used to meet each afternoon over bourbon and water to talk politics. Fifteen years after Rayburn's death the star of Texas is still there, painted in ornate style on the far wall.

From *Playing for Keeps in Washington* by Laurence Leamer. Copyright © 1977 by Laurence Leamer. Permission granted by The Dial Press.

On the Senate side of the Capitol there are fifty-four private rooms used by senators. Some are no more than rude accumulations of government-issue desks, chairs, and paintings. Others are exquisitely decorated with antiques, political memorabilia, ornate telephones. The largest office is a three-room suite that can be reached by going down a narrow staircase just off the main corridor. These are the offices out of which Bobby Baker, the assistant to Senate majority leader Lyndon Johnson, operated. Baker had worked there until he was convicted of abusing his position and sent to prison.

These are the rooms that Edward "Ted" Kennedy of Massachusetts claimed as his own in 1969 when he was elected Democratic whip, the number-two position in the Democratic leadership. Then the offices had all the sweaty urgency of a political boiler room. The suite was full of Kennedy people. The phones rang constantly. Journalists hurried in and out. Now and again Kennedy came bursting in for a few minutes before rushing off somewhere else. There was always something happening. There had never been anything quite like it in the Senate.

In 1971 Robert C. Byrd of West Virginia defeated Kennedy and took over the suite. From all appearances, Byrd did not think the suite a grand prize but more a gift kept for occasional use. The doors might stay locked for days. Byrd decorated the rooms with just enough pictures and artifacts so that the suite became indisputably his. On the wall he put mounted whips that Senator Joseph Montoya of New Mexico had given him and a copy of a *Parade* magazine story about himself ("Senate Whip Bob Byrd: From Poverty to Power").

On the wall of the outer office hung pictures of the fourteen men who had served as Democratic whip. From Jay Hamilton to Hubert Humphrey, from Morris Sheppard to Russell Long, from Lister Hill to Lyndon Johnson, the first twelve faces looked forth with the fleshy, canny confidence of the prefessional politician. But Kennedy and Byrd were different. Kennedy's picture had the perfect looks of a Hollywood publicity glossy. Byrd, for his part, looked half-embarrassed, as if in the act of allowing himself to be photographed he was giving away something that he did not want to give away.

As much as Kennedy and Byrd were different in appearance from the twelve men who preceded them, so were they different from each other. They were two of the most powerful men in Washington. They did not like each other. They did not like each other's politics. In their distinct ways they symbolized what power had become in the modern Senate.

Senator Robert Byrd walked down the main corridor of the Capitol, down a narrow staircase, and unlocked the door to the whip's office. Many senators travel with a flotilla of aides, but Byrd almost always walks alone. He is a little man with a chalk-white face and black-and-white streaked hair swept back in a high pompadour. He looks like a wary sparrow, with a face that could be found up most any hollow in Appalachia, the face of a man who had missed some basic nutrient. It belonged to the man who was on the verge of becoming the Senate majority leader — the most powerful and prestigious position in Congress.

Byrd is a man of religious intensity, both public and private, the personification of the self-made man, a man of deep, unfathomable ambition, beyond perhaps anyone else's in the Senate. He sought power, wooed power, lived with and for power. . . .

The Senate that Byrd was sworn into in January 1959 was still dominated by Southerners like Lyndon Johnson of Texas and Richard Russell of Georgia. A conservative might believe that a certain lassitude and the petty corruption of privilege were merely the exhaust fumes given off by the Senate as it made its stately way through history. Senator Thomas Dodd of Connecticut, for instance, had an elderly retainer known as the "judge" who slept blissfully at a desk outside the senator's office.

The Senate had not yet spread out into the nearly completed New Senate Office Building. Donald R. Matthews, an academician, was finishing work on a book on the Senate, *U.S. Senators and Their World*. He broke Senate offices down into two general types: the bureaucratic and the individualistic. In the bureaucratic offices, "the senator has delegated considerable nonroutine responsibilities to his staff, established a fairly clear-cut division of labor and chain of command." The individualistic offices were "vest pocket operations in which the senator has delegated only routine tasks and in which the staff has little influence and less authority."

Byrd was arriving in the Senate as it was going through a profound evolution. The old Senate, the Senate of "individualistic" offices, had just been portrayed in *Citadel: The Story of the United States Senate*, a book by William S. White. White wrote of the U.S. Senate as "an institution that lives in an unending yesterday where the past is never gone, the present never quite decisive, and the future rarely quite visible. It has its good moments and its bad moments, but to the United States it symbolizes, if nothing else at all, the integrity of continuity and wholeness." This Senate was an institution where, when a man was sworn in, he assumed a mantle of dignity and honor. It was honor enough for any man to be in this body.

When the *Citadel* came out, Senator J. William Fulbright noticed that for a few days some of his colleagues attempted to play senator, walking the halls of Congress as if they were wearing togas. On January 15, 1957,

Lyndon B. Johnson had a luncheon for the six new Democratic senators. He gave the six freshmen autographed copies of *Citadel* and he told them that they should think of the book as a kind of McGuffey's *Reader*.

Johnson knew that White's Senate was not his, but he may have found a certain comfort in that mythical body. To White, the Senate was a great conservative body, the naysayer and watchman of democracy. But what gave the Senate its greatness were individual senators with individual ideas. They worked in the body of Congress to transform their ideas into legislation that would affect the nation. When Johnson had come to Washington, George Norris of Nebraska was still in the Senate. For years Norris had studied how to protect the land and the people. He had prepared his bill for the Tennessee Valley Authority, and he had defended it as if it were a part of his very being, which in a sense it was. Robert Wagner of New York was in the Senate too. For years he worked on the great legislation of the New Deal, including the labor bill that bears his name. Bob La Follette and Robert Taft were also in the Senate in those years. What these senators had in common was an organic relationship between what they believed, the people they served, and what they did and said to achieve their ends.

When Robert Byrd entered the Senate, he accepted the life of the Senate as the central reality of his being. "Over the years he has cloaked himself in what he perceives to be senatorial dignity and aura," said one of Byrd's former aides, "but even when he arrived, there really was very little dignity left and the aura was gone."

Byrd allied himself with Lyndon Johnson of Texas and more closely yet with Richard Russell of Georgia. Those who watched Byrd often thought him great only in petty things. But to a man who revered the Senate as much as Byrd, there were no petty duties. In 1960, during an all-night civil rights filibuster, Byrd talked for a record twenty-one hours. Five years later in another filibuster, he talked for fifteen hours. Byrd was always ready to volunteer for the KP duty of legislative life. The Senate was based on rules and precedents. And Robert Byrd, alone of his generation, was willing to learn the rules and the precedents. He studied them until he knew them as did no one else and then he studied them some more.

Byrd performed duties, great and small, for senators of every persuasion, North and South, Democrat and Republican. He helped colleagues whenever he could. When he had helped, he sent them notes saying that he had been glad to be of service. These he filed away. In 1967 he was elected Secretary of the Democratic Conference, the number-three position in the Senate Democratic leadership. Four years later he defeated Ted Kennedy and became senate whip, the number-two position in the Senate Democratic leadership.

As a Senate leader, Byrd worked even harder. He knew the Bible, the book of Senate rules and the book of precedents, and these were just about the only books he figured he would ever have to know. He had read the 900-page collection of precedents cover to cover, two times, and late at night at home he was reading it for the third. When the Senate was planning to go into closed session on matters of national security, he would go over Rule 35 once again. When there was going to be a vote on cloture, he would read the rule on cloture. Byrd knew the rules and he knew the precedents and could make them turn upside down and dance on their heads. It was *his* Senate now, and he left the floor rarely.

The Washington monument splits the window of his vast inner office in the Capitol. Senator Byrd speaks quietly, the twang of the hills in his voice: "The Senate is a forest. There are ninety-nine animals. They're all lions. There's a waterhole in the forest. I'm the waterhole. They all have to come to the waterhole. I don't have power but I have knowledge of the rules. I have knowledge of the precedents. I have knowledge of the schedule. So I'm in a position to do things for others.

"Now the majority leader is the dispatcher, the engineer, the fellow at the head of the engine who's looking out from the dark night at the headlight down the railway, pulling on the throttle a little harder, push-ing on the throttle a little, or leveling off a little, moving it along. Or he determines to move over on this sidetrack or that sidetrack. This legis-lative organism, with its power, has to have direction. It has to have a leader, but he doesn't have the power. He's the umpire, the referee. He doesn't have any more of that raw power than any other senator has.

"The president, he has power. He's the chief executive of this coun-try. The presidency of the United States should in reality seek the man. Someone said that. That's the way it ought to be. People ought not to be persuaded by a person's pretty teeth, by his smile, or by the way he cuts his hair — by his charisma. That's misleading. That's not to say that a person with pretty teeth and a pretty smile and a handsome build and charisma may not have the ability. But they don't necessarily go to-gether either."

Talking about pretty teeth and a pretty smile and the cut of a man's hair, Robert Byrd could have been sketching a caricature of Edward Ken-nedy. Byrd and Kennedy were the two Janus faces of the Senate, Byrd often looking backward to a past that had never been, Kennedy looking forward to a future that might never arrive. They approached their work as differently as two men in the same profession possibly could. They also had different conceptions of power and how to use it.

Edward Moore Kennedy walked down the center aisle of the Senate to be sworn in as the junior senator from Massachusetts on January 9, 1963. He had the accent and bearing of the Kennedys, but was a big, brawny fellow with a rousing, friendly manner that suggested an Irish politician of a half century past. He was the scion of a family that seemed destined to dominate American political life in the last decades of the twentieth century as had the Adams family in the first decades of the nation's history. . . .

Kennedy fit unobtrusively into the traditional role of the freshman senator. One morning he went around to see Senator James Eastland of Mississippi, chairman of the Judiciary Committee and champion of the old Senate. He drank bourbon with the senior senator and Eastland discovered that the Kennedys were not all alike. He went around to see Senator Richard Russell of Georgia, Robert Byrd's patron, and he went to the Senate prayer breakfast, too — once at least — and led his colleagues in prayer.

While Kennedy might act out such old-fashioned rituals of the Senate, he was still the most modern of freshmen. A decade later, James Macgregor Burns, a biographer of Kennedy, would call him a "presidential senator." Kennedy was a presidential senator not only in the sense that he had become the sole bearer of the Kennedy legacy and heir apparent to the White House. He was presidential in the way he went about being a senator. He launched a frenetic, permanent presidential-like campaign within the very Senate.

In the favored analogy of his staff, Senator Kennedy stood at the center of a circle of aides who flowed in and around him. The Kennedys had always had a special talent for acquiring and using people whose talents met the needs of the moment. They attracted members of that natural aristocracy of the able and the ambitious. These aides were perhaps no more talented than those around other contenders for the ultimate prize in American politics. But in the livery of the Kennedys, they seemed to serve with extraordinary energy and devotion, and in the end they were, in one way or another, rewarded in kind.

One of those who was there when Kennedy entered the Senate was Milton Gwirtzman, now a Washington lawyer.

"From the beginning Kennedy knew how to use his staff," Gwirtzman observed. "Even in his first term he had that lineup outside his office. There were perhaps six professionals then and Kennedy used them as a multiplier." To a Borah or Taft or Wagner, the idea of a senatorial multiplier would have been absurd. It would, indeed, have been impossible, for until the Legislative Reorganization Act of 1946, most senators had only a clerk and a secretary.

Kennedy was one of the first senators to employ his staff so systematically that he helped create a new definition of "senator." Kennedy not only used the half dozen or so aides who were his natural due, but he subsidized two others. Gwirtzman, for one, left the staff in 1964 but for the next six years was paid $18,000 a year by the Park Agency, a Kennedy family conduit, for speeches and advice. Kennedy, moreover, had a press secretary. That itself was a relatively new position on the Hill: a media-savvy specialist who measured success in newsprint and television time, not merely in a product called legislation.

Kennedy understood how to develop his staff so that they would serve him. He did not want any one Super Aide around him who might become for him what Ted Sorensen had been for Jack. He did not want an alter ego. What he did want was a group of people who could work on their own, self-motivated young men ambitious for themselves and for him, men whose competitiveness with one another might sometimes spill over into jealousies, but whose energies and ideals could be channeled into furthering Senator Ted Kennedy and his career.

In those first years in office, Kennedy did not draw on his name. He did not use his power in ways that were memorable or important. He had a quotation from Machiavelli as his maxim: "Power not used is power saved." Machiavelli, however, was writing about power that had once been used. Kennedy was hoarding a commodity whose worth he could not know until he used it. He was acting as if even he accepted the common definition of himself as the last and the least of the Kennedys — the kid brother.

During the day Kennedy abided by all the rituals of egalitarianism: bantering with aides, employing the ersatz intimacy of first names. However, if an aide stepped over a certain line, visible only to Kennedy, that aide learned to regret it. By day they might be members of a team but not in the evening. It was simply understood that if you worked for Ted Kennedy you did not go to social gatherings that he attended. You learned to treat his family in a special way. An aide had taken a phone call from Rose Kennedy in Hyannis Port one day. "Your mother called," the aide said when Kennedy returned to the office. "You mean *you* talked to *my* mother?" Kennedy said. If politics was one world, and social life another, then the family was yet a third and the most exalted of Kennedy's worlds. Here the subordinates were not allowed to trespass, even for a moment.

On that November afternoon in 1963 when President John F. Kennedy was assassinated in Dallas, Ted Kennedy was performing that most thankless of tasks foisted on the freshman: presiding over a nearly empty Senate. When he learned of the shooting and he finally reached his brother on the telephone, Robert Kennedy told him, "You'd better call your mother and your sisters." In their division of the duties of mourning, it fell to Ted Kennedy to comfort the family.

By that next June, Kennedy had prepared his public face. His party back in Massachusetts was preparing to nominate him for his first full term in office. Kennedy, however, was still on the floor of the Senate waiting to vote on the civil rights bill. It was so typical of his life to have a dozen people, a dozen decisions, a dozen proposals backed up waiting for him.

Kennedy finally left Washington for Massachusetts by private plane, accompanied by Senator Birch Bayh of Indiana and his wife Marvella, and aide Ed Moss. It was no kind of weather to be flying in a private plane, but Kennedy lived in a world of days that were scheduled too tight, cars that were driven too fast, planes that were flown when they shouldn't have been. On the approach to the airpost outside Springfield, the plane crashed. The Bayhs were injured, the pilot was dead, Moss would die soon afterward, and Kennedy had cracked ribs, a punctured lung, and three damaged vertebrae.

Kennedy spent the next six months in bed. . . .

While still in the hospital, Kennedy won reelection in Massachusetts with 74.4 percent of the votes. In New York, his brother Bob defeated Kenneth Keating for a Senate seat by a much closer margin. Afterward his brother had come up to visit in the hospital. The two Kennedys had posed for the photographers. "Step back a little, you're casting a shadow on Ted," one of the photographers said to Bob Kennedy.

"It'll be the same in Washington," Ted Kennedy said laughing.

During the nearly four years that the two Kennedys served together in the Senate, Ted Kennedy largely deferred to his brother and to his leadership. In 1965 he took over the chairmanship of the Subcommittee on Refugees and Escapees. This was his first chairmanship, the natural legacy of the seniority system. It was a moribund subcommittee concerned largely with refugees who had fled Communist Europe. But it represented more staff and an area that he could now legitimately make his own.

Ted took the subcommittee and expanded its mandate to the refugees of Southeast Asia. He used it as his ticket of admission to the issue of Vietnam. He went to Vietnam and the papers were full of the poignant testimony of human suffering. . . .

It was not until after the murder of his brother Bob in 1968 that Ted Kennedy, the senator, began to fully emerge. In his time of mourning he had gone sailing for days on end, and drinking, and carousing. Then in August in Worcester he had given a speech important enough to be televised nationally. He told his audience that he had been at sea. But he said, "There is no safety in hiding. Not for me, not for any of us here today . . . like my brothers before me, I pick up a fallen standard." He went on to talk about the Vietnam war and all it had cost in money and blood. He proposed that the United States unconditionally end the bombing and negotiate a peace. . . .

The next office Kennedy did seek was one that his brothers would never have considered. In January he defeated Russell Long, that son of Louisiana, and son of oil, to become majority whip. The whip had a series of thankless bureaucratic duties such as rounding up senators and arranging schedules. He was, nonetheless, the number-two leader in the Senate. Kennedy set out to make the whip more than that. He brought in some of his own academic and other expert advisors to forge a cohesive policy for the Democrats. Senators, however, are a jealous and self-protective group. A hundred different policies were better than one, if the one came stamped with the mark of a particular senator. Worse yet, Kennedy simply did not perform the mundane, pesky tasks of the whip as they were supposed to be. Bored by them, he foisted such chores as he could onto his staff.

Kennedy was drinking heavily. At times his face had the florid look that showed him a full-blooded member of the race of Irish drinkers. Then in July on vacation he had gone over to Chappaquiddick Island to attend a party for some of Bobby Kennedy's "boiler-room girls." He had left with one of them, Mary Jo Kopechne, and the next morning the police had found her body in Kennedy's overturned Oldsmobile off a bridge on a dirt road on Chappaquiddick Island.

Kennedy, according to his own statement, had dived down to try to get her out and then he had left and gone back to his friends to get help. He had not contacted the police until the next morning. The Kennedys, whatever else one said about them, had always showed the grace under pressure that Hemingway had called the mark of courage, the mark of a man. The private Kennedy had failed that night, as those around him failed. "It was in part a failure of staffing," one of his aides said. "He had no one with him to tell him he was crazy."

Within hours Kennedy had left the island. He retreated into that flimsy story; he made a televised public statement prepared by Ted Sorensen, Gwirtzman, Richard Goodwin, and Burke Marshall and then backed into legal refuges, the power of wealth and position, and the sympathy that people of Massachusetts had for him and for his family. . . .

Until that night at Chappaquiddick, Kennedy had appeared an inevitable choice for the 1972 presidential nomination. But that was all over. When Kennedy returned to the Senate, Mike Mansfield, the majority leader, as goodhearted a man as was to be found in that body, noticed Kennedy pausing for a moment in the cloakroom. "Come here," Mansfield said encouragingly. "Come here, right back where you belong." To the last of the Kennedys, it was a phrase not without its ironies. . . .

O N NOVEMBER 2, 1948, Russell B. Long was elected to the United States Senate to fill the unexpired term of John H. Overton, who was Huey Long's hand-picked candidate in 1932. Overton's seat thus fittingly remained in the hands of the Long organization. Huey Long himself had had a short but flamboyant career as a United States senator, having been elected to the Senate in 1930 while he was governor. He retained both positions until 1932, when he took the senatorial oath, which required him under Louisiana law to relinquish his governorship. His son Russell's Senate "Class of 1948" included Hubert H. Humphrey of Minnesota, Lyndon B. Johnson of Texas, Robert Kerr of Oklahoma, and Paul Douglas of Illinois, all of whom became powerful members.

By 1964, Russell Long was the ranking member of the Senate Finance Committee. He used his position of power and prestige in the Senate to launch a successful drive to become majority whip in 1965. He became chairman of the Finance Committee in 1966. At that time, Long's personal style, a combination of effective wheeling and dealing and highly powerful oratory, was able to gain him widespread Senate support. He was not, however, nearly as flamboyant as his father, and his quiet, reasonable, and flexible maneuvering behind the scenes was in line with Senate traditions.

After he became majority whip Long's style changed. Robert Peabody describes Long's post-1965 period as follows:

Throwing most of his energies into his prime love, the chairmanship of the Finance Committee, Long managed over the next three years to (1) incur the increasing displeasure of the Majority Leader, (2) please few of the colleagues with his performance as Majority Whip, (3) tie up the entire Senate for six weeks in an attempt to promote a presidential election campaign fund, (4) defend the unpopular cause of Senator Thomas Dodd, (5) antagonize a number of liberals with rather heavyhanded and arbitrary floor maneuvering, (6) aggravate a drinking problem, and (7) neutralize the backing of several of the most important senior oligarchs in the Senate.[1]

Russell Long lost his position as whip to Senator Edward Kennedy in 1969, who in turn lost his position to Senator Robert C. Byrd in 1971. The defeats of Long and Kennedy were mainly due to personal factors, and resulting leadership styles that were unacceptable to many Senate colleagues.

Although Long lost the post of majority whip in 1969, it was a close vote, thirty-one to twenty-six. The defeat in no way affected his position as chairman of the Finance Committee, which guaranteed him a solid base for expansion of his power if he wished. Losing the position of majority whip was only a temporary loss of power for Russell Long in the Senate. He quickly retrenched, and soon was able to renew the personal style that had led to his rise to power. By the mid-1970s Long was again a major force in

[1] Robert L. Peabody, *Leadership in Congress* (Boston: Little, Brown, 1976), p. 366.

the Senate. Under his chairmanship the Finance Committee became a power in determining tax legislation, and in the Ninety-fourth Congress (1976) he defeated a major attempt by Senator Edmund Muskie of Maine, chairman of the Senate Budget Committee, to force the Finance Committee to comply with the wishes of the Budget Committee.

Just as Long had maintained his independence within the Senate, he was determined not to be dominated by "the other body." The Finance Committee had operated for many years in the shadow of the House Ways and Means Committee, but under Long it was revitalized.

The major confrontations between the House and the Senate often comes in conference committees, and Russell Long had become a master of conference committee technique. His skill in handling Senate-House negotiations often assured victory for the Senate side. The following selection is a case study of Russell Long's style and of his methods in making his personal imprint on legislation.

24   Aaron Latham
RUSSELL LONG

Richard Nixon probably spent too much time studying football. But Al Ullman (D., Ore.), the new chairman of the Ways and Means Committee, may have spent too little. If Ullman had known more about football strategy, he would never have committed the classic coach's blunder: publicly knocking the other team on the eve of the big game. That tends to get the other side riled up.

Ullman's indiscretion occurred on ABC's "Issues and Answers" show. The day was Sunday, March 23, the day before a House-Senate conference committee was scheduled to begin reconciling the differences between the House and Senate versions of the tax-cut bill. Since the two houses of Congress almost never pass exactly the same bill, such conference committees are necessary to work out a compromise. And in these conferences, Senate and House chauvinism often plays a role. In this case the trouble started when ABC's Bob Clark asked what would happen to the long list of amendments which the Senate had tacked onto the bill.

Ullman said, "We think many of the amendments added in the Senate cannot be justified. We think there is a real danger in being irresponsible here, and doing the things that might lead to an inflationary spiral. So, many of the Senate amendments will be cut back."

Clark asked for Ullman's assessment of a Senate amendment which would allow a tax credit of up to $2,000 to anyone who bought a new home.

Ullman said, "I personally think that that is not the right way to approach the housing problem."

The problem was that the housing credit was one of the amendments sponsored by Huey Long's son Russell, the leader of the Senate conferees, a paradigm of the Southern politician who hides his consummate legislative mastery in a good-ol'-boy verbal briar patch.

For years, when Senate and House conferees met to wrestle over money bills, Russell Long (D., La.), the chairman of the Senate Finance Committee, had been eclipsed by Wilbur Mills (D., Ark.), the long-reigning chairman of the House Ways and Means Committee. But now Mills was gone. Now Russell Long, the cagey veteran, would be up against Al Ullman, the new boy. Long looked forward to eclipsing Ullman the way Mills had eclipsed him.

And yet it wasn't working out quite that way. The media tended to treat Ullman as if he were Mills — and Long got left out. Ullman was always on the television shows. And now, on the eve of the conference, here was Ullman, basking in the "Issues and Answers" limelight, saying Long's housing amendment would have to go.

This would be the first conference where Long and Ullman would be pitted head to head. Whoever won this one might just go on winning for the next decade, so Long was determined to prove he couldn't be run over.

Long's strategy was based in part on all those Senate amendments to which Ullman objected. Long was a horse trader and the amendments were his horses. If Ullman wanted any of them dropped, he would have to make concessions.

The total cost for all those amendments, if approved, would add billions to the tax-cut bill, which reminded Long of a story. He told reporters that when Clinton Anderson was on the Finance Committee, he had suggested that they install a gong which would be rung every time the committee gave away a billion dollars. He thought that such a gong would help provide some sense of reality. If the Senate Finance Committee had had a gong when it was tacking amendments onto the tax-cut bill, it would have rung as follows: *Bong . . . bong . . . bong . . . bong . . . bong . . . bong . . . bong . . . bong . . . bong . . . bong.* Ten times in ten hours.

The Senate had taken the $20-billion tax-cut bill voted by the House and added another $10 billion or so. That meant that, going into the conference committee, Russell Long had 10 billion chips to play with. So, ask not for whom the gong bonged. The gong bonged for Al Ullman.

The First Day

Russell B. Long, fifty-six, who has been a senator since he was thirty, moves with the inevitability of the Mississippi River. Sometimes he overflows with sentiment. Sometimes he simply drowns you in words. But he keeps on rolling. One of his colleagues says, "Long is the most colorful man in the Senate." Some reporters will tell you Long, whose ADA rating hovers under twenty, is their favorite senator, although they often disagree with him. Linda Wertheimer, who covers the Hill for National Public Radio, says, "In the Senate, you've got all these presidential hopefuls standing around saying presidential things, and then you've got Long, who knows how to get things done. It's often not passion but presidential passion guiding these other senators, but Long's passion seems real."

Long, like Mills, used to have a drinking problem. It almost seems to go with the job. The difference is that Long licked his with the help of his second wife, who often sits up in the gallery during late sessions as if to watch over him. Long still has something of a W. C. Fields nose and can be almost as funny, but he has been sober for years. He may look a little sleepy, but he isn't.

On the first day of the conference, Russell Long got up at 5:30 in the morning. He was on Capitol Hill by 7 A.M. Before the conference started, Long caucused with the Senate's Democratic conferees in his office. The Senate was allowed ten members on the conference committee — six Democrats and four Republicans. If the six Senate Democrats did not get their way, they could simply stalemate the conference, provided they voted as a bloc.[1]

In the caucus, Long did just what a football coach would have done: He gave a pep talk in which he pointed out that the other side's coach had been mouthing off about the Senate team. He said that if the Senate Democrats did not stick together, the House would "run them right off Capitol Hill."

The Senate Democrats agreed to stick together. Moreover, they promised that, come what may, Al Ullman was going to accept the housing-credit amendment he had rejected on national TV.

[1] The Senate conferees were Long, Herman Talmadge (D., Ga.), Vance Hartke (D., Ind.), Abraham Ribicoff (D., Conn.), William Hathaway (D., Me.), Floyd Haskell (D., Colo.), Carl Curtis (R., Neb.), Paul Fannin (R., Ariz.), Clifford Hansen (R., Wyo.), Robert Dole (R., Kan.). The House conferees were Ullman, James Burke (D., Mass.), Dan Rostenkowski (D., Ill.), Phil Landrum (D., Ga.), Charles Vanik (D., Ohio), Herman Schneebeli (R., Pa.), Barber Conable, Jr. (R., N.Y.).

The conference committee met that morning in H208, a small room just outside the House chamber. In years past, the door bore the name "Mr. Mills," and tourists posed next to it to have their pictures taken. Now the door bears the name "Mr. Ullman," and the tourists don't take pictures anymore.

The House and Senate, for the first time in history, had both held their markups on the tax-cut bill in public session, but when they went into conference, they closed the door, making a lot of reporters mad. As the conference was getting under way, the conferees could hear reporters grumbling through the louvered door. So they closed the louvers. Then there was no air; some reporters thought that was poetic justice.

Inside tiny H208, the conferees were incredibly cramped, with one lawmaker's knees jammed into another lawmaker's back. There was no oxygen. And, as one participant put it, "There was a lot of 'bad air,' as the French say." He meant there was a lot of hostility bordering on rudeness.

Russell Long kept needling Al Ullman about his appearance on "Issues and Answers." Long boasted that since he had not taken any positions on TV the day before, he could approach the conference with an open mind.

Only Long's mind really wasn't all that open. He had determined not to give in on anything that first day. Like any good coach, he knew that if you could stop your opponents cold in the first quarter, it might break their spirit.

One of the first issues taken up by the conference was relatively trivial but hotly contended. Al Ullman proposed that the conferees meet late into the evenings. Long objected. After all, he felt that time was on his side. With the whole Congress eager to take an Easter recess, the longer the conference, the greater would be the pressure to compromise. Long, who was prepared to outstall Ullman, definitely did not want to work late. He got his way.

The rest of the morning, the House side offered the Senate side compromises, And the Senate side stonewalled.

Just before lunch, Long complained that there was no air in the room and everyone was getting red in the face. He proposed that they meet in a larger room. For once, the Senate and House sides found themselves in agreement.

After lunch, the conferees reconvened in the Ways and Means hearing room in the Longworth Building. It is enormous. The move to the larger room seemed to open up the atmosphere. That afternoon, the House gave way on some minor points, but the Senate, although more amicable, refused to give on anything.

The Second Day

The conference's first major breakthrough came on the second day, when the House made a concession to Long. Russell Long, the son of a populist and a populist himself, had sponsored an amendment which he called the "work bonus" plan. He proposed to pay the working poor with dependent children a bonus amounting to 10 percent (up to $400) of their income. The House conferees knew that Long had a substantial investment in this amendment, so they let him have it.

Long responded by giving up some amendments — ones he had not sponsored. He agreed to knock out an amendment providing a tax credit for people who installed insulation or solar heating in their homes. He agreed to throw out an amendment lifting the excise tax on trucks. He agreed to reduce the scope of an amendment which would have allowed all working parents to deduct the cost of child care as a regular business expense. (Under the old law, only working parents earning under $18,000 qualified for the full deduction. The conference committee simply agreed to raise this ceiling to $35,000.) And then Long agreed to give up the so-called "Chrysler bailout" amendment which would have allowed a company to write off current losses against profits way back in 1967, 1968, and 1969 — thereby qualifying for a refund of past taxes. So, in effect, Russell Long sacrificed a tax break for big corporations in order to assure one for the working poor. His old daddy would have been proud.

The Senate conferees also agreed to accept the House formula for a rebate to individual taxpayers. The Senate version called for a rebate of 12 percent, but not more than $240, on 1974 taxes. The House version called for a rebate of 10 percent, but not more than $200 — total cost $8.1 billion. *Bong . . . bong . . . bong . . . bong . . . bong . . . bong . . . bong . . . bong.*

The Senate and House conferees agreed to compromise on an investment tax credit for new machinery. This credit was raised from 7 to 10 percent for the next two years, giving business slightly more than the House bill, slightly less than the Senate bill.

But tacked onto this provision was a major victory for Long. The senator from Louisiana calls it his "share the wealth" plan. This allows businesses an additional 1 percent tax credit if they will invest that money in an employee stock-ownership plan. This idea originated with an economist named Louis Kelso, who persuaded Long to back it. For years, Long has crusaded for this idea with the fervor of a new convert. Long reels off statistics the way an evangelist reels off Scripture: "Three percent of the people own 70 percent of the country's net worth." The Aesop plan illustrates the power of an idea which has just one true believer pushing it. The other conferees let Long have his way. Long says, "The most significant thing in that bill is the Aesop plan." To him, the biggest tax cut in the history of the United States is eclipsed by his amendment.

The House-Senate conferees made good progress all morning, but after lunch they completely bogged down in an oil quagmire. The House of Representatives had given Al Ullman a mandate: Put an end to the oil-depletion allowance. But Russell Long, who has invested in oil wells himself, whose family is in the oil business, and whose campaigns have been enriched with oil money, refused.

Actually, Long more than refused. He went into his act. He told stories. He philosophized. He filibustered. One person at the conference said, "Trying to pin Long down was like trying to grab 100 pounds of Jell-O."

For many years, oil companies were allowed to write off 22 percent of their profits from their drilling operations. But the House had voted to shut off this allowance. When the House bill reached the Senate, it set off some Byzantine politics. On the Senate floor, Senator Ernest Hollings (D., S.C.) rose to move for an end of the oil-depletion allowance. Before he could make his motion, however, Senator Mike Gravel (D., Alaska) managed to offer an amendment which was itself amended by Senator Alan Cranston (D., Cal.). This amended amendment sought to preserve the oil-depletion allowance for independent producers. This was all an elaborate ruse worked out ahead of time, for the Senate rules stipulate that you cannot amend beyond the second degree, meaning that you can amend an amendment but you cannot amend an amendment of an amendment. So Hollings was shut out cold.

This trick made Hollings hopping mad. When the parliamentary dust had settled, this maneuver was ruled out of order. Eventually a compromise was worked out which was sponsored by Hollings, Cranston, and Edward Kennedy. This compromise ended the oil-depletion allowance for the majors but retained it in a limited form for independent oil producers, who were allowed to write off 22 percent of their profits on 2,000 barrels a day. Since twenty-eight states have independent oil companies, this provision passed the Senate.

It was this amendment which Russell Long carried into the conference committee. The oil-depletion allowance for the majors was dead, but he was determined to keep it alive for all the little independent "mom and pop millionaires" and "storefront barons."

In the conference, Long attempted to use Kennedy's sponsorship of the amendment to his advantage. At one point, Long accused Ullman of not understanding the Democratic caucus in the House. Long said, "Just go back and tell them that Kennedy is for it and they'll love it."

When that argument failed, Long retreated into storytelling. He talked so much and in so many circles that Ullman seemed disoriented, confused. Which was just what Long wanted. He rules by confusion. During the Finance Committee markups, several senators complained that they did not understand what they were being asked to vote on. Long replied, "If every man insists on knowing what he's voting for before he votes, we're not going to get a bill reported before Monday." In the land of the confused, the man who has some idea what is going on is king.

And now Russell Long had Al Ullman's head spinning. Ullman could simply never catch Long as he darted here and there in his briar patch.

Long told a story about a woman who went to the store to buy some eggs. She asked the storekeeper how he had the gall to sell eggs for 40 cents a dozen when the grocer down the street wanted only 30 cents a dozen. The storekeeper asked the woman why she didn't buy her eggs down the street. The woman said, "Because he's out of eggs." The storekeeper said, "Well, if I were out of eggs, I'd sell them for 10 cents a dozen." The moral of the story, according to Long, was that if you wanted something, like, for instance, oil, then you had to pay the price, and part of that price was oil depletion.

When the House conferees saw that they had no chance of ending the oil-depletion allowance forthwith, they proposed a compromise. Charles Vanik (D., Ohio) suggested that the allowance be phased out over twelve years.

Which reminded Long of another story. This one was about a sheik who caught a young courtier making love to his daughter. The sheik ordered the young man executed at dawn. The boy said, "If you'll give me three months, I'll teach an ass to talk." The sheik was intrigued by the idea, and so put him in a cell with an ass. One of the boy's friends came by the prison and asked why the boy had claimed he could teach the ass to talk. The boy said, "Because it got me three months. In that time, the sheik might die, or I might die, or I might just teach the ass to talk." The moral of the story, according to Long, was that it made no sense to phase out oil depletion over the years because you never could tell what was going to happen. You never knew what future Congresses or future presidents might want to do about the matter. (Listening to Long, some of the conferees felt that the young courtier had succeeded in his task.)

After hearing Long defend the oil-depletion allowance for hours, the House conferees finally backed down and proposed to continue the independents' depletion allowance but to phase it down over the years from 2,000 barrels a day to 500 barrels a day. Long seemed interested, but said he would have to check with his people. The conference broke up for the day.

Russell Long went home to his apartment in the Watergate complex. That evening, Long called Senator Clifford Hansen (R., Wyo.), another member of the conference committee who also lives in the Watergate, and invited him to drop up for a visit. Long and Hansen belong to different parties but are allies on the oil-depletion question. They are also friends. Long sold Hansen his apartment. While the two senators were visiting, Long's telephone rang.

The president of the United States was calling. Gerald Ford wanted to discuss the tax-cut bill, but his tone was almost jocular. The president instructed Long more or less as follows: "If the tax-cut bill is over $25 billion, please make it as big as possible, because then it will be that much easier to veto."

Long told the president that Hansen was there. Ford, a gregarious president, asked to speak to Hansen and gave him a pep talk on reporting out a good bill.

After his chat with the president, Long never again took seriously all the White House threats to veto the tax cut. Long knew that the bill would come in well under twenty-five bongs.

The Third Day

On Wednesday morning, the conferees reported to the Ways and Means hearing room in an optimistic mood. They felt they were on the verge of wrapping up the tax cut. But before the conference got under way, Long and Ullman sat down together to talk. It was a private conversation, but their mikes were on. So the others knew that Long's answer was no. Gloom settled over the conferees once again.

The conference moved on to a discussion of Senator Vance Hartke's (D., Ind.) amendments to close loopholes which have saved multinational companies billions in taxes. Hartke's main points were dropped from the bill, but a few provisions were allowed to remain. The conference agreed to end both the tax break given money channeled through underdeveloped countries and the tax break on shipping income. And they restricted the size of the tax credit oil companies may take when they pay foreign taxes.

But then the conference seemed to bog down completely. Some conferees began to fear that the conference might fail to report out a bill at all.

Long and Ullman moved out into the seats where the audience would have been if the conference had not been closed. They bargained head to head, but still reached no compromise.

By noon, the conference seemed completely stalemated. It was a hung jury. Abraham Ribicoff (D., Conn.) chose this moment to speak. None of the senators except Long had said much during the conference, but Ribicoff had been especially quiet. Breaking his silence at last, Ribicoff observed that they seemed to have come to the end of the road. As one last effort to avoid failure, he suggested that Long and Ullman go to lunch together and try to come back with some sort of compromise.

The conference voted unanimously in favor of Ribicoff's suggestion. One conferee offered to pay for the lunch.

Everyone left the room except Long, Ullman, and Laurence Woodworth, the brilliant chief of staff of the Joint Committee on Taxation. In a trivial sense, Long and Ullman double-crossed the others: They didn't go to lunch together. Instead, they stayed right there in the room and cut their compromise.

Sitting down together at the dais, they went to work. Long said that neither of them was going to convince the other, so, "Why don't we just split the difference?" And with Woodworth working as a catalyst, they did just that.

The Senate wanted to pay $100 to people on Social Security. The House didn't want to pay anything. So they settled on $50.

The Senate wanted to allow people who bought new homes in 1975 a 5 percent tax credit up to $2,000 — estimated total cost: $1.1 billion. The House wanted no housing credit at all. So they settled on a housing credit for homes under construction by March 25 — estimated total cost: $600 million.

The Senate wanted to allow taxpayers to take a $200 tax credit rather than a $750 deduction if that made their taxes lower. Since the deduction is regressive, saving those in a lower bracket less than those in a higher bracket, this credit was supposed to help even out this inequity. Long and Ullman agreed to give every taxpayer a $30 credit on top of a deduction.

The Senate bill allowed independent oil producers a depletion allowance on 2,000 barrels a day. The House wanted to cut it out altogether. So they decided to phase down the depletion allowance from 2,000 barrels a day in 1975 to 1,000 barrels a day in 1980. They further agreed to phase down the percentage of income on these barrels which could be written off. This percentage would hold firm at the old 22 percent until 1980, but between 1980 and 1984 it would phase down to 15 percent.

Done and done.

After the lunch recess, the conference committee reconvened not in the Ways and Means hearing room but in S207 just off the Senate floor. This room is similar to H208, where the conference had started, but it is larger. Also, it is on the other side of the Capitol. This move seemed symbolic. In three days, the conference had migrated from the House side to the Senate side.

In its new digs, the conference committee immediately agreed to accept the oil-depletion compromise. Everyone felt like celebrating. It seemed to be all over but the easy items.

Then a house — or rather 400,000 houses — fell on them. The House conferees still would not accept the housing credit. It was all coming apart all over again.

Ribicoff spoke again. He made what bordered on a patriotic speech. He spoke of chaos in the economy. He spoke of a lack of leadership. He spoke of a need to take hold. He suggested that they vote all remaining provisions — the oil, Social Security, $30 credit, and housing — up or down as one complete package.

Then Phil Landrum (D., Ga.), a conservative Southerner who is in many ways Ribicoff's opposite, took the floor to make a speech much like Ribicoff's.

The liberal Northern senator and the conservative Southern representative carried the day. The conference committee voted to accept the whole Long-Ullman lunch-break package. The conference, which Ullman calls "one of the toughest I've ever been in," was over.

Ullman had managed to pare down the cost of the tax cut, but Long had retained all of the amendments about which he really cared. If you looked only at the price tag, then Ullman had won the conference. If you looked only at the provisions, then Long had won. So in a sense it was a compromise. However, Russell Long had never really expected, or even wanted, to get the full $30-billion Senate-approved tax cut. What he really wanted, he got. On Capitol Hill Russell Long was generally awarded the conference.

Mills is "dead" — long live Long.

In the hall, the reporters had organized a pool on the cost of the tax cut. The winners were Marya McLaughlin of CBS and Chuck Van Dyke of AP. Al Hunt, the *Wall Street Journal* reporter who acted as banker, threw the money at them. The tax-cut conference ended in a shower of dollar bills.

And what was the winning bet?

Bong, bong.

THOMAS P. ("TIP") O'NEILL IS the epitome of the Massachusetts politician, which according to some political observers is a unique breed. O'Neill was born in 1912, into a second-generation Irish immigrant family. His father was a Cambridge politician, and by the time Tip O'Neill was in his teens, he was actively involved in political campaigns. He was elected to the Massachusetts legislature in 1936, the same year he graduated from Boston College. He served in the state legislature until 1952, having been chosen minority leader in 1947 and 1948, and Speaker of the House from 1948 until 1952. In 1952 he ran for John F. Kennedy's vacated House seat (Kennedy was running a successful senatorial campaign against Henry Cabot Lodge, Jr.), and after a close primary win he won the general election by a large majority, which was the case in all of his subsequent elections to the House.

Tip O'Neill advanced rapidly in the House, not only because of his own consummate skill as a politician, but because he was aided by another Massachusetts politician, John F. McCormack. In 1955, McCormack, who was majority leader, appointed O'Neill to the powerful House Rules Committee. When McCormack became Speaker of the House in 1962, O'Neill served as an informal majority leader until the selection of Carl Albert. Tip O'Neill himself became majority leader in January 1971, after the untimely death of Majority Leader Hale Boggs of Louisiana, who was lost on a plane flight over Alaska. The backing of Boggs's people in the House helped to give O'Neill the majority leadership. O'Neill conducted the same kind of highly effective personal campaign for the House leadership that had always guaranteed him success with the regular electorate. Within the House, O'Neill's personal friendship with McCormack and his close working relationship with Carl Albert, both when Albert was majority leader and when he was Speaker, reflected O'Neill's effective personality and style. By the time the Democratic caucus met in January 1973 to choose its new majority leader, Tip O'Neill was unopposed. From the position of majority leader it was only one short step to the Speakership in 1977 after Albert retired. In the following selection we see why Tip O'Neill is truly a master politician; we are given a close look at his two major assets, his personality and style.

25 Jimmy Breslin
THE POLITICIAN

The hand that rocked the bureaucracy into motion was found, of a Saturday night in June 1974, wrapped around a glass.

"Will you drink a Manhattan?" Tip O'Neill asked a man joining the party.

The man thought about it.

"I asked you, will you drink a Manhattan?"

The man thought more about it. Agitation showed in O'Neill's face.

"The reason I'm asking if you take a Manhattan is that there's no bar here and it takes them too long to bring us back a drink. So I ordered two Manhattans for myself and you can have one of them if you want."

This was in the early part of the evening, when more than forty people came into the private dining room of the Wayside Inn, at Chatham, on Cape Code, the people gathering there in celebration and admiratimn of the thirty-third wedding anniversary of Tip and Milly O'Neill and simultaneously the sixtieth birthday of Milly O'Neill, that number being loudly announced to all by her husband.

O'Neill was standing in a circle of people, everybody talking, O'Neill talking back to everybody, when his son Tom — who was running, successfully it turned out, for lieutenant governor of Massachusetts — placed a hand on his father's elbow. "Dad, I just want to tell you this one thing."

O'Neill, looking straight ahead, the eyes taking in the entire room — politics is for backcourt men — said out of the corner of his mouth to his son, "Hey, I can listen to five conversations at once. Just keep telling me what you want me to know."

His father went back to the group. "Chuck, is the weather really that bad? I thought Bantry was part of Cork. Cork's not supposed to be that bad. Oh, it's in West Cork? Oh, they have bright spells. That's good. Bright spells. Dick, old pal, you look good. Mary, darling! How are you? What will you have to drink, dear? Are you playing any golf, Paul? Well, I played today. You know what happened the other day out there? I'm on the third hole and there's a ball on the fairway and I don't know where the hell it came from. And here coming through the woods from the other fairway is Jim St. Clair. I said to him, 'Hey, Jim, what are you doing over here?' He just gave me this shrug and I kept going my way. Stop to talk to him? Oh, I wouldn't do that. It just so happens that we're both members of Eastward Ho. Do I know him? I'll tell you a story about

From *How the Good Guys Finally Won* by Jimmy Breslin. Copyright © 1975 by Jimmy Breslin. Reprinted by permission of Viking Penguin, Inc.

Jim St. Clair. One day a long time ago I got a call on a Sunday morning from a man whose son was arrested for drunken driving the night before. The boy was a senior at West Point. He was taking a summer course at MIT. The boy had been out and he'd had a few and the officer arrested him in Central Square for drunk driving. Well, I get a call from the father. He said the son'll be thrown out of West Point. Could I help? Well, geez, a kid goes to his last year in the Academy. I'm not going to let him get into trouble over a few drinks. Of course, I'll try to help. I told him I'd get my brother Bill, who was alive then. Practicing law, you know. Well, Bill calls the guy and the father says there's ten thousand in it if you could get my son off. My brother says, no, one thousand will be the charge, and I *cahn't* guarantee you anything but a pretty good try. The father said, no, it has to be ten thousand. My brother Bill says, no, I'll charge you a thousand. So on a Sunday morning we all come to court. I take a seat and the clerk comes up to me and says the judge wants to see me in the back. So I go back there and the judge says, 'Tip, what are you doing in here?' So I tell him the story of this West Point lad. When I finish I go outside and by now the father and the boy are in court. And with them is Jim St. Clair. During the night, it seems the father had gotten nervous after he arranged to have my brother Bill. And the father asked for the name of the biggest lawyer in Boston and they told him Jim St. Clair. So Jim St. Clair sees Bill and I starting to leave and he says to the father, 'You know, I'm not as experienced in a city court like this one. I think you're better off with Bill O'Neill here.' So the father said all right, and Jim St. Clair went off to play golf and my brother handled the case. Well, it was in Cambridge, and you got to know Cambridge. The policeman got up on the stand and my brother asked him, 'Did you know that this boy was a senior at West Point and that he is taking summer courses at MIT in order to better prepare himself to defend his country, and that he just pulled off to the side of the road on Saturday night to sleep off the exhaustion?' And the cop said, 'No, I didn't. If I had known it, I never would have allowed the court clerk to issue the sommons.' Now you see, in Cambridge at the time the cop did not issue the summons. The court clerk did. So now the cop decided not to press the matter anymore. At the same time he himself didn't have to rip up any ticket or anything. It was up to the court clerk to revoke the summons. Which of course he did and the case was over. And now I'm going to show you where Jim St. Clair is so smart. Remember the father telling my brother Bill about ten thousand dollars for the case? Well, he gave Bill three hundred dollars on the first day. Now for the rest of the bill, seven hundred, it was pulling teeth to get it out of him. Anyway, Paul, old pal, you look marvelous. Hey, what about all this food? Come on now, let's eat.'' He began steering people toward the buffet table.

At the end of the night, on his way to the car, O'Neill led his wife into the crowded smoky taproom of the Wayside Inn. He waited until George McCue, who plays the piano, finished a song. Then he came through the tables and up onto the small bandstand. He wanted to do one thing before the evening was over.

"My name is Tip O'Neill and I fool around in politics. I just want to sing a song for my wife, Milly, on her thirty-third wedding anniversary. I want to sing the song they played on the day we were married. The name of the song is 'Apple Blossom Time.' "

George McCue began to play the song on the piano and O'Neill's barbershop voice boomed out the start of the song.

> *I'll be with you in apple blossom time,*
> *I'll be with you*
> *To change your name to mine. . . .*

He sang through the smoke to his wife, selling her a love song in front of strangers. You thought automatically of Nixon and his Haldeman and Ehrlichman, standing in the doorway of the amber light of the room, smirking and starting to leave, secure in the absolute belief that no such open, old-fashioned people could be dangerous. If O'Neill was Congress's idea of a leader, how could they be hurt? How could a man who sings to his wife in public ever qualify as an opponent? At the last note, O'Neill broke into a neighborhood cheer, his voice coming up from the sandlots:

"Milly Miller O'Neill! Yeah!"

The next day he went to Washington, taking with him in all his mannerisms and speech the loud, crowded life of the streets and of the frame houses of Cambridge and Boston, and the life as a politician that is much a part of the area. There is no way to understand what went on in Washington in the summer of 1974 unless you realize that what happened was because of politicians. Ask Peter Rodino what was the single most important thing he had to do to bring about the impeachment vote against Richard Nixon and watch the Constitutional scholars pack around to hear his answer:

"When I was able to hold Mann, Thornton, and Flowers, then I knew it could be done," Rodino tells you. "I had to have them. Once I had them I could start to put it together."

Put it together. A vote. The basics of clubhouse politics. He had to know that he had the votes of James Mann of South Carolina, Walter Flowers of Alabama, and Ray Thornton of Arkansas. With these Southerners for impeachment, the needed Republican votes would not be impossible to obtain. Let the scholars debate the narrow versus broad interpretations of the Constitution as the most meaningful thing to come out of the impeachment. Peter Rodino knew it was the votes that did it. The politics, not the scholarship of the matter.

And, from his position, Tip O'Neill knew it was the job of causing the bureaucracy to move that enabled everything else to happen. He knew this because he was a professional politician, and you might as well know a little bit of what these people are and where they come from.

For a little island, it has caused so much pain. In 1845, there was a great potato famine in Ireland, people in remote areas trying to subsist on yellow winter grass and, finally, crazed, entering the black torture of cannibalism. Everywhere in the country there were children unable to close their mouths, the lack of calcium in their bones preventing their jaws from working. Three O'Neills — Pat, John, and Mike — left Cork City for the terrible ocean crossing to Boston, and the promise of jobs with the New England Brick Company. In Boston, the first money the brothers gathered that was not needed for food went directly into the Irish stock market — cemetery plots. The next money Pat O'Neill had — in 1855 — was spent going home to Ireland and bringing back a wife to America. A son from this marriage was Thomas P. O'Neill, Sr. He was raised to be a bricklayer. In 1900, he won a seat on the Cambridge City Council. On the day his son was born — Thomas P. O'Neill, Jr. — the father was picketing Harvard with people from the bricklayers' union. The only thing better a man from Cambridge could say about his father is that the father was elected president on the day he was born. For Harvard, until it began to grow up in the last fifteen years, always regarded the people outside its gates as leaves upon the streets.

In 1914, Thomas P. O'Neill, Sr., received the highest mark in a Civil Service test for the job of superintendent of sewers and sanitation for Cambridge. There were 1700 men on the payroll, none of them Civil Service, which meant that O'Neill was in charge of hiring and firing. His hand immediately reached out to touch more jobs. He married the executives of the Edison Cambridge Gaslight Company, a joining together worth hundreds of jobs to O'Neill, Sr. In North Cambridge, he became known as "The Governor." He ran the North Cambridge Knights of Columbus baseball team, was president of St. John's Holy Name Society and — strict Irish rather than dreaming Irish — head of the St. Matthew's Temperance Society. Nobody in his house was allowed to wear anything that did not have a union label on it. No clothes were ever thrown out — there always was a society for the needy. And all the children in the household were brought up to regard the first Tuesday after the first Monday in November as the most important day of the year. When Tip O'Neill was fifteen, he was out ringing doorbells to pull people out of their houses to vote for Al Smith for president and Charley

Cavanaugh for Massachusetts state representative. Tip O'Neill, in charge of half a precinct, reported at the end of the day that only four people in his area did not vote, and they were out of town.

Tip O'Neill hung out with a large crowd of kids at a place called Barry's Corner, and without anybody mentioning the fact, O'Neill was the leader. One of them, Red Fitzgerald, remembers his mother saying that Tip O'Neill was going to be a bishop. "He never pulled a dirty trick in his life, so how could he miss?" Red Says. O'Neill always had a way to keep the crowd around him, and also be useful to them. He had a job as a night watchman at a brickyard, and he fixed up the outdoor telephone pay station with a nail into the contact so that his nightly crowd of visitors had free phone service. It was in the middle of the Depression and nobody had the nickel for a call.

By 1931, O'Neill was out of high school and earning $21 a week as a truck driver for a brick company. November of that year was cold and work was slow. O'Neill took courses at Boston College High School at night, then entered Boston College. Neither the college nor the O'Neill family publicizes his scholastic achievements, although Boston College prints his picture on its literature and considers him as perhaps the school's most important alumnus. Meanwhile, if Boston College ever were to falter, Harvard would be more than happy to claim O'Neill as its own. The matter of academic brilliance was brought up over the summer in Washington, when Peter Rodino (who never went to college) and John Sirica (scholastic background at best vague) were busy showing the nation that honesty might be important.

"The night-school students are saving the country," Mary McGrory, the writer, was saying one day. "I don't think Sirica or Rodino spent a day in a regular undergraduate school. And I'm certain that Tip did not."

"Oh, no, he went to Boston College," she was told.

"Oh, yes, but thank God it wasn't serious," Mary McGrory said.

In his education O'Neill did himself and the country a favor by not following the traditional path of entering law school before going on to politics. During the early months of 1973, a Tip O'Neill, attorney at law, trained in the deviousness and tiny facts of the law, never would have come walking into Carl Albert's office saying that Richard Nixon was going to be impeached. That was too outrageous, and also too true, for a lawyer. Tip O'Neill, attorney, would have had instilled in him by professors the knowledge that he had not a scintilla of evidence upon which to base any judgment at all of Richard Nixon's status in February of 1973. O'Neill, not being a lawyer, did not know that he was using such terribly unsure methods as instinct, a little anger, and a boxcar full of common sense.

The fact that O'Neill is not a lawyer gives singularity to his success.

It always has been extremely difficult for legitimate people to get into politics because the base of the American political system has been built on the needs of lawyers. They come out of offices that are one flight over a drugstore and have gold lettering on the windows that says "Attorney at Law," and they come into the political system because time and occupation make it the place to be. Lawyers are not lashed to a normal person's work schedule. Always, a lawyer can switch his schedule around so he may attend a city council meeting at one-thirty on Thursday afternoon. Also, as the nation grew and started its sprawl at the turn of the century, the lawyers then in command drew up codes so intricate, so tangled that no citizen could ever do business with a government agency of any size, from town to federal, without the service of a lawyer. Particularly a lawyer involved in politics. Many of the rules and regulations adopted throughout the country, most still in effect today, carried with them the unwritten admonishment, "Bring Extra Money!" This, in envelopes, for sliding under the table. Corruption to benefit lawyers was built into the government structure as if it were notarized. Today in politics, at the place where most men must start, it seems to be almost solely a place for lawyers. Judges appoint referees, lawyers, for mock-auctions of foreclosed properties. The judges appoint lawyers known in the business, and politics is the business of judges. The items spiral upward to a point where you have foreclosure proceedings on multimillion-dollar mortgages and the judge appoints a referee, a monitor, again a clubhouse lawyer who receives as high as $30,000 on a million-dollar matter; receives the $30,000 for doing approximately nothing. How much of this does the lawyer keep for himself and how much does he hand back to the judge? That depends upon the bargaining ability of both. If they were to strike a poor deal, a quarrelsome deal, somebody might hear of it and a district attorney would consider the subject a prime opportunity for career advancement. Other matters between lawyer and judge can be settled in ways that almost can be traced; the judge has a son and daughter who attend expensive colleges, all bills paid from a sort of scholarship set up by a lawyer.

Because there is money to be made from the system, lawyers get into politics as a business necessity. The reasoning is that lawyers are necessary in government because government makes and deals with laws, and lawyers are best equipped for this. But laws are things to be understood and obeyed by everybody, so why should the making of laws be left to a small inbred system? The major reason for the presence of so many lawyers in government is, of course, the economics. Less than 5 percent of the lawyers in the nation ever stand on their feet in a courtroom. That is too unsure a life. A public payroll, however, is very sure. Representing a contractor who does business with government agencies — where the lawyer knows many people through his political life —

also can be considered a certainty. And then the financial structure of public life makes officeholding a dream for a lawyer. Most local and state and many federal elective posts allow a person to practice law on the side. Senator Jacob Javits has a law firm on Park Avenue in New York City. State Representative Michael LoPresti has a law practice in Boston. The rewards produced by the situation cannot be counted. Therefore, at the start of a career, it bothers not a politician to have to live in the state capital for four or five months a year, at a salary of perhaps less than $15,000, because his law office in his home district is producing a living for him. But for a college teacher with ideas, or a steamfitter with ideas, it is financially impossible to serve in a state legislature. Some think or dream or even try. Always the result is the arithmetic of family bills makes politics impossible.

Left mainly to lawyers, then, the pursuit among most politicians on a local level is for the great prize: a judgeship. Judges receive excellent money, serve lengthy terms, and have short working hours and long vacations. In New York, higher courts pay up to $49,000 for terms of fourteen years. Foraging rights appear to be limitless. The scramble for a judicial vacancy becomes so intense that the entire political structure of a county can be frozen while councilmen and assemblymen and leaders push and swirl and bargain — often openly passing money about — for the judgeship.

Tip O'Neill represents the ones who came another way. If you see the system work on a local basis, you wonder how anybody worth while ever lasts through it and gets anyplace. But for O'Neill, there was no way he could not be a lifetime politician. Clearly, the viral containers in his genes held, who knows, a couple of thousand years of the ability to control, to calm others, to decide without being abrasive, to be affable while the insides boil. For good politicians, real politicians, are not created in law school or in bank vaults. They are born, as their fathers were born, and the father of the father before them, and then back through the ages, with this viral container of public life in the genes. Just as the ability to play a piano in concert or to write a lasting novel is present at birth.

As a senior at Boston College he ran for Cambridge City Council. His father did virtually nothing to help him, and he lost the election by a hundred and fifty votes. The arithmetic still is fresh. "I got four thousand votes," he says quickly, "and thirteen hundred of them were from North Cambridge. I should have gotten eighteen hundred votes there. That's if I pulled what I should have in wards seven, eight, nine, ten and eleven. What happened? My father said to me at the end of the election, 'You know, you never asked me for help.' The woman across the street said the same thing to me on election day. Her name was Mrs. Elizabeth O'Brien. She was an elocution teacher. She called over to me in the morning, 'Good luck, Thomas, I'm going to vote for you even though you didn't ask me.' I told her I'd known her all my life. 'Mrs. O'Brien, I used to run to the store for you. I didn't think I had to ask you.' And she said to me, 'Tom, people always like to be asked.' Well, you could of punched me right in the nose and I wouldn't of felt it."

The next time he ran he was working in a small insurance brokerage and real-estate office in Harvard Square. The insurance business can serve the same purpose as a law degree to a politician, but he never did very much with it. In the election this time, there was a candidate named Tierney who had to be beaten for a seat in the state legislature. A few days before the election, an old pro named Foley said to O'Neill, "You've done well for a beginner. I don't want you to feel bad when you lose." O'Neill began to come continually late to street-corner rallies. He was too busy working the side streets and asking housewives to vote for him.

On election night, Tierney took a hotel room, had a few drinks, then slept for an hour. He showered and changed his clothes in order to look fresh and vibrant when acknowledging the cheers later on. Tierney came to his headquarters and, whistling softly, asked to see the results from his prime area, Ward 11, Precinct 3. Eleven-three contained St. John's School, its rectory and convent. Tip O'Neill had worked the area so thoroughly he owned it. The slip of paper for 11-3 was handed to Tierney. Tierney's soft whistle stopped, as did his heart. The results from 11-3 showed O'Neill with 712 votes and Tierney with 163. Rested, showered, Tierney went out in search of a pulmotor. And in his own headquarters, a rumpled, sweaty, flushed Tip O'Neill let out the first of what were to become a lifetime of election-night laughs.

Some years later, 11-3 was given a thorough campaigning by Congressional candidate John F. Kennedy. The area is changing now, with college students moving into houses that have been cut into small apartments; but if you walk into the kitchen of a house where lifelong residents live, the woman will point to a chair at the kitchen table and tell you, "He came in here and he sat right there. God rest his soul."

One day after the 1962 Congressional elections, Jack Kennedy saw O'Neill in the White House, and he said, "Say, Tip, how did you do in 11-3?"

"You know, only thirty-four people voted against me," O'Neill said.

"And I'm sure you have the names and addresses of every one of them," Kennedy said.

In 1935 O'Neill was almost twenty-three when he won this first election. Also in that election, up in another section of Cambridge called Greasy Village, Leo Edward Diehl, twenty-two, won a seat in the legislature. He won as much by his powers of observation as anything else. One morning, at the start of the campaign, Leo was out in the streets in time to see one Father John Geoghegan driving a woman named Peggy Dolan in the general direction of Peggy Dolan's job in Boston. You would have had to cut off Leo Diehl's head to make him forget this.

Some mornings later, Leo Diehl was on the same street at the same time and here was Father Geoghegan again driving Peggy Dolan to work. Leo grunted.

It then happened that in the core of the campaign, Leo Diehl heard that Father Geoghegan was going door to door on behalf of Leo's opponent, a man named Hillis. When this news was brought to Leo Diehl, the candidate showed no outrage. He simply asked for somebody to give him a lift. As the car pulled away, everybody on the sidewalk was surprised at the calmness with which Leo received the news, very bad news for his campaign because in Cambridge a priest's word had power second only to money.

The friend driving Leo Diehl said to him. "Where are we going?"

"I want to drop by and say hello to Peggy Dolan."

Peggy Dolan was shocked by Leo Diehl's accusations. "I do not go out with Father Geoghegan! I just let him drive me to work.

"Besides," she said, "Father Geoghegan goes steady with Theresa MacNamara."

Theresa MacNamara was a local dance instructress who had danced the parish to death. Leo immediately had his friend drive over to Theresa MacNamara's dance studio.

"We do not!" Theresa MacNamara squalled. "All we do is the Texas Tommy together."

Leo Diehl persisted. Soon, in tears, Theresa MacNamara said:

"He calls me Pussy Cat."

Later that night, grunting, grimacing, Leo Diehl pulled himself up the rectory steps and rang the doorbell. When Father Geoghegan appeared, Leo Diehl said, "I just wanted your permission for Theresa MacNamara to come around with me tonight and tell all the people that she's your best girl and that she wants them all to vote for me."

Father Geoghegan started to faint. He pulled himself together long enough to agree that he would make the rounds on behalf of Leo Diehl himself.

"Make sure you do," Leo said. "By the way, I don't know what's the matter with you. I'd rather jump on top of Peggy Dolan than Theresa MacNamara any day."

In January of 1936, O'Neill and Diehl entered the State House for the first time. It was the beginning of a relationship which is closer today than it ever was. And it also was the true beginning of a political career for Tip O'Neill.

There is in this country no place that could even be suggested as being anywhere near the Massachusetts State House for bone politics.

Throughout the nation, the complaint with state legislatures is that they are part-time bodies. Not even that in many places. New York, supposedly so efficient, has a state legislature which meets in January and averages three days a week until the late spring. After which it is regarded as a criminal offense for the legislature not to be recessed well in advance of the closing days of the school year, thus giving legislators time to open summer houses, pack their kids' clothes for camp, and plan vacation trips. In Massachusetts, the legislators prefer to sit forever. They usually have to be driven out of the building, practically at gunpoint. If a Massachusetts legislator is removed from his game, his sport, his very life, then all that is left for him to do is return home to his wife and family, and in Massachusetts anybody can have a family but the true goal of life is to be a politician; or, true term, a Pol. It is not uncommon for the Massachusetts Pols to sit in the state house throughout the summer, arguing, spreading rumors, using the phones, and — true glory — plotting against each other.

But in this they are so right. For who would leave a building, and what possible reason could he give, where the life in its halls is dedicated to the memory of the actions of such as former governor — among other things — James Michael Curley? Ask anybody in Boston about Curley and they will grope for a place to begin; there is so much to tell. Well, in 1933 new President Franklin D. Roosevelt offered Curley the post of United States Ambassador to Poland. From the state house there came a great cry, "He'll pave the Polish Corridor." And from James Michael Curley himself, in a face-to-face meeting with Roosevelt, there came, "If Poland is such a great place, why don't you resign and go there yourself?"

ES ASPIN WAS AN ASSISTANT professor of economics at Marquette University when he decided to run for Congress in the First District of Wisconsin in 1970. As a liberal Democrat he rode the wave of anti-Vietnam war sentiment and was elected overwhelmingly in what had been a marginal district. He was no stranger to Capitol Hill or Washington. He had worked on Senator William Proxmire's (D., Wis.) staff, and later for Walter Heller when he was chairman of the President's Council of Economic Advisors. During a two-year stint in the army from 1966 to 1968, he became one of Defense Secretary Robert McNamara's "Whiz Kids."

His experience with McNamara, combined with a bit of luck, helped gain him a seat on the prestigious Armed Services Committee. Aspin was a liberal whose dovish views did not fit in with the mostly hawkish committee. He became a gadfly who made a career out of criticizing Pentagon inefficiency. After several terms, however, he realized that simply playing the role of critic would not serve his House career. He developed an expertise in military matters that gained him the respect of his colleagues on the committee and in the House. He supported both a strong defense posture and arms control. The following selection describes Aspin's transformation from political outsider to insider on Capitol Hill.

26 Fred Kaplan
GOING FROM OUTSIDER TO INSIDER ON CAPITOL HILL: LES ASPIN AND THE CASE OF THE MX

What is Les Aspin up to?

A lot of his friends and colleagues shake their heads in wonder and sadness. Representative Thomas Downey (D., N.Y.), who has usually been in accord with Aspin's views, says, "I can't imagine the Aspin of a few years ago doing this. I just don't get it and never have." Representative Nicholas Mavroules (D., Mass.) is similarly baffled: "I told him, 'Someday, Les, you've got to tell me why you did this' . . . This is not the Les Aspin I used to know."

These and other liberal Democrats are perplexed by the recent behavior of Representative Les Aspin (D., Wis.), once the House of Representatives' most articulate critic of the Pentagon. Last month, Aspin singlehandedly rescued the MX missile from defeat. His colleagues are puzzled and distressed by this feat because the MX was the number-one target

From *The Boston Globe*, Sunday, 3 June 1984. Reprinted by permission.

of the House Democrats this year and the one major weapon system they had a chance of killing.

The missile also was regarded as a symbol of the Reagan administration's extravagant arms program and of its failure to treat arms control as a serious subject. And yet, here was one of the Democrats' leading arms experts and liberals coming to the aid of the Republicans, defusing the MX as a political issue — and in an election year, no less, when every Democratic presidential candidate had publicly opposed the missile.

What *is* Les Aspin up to?

One thing is clear. By conceiving a compromise position on such a polarized issue, and winning with it, Aspin, at forty-five, has emerged as a major leaguer in House politics — a congressman whose views are respected by all sides, whose talents as a coalition builder are incontestable and whose approval or rejection could now mean the victory or defeat of a weapons program, at least if the margin of votes is not too lopsided to begin with.

A sign of Aspin's status can be read in the list of VIPs sponsoring his upcoming annual Washington fund raiser: former defense secretaries Harold Brown, Robert McNamara, and James Schlesinger, former national security adviser Brent Scowcroft, former Secretary of State Cyrus Vance, former SALT II arms control negotiator Paul Warnke, and the ranking Democrat on the Senate Armed Services Committee, Sam Nunn. Talk about an insider's network. Talk about coalition building.

A Classic Washington Success

It wasn't always this way. The story of how Aspin got there is, in many ways, a classic Washington story — young gadfly comes to town eager to raise hell, gains a reputation, grows older, acquires seniority, adjusts to "the consensus," meets people in very high places, discovers that power can be more fun than press releases and becomes "respectable."

Or, as James Schlesinger, defense secretary during the Nixon and Ford administrations, says, "Les was kind of a maverick and a cut-up while I was secretary of defense. Now he's become a bloody statesman."

In the mid 1960s, Aspin, then in his late 20s, was a systems analyst, one of Robert McNamara's "whiz kids," in the Pentagon. A few years earlier, he was an aide to Senator William Proxmire (D., Wis.). From Proxmire, Aspin learned how to become famous in Congress — find out about some outrage in the bureaucracy, write up a stinging press release with lots of witty quotes, send it out to all the right reporters and call their editors on the phone. When Aspin first came to Congress, he made lots of headlines with this technique. One much-celebrated Aspin release chided Alexander Haig, then commander of NATO, for using taxpayer dollars to fly his dog to Europe.

By the mid 1970s, Aspin still was lambasting the Pentagon, but in a more sophisticated fashion, writing lengthy analyses that attacked official exaggerations of the Soviet military threat, proposals for higher defense budgets, and rationales for new, more powerful nuclear weapons systems.

In the late 1970s, things began to change. The Soviets deployed big land-based missiles and invaded Afghanistan. The shah of Iran was overthrown in revolution. Americans came to sense that the United States was weak — or, at least, could no longer dominate the world, which, to many, meant the same thing. Congress shifted sharply to the right on national security issues. The SALT II treaty lay dead in the Senate. The defense budget started to skyrocket.

The Political Pathfinder

One of Aspin's chief talents has always been to figure out where things were moving politically and to get out in front of the wave before anyone else did. He has never been a radical; perhaps left of center on occasion but always well within the boundaries of the consensus. Now the consensus was shifting, and, in order to stay in the ballgame, Aspin felt he had to shift, too.

Another factor: Aspin was a good friend of President Jimmy Carter's defense secretary, Harold Brown. They had met in the 1960s, when Aspin was a McNamara whiz kid and Brown was secretary of the air force. According to former Carter administration officials, Brown convinced Aspin of the virtues of the MX missile — that it was needed as a bargaining chip in future arms negotiations both with the Soviets and with the U.S. Senate; that for purposes of political perceptions, the U.S. had to match the Soviets' monster SS-18 and SS-19 ICBMs; that without the MX those Soviet missiles would soon be able to destroy U.S. land-based missiles in a first strike. (This was still when the MX was going to be moved about on a racetrack from one hole-in-the-ground to another.) Friends of Aspin say that his respect for Brown on defense issues is almost boundless. "He worships Harold Brown" is the way one put it.

In 1980, Aspin started voting against amendments to kill the MX. Still, he made no big deal of his shift, did not help organize pro-MX forces, in fact made no effort to get involved in much action on the House floor at all. That change — more in style than in substance — came a few years later.

In December 1982, Congress seemed to be on the verge of killing the MX. In desperation, President Reagan appointed a commission to figure out what to do. Headed by Scowcroft, the panel was ostensibly bipartisan but was, in fact, filled with MX supporters.

Harold Brown was one of the panelists. So was former navy undersecretary R. James Woolsey, another Aspin friend. In January 1983, Aspin and Woolsey — with, later, Scowcroft joining in — began having informal chats on how to sell the MX to Congress. The final Scowcroft report, which provided a new rationale for the MX, was composed mainly by Woolsey and incorporated Aspin's views of what would go over on Capitol Hill.

Aspin led the way on the House floor fight, organizing, hand in hand with the Reagan White House, the winning coalition of conservatives and moderates that saved the MX last year — much to the anger of his liberal colleagues.

A More Remarkable Performance

This year, from a strictly legislative point of view, Aspin's performance was even more remarkable. The MX was teetering toward oblivion once again, in the House anyway. The Reagan administration wanted to produce forty missiles; the House Armed Services Committee had whittled that down to thirty. And an amendment to cut it to zero, offered by Representatives Charles Bennett (D., Fla.) and Nicholas Mavroules (D., Mass.), seemed sure to win.

Aspin fashioned an ingenious compromise: Produce only fifteen missiles; forbid any spending on those until April 1985; if the Soviets have come back to the strategic arms talks in Geneva by then, funding is further delayed; if not, the money can be released. Aspin's argument: Why give the Soviets something for nothing? Why not demand a sacrifice from them in return for delay on the MX? It was compelling. The zero-MX amendment lost by six votes.

A few days later, Representative George Brown (D., Calif.) offered an amendment to forbid U.S. testing of antisatellite weapons against an object in space as long as the Soviets continue to abide by their moratorium on such testing. Aspin and his coalition of moderate Democrats got behind Brown's amendment, and it won by a hefty margin. At a press conference afterwards, Brown attributed his success, at least in part, to "the Aspin machine."

A Week of Amazing Work

Within one week, then, Aspin accumulated a dazzling record, pulling the MX through against everyone's expectations and then reestablishing his bona fides as an arms controller by working the floor on an antisatellite-weapons test ban.

As one of his aides said a few days later, "He's having a great time."

The successful effort early Friday morning to change Aspin's amendment slightly — giving Congress another chance to vote on the MX next April, rather than leaving the matter in the hands of the Soviets and the president — takes a bit of the luster off Aspin's shine, but only a bit. The practical consequence of the change, as even some of its advocates admit, is to strengthen the chances of Aspin's language being approved in the House-Senate conference committee on the defense bill.

Yet many Democrats are angry at Aspin. Certainly he's not on House Speaker Thomas P. (Tip) O'Neill's list of favorites. (O'Neill had predicted a few days before the vote that the zero-MX amendment would win.) Representative Downey adds, "He's alienated the liberals irremediably . . . In the eyes of a lot of [antinuclear] activists, he's indistinguishable from Ronald Reagan. That's unfortunate, that's unjust — but I don't think he knows how serious it is."

Aspin says his MX amendment will, in fact, help the Democratic party in the 1984 elections. President Reagan had insisted that he needed the MX to force the Soviets to negotiate seriously in arms talks. Had Congress killed the MX, Aspin says, Reagan would have blamed the Democrats for his failure to get an arms control agreement; now, he says, Reagan must accept the blame himself.

Former SALT II negotiator Paul Warnke sees Aspin's point: "Les was in a very difficult position . . . Do I agree that he's doing the right thing? No. But I can understand it." Others are less sympathetic. Says Representative Les AuCoin (D., Ore.), "Parties are supposed to differ on some things . . . Some things are worth fighting for, and this was definitely one of them."

Purpose of the Position

AuCoin's comment hints at something fundamental. In interviews with Aspin, it becomes difficult to tell whether he takes a position because it has merit or because it is, to his mind, the politically shrewd thing to do. Several of his colleagues wonder whether Aspin might be enthralled with the political process, with the idea of conceiving a clever compromise and the parliamentary maneuverings of pushing it through, for its own sake.

Says an aide in the House leadership, "He's the classic technocrat, the man who gets caught up in the how and forgets the why. He's like the guy in 'The Bridge on the River Kwai' who gets so caught up in building the bridge [as a WWII prisoner of war] that he forgets he's building it for the Japanese."

The final verdict on Aspin must remain open, and almost all of his colleagues know it. Even his critics volunteer that he is "brainy," "extremely bright," "one of the smartest members of the House," who has "an incredibly winning personal way about him." Whether he can hold on to his new power — more important, what he does with it — is something that everyone is waiting to find out.

THE COURTS

Chapter Six

Character, personality, and style help to shape the judiciary at all levels. A true picture of the judicial process would not be complete without a personality profile of the actors that are involved, including judges, prosecuting attorneys, lawyers for the defense, plaintiffs and defendants, and, in some cases, jurors. At the trial level the drama of the courtroom is shaped by all of the personalities that are involved. The full-fledged and celebrated criminal trial is, however, a rarity, and personality usually affects the judicial process outside of public view.

The character of judges inevitably has a profound effect on the judicial process. At the trial court level their personalities determine the way in which they run their courts. At the appellate level, and particularly on the Supreme Court, their personalities and styles determine the effect they will have on colleagues. The character of judges has been molded long before they reach the bench. Certainly it would be profitable to apply James Barber's character classification of presidents to judges. An active-positive judge would deal with cases quite differently than would an active-negative judge. The value system of the former would be better developed and more likely to affect opinions without at the same time being rigid. An active-negative judge would be opportunistic on the bench, and particularly below the Supreme Court, would always be keeping an eye out for the possibility of higher judicial or political office. The character of some judges will cause them to seek the emulation of colleagues, and others will exhibit a strongly independent and iconoclastic streak. Some judges will attempt to control everything that goes on in their courts and will seek rights of defendants who they feel deserve a break. The character of every courtroom will reflect the personality and style of the presiding judge.

The Supreme Court is unique, not only because its decisions are far-reaching, but also because it is affected more by group dynamics among the justices than other courts are. Coalitions are formed, and pressures are used to change minds. The effectiveness of the chief justice and the influence of other justices largely depends on their personalities.

A strong and persuasive personality can often change colleagues' minds. The chief justice is potentially an important leader. He presides over the weekly, secret conferences of the justices, gives his opinion first, and votes last. When he votes with the majority he determines which majority justice will write the opinion. A forceful chief justice can bring unity to a divided Court, and in some cases bring about unanimity on politically crucial decisions, such as the desegregation decision in *Brown v. Board of Education*, decided in 1954. At that time, Chief Justice Earl Warren, who assumed office in October 1953 after the Brown case had been taken up by the Court, used his considerable powers of persuasion and his highly personal leadership style to bring unanimity to a highly divided Court.[1]

Judicial decision making, at both Supreme Court and lower levels, is a far more fluid process than is commonly known. In commenting on Supreme Court decisions in the decade that ended with the *Brown* decision, one scholar concludes on the basis of reviewing the private papers of Supreme Court justices that "hardly any major decision in this decade was free of significant alteration of vote and language before announcement to the public."[2] Justices often change their minds regardless of their seeming ideological commitment. Group pressure has its effects on Supreme Court justices as on ordinary human beings. The "Freshman effect" causes instability in voting patterns among new justices to the Supreme Court.[3] Freshman justices may follow rather than lead their colleagues during their initial period of assimilation onto the Court, although this certainly was not true of Chief Justice Earl Warren, who was a pivotal justice from the time he was appointed in 1953.

Most Supreme Court justices have had little or no prior judicial experience before joining the Court and almost without exception those justices ranked as great or near-great have been more "political" than "judicial" in their styles.[4] Many of the most effective justices from John Marshall to Earl Warren held elected or appointed political offices, and often were highly partisan politicians. This political experience helped

[1] See S. Sidney Ulmer, "Earl Warren and the Brown Decision," *Journal of Politics* 33 (1971):689–702.

[2] J. Woodford Howard, Jr., "On the Fluidity of Judicial Choice," *The American Political Science Review* 52 (March 1968):43–56, at p. 44.

[3] Ibid., p. 45.

[4] An interesting rating of Supreme Court justices by law school deans and professors of law, history, and political science, undertaken in 1970, may be found in Henry J. Abraham, *Justices and Presidents* (New York: Oxford University Press, 1974), pp. 289–90. Holmes and Cardozo were notable exceptions to the usual lack of prior judicial experience among justices ranked as great.

to shape their style of operation once on the Court. The Court was viewed as a political arena, in which pressure and persuasion could be used to change the minds of colleagues on cases that had far-reaching political ramifications.

Although the Supreme Court is somewhat more cloistered than the other branches of the government, the justices do not remain in isolation from each other or from Congress, the president, and administrative officials. Conflicts between the Court and other branches is often smoothed through personal contacts. While the New Deal Court was turning down much of Roosevelt's New Deal legislation, Justice Harlan F. Stone, at an informal party, gave Frances Perkins, FDR's secretary of labor, the idea to use the taxing and spending authority of Article I to support the Social Security Act.[5] The Court is not supposed to give advisory opinions, but nothing prevents a justice from informally communicating his ideas to the president or a member of his administration. Justice Felix Frankfurter remained a close personal friend of Franklin Roosevelt after he was appointed to the Court, and Abe Fortas was a constant political adviser to President Lyndon B. Johnson. Hugo Black, who wrote the majority opinion in the 1952 *Steel Seizure* case, which held that President Truman did not have independent constitutional authority to seize the steel mills, invited President Truman to dinner to help keep the president and the Court on good terms with each other. Justice William O. Douglas was present, and he described the incident in his autobiography as follows:

> Hugo loved company and long conversations. His spacious garden in his exquisite Alexandria home was ideal for that purpose during spring and summer. He loved to entertain there; and when, during the Korean War, the Court held on June 2, 1952, that Truman's seizure of the steel mills was unconstitutional, Hugo asked me what I thought of his idea of inviting Truman to his home for an evening after the decision came down. I thought it a capital idea. So in two weeks Hugo extended the invitation and Truman accepted. It was stag dinner, and only Truman and members of the Court were present. Truman was gracious though a bit testy at the beginning of the evening. But after the bourbon and canapes were passed, he turned to Hugo and said, "Hugo, I don't much care for your law, but, by golly, this bourbon is good." The evening was a great step forward in human relations, and to Hugo Black, good human relations were the secret of successful government.[6]

As this anecdote has shown, the personalities and styles of the justices affect external as well as internal relationships.

---

[5] Frances Perkins, *The Roosevelt I Knew* (New York: Viking, 1946), p. 286.
[6] William O. Douglas, *Go East Young Man* (New York: Random House, 1974), p. 450.

NOWHERE IN GOVERNMENT is the impact of character and personality more important than on the Supreme Court. Each week while the Court is in session, the justices meet secretly in conference to deliberate their decisions on cases involving some of the most important issues that confront our government, such as discrimination, freedom of speech and press, the death penalty, the busing of school children, executive privilege, the separation of church and state, and abortion. The decisions of the Court take precedence over those of the president, the Congress, and the state legislatures, and the actions of the Court are unreviewable.

The scales of justice are supposed to be balanced through a rational, deliberative process that carefully and objectively ascertains the facts of individual cases and applies the law. However, the law is not readily defined objectively but requires interpretation to give it meaning. The process of judicial interpretation necessarily involves a highly subjective element. It is the subjectivity of the law that permits and even encourages judges to apply their own values and prejudices in making decisions. And, on the Supreme Court, where the justices must work in close contact with their colleagues, interpersonal relationships among "The Brethren" may influence the outcome of a case as much as the ideological orientation of the justices.

The private world of the Supreme Court, like that of the other branches of the government, is characterized by maneuvering among the justices to gain internal power and status. The highly personal and political dimension of Supreme Court decision making has generally been overlooked in the study of constitutional law. The following selection gives a behind-the-scenes view of the role of personalities in the historic Supreme Court decision that held that women have a constitutional right to obtain abortions.

27 Bob Woodward and Scott Armstrong
THE BRETHREN AND THE ABORTION DECISION

Douglas had long wanted the Court to face the abortion issue head on. The laws in effect in most states, prohibiting or severely restricting the availability of abortions, were infringements of a woman's personal liberty. The broad constitutional guarantee of "liberty," he felt, included the right of a woman to control her body.

Douglas realized, however, that a majority of his colleagues were not likely to give such a sweeping reading to the Constitution on this increasingly volatile issue. He knew also that the two cases now before the Court — challenging restrictive abortion laws in Georgia and Texas *(Doe* v. *Bolton* and *Roe* v. *Wade)* — did not signal any sudden willingness on the part of the Court to grapple with the broad question of abortions. They had been taken only to determine whether to expand a series of recent rulings limiting the intervention of federal courts in state court proceedings. Could women and doctors who felt that state prosecutions for abortions violated their constitutional rights, go into federal courts to stop the state? And could they go directly into federal courts even before going through all possible appeals in the state court system? Douglas knew the Chief wanted to say no to both these jurisdiction questions. He knew the Chief hoped to use these two cases to reduce the number of federal court cases brought by activist attorneys. The two abortion cases were not to be argued primarily about abortion rights, but about jurisdiction. Douglas was doubly discouraged, believing that his side was also going to lose on the jurisdiction issue.

These are difficult cases, the Chief said. No one could really tell how they would come out until the final drafting was done. . . .

Brennan and Marshall counted the vote five to two — Douglas, Brennan, Marshall, Stewart, and Blackmun for striking the laws; the chief and White dissenting.

Douglas, however, thought there were only four votes to strike the laws. Blackmun's vote was far from certain. He could not be counted on to split with the Chief on such an important issue.

For his part, Blackmun was for some kind of limited ruling against portions of the laws, but he had not decided what to do. . . .

. . . The puzzle was Blackmun.

The Chief's assignment sheet circulated the following afternoon. Each case was listed on the left side in order of the oral argument, the name of the Justice assigned to write each decision on the right.

It took Douglas several moments to grasp the pattern of the assignments, and then he was flabbergasted. [Flouting Court procedure] the Chief had assigned four cases in which Douglas was sure the chief was not a member of the majority. These included the two abortion cases, which the Chief had assigned to Blackmun. He could barely control his rage as he ran down the list. Was there some mistake? He asked a clerk to check his notes from the conference. Douglas kept a docket book in which he recorded his tabulation of the votes. It was as he suspected. . . .

Never, in Douglas's thirty-three years on the court, had any chief justice tried to assign from the minority in such fashion. For two terms now there had been incidents when the Chief had pleaded ignorance, had claimed he hadn't voted, had changed his vote. Until now they had been isolated instances.

On Saturday, December 18, Douglas drafted a scathing memo to Burger, with copies to the other justices. He, not the Chief, should have assigned the opinions in four of the cases. And, Douglas added, he would assign the opinions as he saw fit.

The Chief's response was back in a day. He conceded error in two of the cases, but insisted that the voting in the two abortion cases was too complicated. "There were . . . literally not enough columns to mark up an accurate reflection of the voting," Burger wrote. "I therefore marked down no votes and said this was a case that would have to stand or fall on the writing, when it was done.

"This is still my view of how to handle these two sensitive cases, which, I might add, are quite probable candidates for reargument."

Douglas ascribed to Burger the most blatant political motives. Nixon favored restrictive abortion laws. Faced with the possibility that the Court might strike abortion laws down in a presidential-election year, the Chief wanted to stall the opinion, Douglas concluded.

Blackmun was by far the slowest writer on the Court. The year was nearly half over and he had yet to produce a first circulation in a simple business case that had been argued the first week. . . . It was the kind of case in which Douglas produced drafts within one week of conference. But in the abortion cases, Douglas had a deeper worry. The Chief was trying to manipulate the outcome.

Blackmun might circulate a draft striking portions of the restrictive abortion laws. But as a judicial craftsman, his work was crude. A poor draft would be likely to scare off Stewart, who was already queasy, and leave only four votes. Or if Blackmun himself were to desert the position — a distinct possibility — precious time would be lost. Either defection would leave only a four-man majority. It would be difficult to argue that such a major decision should be handed down on a four-to-three vote. There would be increasing pressure to put the cases over for the sort of case that Nixon had in mind when he chose Powell and Rehnquist.

Blackmun was both pleased and frightened by the assignment. It was a no-win proposition. No matter what he wrote, the opinion would be controversial. Abortion was too emotional, the split in society too great. Either way, he would be hated and vilified.

But from Blackmun's point of view, the Chief had had little choice but to select him. Burger could not afford to take on such a controversial case himself, particularly from the minority. Douglas was the Court's mischievous liberal, the rebel, and couldn't be the author. Any abortion opinion Douglas wrote would be widely questioned outside the Court, and his extreme views might split rather than unify the existing majority. Lastly, Blackmun had noticed a deterioration in the quality of Douglas's opinions; they had become increasingly superficial.

Brennan was certainly as firm a vote for striking down the state abortion laws as there was on the Court. But Brennan was the Court's only Catholic. As such, Blackmun reasoned, he could not be expected to be willing to take the heat from Catholic antiabortion groups. Marshall could not be the author for similar reasons: an opinion by the Court's only black could be unfairly perceived as specifically designed for blacks. That left only Stewart. Blackmun believed that Stewart would certainly relish the assignment, but he clearly had trouble going very far.

Blackmun was convinced that he alone had the medical background and sufficient patience to sift through the voluminous record for the scientific data on which to base a decision. He was deeply disturbed by Douglas's assumption that the Chief had some malicious intent in assigning the abortion cases to him. He was *not* a Minnesota Twin.

True, Blackmun had known the Chief since they were small children and had gone to Sunday school together. They had lived four or five blocks apart in the blue-collar Daytons Bluff section of St. Paul. Neither family had much money during the Depression. The two boys had kept in touch until Blackmun went to a technical high school.

Blackmun's seven years at Harvard, however, put the two men worlds apart. Burger had finished local college and night law school in six years and was already practicing law when Blackmun came back to clerk for a judge on the Court of Appeals. Blackmun was best man at Burger's wedding, but the two drifted apart again as they established very different law practices.

Blackmun tried to tell his story every chance he got. His hands in his pockets, jingling change uncomfortably, he would explain how he had practiced in Minneapolis, where large law firms concentrated on serving major American corporations. Burger had practiced in St. Paul, across the river, in the political, wheeler-dealer atmosphere of a state capital.

"A Minneapolis firm," Blackmun would say, "will never practice in St. Paul or vice versa." Left unsaid was the disdain so obvious in the Minneapolis legal community for St. Paul lawyers.

But Blackmun was a hesitant and reserved storyteller, and he was never sure that the others got the message. Douglas, however, should have realized by now that Harry Blackmun was no Warren Burger twin.

Blackmun had long thought Burger an uncontrollable, blustery braggart. Now, once again in close contact with him, he was at once put off and amused by the Chief's exaggerated pomposity, his callous disregard for the feelings of his colleagues, his self-aggrandizing style. "He's been doing that since he was four," he once told Stewart.

Blackmun was just as aware as Douglas was of the Chief's attempts to use his position to manipulate the Court. Douglas was correct to despise that sort of thing. But this time, Blackmun felt, Douglas was wrong. When he arrived at Court, Blackmun had assumed the Chief's job as scrivener for the conference. Burger had finally given up trying to keep track of all the votes and positions taken in conference, and had asked Blackmun to keep notes and stay behind to brief the Clerk of the Court. Even then the Chief sometimes misstated the results. Blackmun would deftly field the Chief's hesitations, filling in when he faltered. When Burger misinformed the Clerk of the Court, Blackmun's cough would cue him.

"Do you recall what happened there, Harry?" the Chief would then say. "My notes seem to be a bit sporadic."

Blackmun would fill in the correct information as if Burger had initiated the request.

Part of the problem was that the Chief spread himself too thin. He accepted too many social, speaking, and ceremonial engagements, and exhibited too little affection for the monastic, scholarly side of the Court's life. As a result, Burger was often unprepared for orals or conference. Too often, he had to wait and listen in order to figure out which issues were crucial to the outcome. His grasp of the cases came from the summaries, usually a page or less, of the cert. memos his clerks prepared. The Chief rarely read the briefs or the record before oral argument.

The problem was compounded by Burger's willingness to change his position in conference, or his unwillingness to commit himself before he had figured out which side had a majority. Then, joining the majority, he could control the assignment. Burger had strained his relationship with everyone at the table to the breaking point. It was as offensive to Blackmun as it was to the others. But one had to understand the Chief. For all his faults, here was a self-made man who had come up the ladder rung by rung. Blackmun did not begrudge him his attempts at leadership.

The abortion assignment really amounted to nothing more than a request that Blackmun take first crack at organizing the issues. It was one of those times when the conference had floundered, when the briefs and oral arguments had been inadequate, when the seemingly decisive issue in the case, jurisdiction, had evaporated. The Court had been left holding the bull by the tail.

Blackmun was not so naïve as to think that the Chief had given him the abortion cases with the intention of having him find a broad constitutional right to abortion. But he was distressed by Douglas's implicit suggestion that he was unfit for the assignment or was somehow involved in a deception.

Blackmun also knew that he, after all, had a unique appreciation of the problems and strengths of the medical profession. At Mayo, he had watched as Doctors Edward C. Kendall and Philip S. Hench won the Nobel Prize for research in arthritis. He rejoiced with other doctors after their first successful heart-bypass operation, then suffered with them after they lost their next four patients. He sat up late nights with the surgical staff to review hospital deaths in biweekly meetings, and recalled them in detail. He grew to respect what dedicated physicians could accomplish. These had been terribly exciting years for Blackmun. He called them the best ten years of his life.

If a state licensed a physician to practice medicine, it was entrusting him with the right to make medical decisions. State laws restricting abortions interfered with those medical judgments. Physicians were always somewhat unsure about the possible legal ramifications of their judgments. To completely restrict an operation like abortion, normally no more dangerous than minor surgery, or to permit it only with the approval of a hospital committee or the concurrence of other doctors, was a needless infringement of the discretion of the medical profession.

Blackmun would do anything he could to reduce the anxiety of his colleagues except to spurn the assignment. The case was not so much a legal task as an opportunity for the Court to ratify the best possible medical opinion. He would take the first crack at the abortion case. At the least, he could prepare a memo to clarify the issues.

As was his custom, Douglas rushed through a first draft on the cases five days after conference. He decided not to circulate it, but to sit back and wait for Blackmun. He was still bitter toward Burger, whom he had taken to calling "this Chief," reserving "The Chief" as an accolade fitting only for retired Chief Justice Earl Warren. But Douglas broke his usual rule against lobbying and paid a visit to Blackmun. Though he would have much preferred that Brennan write the draft, he told Blackmun, "Harry, I would have assigned the opinion to you anyway."

Reassured, Blackmun withdrew to his regular hideaway, the justices' second-floor library, where he worked through the winter and spring, initially without even a law clerk to help with research.

Brennan, too, had little choice but to wait for Blackmun's draft. But in the interval, he spotted a case that he felt might help Blackmun develop a constitutional grounding for a right to abortion. Brennan was writing a majority opinion overturning birth-control activist Bill Baird's conviction for distributing birth-control devices without a license (*Eisenstadt* v. *Baird*). He wanted to use the case to extend to individuals the right to privacy that was given to married couples by the 1965 Connecticut birth-control case.

Brennan was aware that he was unlikely to get agreement on such a sweeping extension. He circulated his opinion with a carefully worded paragraph at the end. "If the right to privacy means anything, it is the right of the individual, married or single, to be free from unwarranted governmental intrusion into matters so fundamentally affecting a person as the decision whether to bear or beget a child."

That case dealt only with contraception — the decision to "beget" a child. He included the reference to the decision to "bear" a child with the abortion case in mind. Brennan hoped the language would help establish a constitutional basis, under the right to privacy, for a woman's right to abortion.

Since the last paragraph was not the basis for the decision, Stewart could join it without renouncing his dissent in the 1965 case. Brennan got Stewart's vote.

But Blackmun was holding back. The Chief was lobbying Blackmun not to join Brennan's draft. Brennan's clerks urged their boss to lobby Blackmun.

Brennan refused. Blackmun reminded him, he said, of former Justice Charles E. Whittaker, who had been paralyzed by indecisiveness. Whittaker's indecision had ended in a nervous breakdown and his resignation. Former Justice Felix Frankfurter had misunderstood Whittaker's indecision and had spent hours lobbying him. Instead of influencing him, Frankfurter had drawn Whittaker's resentment. No, Brennan said, he would not lobby Blackmun.

Blackmun finally decided not to join Brennan's opinion, but simply to concur in the result. That worried Brennen. Without adopting some logic similar to that provided in the contraception case, Blackmun would have difficulty establishing a right to abortion on grounds of privacy.

With the official arrival of Powell and Rehnquist, the Chief scheduled a January conference to discuss which cases should be put over for reargument before the new nine-man Court. Burger suggested that cases with a four-to-three vote should be reargued. His list included the abortion cases, . . .

Blackmun spent his time — apart from oral argument, conferences, and a bare minimum of office routine — in the justices' library. Awesome quantities of medical, as well as legal, books were regularly carried in. But all indications pointed toward no circulation of a first draft until much later in the spring. . . .

Blackmum began each day by breakfasting with his clerks in the Court's public cafeteria, and clerks from the other chambers had a standing invitation to join them. Blackmun would often spot a clerk from another chamber eating alone and invite him over. He seemed, at first, the most open, unassuming, and gracious of the justices.

Breakfast-table conversation generally began with sports, usually baseball, and then moved on to the morning's headlines. There was an unspoken rule that any discussion of cases was off limits. Where other justices might openly debate cases with the clerks, Blackmun awkwardly side-stepped each attempt. The law in general was similarly out of bounds. Blackmun turned the most philosophical of discussions about law around to his own experience, or to the clerk's family, or the performance of a younger sibling in school.

The clerks in his own chambers saw a different side of Blackmun which betrayed more of the pressure that he felt. The stories were petty. An office window left open all night might set him off on a tirade. It was not the security that worried Blackmun, but the broken social contract — all clerks were supposed to close all windows each night. Number-two pencils, needle-sharp, neatly displayed in the pencil holder, need include only one number three or a cracked point to elicit a harsh word. If Blackmun wanted a document photocopied, and somehow the wrong one came back, he might simply fling it aside. An interruption, even for some important question, might be repulsed testily.

The mystery of the Blackmun personality deepened. His outbursts varied in intensity and usually passed quickly. "Impatient moods," his secretary called them. But they made life more difficult; they added an extra tension.

Yet none of his Court family — clerks, secretaries, or his messenger — judged Blackmun harshly. They all knew well enough the extraordinary pressures, real and imagined, that he worked under.

From his first day at the Court, Blackmun had felt unworthy, unqualified, unable to perform up to standard. He felt he could equal the Chief and Marshall, but not the others. He became increasingly wihhdrawn and professorial. He did not enjoy charting new paths for the law. He was still learning. The issues were too grave, the information too sparse. Each new question was barely answered, even tentatively, when two more questions appeared on the horizon. Blackmun knew that his colleagues were concerned about what they perceived as his indecisiveness. But what others saw as an inability to make decisions, he felt to be a deliberate withholding of final judgment until all the facts were in, all the arguments marshaled, analyzed, documented.

It was a horribly lonely task. Blackmun worked by himself, beginning with a long memo from one of his clerks, reading each of the major briefs, carefully digesting each of the major opinions that circulated, laboriously drafting his own opinions, checking each citation himself, refining his work through a dozen drafts to take into account each Justice's observations. He was unwilling, moreover, to debate the basic issues in a case, even in chambers with his own clerks. He preferred that they write him memos.

Wearing a gray or blue cardigan sweater, Blackmun hid away in the recesses of the justices' library, and his office had instructions not to disturb him there. The phone did not ring there, and not even the Chief violated his solitude. Working at a long mahogany table lined on the opposite edge with a double row of books, Blackmun took meticulous notes. He spent most of his time sorting facts and fitting them to the law in a desperate attempt to discover inevitable conclusions. He tried to reduce his risks by mastering every detail, as if the case were some huge math problem. Blackmun felt that if all the steps were taken, there could be only one answer.

These abortion cases were his greatest challenge since he came to the Court. Beyond the normal desire to produce an opinion that would win the respect of his peers in the legal community, Blackmun also wanted an opinion that the medical community would accept, one that would free physicians to exercise their professional judgment.

As general counsel at the Mayo Clinic, Blackmun had advised the staff on the legality of abortions the hospital had performed. Many of them would not have qualified under the Texas and Georgia laws now in question.

Blackmun plowed through both common law and the history of English and American law on the subject. He was surprised to find that abortion had been commonly accepted for thousands of years, and that only in the nineteenth century had it become a crime in the United States. At that time, abortion had been a very risky operation, often fatal. The criminal laws had been enacted largely to protect pregnant women.

The use of antiseptics and the availability of antibiotics now made abortion relatively safe, particularly in the first few months of pregnancy. The mortality rates of women undergoing early abortions were presently lower than the mortality rates for women with normal childbirths. That medical reality was central for Blackmun. It was itself a strong medical justification for permitting early abortions.

A decision to abort was one that Blackmun hoped he would never face in his own family. He presumed that his three daughters felt that early abortions should be allowed. He claimed to be unsure of his wife Dottie's position. But she told one of his clerks, who favored lifting the restrictions, that she was doing everything she could to encourage her husband in that direction. "You and I are working on the same thing," she said. "Me at home and you at work."

By mid-May, after five months of work, Blackmun was still laboring over his memorandum. Finally, he let one of his clerks look over a draft. As usual, he made it clear that he did not want any editing. The clerk was astonished. It was crudely written and poorly organized. It did not settle on any analytical framework, nor did it explain on what basis Blackmun had arrived at the apparent conclusion that women had a right to privacy, and thus a right to abortion. Blackmun had avoided extending the right of privacy, or stating that the right to abortion stemmed from that right. He seemed to be saying that a woman could get an abortion in the early period of pregnancy. The reason, however, was lost in a convoluted discussion of the "viability of the fetus," the point at which the fetus could live outside the womb. Blackmun had added the general notion that as the length of the pregnancy increased, the states' interest in regulating and prohibiting abortions also increased. But there was no real guidance from which conclusions could be drawn. Blackmun had simply asserted that the Texas law was vague and thus unconstitutional.

The clerk realized that the opinion could not settle any constitutional question. It did not assert, or even imply, that abortion restrictions in the early months of pregnancy were unconstitutional. The result of this opinion would be that restrictive laws, if properly defined by the states, could be constitutional.

The draft seemed to fly in the face of Blackmun's statements to his clerks. "We want to definitely solve this," he had told them. But he seemed to be avoiding a solution.

In the Georgia case, he had found that the law infringed on a doctor's professional judgment, his right to give advice to his patients. Blackmun proceeded from the doctor's point of view; a woman's right to seek and receive medical advice did not seem an issue.

Blackmun's clerk, who favored an opinion that would establish a woman's constitutional right to abortion, began the laborious task of trying to rehabilitate the draft. But Blackmun resisted any modification of his basic reasoning or his conclusions. He circulated the memo to all chambers with few changes.

Stewart was disturbed by the draft. Aside from its inelegant construction and language, it seemed to create a *new* affirmative constitutional right to abortion that was not rooted in any part of the Constitution. Stewart had been expecting a majority opinion. Blackmun's memo did not even have the tone of an opinion, merely of a tentative discussion.

Stewart decided to write his own concurrence, specifying that family-planning decisions, including early abortions, were among the rights encompassed by the Ninth Amendment, which says that all rights not specifically given to the federal or state governments are left to the people. Rather than identify the rights that women or doctors have, Stewart preferred to say that states could not properly interfere in individuals' decisions to have early abortions. He circulated his memo two weeks after Blackmun's but immediately joined Blackmun's original.

Douglas saw no shortage of problems with the Blackmun draft, but Blackmun had come a long way. At least it was a step in the right direction. Though Douglas was still holding on to his concurrence, he did not circulate it. Instead, he joined Blackmun.

At the time, the Court was considering an antitrust case against a utility company, the Otter Tail Power Company, which operated in Minnesota. Douglas saw an opportunity to flatter Blackmun. "Harry, you're not a Minnesota Twin with the Chief," he told him. "I am the real Minnesota Twin. . . . We were both born in Minnesota and you were not."

Blackmun appreciated the point.

"Furthermore, Harry, I belong to the Otter Tail County regulars. You can't belong, because you weren't born there."

Douglas regaled Blackmun with stories of his father's life as an itinerant preacher in Otter Tail County, and he praised Blackmun's abortion draft. It was one of the finest presentations of an issue he had ever seen, he said.

Blackmun was ecstatic. Douglas, the greatest living jurist, had freed him of the stigma of being Burger's double. Soon, Blackmun had five votes — his own and those of Douglas, Brennan, Marshall, and Stewart. It was one more than he needed; it would have been a majority even if Powell and Rehnquist had participated.

For White the term had its ups and downs like any other year at the Court. He had been a fierce competitor all his life. He loved to take control of a case, pick out the weaknesses in the other Justices' positions, and then watch them react to his own twists and turns as he pushed his own point of view. When he could not, which was often, he took his frustrations to the third-floor gym to play in the clerks' regular full-court basketball game.

Muscling out men thirty years his junior under the boards, White delighted in playing a more competitive game than they did. He dominated the games by alternating savage and effective drives to the basket with accurate two-hand push shots from twenty feet. White consistently pushed off the clerk trying to cover him, calling every conceivable foul against the hapless clerk, while bitching about every foul called against himself. He regularly took the impermissible third step before shooting. The game was serious business for White. Each man was on his own. Teamwork was valuable in order to win, not for its own sake.

One Friday afternoon White was out of position for a rebound, but he went up throwing a hip. A clerk pulled in the ball and White came crashing down off balance and injured his ankle.

The Justice came to the office on crutches the next Monday: He would be off the basketball court for the rest of the season. He asked the clerks to keep the reason for his injury secret. The clerks bought him a Fussball game, a modern version of the ancient game of skittles. It was competition, so White enjoyed it, but it lacked for him the thrill of a contact sport like basketball — or law.

On Friday, May 26, Byron White read a draft dissent to Blackmun's abortion decision that one of his clerks had prepared. He then remolded it to his liking. The structure of Blackmun's opinion was juvenile; striking the Texas law for vagueness was simply stupid. The law might have several defects, but vagueness was not among them. The law could not be more specific in delineating the circumstance when abortion was available — it was only to protect the life of the mother.

Blackmun was disturbed by White's attack, but whether it made sense or not, it showed him that he had more work to do. The more he studied and agonized over his own memo, the less pleased he was. He needed more information, more facts, more insight. What was the history of the proscription in the Hippocratic oath which forbade doctors from performing abortions? What was the medical state of the art of sustaining a fetus outside the womb? When did life really begin? When was a fetus fully viable? What were the positions of the American Medical Association, the American Psychiatric Association, the American Public Health Association?

These and dozens of other questions plagued Blackmun. His opinion needed to be stronger. It needed more votes, which could mean wider public acceptance. A nine-man court was essential to bring down such a controversial opinion. "I think we can get Powell," he told his clerks.

One Saturday toward the end of May, the Chief paid Blackmun a visit, leaving his armed chauffeur-bodyguard in the outer office. Blackmun's clerks waited anxiously for hours to find out what case the Chief was lobbying. The Chief finally left, but Blackmun also departed without a word to his clerks. The next week, the Chief shifted sides to provide the crucial fifth vote for Blackmun's majority in an antitrust case against professional baseball (*Flood* v. *Kuhn*).

The following Saturday, June 3, Blackmun drafted a memorandum withdrawing his abortion opinion. It was already late in the term, he wrote. Such a sensitive case required more research, more consideration. It would take him some time both to accommodate the suggestions of those in the majority, and to respond to the dissenters. Perhaps it would be best if the cases were reargued in the fall. He asked that all copies of his draft memo be returned.

Douglas was once again enraged. The end of the year always involved a crunch. Of course, there was tremendous pressure to put out major opinions without the time to fully refine them. That was the nature of their work. The pressure affected them all. It was typical that Blackmun could not make up his mind and let his opinion go. Douglas had heard that the Chief had been lobbying Blackmun. This time, Burger had gone too far. The opinion had five firm votes. It ought to come down. It was not like cases with only four votes that might change when Powell's and Rehnquist's votes were added. Douglas also did not want to give the Chief the summer to sway Blackmun.

Burger was taking the position that there were now five votes to put the case over to the next term — Blackmun, White, Powell, Rehnquist, and himself. Douglas couldn't believe it. Burger and White were in the minority; they should have no say in what the majority did. And Powell and Rehnquist had not taken part; obviously they could not vote on whether the case should be put over.

The looming confrontation worried Blackmun. There were no written rules on such questions, and Douglas's apparent willingness to push to a showdown would further inflame the issue. Finally, Blackmun turned to Brennan, who was sympathetic. Obviously the opinion could not come down if its author did not want it to come down. But Brennan also wanted it out as soon as possible.

Blackmun said he understood that Douglas did not trust him, but insisted that he was firm for striking down the abortion laws. The vote would go the same way the next year. They might even pick up Powell. That would make the result more acceptable to the public. He would be able to draft a better opinion over the summer.

Brennan was not so certain of Blackmun's firmness. At the same time, he did not want to alienate him. He agreed to tell Douglas that he, too, was going to vote to put the case over for reargument. He was fairly certain Marshall and Stewart would join. That would leave Douglas protesting alone.

Douglas was not pleased by the news of Brennan's defection. But the battle was not yet over. He dashed off a memo, rushed it to the secretaries for typing and to the printers for a first draft. This time, Douglas threatened to play his ace. If the conference insisted on putting the cases over for reargument, he would dissent from such an order, and he would publish the full text of his dissent. Douglas reiterated the protest he had made in December about the Chief's assigning the case to Blackmun, Burger's response and his subsequent intransigence. The senior member of the majority should have assigned the case, Douglas said, . . .

Douglas knew a fifth Nixon appointment was a real possibility on a Court with a seventy-four-year-old man with a pacemaker; with Marshall, who was chronically ill; and with Brennan, who occasionally threatened to quit. . . .

Borrowing a line from a speech he had given in September in Portland, Douglas then made it clear that, despite what he had said earlier, he did in fact view the Chief and Blackmun as Nixon's Minnesota Twins. "Russia once gave its Chief Justice two votes; but that was too strong even for the Russians. . . .

"I dissent with the deepest regret that we are allowing the consensus of the Court to be frustrated."

Douglas refined his draft three times, circulated it, and left for Goose Prairie.

The Court erupted in debate over whether Douglas was bluffing or was really willing to publish the document. Though sympathetic to his views, Brennan, Marshall, and Stewart could not believe that Douglas would go through with it. No one in the history of the Court had published such a dissent. The Chief might be a scoundrel, but making public the Court's inner machinations was a form of treason. And the reference to the Russian Chief Justice with two votes was particularly rough. They pleaded with Douglas to reconsider. His dissent would undermine the Court's credibility, the principal source of its power. Its strength derived from the public belief that the Court was trustworthy, a nonpolitical deliberative body. Did he intend to undermine all that?

Douglas insisted. He would publish what he felt like publishing. And he would publish this if the request to put over the abortion decision was not withdrawn.

But, the others argued, what good would it do to drag their internal problems into public view?

It would have a sobering influence on Blackmun, Douglas retorted. It would make it harder for him to change his mind over the summer.

Brennan's impatience with Douglas turned to anger. Douglas had become an intellectually lazy, petulant, prodigal child. He was not providing leadership. Douglas was never around when he was needed. His departure for Goose Prairie was typical. He was not even, for that matter, pulling his share of the load, though he certainly contributed more than his share to the tension. The ultimate source of conflict was the Chief. But Douglas too was at fault.

Finally, Brennan gave up arguing.

Blackmun then took it up, pleading with Douglas to reconsider. He insisted that he was committed to his opinion. He would bring it down the same way the next term; more research would perhaps pick up another vote.

Douglas was unconvinced. He needed time to think it over. His clerks would remain instructed to publish the opinion if the cases were put over for reargument.

But Blackmun had made his point. Douglas finally decided that he couldn't publish. It would endanger next term's vote on the abortion cases.

No longer speaking to his own clerks, whom he blamed for slow mail delivery to Goose Prairie, Douglas called Brennan and told him to have his dissent held. A memo came around to the Justices from Douglas's chamber asking for all the copies back.

The conference agreed to put over the abortion cases, but they would not announce their decision until the final day of the term. . . .

Harry Blackmun returned to Rochester, Minnesota, for the summer of 1972, and immersed himself in research at the huge Mayo Clinic medical library. Rochester and the clinic were home to Blackmun, a safe harbor after a stormy term. He worked in a corner of the assistant librarian's office for two weeks without saying a word to anyone on the Mayo staff about the nature of his inquiry.

In his summer office in a Rochester highrise, Blackmun began to organize the research that would bolster his abortion opinion. He talked by phone nearly every day with one of his clerks who had agreed to stay in Washington for the summer. . . .

The clerk who was working on the opinion began to worry that one of the other clerks, strongly opposed to abortions, might try to change their boss's mind. He took no chances. Each night he carefully locked up the work he had been doing for Blackmun. At the end of the summer, he carefully sealed the latest draft in an envelope, put his initials across the tape, and had it locked in Blackmun's desk. Only Blackmun's personal secretary knew where it was.

Powell also made abortion his summer research project. As a young lawyer in Richmond in the 1930s, Powell had heard tales of girls who would "go away" to Switzerland and New York, where safe abortions were available. If someone were willing to pay for it, it was possible to have an abortion.

Powell understood how doctors viewed abortion. His father-in-law had been a leading obstetrician in Richmond, and his two brothers-in-law were obstetricians. Powell had heard all the horrifying stories of unsanitary butchers and coat-hanger abortions.

Nevertheless, Powell came quickly to the conclusion that the Constitution did not provide meaningful guidance. The right to privacy was tenuous; at best it was implied. If there was no way to find an answer in the Constitution, Powell felt he would just have to vote his "gut." He had been critical of justices for doing exactly that; but in abortion, there seemed no choice.

When he returned to Washington, he took one of his law clerks to lunch at the Monocle Restaurant on Capitol Hill. The abortion laws, Powell confided, were "atrocious." His would be a strong and unshakable vote to strike them. He needed only a rationale for his vote.

In a recent lower court case, a federal judge had struck down the Connecticut abortion law. This opinion impressed Powell. The judge had said that moral positions on abortion "about which each side was so sure must remain a personal judgment, one that [people] may follow in their personal lives and seek to persuade others to follow, but a judgment they may not impose upon others by force of law." That was all the rationale Powell needed.

Brennan and Douglas worried that votes might have shifted since the previous spring. Blackmun remained a question mark, Stewart might defect, and they were not sure what Powell would do.

At conference on October 12, Blackmun made a long, eloquent, and strongly emotional case for striking down the laws. Stewart too seemed ready to join. But the big surprise was Powell. He made it six to three.

Immediately after conference, Douglas called Blackmun to tell him that his presentation had been the finest he had heard at conference in more than thirty years. He hoped the call would sustain Blackmun for the duration.

Before the end of October, Blackmun's new draft in the abortion case was circulated to the various chambers. . . .

The clerks in most chambers were surprised to see the justices, particularly Blackmun, so openly brokering their decision like a group of legislators. There was a certain reasonableness to the draft, some of them thought, but it derived more from medical and social policy than from constitutional law. There was something embarrassing and dishonest about this whole process. It left the Court claiming that the Constitution drew certain lines at trimesters and viability. The Court was going to make a medical policy and force it on the states. As a practical matter, it was not a bad solution. As a constitutional matter, it was absurd. The draft was referred to by some clerks as "Harry's abortion." . . .

By early December, Blackmun's final draft had circulated. Stewart's and Douglas's concurrences were finished, and White's and Rehnquist's dissents were ready. There was still nothing from Burger. . . .

Stewart and Brennan thought he was stalling. The Chief was scheduled to swear in Richard Nixon for his second term as president on January 20. It would undoubtedly be embarrassing for Burger to stand there, swearing in the man who had appointed him, having just supported a sweeping and politically volatile opinion that repudiated that man's views.

At the Friday, January 19, conference, the Chief said that his schedule had been busy, and he still had not gotten to the abortion decision. Stewart figured that, having manipulated a delay until after the inaugural, Burger would acquiesce. The others wanted a Monday, January 22, announcement, three days later, and Burger said that he would have something.

Over the weekend, he wrote a three-paragraph concurrence. Ignoring the sweep of the opinion he was joining, Burger said that one law (Texas) was being struck because it did not permit abortions in instances of rape or incest, and he implied that the other law was being struck because of the "complex" steps that required hospital board certification of an abortion. He did not believe that the opinion would have the "consequences" predicted by dissenters White and Rehnquist, and he was sure that states could still control abortions. "Plainly," he concluded, "the Court today rejects any claim that the Constitution requires abortion on demand."

The day of the scheduled abortion decision the Chief sat in his chambers reading the latest edition of *Time* magazine. "Last week *Time* learned that the Supreme Court has decided to strike down nearly every antiabortion law in the land," an article said. The abortion decision had been leaked.

Burger drafted an "Eyes Only" letter to the other justices. He wanted each justice to question his law clerks. The responsible person must be found and fired. Burger intended to call in the FBI to administer lie-detector tests if necessary.

Dutifully, Rehnquist brought up the matter with his clerks. It was harmless in this case, he said. But in a business case, a leak could affect the stock market and allow someone to make millions of dollars. None of Rehnquist's clerks knew anything about the leak, but they asked him if it were true that the Chief was thinking of lie-detector tests. "It is still up in the air," Rehnquist said. "But yes, the Chief is insisting."

Rehnquist's clerks were concerned. Such a witch hunt would be met with resistance. Certainly, some clerks would refuse to take such a test and would probably have to resign. The Chief is mercurial, Rehnquist explained. "The rest of us will prevail on him."

Brennan summoned his clerks and read them the Chief's letter. It was another example, he said, of the Chief usurping the authority each justice had over his own clerks. "No one will question my law clerks but me," Brennan said. Then in a softer voice, he added, "And I have no questions." The real outrage for Brennan was not the leak but the delay. If the Chief had not been intent on saving himself and Nixon some embarrassment on Inauguration Day, there probably would have been no damaging leak.

Marshall asked what his clerks knew about the incident. When he was assured that they knew nothing, he told them to forget it.

Douglas treated the letter as he had treated a request from the Chief the previous term that all clerks be instructed to wear coats in the hallways. He ignored it.

Powell was out of town, so one of his clerks opened the Chief's letter. The clerk had talked to the *Time* reporter, David Beckwith, trying to give him some guidance so he could write an intelligent story when the decision came down. But the delay in announcing the decision had apparently left *Time* with a scoop, if only for half a day.

The clerk called Powell and told him about the Chief's letter and his own terrible mistake in talking with Beckwith. He volunteered to resign.

That would not be necessary, Powell said. But a personal explanation would have to be given to the Chief.

Powell called Burger and explained that one of his clerks, a brilliant and talented young lawyer, was responsible. The clerk realized his mistake and had learned his lesson. The clerk went to see the Chief.

Burger was sympathetic. Reporters were dishonest and played tricks, he said. It was a lesson everyone had to learn.

Apparently never expecting to learn so much about the little deceptions of both reporters and sources, Burger pressed for all the details. It took nearly forty-five minutes to satisfy his curiosity.

The clerk concluded that Burger understood, that he was being a saint about the matter. Burger wanted a memo detailing exactly what happened. The clerk would not have to resign.

Later, the Chief met with top editors of *Time* in an off-the-record session. He labeled Beckwith's efforts to get inside information at the Court improper, the moral equivalent of wiretapping.

Blackmun suggested to his wife, Dottie, that she come to Court to hear case announcements on Monday, January 22. He did not tell her why. As Blackmun announced the decisions, Powell sent a note of encouragement to Blackmun's wife. Powell suspected they were about to witness a public outcry, the magnitude of which he and Blackmun had not seen in their short time on the Court.

"I'm very proud of the decision you made," Dottie later told her husband.

After the abortion decision was announced, Blackmun took congratulatory calls through most of the afternoon. But former President Lyndon Johnson died that same day, and the news of his death dominated the next morning's newspapers.

Blackmun was unhappy that the abortion decision did not get more attention. Many women, especially the poor and black, would not learn of their new rights. But the outcry quickly began, led by the Catholic Church. "How many millions of children prior to their birth will never live to see the light of day because of the shocking action of the majority of the United States Supreme Court today?" demanded New York's Terence Cardinal Cooke.

John Joseph Cardinal Krol, of Philadelphia, the president of the National Conference of Catholic Bishops, said, "It is hard to think of any decision in the two hundred years of our history which has had more disastrous implications for our stability as a civilized society."

Thousands of letters poured into the Court. The guards had to set up a special sorting area in the basement with a huge box for each justice.

The most mail came to Blackmun, the decision's author, and to Brennan, the Court's only Catholic. Some letters compared the justices to the butchers of Dachau, child killers, immoral beasts, and Communists. A special ring of hell would be reserved for the justices. Whole classes from Catholic schools wrote to denounce the justices as murderers. "I really don't want to write this letter but my teacher made me," one child said.

Minnesota Lutherans zeroed in on Blackmun. New Jersey Catholics called for Brennan's excommunication. Southern Baptists and other groups sent over a thousand bitter letters to Hugo Black, who had died sixteen months earlier. Some letters and calls were death threats.

Blackmun went through the mail piece by piece. The sisters of Saint Mary's hospital, the backbone of the Mayo Clinic, wrote outraged letters week after week. He was tormented. The medical community and even his friends at Mayo were divided. Blackmun encountered picketing for the first time in his life when he gave a speech in Iowa. He understood the position of the antiabortion advocates, but he was deeply hurt by the personal attacks. He felt compelled to point out that there had been six other votes for the decision, besides his, that the justices had tried to enunciate a constitutional principle, not a moral one. Law and morality overlapped but were not congruent, he insisted. Moral training should come not from the Court but from the church, the family, the schools.

The letters continued to pour in. Every time a clergyman mentioned the decision in his sermon, the letters trickled in for a month from members of the congregation. The attack gradually wore Blackmun down. At breakfast with his clerks, when the discussion turned to the decision, Blackmun picked up his water glass reflectively, turning it slightly on edge and staring into it in silence.

The criticism also drew Blackmun and Brennan closer. Blackmun wrote Brennan a warm thank you note: "I know it is tough for you, and I thank you for the manner in which you made your suggestions."

Brennan tried to cheer up Blackmun. Doing the right thing was not often easy, he said. The one thing in the world Brennan did not want known was his role in molding the opinion.[1]

Blackmun did not cheer up easily. The hysteria on each side of the issue convinced him that any decision would have been unpopular. However, the deepest cut came when the state of Texas filed a petition for rehearing that compared Blackmun's conclusion, which held that a fetus was not a person, to the Court's infamous 1857 decision that said that Dred Scott, a slave, was not a citizen or person under the Constitution. Blackmun thought that comparing his opinion with the Court's darkest day of racism was terribly unfair. And, after all, it had been Stewart who had insisted on that part of the opinion.

Months later, Blackmun gave a speech at Emory Law School in Atlanta. He was chatting with students and faculty when a petite young woman with black curly hair ran up the steps to the stage. She squeezed

[1] When the clerks later put together bound volumes of the opinions Brennan had written that term, they included the abortion opinions, and on page 156 they wrote, "These cases are included with Justice Brennan's opinions for the October term 1972 because the opinions for the Court were substantially revised in response to suggestions made by Justice Brennan."

through the group, threw her arms around Blackmun and burst into tears. "I'll never be able to thank you for what you have done. I'll say no more. Thank you."

The woman turned and ran from the room.

Blackmun was shaken. He suspected that the woman was probably someone who had been able to obtain an abortion after the Court's decision. He did not know that "Mary Doe," the woman who had filed one of the original suits in Texas under a pseudonym, had just embraced him.

ARL WARREN PRESIDED OVER the Supreme Court during its most active and controversial period. Named as chief justice by President Eisenhower in 1953, Earl Warren served until 1969. The decisions of the Court during this time caused major changes in constitutional law, and eventually, they resulted in the desegregation of public education in the South, the reapportionment of state and congressional legislative districts, and the widening of most of the protections of the Bill of Rights to limit state action. Before becoming chief justice, Earl Warren had an extensive career in public office. He was attorney general of California from 1939–43 and was elected governor in 1943, a position he held until he was appointed to the Court in 1953. He was one of the most popular governors in the history of California and received widespread support from both parties. He brought a political approach to his job as chief justice, and as the following selection reveals, his political background, style, and personality had a strong effect on the direction the Court took while he was chief justice.

Although Warren was to become one of the most forceful chief justices in the history of the Supreme Court, he did not come to the Court with firm goals in mind. "The day of my induction as chief justice of the United States Supreme Court was for me at once the most awesome and the loneliest day of my public career," wrote Warren. "I approached the high office with a reverential regard," he continued, "and with a profound recognition of my unpreparedness to assume its obligations in such an abrupt manner." Warren was unacquainted with Washington, knew only a few members of the Supreme Court personally, and had long been absent from the courtroom. "Since becoming governor," Warren said, "I had not been engaged in handling legal matters except to study contracts of the state with other parties to see that they were consistent with my policies and to study all bills passed by the legislature to determine, among other things, if they conformed to the state and federal constitutions."[1] Although Warren's experience in dealing with the more technical aspects of state and federal court procedure was limited, his experience as governor in judging the constitutionality of legislation was, he felt, a valuable background for his future career on the Supreme Court.

The following selection is a personal account by Warren of his role on the Supreme Court as it faced a number of difficult issues, including the desegregation cases of 1954.

[1] Earl Warren, *The Memoirs of Earl Warren* (Garden, City, N.Y.: Doubleday, 1977), pp. 275–276.

28

Earl Warren
A CASE OF EMOTIONAL IMPACT

The home of the Supreme Court of the United States, facing Capitol Plaza, has often been called the most beautiful building in Washington, D.C. It is indeed an awesome sight as one stands before its Grecian serenity and reads the words chiseled in white marble above the main entrance. Like the building itself, the words are inspiring. They say: "Equal Justice Under Law."

As one enters through the massive bronze doors and passes down a lofty hallway to the courtroom around which the building was designed, a feeling of solemnity and a sense of history build until the visitor arrives at the Supreme Court room itself. Inside, the stately side columns of Italian marble, the polished mahogany furnishings and the red velour hangings induce a self-imposed, respectful silence. This silence invariably prevails in deference to the cause of justice whether the Court is in session or not. Thousands of visitors come each month; on some individual days as many as twenty thousand. Yet one almost never hears a discordant sound. In the entire sixteen years that I presided as chief justice of the Supreme Court, I never heard an unauthorized voice raised during a session.

Rarely, in fact, did there appear to be even an air of tension in the courtroom, regardless of the importance of the case being argued or reported.

It was very different, however, on May 17, 1954.

That was the day when the historic school segregation case of *Brown* v. *Board of Education* was reported to an expectant American public. Seventeen of our states, by their own laws, had racially segregated public schools. A number of others had *de facto* segregation because of the rapid growth of ghettos which concentrated minority groups in the larger cities. The *Brown* case, when it came before the Supreme Court, challenged such discrimination in public schools as being unconstitutional.

For weeks before the announcement of our decision, the courtroom had been jammed with people; anticipation had been mounting and political writers had been hazarding all kinds of guesses as to why the opinion had been delayed from December 8, 1953, when the case had been argued, until this momentous day in May of the following year.

Contrary to speculations in the press, there had *not* been a division of opinion expressed on the Court at any time. At the weekly conference after arguments in the case, the members, conscious of its gravity and far-reaching effects, decided not to put the case to a vote until we had thoroughly explored the implications of any decision. As a result, we discussed all sides dispassionately week after week, testing arguments of counsel, suggesting various approaches, and at times acting as "devil's advocates" in certain phases of the case, but not stating our final decision until February of 1954.

At that time we voted unanimously among ourselves to declare racially segregated public schools to be unconstitutional.

Although the chief justice always assigns opinions when he is with the majority, I neither assigned nor pre-empted the writing of this one. Some of the senior members of the Court voluntarily suggested that I write it. The others agreeing, I did so. The opinion was submitted to the Court in conference, and, after suggestions were incorporated into it, it was officially reported, as I have noted, on May 17.

I write this at some length to emphasize that there was no dissension within the Court in connection with the *Brown* case. There was not even vigorous argument. Our decision represented the judgment of every justice independently arrived at in the finest collegiate tradition. In my entire public career, I have never seen a group of men more conscious of the seriousness of a situation, more intent upon resolving it with as little disruption as possible, or with a greater desire for unanimity. To show how desirous we all were to present a united front, Justice Robert Jackson, who had been in the hospital for a month or so as the result of a heart attack, surprised us all by insisting on dressing and coming to the Court for the announcement. I showed concern about the danger of his overdoing, but he insisted that the case was of such importance as to call for a full Court, and he prevailed.

The lawyers and the public knew in advance that the decision must soon be reported because the usual date for adjournment of the term was not far distant.

As we justices marched into the courtroom on that day, there was a tenseness that I have not seen equaled before or since. When I announced that I was about to report the judgment and opinion of the Court in *Brown* v. *Board of Education of Topeka, Kansas*, there was a general shifting of positions in the crowded room and a rapt attention to my words. It was not a long opinion, for I had written it so it could be published in the daily press throughout the nation without taking too much space. This enabled the public to have our entire reasoning instead of a few excerpts from a lengthier document.

In the middle of the opinion, I read:

"We come then to the question presented: Does segregation of children in public schools solely on the basis of race, even though the physical facilities and other tangible factors may be equal, deprive the children of the minority group of equal educational opportunities? We unanimously believe that it does."

When the word "unanimously" was spoken, a wave of emotion swept the room; no words or intentional movement, yet a distinct emotional manifestation that defies description. Some of it undoubtedly was occasioned by relief that the case was decided in such a manner; some of it because of disagreement with the result; but I am sure that much of it stemmed from the word "unanimously," which flew in the face of previous news stories about dissension on the Court with regard to this case. I assume this because for weeks thereafter people would phone the clerk's office and demand to see the dissenting opinion. When informed that the decision was unanimous and, therefore, there could be no dissenting opinion, they would demand to know, "By what right is the dissenting opinion withheld?" or "Who outlawed dissenting opinions?"

Much has been said and written concerning this unanimity. I have been praised by many who favor the opinion for bringing it about, and I have been condemned by others who object to it. But I am entitled to neither approbation nor condemnation. The real credit for achieving unanimity, in my opinion, should go to the three justices who were born and reared in that part of the nation where segregation was a way of life and where everyone knew the greatest emotional opposition to the decision would be forthcoming. They were Justices Hugo L. Black of Alabama, Stanley F. Reed of Kentucky, and Tom C. Clark of Texas. The others of us, while enthusiastic in our adherence to the decision and fervent in our desire for unanimity, were not in danger of being faced with animosity and harassment in our home states because of centuries-old patterns of life.

Incidentally, this was the genesis of the phrase "The Warren Court." It was coined not as a symbol of achievement or endearment, but as an indication of scorn by those who resented the decision. Since that time, it has been used in various senses. I say this advisedly because, shortly after *Brown*, Southern congressmen signed and introduced into the *Congressional Record* the so-called "Southern Manifesto," pledging that they would use every means at their command to overcome the *Brown* decision. Several of them told me personally that I had "stabbed them in the back." I know of no reason why they should have thought me ever to have been in favor of segregation in the first place. As far as I am aware, there was nothing in my career that would convey such an impression. I had been born and reared in California where there was no accepted policy of school segregation. I had attended public schools and the University of California, and had sat in classrooms with blacks and members of almost every minority group. I never gave it a second thought.[1]

As the wartime governor of California, I had integrated the National Guard shortly after its return from the war. In fact, I was one of the first, if not the first, governor to do so. I appointed some Negroes as judges. Walter Gordon, a Negro who later distinguished himself as governor of the Virgin Islands and as a United States district judge, was appointed by me to the important position of chairman of the California Adult Authority, which fixed the sentences and determined the paroles of all the prisoners in our state penitentiaries. I saw to it that Negroes and all minority groups shared in the employment benefits of our Civil Service of sixty thousand employees. All of this could hardly have been reasonably interpreted as a bias in favor of segregation.

But people do misinterpret a public figure's instincts and motivations, and I have often encountered this in my career. It has been written that there was nothing in my background to presage my so-called "liberal" decisions on the Supreme Court. This notion has always been something of a mystery to me. Of course, I could well have some prejudice, as most of us do, in favor of my own consistency, but my actions have been exposed to the public constantly for more than half a century, and I feel that my views and actions in later years are but an outgrowth of the earlier ones.

Many people believe that my views on crime are radically different from those of my district attorney and attorney general days. I have been accused of being "soft on crime" and "in favor of permissiveness." Senator Joseph McCarthy once said on the floor of the Senate, "I will not say that Earl Warren is a Communist, but I will say he is the best friend of Communism in the United States."

I have also had the experience of having two presidential candidates, George Wallace and Richard Nixon, work against me and the Court over which I presided by conveying the impression that we were a menace to the internal security of the nation and pledging themselves to undo our work of sixteen years. Even the fatherly President Dwight Eisenhower was widely quoted as having said that his appointment of me as Chief Justice "was the biggest damn fool thing I ever did."

I knew he had some such opinion because we once discussed his view of the opinions of the Court which I either wrote or joined. On this occasion, President Johnson had appointed me to head the United States delegation to the funeral service of Sir Winston Churchill in London. He assigned his Air Force One plane for the use of the delegation, and for-

[1] Ed. note in *The Memoirs of Earl Warren:* In the preceding the author uses the more modern and socially aware term "black," but elsewhere interchanges it with "Negro." For him, the latter was never a pejorative word; it was simply the usage of his time and in his mind carried recognition of class dignity and due respect.

mer President Eisenhower accompanied us. Eisenhower was not a member of the delegation, but he was invited by the Churchill family to the ceremony. I do not recall how the conversation started, but Eisenhower said he had been disappointed in Justice Brennan and me; that he had mistakenly thought we were "moderate" when he appointed us, but eventually had concluded otherwise. I replied that I had always considered myself a moderate, and asked him what decisions he was referring to.

He said, "Oh, those Communist cases."

"What Communist cases?"

"All of them."

I pursued the discussion, and asked if he had read the opinions. He said he had not, but he knew what was in them. I then suggested that he must have some particular case in mind, and he said, "The Communists in California." I knew he probably meant the *Yates* case, which involved some garden variety Communists of no great importance. Ironically, he had just praised Justice Harlan, whom he had also appointed, for his moderation, so I said with some satisfaction, "John Harlan wrote that one." He responded that it didn't make any difference who wrote it. I tried to explain that in the judging process we were obliged to judge Communists by the same rules that we applied to all others. He refused to accept this statement, and I asked him:

"What would you do with Communists in America?"

"I would kill the S.O.B.s," he said.

I was sure this remark was merely petulant rather than definitive, so I replied, "Perhaps that could be done in the army, but it could not be done through civilian courts."

It being dinnertime, the conversation ended. It was not a pleasant session. However, I was glad that it occurred, not only because I was always fond of the general and appreciated his having given me the opportunity to serve on the Supreme Court, but also because it afforded me the first opportunity I had had in years to explain to him my views on the difference between moderation in the political process and in the judicial processes. Through politics, which has been defined as the art of the possible, progress could be made and most often was made by compromising and taking half a loaf where a whole loaf could not be obtained. The opposite is true so far as the judicial process was concerned. Through it, and particularly in the Supreme Court, the basic ingredient of decision is principle, and it should not be compromised and parceled out a little in one case, little more in another, until eventually someone receives the full benefit. If the principle is sound and constitutional, it is the birthright of every American, not to be accorded begrudgingly or piecemeal or to special groups only, but to everyone in its entirety whenever it is brought into play. I think of this principle often because many people have said to me concerning our civil rights decisions, "I agree that everyone should have equal rights, but don't you think we are going too fast?" This is but another way of saying that moderation calls for doling out rights only a little at a time to the minority groups, the poor, the uneducated, and the otherwise underprivileged. It was this misunderstanding that was responsible for the outburst of emotion in some quarters when *Brown* v. *Board of Education* was decided.

In my more than fifty years of public service, I have been exposed to both processes, the political and the judicial, and to the interrelationship between the two, until I have what I believe is a clear concept of each in the administration of justice. In those official positions I have held, I have tried to carry this distinction in mind, and to honor both sides as essential ingredients of our governmental system. One is not born with such a concept, nor is it acquired overnight. It is an evolving thing that stems from one's experiences in life and from interpretations he or she gives them, particularly when the paths of the two processes cross.

My years on the Court were crowded with cases involving segregation, voting rights, and other civil rights, malapportionment of representative bodies, incursions on the Bill of Rights, and so forth — all of which had an emotional impact on large segments of the nation. Such cases would provoke controversy regardless of the way they might be decided. I, of course, understood that it was in the nature of the judicial process to evoke criticism because no judge can satisfy both sides, particularly in emotion-charged cases. Therefore, I never took objection to the criticism leveled at me or the Court, and made no attempt to justify publicly any of our decisions. On the other hand, I did want General Eisenhower, who had appointed me to the Court, to know from me that I had not changed my spots; that I was acting from conscience in accordance with my view of the judicial process, even though doing so resulted in unpopularity in some circles.

THE BUREAUCRACY

Chapter Seven

The bureaucracy is usually thought of as consisting of hordes of civil servants whose greatest interest is in job security, and who spend their lives in eight-hour days engaged in routine matters, never taking a chance, hoping to reach retirement safely. Whatever ripples bureaucrats are supposed to cause on the political scene are generally thought to go no further than the invention of ingenious ways of increasing red tape and regulations that irritate the public. Bureaucrats are seldom pictured in the grandiose terms that are used to describe presidents, members of Congress, Supreme Court justices, and the leaders of parties and pressure groups. The bureaucracy and the people that serve within it may not seem as dynamic and forceful as the charismatic leaders that populate the political scene elsewhere, but the personalities and styles of bureaucratic leaders have had a profound effect on the political system and public policy over the years.

The great size and diversity of the bureaucracy, and the many functions it performs, allows many kinds of personalities to be effective. There is greater movement into and out of the bureaucracy from the private sector than is the case with other governmental branches. The infusion of new personalities into the bureaucracy may cause changes in methods of operation and may cause different policies to be adopted or emphasized. There is a constant struggle in the administrative branch between defenders of the status quo and incoming or even permanent members of the bureaucracy who wish to innovate. The personality of bureaucrats goes a long way toward explaining such conflicts.

Contrasting personalities and styles are readily observable throughout the bureaucracy. There is the cautious bureau chief, who over the years has developed careful relations with the chairmen of the congressional committees that have jurisdiction over his agency. He will not make a move without consulting them and may have developed close personal friendships with them. Other administrative officials may pay only token attention to Congress, going to Capitol Hill only when it is absolutely necessary. Some officials may try to cultivate power relationships within the bureaucracy, whereas others may seek public acclaim and outside support. Some officials, when dissatisfied with policies that they see being implemented by the White House or by their agency, may resign in protest, making their dissatisfaction known to the press and the public. Other bureaucrats in the same position will try to change the policy from within, and if they resign will keep their discontent to themselves, knowing that in some agencies a public attack on the bureaucratic establishment will close the doors to future employment there. Differing bureaucratic personalities will result in a wide variety of styles, including playing it safe, playing an external or internal power game, becoming a bureaucratic politician, and seeking power and status through expertise. The positive and negative character attributes of administrators at all levels of the bureaucracy greatly affect government.

CERTAINLY NO ONE WOULD have predicted, when J. Edgar Hoover was born in 1895 in Washington to a family of undistinguished civil servants, that he would become one of the most powerful men in the federal bureaucracy, using the Federal Bureau of Investigation as his power base. The Bureau of Investigation within the Justice Department was created in 1906 and expanded during World War I; it was taken over by J. Edgar Hoover in 1924 when he was appointed its acting director by Attorney General Harlan Fiske Stone, who was shortly to join the Supreme Court.

Hoover had been working as a lawyer in the Justice Department, when he became an assistant in 1918 to the director of a newly created General Intelligence Division, which had been assigned the task of compiling information on alleged radicals. During this period, A. Mitchell Palmer, the attorney general, used the bureau to carry out the infamous "Palmer Raids" on radicals throughout the country. Thousands of people, particularly new immigrants, were arrested without warrants, and thrown into seamy jail cells. Most were eventually released, although some noncitizen anarchists were deported. The raids brought the Bureau of Investigation into disrespect in many quarters of the country. When President Warren G. Harding assumed office, a new director of the bureau was appointed, William J. Burns, who had once been head of the Secret Service, and had established the William J. Burns National Detective Agency in 1909 after his retirement. As a private detective he had been convicted of a misdemeanor charge after illegally entering a New York law office. Sanford J. Ungar notes, however, that to the Harding administration the conviction

> seemed to be taken as a qualification rather than as a blot on his record, and it became widely known that Bureau men, under Burns's leadership, randomly wiretapped, broke into offices, and shuffled through personal files, and kept tabs on people's private lives. The most likely targets were "enemies" — persons who criticized [Attorney General] Daugherty, the Department of Justice, and the Bureau of Investigation; Senators who asked too many questions; and other competing government departments.[1]

The bureau continued to be deeply involved in political activities under the directorship of Burns, and attacks were launched on alleged radicals within and without government. When Democratic Senator Burton J. Wheeler of Montana attacked corruption in the Justice Department after his election in 1922, the bureau used every device possible to discredit him, including supplying information to the Republican National Committee on the senator's alleged radicalism, spying on his Washington home, and attempting to lure him into a compromising situation with a woman. But the bureau was not to stop there; it even aided the Justice Department in securing an indictment against Wheeler from a federal grand jury in Montana for influence peddling. The attempt by the bureau to frame Wheeler failed, and the senator was acquitted.

[1] Sanford J. Ungar, *F.B.I.* (Boston: Atlantic-Little Brown, 1975), p. 45.

When Calvin Coolidge assumed the presidency after the death of Harding, he replaced Attorney General Daugherty, who had been implicated in the Teapot Dome scandals, with Harlan Fiske Stone. Burns was forced to resign. It was Stone who chose Hoover to clean up the bureau. When Stone called Hoover into his office in May of 1924 to offer him the job, the following exchange took place:

> Hoover said, "I'll take the job, Mr. Stone, on certain conditions."
> "What are they?" the Attorney General asked.
> "The Bureau must be divorced from politics and not be a catch-all for political hacks. Appointments must be based on merit. Second, promotions will be made on proved ability and the Bureau will be responsible only to the Attorney General," Hoover replied brashly.
> As this account has it, Stone was delighted with the terms and said, "I wouldn't give it to you under any other conditions. That's all. Good day."[2]

With that, J. Edgar Hoover became director of the Bureau of Investigation, and was to turn the FBI into one of the most politically oriented agencies of government under the guise of maintaining political neutrality at all costs, and operating solely as a highly efficient federal police force.

Hoover proceeded cautiously after taking over the Bureau of Investigation, but soon he was to involve it in extensive public relations to fortify its image. Both he and the bureau were to become invincible in the minds of both the public and Congress. The agency was always treated with extreme favoritism by most senators and congressmen. Within the bureau, Hoover tried to rule over every detail, and he was to develop a cult of personality that has never been seen in the bureaucracy before or since. In the end, J. Edgar Hoover became more powerful in many ways than the presidents he served. During the Nixon years, he single-handedly vetoed a White House-sponsored plan to establish extensive domestic political surveillance, using the FBI, because he felt that it would not serve his purposes, but the president's. Hoover had for many years used the FBI for political surveillance.

In the following selection, we see how complete Hoover's domination was. For many years the FBI was run on the basis of Hoover's supposed strengths. In this selection Ungar shows that bureau operations equally reflected Hoover's many weaknesses.

[2] Ibid., p. 48.

29 Sanford J. Ungar
THE KING:
J. EDGAR HOOVER

FBI Director Clarence M. Kelley came to the office of Senator James O. Eastland (D., Miss.), chairman of the Senate Judiciary Committee, one day in June 1974 for a little ceremony in which Eastland presented Kelley with the first copy of a handsome black volume in memory of J. Edgar Hoover, containing *Memorial Tributes in the Congress of the United States and Various Articles and Editorials Relating to His Life and Work.* The following exchange occurred, as Kelley sought to turn a rather stiff and formal occasion into a relaxed and social one:

KELLEY: "Senator, there's an awful lot about J. Edgar Hoover in this book."

EASTLAND: "Chief Kelley, there's an awful lot about J. Edgar Hoover that ain't in this book."

There is a treasury of jokes about J. Edgar Hoover in FBI folklore, stories that agents tell each other during long, uneventful surveillances while they wait for things to happen and that assistant directors use to cheer each other up in moments of exasperation. In one, the Director is at the beach with his constant companion, Clyde Tolson. Tolson agitatedly scans the shoreline back and forth and finally says with a sigh of relief, "Okay, Boss. The coast is clear. Now you can practice walking on the water." Another tale has it that Hoover and Tolson, as they became older, decided to check into the cost and availability of cemetery plots. When Tolson reported back to him on the high price, Hoover, a notorious cheapskate, was outraged. "Never mind, Clyde," he declared. "You buy yours. But I'll just rent a crypt. I don't plan to be there for more than a few days anyway." Yet another related that whenever Tolson became depressed or dispirited, which was apparently often, the Director would seek to cheer him up by saying, "Clyde, why don't you transfer somebody?" If that didn't do the trick, Hoover would escalate the suggestion: "Go ahead, fire someone." And if Tolson still complained that this didn't help, the Director would add, "Fire him with prejudice" — a device that made it nearly impossible for the victim to find another job. Only then, went the story, did Tolson feel better.

Such bizarre fantasies conjure up the image of a man who regarded himself as infallible and godlike and who exercised arbitrary and sometimes inexplicable control over thousands of lives. J. Edgar Hoover had a degree of authority and prerogative seldom seen in democratic governments. The longer he stayed in power, the greater these prerogatives became and the more inconceivable it became that he might ever be removed; the phenomenon seemed at times to grow out of the medieval notion of the divine right of kings. Indeed, some suggested that, in times of trouble, the elevation of Hoover was just what the country needed, and his friend, Senator Joseph McCarthy of Wisconsin, tried more than once in the 1950s to launch Hoover-for-President boomlets.

But Hoover disavowed any such ambition. He was content to stay where he was, ruling over a limited but significant realm — an agency that he had salvaged from the depths of scandal and raised to the heights of honor and influence. The Director turned away other job offers — to become national baseball commissioner or head of the Thoroughbred Racing Association. Hoover put his own distinct imprint on the FBI and then turned himself into an institution. It became a tradition — and a necessity for those who sought to advance through the ranks — to say what the Director wanted to hear. By definition, it was right. It also became a tradition, as one FBI official put it, "that you do what the Director says without really agreeing with him." Hoover's words and acts were converted into legends, and some of them came out sounding as stiff and unreal or as difficult to believe as those of such other authoritarian leaders as Chairman Mao Tse-tung of the Chinese Communist party. If an attorney general or a president made him angry, the Director could just threaten to resign, and that was usually enough to bring the offender back into line. No president could afford to lose him.

Reflecting on the reverence that came to be accorded Hoover, Clarence Kelley, his successor, says, "His most casual remark [to a member of the FBI leadership] would be turned into a point of philosophy. They would even go out and document it and build it up, so it could aid them at a future time."

This treatment could be taken to laughable extremes. Once asked how he got along so well with the Director, Sam Noisette, Hoover's black retainer who was an "honorary agent," replied, "It's easy. . . . If it's snowing and blowing outside and the Director comes in and says it's a beautiful, sunny day, it's a beautiful, sunny day. That's all there is to it."

John Edgar Hoover — he abbreviated his name when he learned of a namesake who had large debts — was born the third child of an obscure family of civil servants in Washington on the first day of 1895. His father, like his father before him, worked for the Coast and Geodetic Survey, and his brother, Dickerson N. Hoover, Jr., became inspector general of the Steamboat Inspection Service in the Department of Commerce. In high school Hoover distinguished himself as a good student, a debater (overcoming an early childhood stutter and arguing, on occasion, in favor of American annexation of Cuba and against women's suffrage), and a member of the cadet corps. He had to work for anything he obtained after his high school graduation in 1913, and while studying law at night at George Washington University he had a daytime job, for thirty dollars a month, as an indexer at the Library of Congress.

After obtaining two degrees, a bachelor's and a master's of law, and passing the District of Columbia bar exam, he went to work in 1917 as a law clerk in the Justice Department. As Jack Alexander noted in a unique and intimate 1937 profile of Hoover in *The New Yorker*, from his earliest days in the department,

> certain things marked Hoover apart from scores of other young law clerks. He dressed better than most, and a bit on the dandyish side. He had an exceptional capacity for detail work, and he handled small chores with enthusiasm and thoroughness. He constantly sought new responsibilities to shoulder and welcomed chances to work overtime. When he was in conference with an official of his department, his manner was that of a young man who confidently expected to rise. His superiors were duly impressed, and so important did they consider his services that they persuaded him to spend the period of the [First] World War at his desk.

Rise he did. By 1919, at the age of twenty-four, Hoover became a special assistant attorney general in charge of the General Intelligence Division of the Bureau of Investigation. In that position, he was responsible for assessing the threat to the United States from communists and other revolutionaries, and the information he developed became essential background for the "Red raids" conducted by Attorney General A. Mitchell Palmer in 1920. Few of the ten thousand persons arrested and detained in the raids were ever convicted under the wartime Sedition Act, but Hoover was successful in his personal efforts before a Labor Department tribunal to have at least three well-known figures deported: radicals Emma Goldman and Alexander Berkman as well as Ludwig Martens, the unofficial representative in the United States of the new Soviet government. Hoover became an assistant director of the Bureau of Investigation under Director William J. Burns during the presidency of Warren G. Harding; but his patience and freedom from association with the Harding scandals were rewarded when after his exchange with Coolidge's new attorney general, Harlan Stone, about the need to keep politics out of the Bureau, Stone named Hoover its acting director at age twenty-nine.

Before and after he took over the troubled Bureau of Investigation in 1924, Hoover was something of a mystery man in Washington. He kept very much to himself, living in the house where he was born and caring for his mother, the descendant of Swiss mercenary soldiers and a strong disciplinarian, until her death in 1938. But although he remained close to her, Hoover apparently shunned the rest of his family. His sister Lillian fell upon hard times, but got no help from him. "J.E. was always accessible if we wanted to see him, but he didn't initiate contacts with his family," said Margaret Fennell, his niece to interviewer Ovid Demaris. Indeed, even Hoover's most persistent admirers and defenders within the FBI complained occasionally that the absence of any family devotion on his own part contributed to his lack of compassion toward or understanding of strong family men who worked for him. "Hoover couldn't have a family-type feeling toward anyone," observed one agent long stationed in New York; "a man who has never been a father cannot think like a father." The wife of a former assistant director of the FBI said that "the man just had no feeling at all for families." There was a certain paradox to this attitude, as Hoover expected his married agents to be loyal family men.

Hoover's coldness to his own family could not be readily explained by a busy schedule of other commitments and associations. For a time, especially in the 1930s, he was seen frequently with well-known writers and other friends on the New York nightclub circuit; and sometimes he went with bachelor friends to baseball games and other sports events (he was occasionally joined on excursions to watch the Washington Senators in the 1950s by then Vice-President Richard M. Nixon); but Hoover generally turned away all other social engagements, unless they involved official business at the Justice Department. There was little socializing in the top ranks of the bureau itself, and relations between Hoover and his associates were intentionally kept on a businesslike level. The only woman in the Director's life, it was often said, was Shirley Temple, his favorite actress and then a child. His most frequent and celebrated diversion, especially as he became older, was horse races, where he generally placed small, losing bets and sometimes presented trophies in the winner's circle.

The replacement for family, and eventually for everyone else, in Hoover's celibate life was Clyde A. Tolson, a native of Missouri who came to Washington at the age of eighteen to work as a clerk in the War Department. He eventually became confidential secretary to Secretary of War Newton D. Baker and two successors, but after getting a law degree in night school at George Washington University, he joined the bureau in 1928. He originally planned to move on to practice law in Cedar Rapids, Iowa, where he once attended business college for a year. But for reasons that were never entirely clear, Tolson rose quickly and was soon working at the Director's side. Hoover and Tolson became so close that, as Don Whitehead put it in his history, "They have even reached the point where they think alike." They also came to spend a great deal of time together, including, on most days, lunch at a restaurant and dinner at one or another's home. When Hoover appeared at an official function,

Tolson was invariably a few steps behind and to the right of him, almost like a courtier carrying a king's cloak. As associate director, a title Hoover finally gave him in 1947, Tolson was in effect the Director's chief of staff and his mouthpiece. He chaired the bureau's executive conference of assistant directors. Many of Hoover's attitudes and opinions, his wrath or his satisfaction, were transmitted through Tolson, who, as the years went on, seemed to do very little thinking or acting on his own. Tolson would invariably write his comments on a memorandum in pencil rather than in pen, so that he could change them to conform with the Director's point of view if necessary. If the executive conference voted unanimously on a matter but Hoover was later found to disagree,[1] Tolson would take it upon himself to solicit unanimity for the "correct" position, and he usually got it. Long-time bureau officials, asked to list Tolson's contributions and innovations to the service, are generally unable to come up with any. And even to those who worked for years near his office, he remained an enigma. Efforts to fraternize with him were turned away abruptly, and any other bureau executive presumptuous enough to try to join him and the Director for their ritual daily lunch at Harvey's Restaurant or the Mayflower Hotel risked disciplinary action or some more subtle punishment.

Tolson's only known diversion was to dream up obscure inventions, and he actually obtained patents on a few, including a mechanism to open and close windows automatically. Hoover usually agreed to try out Tolson's inventions, either in the bureau or at home.

According to the persistent gossip in Washington for decades, Hoover and Tolson were homosexuals; and — according to this interpretation — their attempt to repress and conceal their relationship helped explain the bureau's vigilant, even hysterical bias against men of that sexual orientation. In fact, any such relationship between the two was never acknowledged or discovered. As one former ranking official put it, "If it was true, they were never caught. And you know how we feel in the bureau: you are innocent until proven guilty." Another debunked the rumors about their relationship on the basis of the fact that Hoover "liked to crack jokes about sex."

Tolson was always the more sickly of the two men, and whenever he fell ill, he would move into Hoover's home to be nursed back to health by the Director's servants. When Hoover died suddenly in May 1972 Tolson was grief-stricken, and after going through the formality of being acting director of the FBI for about twenty-four hours, he announced his retirement. But for a few token items and sums of money willed to others, Hoover left all of his worldly possessions — an estate valued at half a million dollars — to Clyde Tolson. Tolson, increasingly ill, closed him-

[1] The Director's famous euphemism was to say, "I approve the minority view."

self up in Hoover's home and declined to talk with anyone, even most of his former bureau colleagues. He died on April 14, 1975, at the age of seventy-four, passing most of the fortune on to other loyal bureau folk.

From all accounts, of those who knew Hoover and those who studied him, the Director was a cold and self-indulgent man. His expressions of warmth were few and far between and private — friendship with neighborhood youths whom he invited into his house; a gift of a beagle pup to replace one that died which had belonged to his neighbors in the 1950s, Senator and Mrs. Lyndon B. Johnson; offers to pay a hospital bill for one of the children of Assistant Director Cartha D. DeLoach. But according to one official who was sometimes the beneficiary of such largess from Hoover, "He extracted a pound of flesh for every ounce of generosity," especially from those who worked for him. From them he expected repayment in the form of intensified loyalty and utter obeisance. From someone like Johnson he wanted political capital; from other neighbors he seemed to require only respect and deference. Seldom did his gestures seem to be motivated simply by unselfishness or humanitarian concern toward others.

Hoover moved only once in his life — after his mother's death in 1938, from the family home in Seward Square on Capitol Hill to a large red-brick house that he bought on 30th Place in Northwest Washington, near Rock Creek Park. There he built a huge collection of antiques, art objects, and pictures, mostly of himself with other famous people. According to his neighbors, the position of each item, once settled upon, remained the same year after year. Each time a new president was elected, Hoover would move a photograph of himself with that president into a place of particular prominence in the entrance hall. Some of the art objects were fine and valuable, but others, it was discovered when they were auctioned after his death, were peculiar items like an eight-sided basket made of Popsicle sticks; a wooden stork from the old Stork Club, one of the Director's favorite New York nightclubs; a salt shaker with a nude woman on the side; and other assorted bric-a-brac. Hoover's house was impeccably well kept (he had a fear of insects and germs and kept an ultraviolet light in the bathroom) and his Kentucky bluegrass front lawn was the pride of the neighborhood until it was replaced with artificial Astro Turf shortly before his death.

He was a man of habit, leaving the house and returning at precisely the same hour every day. He always ate cottage cheese and grapefruit for lunch. If he ever had serious health problems, beyond an ulcer condition, they were a carefully guarded secret; and he did not even like it to be known that in his later years he took a nap in the office for about two hours each afternoon. Hoover did not smoke, and he took only an occasional drink of bourbon, preferably Jack Daniels, with water.

His life was the FBI and there were few diversions from it. The Director did have pretenses of being a religious man. (As a high school student he sang in a Presbyterian church choir and taught a Sunday school class, and at one point, according to his biographers, he considered becoming a minister.) But one man who worked closely with Hoover for many years claimed in an interview that the Bible on his desk was really just "a prop" and that the Director exploited organized religion and famous preachers and evangelists for his own and the FBI's selfish purposes. Despite his extraordinary power and exposure, in the eyes of most of his associates Hoover seemed to remain a man of small dimensions who never became sophisticated or graceful. He was prejudiced and narrow-minded, overtly biased against black people ("As long as I am Director, there will never be a Negro special agent of the FBI," he was often heard to say in the years before Attorney General Robert F. Kennedy exerted pressure on him to change that policy), distrustful of other minority groups, and intolerant of women in any but subservient positions. Always somewhat defensive and insecure about his own education, Hoover had a notorious distrust of people who had gone to Harvard and other Ivy League universities; he claimed that they had little knowledge of the real world. He was embarrassingly susceptible to manipulation through flattery or fulsome praise and sometimes hopelessly out of touch with the realities of changing times. He was, above all, a lonely man.

When Hoover first took over the bureau, he was little known and seldom noticed. When he was appointed to the job, *Time* magazine remarked only that he was distinguished by "an unusually accurate and comprehensive memory," but most of the press merely ignored him. It was almost five years, in fact, before he ever achieved a distinction symbolic to Washington bureaucrats, mention in the *Congressional Record*. A Democratic congressman from Texas, Thomas L. Blanton, took the floor of the House of Representatives in early 1929 to compliment Hoover for "the high character of the splendid work they are doing" at the bureau. Four years later, during a budget debate, Congressman John McCormack (D., Mass.) — later Speaker of the House and always one of Hoover's staunchest supporters — praised the bureau as "a credit to the federal government" and the Director as "a brilliant young man . . . one of the finest public officials in the service of the federal government."

But before long, once he had consolidated power and genuinely improved the agency, Hoover determined to go public, to build a reputation for the bureau and to construct what came to be a cult around himself. This took the form initially of an anticrime "crusade," a zealous effort to awaken the citizenry to the threat and the consequences of lawlessness and to the need to cooperate with the authorities. The wisdom and invincibility of the "G-men" (a name that gangster George "Machine-Gun" Kelly allegedly gave the bureau agents, who had previously been known mostly as "the Feds") were trumpeted in comic strips; children wore G-man pajamas to bed and took G-man machine guns out to play. Alongside the easy, mass-appeal aspects of the crusade, however, there was also a loftier pitch for the federal police efforts, the development of a philosophy that gave the bureau coherence and lasting importance. The Director came to have the image of an expert, a sage, almost of a saint come to deliver the nation from the forces of evil — even if he had never been out on the street working a case.

Hoover was hardly a scholar, nor was he a particularly literate man. He had made an early effort to "understand" the radical forces in the country, holding long arguments in his Justice Department office, for example, with Emma Goldman and others he had deported during the Palmer Raid era. But he soon abandoned any such dialogue and effort to understand and turned to the attack. Apart from the most important reports crossing his desk, he was said to read very little, and one of the best stories about the Director was that not only had he not written the books published under his name, but he hadn't even bothered to read them. His letters often bordered on incoherence, especially in his last years, and sometimes what semblance of logic and rationality they had came from "corrections" mercifully made by close aides like Louis Nichols and Cartha DeLoach or Hoover's lifelong secretary, Helen Gandy. The Director was notorious for his mispronunciation of words that he used often, such as communist ("cominist") and pseudo ("swaydo"), a term he generally put in front of "intellectual" or "liberal" as an expression of contempt; but it was taboo for anyone who intended to have a bright future in the bureau to correct him on such matters.

Most of Hoover's vocabulary was graphic and quotable, and some of it was crude. Criminals were generally "rats" of one form or another and those who failed to keep them in jail were "yammerheads." One of the greatest threats to the nation came from "venal politicians." Those who criticized him might be diagnosed, as columnist Westbook Pegler was, as suffering from "mental halitosis." The press, for that matter, was full of "jackals." In a speech before the Washington, D.C., chapter of the Society of Former Special Agents of the FBI in 1971, he attacked the "few journalistic prostitutes" who could not appreciate the FBI; in that same appearance, one of his last major public addresses, he insisted that the FBI had no intention of compromising its standards "to accommodate kooks, misfits, drunks and slobs." "It is time we stopped coddling the hoodlums and the hippies who are causing so much serious trouble these days," he declared; "let us treat them like the vicious enemies of society that they really are regardless of their age."

Whatever the level of the discourse, Hoover found respectable forums and outlets for his ghostwritten elegies on law and order. He appeared regularly, for example, in the *Syracuse Law Review*. His treatise there on juvenile delinquency in 1953, replete with footnotes, advised the reader:

> Of primary importance in the child's early environment is a wholesome family life. A happy home which glows with morality provides a healthy atmosphere for the growing child. During the years of accelerated character development, the child quickly learns from observing his parents. As the language of his parents becomes his language, so the cleanliness of body and soul displayed by them exerts early influence on him. The child who is confronted with parental strife, immorality, and unhappiness in the home must look beyond the family circle if he is to develop orderly, wholesome ideals. Too often the child does not find proper guidance when it is not provided in the home.

The same article advised that it was a bad idea for both parents in a family to be employed, that poolrooms and other "hangouts" bred juvenile delinquency, and warned that "law enforcement agencies in various parts of the United States are required to adhere to restrictions which hamper policy efficiency. . . . the tendency to discount juvenile crime and to assume an overly protective attitude toward the juvenile offender is dangerous." And there were generally a few words on behalf of the old virtues:

> Truthfulness is one of the strongest characteristics of good citizenship. All criminals are liars; their lives are patterned after the deceit which they reflect in both word and deed. Certainly each parent must insist of his children that they be truthful in their every word. A child should be disciplined more severely when he attempts to hide his misconduct behind a lie than when he is guilty of misconduct alone. That truthfulness can best be learned in the everyday association between the child and his parent is self-evident. Likewise the father who is caught in a lie hardly can demand the truth from his child.

Eleven years later, he was back in the same law review on the same subject, with some rather strident warnings:

> There is a growing possibility that Nikita Khrushchev will never be forced to make good his boast of burying us — we may save him the trouble by doing it ourselves through the dissipation of the youth of our country. . . . The moral deterioration in our people is another basic cause for the large juvenile involvement in criminal activity. . . . Either we solve the problem or we may well go down!

In his prime, Hoover gave frequent speeches, and he had something to say about nearly everything:

Corruption. "One of the worst degenerative forces in American life during the past fifty years has been corruption in public office. Corrupt politicians make venal politics, and right-thinking citizens know there is but one answer and one remedy. Corruption must be eradicated. . . . Few communities in the land are free from contamination of the syndicated leeches who masquerade behind the flattering term — 'politician.' " (National Fifty Years in Business Club, Nashville, May 20, 1939.)

American home life. "When the home totters, a nation weakens. Every day it is my task to review the histories of scores who obey only the laws of their own choosing. Always the one thing that stands out is a lack of moral responsibility and any feeling of religious conviction. . . . While we fight for religious freedom, we must also fight the license sought by the atheist and those who ridicule, scoff and belittle others who would seek spiritual strength." (Commencement exercises, St. John's University Law School, Brooklyn, June 11, 1942.)

Loyalty. "In our vaunted tolerance for all peoples the Communist has found our 'Achilles' heel.' The American Legion represents a force which holds within its power the ability to expose the hypocrisy and ruthlessness of this foreign 'ism' which has crept into our national life — an 'ism' built and supported by dishonor, deceit, tyranny and a deliberate policy of falsehood. . . . We are rapidly reaching the time when loyal Americans must be willing to stand up and be counted. The American Communist Party . . . has for its purpose the shackling of America and its conversion to the Godless, Communist way of life." (Annual convention of the American Legion, San Francisco, September 30, 1946.)

Hoover was even sought out by *Parents' Magazine* in 1940 for remarks on "The Man I Want My Son to Be." His answer:

> I would want him to be intelligent, not necessarily possessed of learning derived from reading, but equipped to face the world with a self-reliant resourcefulness that would enable him to solve, in the majority of instances, the problems of human existence. . . . I would want him to realize that nothing in life can be truly gained without paying the equivalent price and that hard, intensive work is necessary.

There were subjects, perhaps, that Hoover, with his accumulation of influence and credibility, could have profitably addressed himself to, but did not. For example, he never wrote or spoke about the need to control the distribution of handguns. Instead, in sensationalized accounts written for *American Magazine* under his byline by Courtney Ryley Cooper, with titles like "Gun-Crazy," he seemed to lend some romanticism to such groups as the "Brady gang," "the gun-craziest gang of desperadoes ever to fall to the lot of the Federal Bureau of Investigation to blast into extinction."

The Director did not hesitate to pronounce his views on other issues of national controversy. He bitterly opposed the visit to this country of Nikita Khrushchev in 1959 (although he would later endorse President Nixon's voyages to Moscow and Peking). He frequently spoke out against the parole system, which he felt was administered by "sob sisters" with irresponsible leniency. "It is time that we approached the parole problem with a little more common sense," Hoover proclaimed in 1939; "it is time that sound practical businesslike methods supersede the whims of the gushing, well-wishing, mawkish sentimentalist. . . . The guiding principle, the basic requirement, the sole consideration in judging each and every individual case in which parole may be administered, should be the protection of the public."

Hoover often made decisions about people and chose his friends on the basis of their conformity with his own ideological attitudes. He was delighted, for example, when federal judge Irving Kaufman in New York gave death sentences to Julius and Ethel Rosenberg, who were convicted of espionage in his courtroom for the alleged leak of U.S. atomic secrets to the Soviet Union. Kaufman and Hoover became fast friends. Whenever the judge went to visit his son at college in Oklahoma, he was chauffeured by agents from the Oklahoma City Field Office; and even into the 1970s, after Hoover was gone, the FBI did special favors for Kaufman, by then chief judge of the U.S. Court of Appeals for the Second Circuit. Just a phone call from the judge to the New York Field Office, complaining about a group that was demonstrating outside his courthouse, was enough to launch a preliminary bureau investigation of the group.

With the help of his publicity-conscious lieutenants, Hoover cultivated his own image as the fearless enemy of every criminal, so effective in his job as to be loathed by them all. The Director always behaved as if there were an imminent danger to his life. He would put his hat on one side of the rear-window ledge in his chauffeured limousine and then sink down in the corner of the other side, on the assumption that any would-be assassin would fire at the hat first. He and Tolson always sat against the wall in a restaurant so they could see anyone approaching them. And whenever Hoover traveled out of town, he invariably had a large retinue of agents from the nearest field office on duty to protect him. On one occasion, Hoover became alarmed over the origin of suspicious stains that appeared on the floor of his limousine. He ordered the FBI Lab to do tests on the carpet. The conclusion: The stains came from a package of bones that he had taken home from a banquet for his dog. As former agent Joseph L. Schott has reported in his light-hearted memoir of life in the bureau, *No Left Turns,* after an incident in California during which Hoover was jostled uncomfortably during a left-hand turn of his car, he issued a strict order of procedure: There would henceforth be no left turns. His drivers would have to learn to chart their routes accordingly.

Occasionally the Director was criticized — for example, by Senator Kenneth McKellar of Tennessee in 1936 — for having little, if any, experience himself in the investigation and detection of crime and for never having made an arrest. As one sympathetic Hoover biographer, Ralph de Toledano, puts it, after McKellar's criticism "Hoover was boiling mad. He felt that his manhood had been impugned." In response, he staged a dramatic trip to New Orleans and supposedly led the raiding party to capture a member of the "Barker gang," Alvin Karpis. Later, thanks to arrangements made by his friend, columnist Walter Winchell, he repeated the performance in New York for the capture of rackets boss Louis "Lepke" Buchalter. Such gestures grabbed headlines and calmed his critics. It was only years later that it became known that Hoover strolled into both situations after all danger was past and that he played a purely symbolic role.

Many of those who worked closely with the Director privately resented his comfortable daily schedule. While he took an interest in all the important matters before the bureau, says one longtime aide, he "never lost sleep" — neither from working around the clock nor from worrying about the progress on cases. While his agents logged the required "voluntary overtime," he usually left the office on schedule at 4:45 P.M. There was a standing order not to call him at home after 9 P.M. He handled bureau affairs in a routine and businesslike manner, apparently leaving most of the stresses and strains to others. Nonetheless, Hoover showed unusual leadership abilities and maintained the undying loyalty of almost everyone in the FBI for nearly half a century. He managed to persuade underlings that he cared deeply about their careers, and there are thousands of people still in the FBI who, like Special-Agent-in-Charge Arnold C. Larson of Los Angeles, attribute their success in life to such inspirational personal advice from Hoover as "Set your goals high. Go to college. Better yourself. Don't remain a clerk forever." Anyone in the bureau who ever had a personal audience with the director remembers it in intimate detail, even if it consisted merely, as it often did, of listening to a Hoover monologue on the evils of communism or the misdeeds of politicians. There was competition among some people to the very end to offer proof of their closeness to the Director; one ex-bureau official, John P. Mohr, asserts that he was the first to be notified of Hoover's death, and John J. Rooney, the New York congressman who supervised the FBI budget for many years, boasted that he was the only member of Congress at the gravesite after Hoover's funeral.

Hoover was often arbitrary and unreasonable, especially with those jockeying for his favor, but they seldom resisted his way of doing things.

"There was a constant desire on your part to please him," explained one man who worked at it for some thirty years. "You wanted to obtain that praise from him, that letter of commendation, that incentive award. When you did, you had a great sense of pride in it. It gave you a feeling of exhilaration; you had accomplished something. He had an ability to keep you at arm's length, yet make you want to work your guts out for him. . . . I rebelled at the idea of working through fear, but I did it anyway. This was my niche. I have always wondered whether the fear was necessary, whether it might have been better to rule on the basis of mutual respect. But it is hard to fight success."

Working for the FBI and for Hoover meant, above all, submitting to discipline and regimentation that sometimes exceeded the military in its severity and lack of compassion. During the Prohibition era, taking a single alcoholic drink was grounds for being fired, if it were discovered. Hoover assumed the right to set standards for his agents' personal lives, and the sexual taboos, for example, were absolute. Not only would young unmarried male and female clerks be dismissed if it were learned that they had had illicit sexual relations, but the same punishment would be dealt to a fellow clerk who knew about any such indiscretion and failed to report it. The rules persisted, at least for agents, well after Hoover's death, and as late as mid-1974 Director Clarence Kelley approved the transfer and demotion to street-agent status for the special-agent-in-charge of the Salt Lake City Field Office because of his alleged amorous adventures.

Cars had to be kept bright and shiny, and agents were to wear conservative suits and white shirts — even though such uniform characteristics often gave them away and made them less effective at their work. Coffee drinking on the job was forbidden, especially at FBI headquarters, and some veterans still tell of "Black Friday," in the 1950s, when a large number of agents were caught drinking coffee in the Justice Department cafeteria after the deadline hour of 9 A.M. and severely punished. The official justification for such harsh standards was that Hoover wanted all his men to have "an unblemished reputation." As one official explained it, "The FBI name was to be so good that whenever an agent went before a jury, he would be believed."

Sometimes Hoover was simply mean; when he discovered that one agent's wife had an alcohol problem and his son was in trouble with drugs, he exiled the family to a small resident agency far away, apparently out of concern that the bureau would be embarrassed if the agent remained where he was stationed. The Director was so angered when he heard that another agent had indiscreetly said he was willing to serve "anywhere but New York or Detroit" that he made a personal effort to guarantee that the man's entire career was spent in those two cities. The no-mistake concept that Hoover constantly preached caused the bureau to lose some valuable people to other agencies. William V. Broe, for example, was an up-and-coming supervisor when one minor error in a report that came to the Director's attention brought him a cut in pay and a transfer. Broe decided he could not afford to accept the punishment and instead resigned and went to the Central Intelligence Agency, where he rose to one of its top positions.

One of the most-publicized disciplinary excesses involved agent Jack Shaw of the New York Field Office, who was taking graduate courses at the John Jay College of Criminal Justice under FBI auspices. Shaw wrote a letter to one of his professors, in part defending the bureau but also criticizing Hoover for concentrating on "dime-a-dozen" bank robbers and neglecting organized crime, and for a "sledgehammer" approach to public relations, among other matters; foolishly, Shaw had the letter typed in the office secretarial pool and its contents became widely known. Hoover, when the matter reached him, sent Shaw a telegram accusing him of "atrocious judgment" and transferring him to the Butte, Montana, Field Office, despite the fact that his wife was dying of cancer. When Hoover learned that the Shaw letter had been stimulated in the first place by remarks critical of the bureau by one of Shaw's professors, he also ordered that no more agents were to attend the John Jay College or any other educational institution where the FBI was not held in appropriate esteem. Shaw sued for reinstatement, and on behalf of agents' freedom of speech, but ultimately dropped his efforts to return to the bureau and settled for damages of $13,000. He eventually came back into the Justice Department after Hoover died, first working for the Office of National Narcotics Intelligence, then the Drug Enforcement Administration, and eventually the department's Office of Management and Finance.[2]

Hoover had some extraordinary fetishes. His dislike for sweaty or moist palms was rumored to be so extreme that some desperate agents with hands that tended to perspire were nearly driven to seek medical or psychiatric assistance in advance of an occasion when they were expected to shake hands with the Director. Jay Robert Nash, in *Citizen Hoover*, tells of an incident in which Hoover, meeting with a new agents class, stared repeatedly at one man in the group who had a sallow complexion. The reason was that the man had been wounded in the face during wartime combat, and plastic surgery had been only partially successful; but Hoover didn't like his men to look that way, and so the prospective new agent, who had previously done well during the training course, was told that he had failed a critical examination. The Director also instituted a stringent "weight-control program" which followed

[2] The bureau can bear a long grudge on its late Director's behalf, however. When it issued passes in 1975 authorizing access to the new FBI building for certain Justice Department personnel, it excluded Shaw.

a life insurance company chart and went well beyond the actual restrictions within which men would be able to perform their jobs effectively. But resourceful individuals sometimes found their way around the rules, and on occasion the nation's number one G-man was easily fooled. Kenneth Whittaker, for example, later special-agent-in-charge of the Miami Field Office, once found himself overweight in advance of a scheduled interview with Hoover. He solved the problem by buying a suit and shirt that were too big for him — to create the impression that he had lost weight, rather than gained it — and personally thanked the Director for "saving my life" with the weight requirements. In another instance a man slated to be assigned to one of the bureau's overseas offices was hesitant to keep an appointment with the Director because he had gone bald since their last meeting and Hoover did not like to promote bald men. Thinking ahead, and with the help of some clever colleagues, the man wrote to Hoover saying he felt that it would be selfish and unfair to take up the Director's precious time just before his annual appearance before the House Appropriations Committee. Hoover agreed and appreciated the man's sacrifice. When the agent later had to visit Hoover on his return from the overseas post, he brought the Director a gift large enough to distract his attention from his offensive hairless scalp.

Gifts to Hoover — and sometimes to Tolson — were the clue to many dramatic promotions and rapid advances within the FBI ranks. One up-and-coming man had especially good luck after giving the Director a custom-made Persian rug with the initials JEH woven into the center. After a time, major gifts to Hoover from the top leadership were, in effect, informally required on such occasions as his birthday and the yearly anniversary of his appointment as Director. Each time his choice, usually things for the home, would be communicated through Tolson, and then the assistant directors would chip in the appropriate amount of money to try to find the item wholesale through bureau contacts. On Hoover's last bureau anniversary before his death, his forty-seventh on May 10, 1971, his aides spent almost two hundred dollars on a trash compacter obtained through an FBI friend at the RCA Whirlpool Corporation. Sometimes, if Hoover was not particularly fond of a gift, he would not hesitate to give it to someone else in the bureau, even though the recipient might have seen it the first time around. It saved him money. On one occasion, office assistant Sam Noisette was surprised and pleased to receive an expensive pair of cuff links from his boss; then he discovered that they were engraved with JEH on the back.

In order to believe that he looked good himself, the Director often needed to hear that others looked bad. Some of his men played up to that need. In an FBI memorandum that became available to Justice Department officials during a court case in the 1960s, an assistant director, James H. Gale, described to Hoover a meeting with the attorney general, in this case Nicholas deB. Katzenbach — Gale wrote that the attorney general "squirmed" in his chair and "turned pale" during the discussion; when they later shook hands, the assitant director said, the attorney general's hand was "cold and clammy." On another occasion Hoover returned from a meeting at the White House with President Truman and was furious — the Director had quoted a passage from the Bible and Truman had insisted he was misquoting and had corrected him. Back at the bureau, Hoover wanted the matter researched. As it turned out, the Director was wrong; but his aides twisted the context and presented their findings to Hoover so that it was the president who seemed foolish.

Others found different routes to favor with the Director. One, Robert Kunkel, spent years as a clerk under the tutelage of Hoover's influential secretary Helen Gandy; she was generally considered to be responsible for his becoming an agent and, eventually, a special-agent-in-charge (although he also gained some leverage by giving good stock market tips to the Director). John F. Malone, long the special-agent-in-charge in Los Angeles and later the assistant-director-in-charge in New York, is another bureau executive who became close to Hoover, in part because of the friendship he developed with bandleader Lawrence Welk, whose television program was one of the Director's favorites.

Even those who admired Hoover's style and tolerated some of his excesses had difficulty with his more irrational and extreme acts. He tended, for example, to go overboard in trying to correct abuses or avoid controversy. After the Central Intelligence Agency was exposed in the late 1960s for having funded the National Student Association and other university groups, the Director for a time withdrew authorization for anyone in the FBI to contact anyone on any campus, a ruling that made it difficult for agents to handle some routine inquiries. Eventually he relented. When Hoover declared in 1969 that agents were forbidden to fly on Trans World Airlines, because a TWA pilot had criticized the FBI's handling of a hijacking crisis, agents simply ignored the order because, as aides had tried to point out to Hoover, there were some air routes covered only by TWA. (In connection with the same incident, Hoover wrote to the president of the airline and, apparently drawing upon confidential files, told of the pilot's earlier "difficulties in the Air Force.") When Hoover was dissatisfied with the cooperation of the Xerox Corporation in the investigation that followed the theft and distribution of documents from the bureau's Media, Pennsylvania, Resident Agency, he sought to have all Xerox photocopying machines removed from all FBI offices and replaced with another brand; that plan was canceled only when assistant directors persuaded him that the change would be cumbersome, time-consuming, and expensive.

It required considerable bureau resources to build and nourish the desired public interest in Hoover. A "correspondence section" handled the replies to incoming mail that sought personal information about the Director, ranging from his favorite recipe for apple turnovers to how he ate his steak and what color neckties he preferred. Sometimes the correspondence was handled in a laughable, almost cynical way. Once, for example, a two-page letter was drafted explaining why Hoover's favorite hymn was "When the Roll Is Called up Yonder." When the Director saw the draft, he changed his mind and ordered up a new one giving his choice as "Rock of Ages." The correspondence section merely substituted the name of one hymn for the other and sent the letter out, with the explanation for the choice left the same.

One of the major occasions for pronouncements of wisdom from the Director was his annual trip to Capitol Hill to justify the bureau's budget request before the House Appropriations Committee. (He testified only occasionally before the parallel Senate committee.) The transcripts of these sessions read smoothly and show Hoover first giving an eloquent statement and then responding with impressive clarity to every question posed by his congressional interrogators. Bureau officials familiar with the closed-door committee meetings, however, say that quite a lot of work went into sprucing up the public version of the transcripts; one told it this way: "There would be serious mistakes every time he appeared, especially before the House committee. The Director would recite the facts concerning particular cases, and he might have them all wrong, even providing false information about individuals. Sometimes he would be completely off base, especially when he attempted to answer the congressmen's questions. . . . So we would always get the record back the next day. and we would work almost around the clock for three or four days to straighten it out. The job was controlled by John Mohr in the Administrative Division. We would take out the garrulous crap and replace it with perfect language and grammar. When the record came out [publicly], it would be beautiful; it had to be, because Hoover would issue it to everyone on the FBI mailing list. . . . The congressmen were proud to be part of it all, and most of them probably didn't even notice the difference."

But some of the Hoover statements were impossible to take out or doctor up, especially if some of the legislators had immediately latched on to them for their own purposes. The story is told of the occasion in the late 1940s when the Director was asked how much crime cost the country each year and he answered, off the top of his head, twenty-two billion dollars. Back at headquarters later, in trying to justify the figure, the best anyone could come up with was eleven billion. But the public record was left to stand, of course, since Hoover's word was assumed to be gospel. That figure was used blindly for years until finally someone wrote in and asked why, in light of the increase in crime, its cost to the nation never changed. From that time on, the bureau began raising the estimate slightly each year.

These slips and quirks were not publicly known, however, and even had they been revealed, they would have posed no serious threat to Hoover's position. He had himself locked securely in place and employed foolproof techniques for keeping himself there. One was to let it be widely known, or at least believed, that his men in the field were collecting juicy tidbits about political figures, unrelated to pending cases but submitted for Hoover's personal interest and, if necessary, his use. Francis Biddle, one of President Franklin Roosevelt's attorneys general with whom Hoover got along well, wrote in his memoirs that the Director, in private sessions with him, displayed an "extraordinarily broad knowledge of the intimate details of what my associates in the cabinet did and said, of their likes, their weaknesses and their associations." Such information was stored in special locked file cabinets in Hoover's inner office. Access was permitted to only about ten Hoover lieutenants through Miss Gandy. The Director's personal files included some political dynamite — allegations about the extramarital affairs of President Roosevelt and his wife Eleanor, the inside story about an undersecretary of state believed to be a homosexual and his alleged attempt to seduce a porter during a train ride to Tennessee, incidents from Richard Nixon's years as vice-president, and the early escapades of John F. Kennedy. The files grew thicker and more significant all the time, because whenever someone entered the running for president, Hoover would have any records on him in the bureau's general files pulled out, updated, and transferred to his office. What use Hoover made of any particular file is a matter of speculation; but what is now clear is that the implicit threat to use them was always there. It was one way of instilling in politicians a special kind of loyalty toward the FBI: fear of what Hoover might have on them and could choose to reveal. What became of each of Hoover's controversial private files after his death is still a subject of some mystery and concern. Miss Gandy and Tolson are each believed to have taken some with them when they left the bureau, and others were moved into the office of W. Mark Felt, who became acting associate director under Acting Director L. Patrick Gray III, and were later inherited by Associate Director Nicholas Callahan. Many of the files are unaccounted for and were probably shredded before Hoover died or shortly after.

Attorney General Edward H. Levi, testifying before the House Judiciary Subcommittee on Civil Rights and Constitutional Rights on February 27, 1975, announced an inventory of the 164 files that had been made available to him from the associate director's office. Classified as Official and Confidential material or marked OC, they included "many routine, mundane and totally innocuous materials," Levi said; but he also acknowledged that at least forty-eight of the folders contained "derogatory information concerning individuals," including members of Congress. It seemed clear that some of the most important OC files were missing — and that there was probably another entire set of delicate Hoover files, perhaps labeled Personal and Confidential, that were missing and were never made available to the attorney general at all. Miss Gandy later admitted destroying the "personal" files.

Another of Hoover's successful techniques was to calculate carefully his relationships with those in power. As one former associate noted, the Director had "many of the attributes of a genius. He could identify people's foibles and weaknesses and play upon them cleverly." He was not particularly fond of the Kennedy brothers, but the brother he liked least was Robert, who sought to assert unprecedented control over the FBI when he became his brother's attorney general. (One irritant, according to those in the Justice Department in the early 1960s, was Kennedy's personal comportment; Hoover felt that he desecrated the hallowed halls of the Justice Department by strolling around in his shirtsleeves and by bringing his dog to the office.) Hoover knew of, and exploited, Lyndon Johnson's distrust of Robert Kennedy, and immediately after John Kennedy's assassination the Director virtually suspended communication with the attorney general. He replaced a Kennedy intimate, Courtney Evans, as White House liaison with a Johnson favorite, Cartha D. DeLoach. Hoover's antennae were excellent and helped him move quickly to keep up with any realignment of power.

Whatever the complaints about Hoover, most observers generally praised him for keeping the bureau honest and above the temptation of corruption to which so many other law enforcement agencies succumbed. But it has become clear that the Director himself did not measure up to the rigorous standards of honesty and avoidance of conflict of interest that he set for others. In an agency where a man could be severely disciplined for taking an office car home overnight without special permission, it was a little difficult to reconcile and justify the fact that the Director had five bulletproof limousines, each worth about $30,000, at his service — two in Washington and one each in Los Angeles, New York, and Miami — and that he regularly used them for personal business, like trips to the racetrack or on his vacations with Tolson. The vacations, in Florida or southern California, were never officially called vacations but "inspection trips" — meaning that Hoover would drop in at a field office or two each time and shake hands. That was enough for him to charge the whole trip to the government.

In Miami Hoover stayed free at a hotel owned by Meyer Schine, who admitted in congressional testimony that he also had ties with big-name bookmakers. (Schine's son, G. David, was counsel to Senator Joseph McCarthy's investigating subcommittee, along with Roy Cohn.) In La

Jolla, California, his stays at the Hotel Del Charro were at no cost, courtesy of the owners, millionaire Texas businessmen Clint Murchison and Sid Richardson. Sometimes they had elaborate parties in La Jolla in Hoover's honor, flying in specially prepared chili from Texas for the occasion; the bills that were never presented to Hoover and Tolson ran into the thousands of dollars. Murchison and Richardson gained control of a nearby racetrack that Hoover frequented; some of the profits from it were supposed to be channeled to a newly established charitable foundation, but prominent members of the foundation board soon quit when they found that this was not happening. Both of these Hoover friends came under investigation in the mid-1950s in connection with a controversial proxy fight to win control of the New York Central Railroad, and it was learned years later that Richardson, who had extensive oil holdings, made payments to Robert Anderson while Anderson was serving as President Eisenhower's secretary of the treasury and was in a position to influence national oil policy. By means that were never publicly known, Hoover himself amassed substantial oil, gas, and mineral leases in Texas and Louisiana — they were valued at $125,000 at the time of his death — alongside his other valuable investments. All the while the Director was growing rich, he never hesitated to accept free accommodations wherever he traveled.

His annual visit to the West Coast became one of the most important events on Hoover's calendar. If the invitation to stay at the Del Charro did not arrive on schedule, the SAC in San Diego was asked to nudge it along. One year the field office there was sent into a frenzy because it had neglected to stock the hotel's freezer with the Director's favorite ice cream. When he asked for it upon arrival, the SAC had to call the ice cream manufacturer to open his plant at night in order to satisfy Hoover's needs. A stenographer from the field office was then dressed up as a waitress and dispatched to the Del Charro to serve the ice cream to Hoover and Tolson.

The Director eagerly used the extensive and sometimes expert facilities of the bureau for his own personal whim and benefit. He was reluctant, ostensibly for security reasons, to permit outside workmen in or near his home, so it was the FBI Laboratory that performed such duties as building a porch or installing new appliances. The Lab was sent in on one occasion because Hoover was impatient with how long it took his television set to start up. The problem was solved by rigging the unit so that it was always on; he just had to turn it up to get the picture. Unknown to Hoover, this just meant that the tubes burned out and had to be changed often — at government expense. Sometimes the Lab's assignments nearly resulted in disaster, as on the occasion Hoover decided that he wanted a new toilet installed. But the Director did not like the new one, because it was too low, and he demanded the old one back. Fortunately, the technicians were able to reclaim it from a junk heap after a search.

In his earliest days at the bureau, Hoover had steadfastly and emphatically declined to profit from the G-man boom, turning back the honoraria when he gave speeches and declining to endorse cigarettes or other commercial products. But as time passed he became avaricious. When the Freedoms Foundation, a conservative organization based in Valley Forge, Pennsylvania, twice gave him its gold medal and five-thousand-dollar award, it called ahead to the Director's aides, pointing out that it was customary for the recipient of the award to donate the money back to the foundation. Both times Hoover refused and said he intended to keep the money for himself. Perhaps the most profitable transactions, however, involved the books published under Hoover's name, especially the enormously successful *Masters of Deceit,* subtitled *The Story of Communism in American and How to Fight It.* The book was written primarily by agent Fern Stukenbroeker, a bureau researcher on subversive groups, but the substantial royalties were divided five ways — one-fifth each to Hoover; Tolson; Assistant-to-the-Director Louis B. Nichols; William I. Nichols (no relation to Louis), editor and publisher of *This Week* magazine, who helped to market the book; and the FBI Recreation Association — which permitted the Director to contend that the profits were going to the hard-working FBI personnel. Hoover aides urged that Stukenbroeker be rewarded for his efforts with an incentive award. Hoover balked, but agreed after a dispute; however, he knocked the amount down from five hundred dollars to two hundred and fifty. Later, when Warner Brothers wanted to launch a television series about the FBI, Hoover's condition was that the film studio purchase the movie rights to *Masters of Deceit.* His price was seventy-five thousand dollars. As the deal was being closed, the Director suddenly got cold feet and worried whether he would be subjecting himself to criticism. He sent Cartha DeLoach to President Johnson to discuss the situation, and Johnson gave his confidential approval. The television series, with Efrem Zimbalist, Jr., as the star, got off to a successful start. Hoover pocketed the money and later left it to Clyde Tolson.

When J. Edgar Hoover died suddenly on May 2, 1972, the news was initially kept from the agents for about three hours; the day began like any other in the bureau, early and busily. When the word finally came out, it was greeted with a combination of shock and relief. Some felt comfort, for Hoover's sake, that he had died painlessly and in the job rather than suffering the indignity of replacement after forty-eight years; others looked ahead to the opportunity, at last, for a review and reconsideration of the FBI and its roles. Many were oblivious to the turmoil Hoover was leaving behind, and few sensed the trouble ahead.

That night, hundreds of agents and former agents, some traveling from far away, gathered at a funeral home in Washington to pay their respects to the Director. One who came from out of town later recalled the scene this way: "They had washed his hair, and all the dye had come out. His eyebrows, too. He looked like a wispy, gray-haired, tired little man. There, in the coffin, all the front, all the power and the color had been taken away."

The next day his body lay in state in the rotunda of the United States Capitol and Hoover was eulogized by Chief Justice Warren E. Burger as "a man who epitomized the American dream of patriotism, dedication to duty, and successful attainment." A day later, in the National Presbyterian Church, President Nixon added his own tribute: "He was one of those individuals who, by all odds, was the best man for a vitally important job. His powerful leadership by example helped to keep steel in America's backbone and the flame of freedom in America's soul." He was buried not at Arlington National Cemetery but, in accordance with his instructions, at the Congressional Cemetery in the Capitol Hill section of Washington, with members of his family.

On the first anniversary of Hoover's death — a day that one can imagine Hoover would have wanted to be elaborately noted — there was no ceremony because the FBI was in disarray. On the second anniversary, Director Clarence M. Kelley led the assistant directors in a solemn, private wreath-laying ceremony at the Director's grave. For the faithful, that made things seem a little better again.

FBI DIRECTOR J. EDGAR HOO-
ver became a legend in his own
time. He was the paradigm of the
bureaucratic politician, building an
empire that transcended and circum-
vented the formal lines of authority
that placed the FBI under the attorney
general. Presidents did not attempt to
fire Hoover, as some of them would
have liked, nor did powerful members of Congress call for the director's resignation. They did not love
Hoover, but feared him and respected his power.

The bureaucracy is highly political
at every level, but especially at the top.
Those who make the bureaucracy a
life-long career must play a particularly astute political game if they want
to maintain and expand the power they
have attained. Civil Service laws protect the lowly bureaucrat, but not the
ambitious one who has achieved a
policymaking position by moving up
from within the bureaucracy.

Outside political appointees, such
as cabinet secretaries, must also be
skilled in making their voices heard at
the White House, on Capitol Hill, and
within their own departments. Unlike
their bureau chiefs and many of their
principal aides, however, cabinet secretaries usually have a firm base outside of the bureaucracy to which they
happily return if trouble overwhelms
them. When President Jimmy Carter
fired Joseph Califano, his secretary of
Health, Education and Welfare, Califano simply returned to his prosper-

ous Washington law practice where he
reportedly makes $1.5 million a year,
a sharp contrast to his $60,000 per year
salary as secretary. There are others
like Califano, such as Caspar Weinberger, Reagan's defense secretary,
and John Connally, former Texas governor and treasury secretary under
Nixon, who move in and out of government with ease, all of the time
maintaining their reputations for
power.

By contrast with the Califanos of the
political world, those who have chosen to make the bureaucracy a permanent career must construct bar-
riers against the winds of political
change, or learn to bend with them.
Those who stay in power often use
their entrepreneurial talents to build
empires that are immune from outside attack. Others learn to serve, or
appear to serve, their master of the
moment. The entrepreneurs, such as
J. Edgar Hoover and Admiral Hyman
Rickover, often become public figures because of their ability to cultivate and manipulate the press. But
there are largely invisible bureaucrats
as well who eschew publicity and remain in power by making themselves
indispensable to their chiefs.

The following selection depicts
both the entrepreneurial, often flamboyant holders of bureaucratic power,
and those that quietly stay at the top
by effectively adjusting to constant
political change.

30 Jonathan Alter
THE POWERS THAT STAY

What's hard, at the political level [of the bureaucracy], is *staying* in — figuring out how to avoid these four-year dry spells when all you can do is write op-ed pieces, agonize over lunch dates, and decide which boring law firm or think tank to bide your time in while waiting for a chance to get back to the action. The real survivors don't have to worry that they're not so terrific at picking *which* obscure former governor will win the Iowa caucuses. Why sweat it? They're still in.

How does this group of high-wire performers do it? Well, most of the survivors themselves aren't of much help beyond a grunt or two and the startling revelations that they "worked hard" or "just outlived 'em." Like other great con men, they can't ever admit their secrets, for if they do — confessing to "gambits" and "techniques" — it's a good bet they've just taken the first step toward permanent retirement. That's because success in this slippery game is determined by whether they have come to believe their own cons, and whether they've so adroitly melded their personalities, instincts, and accomplishments that they fool everybody, even themselves.

But taking that as a given, there are basically two ways of surviving in the government: Call them "ring kissing" and "empire building." Ring kissing is based on the model practiced by low-level civil servants and other prostrate subordinates throughout American society, but at the high levels we're talking about, it must be perfected to an art form. This requires that the aspiring survivor perform all sorts of tasks that convince his superiors (and potential future superiors) that he is indispensable. By making the boss look good, or by simply doing the boss's bidding, the imaginative ring kisser can collect a government check practically forever.

Empire building, by contrast, doesn't require the help of superiors at all. In fact, the best empire builders have prevailed over active opposition from presidents, cabinet secretaries, and others who would prefer they hang up their spikes. They survive by carving out independent power bases that are stronger than normal lines of authority, and by developing constituencies on Capitol Hill and in the press that help them to pursue their own goals. Because these goals are their own and not simply a divining of what the boss wants, the empires often take on a momentum that translates into longevity for the people who build them.

Reprinted with permission from *The Washington Monthly*, March 1982, pages 10–18. Copyright 1982 by The Washington Monthly Co., 2712 Ontario Road, N.W., Washington, D.C. 20009.

Ring kissers, you may have guessed, are by far the more common breed. In fact, most government officials planning a career in survival are only dimly aware that another model exists. This is their loss, for the very greatest of Washington players — the sultans of survival — have rejected supplication as a technique. The career of Hyman Rickover certainly testifies to that. He served in the navy for more than sixty years, at least half of them under chiefs of naval operations who would have preferred he stay submerged for good after one of his sea trials. Or consider J. Edgar Hoover. Almost every president and attorney general he served under during his forty-eight-year career as director of the FBI disliked him, but when he left the bureau, it was on his back. These masters may have been exceptions, but the skills they plied contain some useful lessons about how to complete lengthy service in the U.S. government — and how to do it without acting like a toady.

Shanghai Log Cabins

To get a sense of the real difference between the two kinds of survival, let's look at a few examples of people who fall into the ring-kissing category, who fit the conventional image of how a "Washington survivor" is supposed to behave.

The man believed by himself and some others to be Washington's "ultimate survivor" is Joseph Laitin, a public affairs officer who survived at a high level from Kennedy to Johnson to Nixon to Ford to Carter. Laitin's aim was to serve his "client," as he put it, the point being that clients tend to appreciate good service and respond with job security. His biggest client was Lyndon Johnson, and his idea of serving him — in fact the principal Joe Laitin accomplishment of the years he spent as deputy White House press secretary — was to feed the president gossip. When LBJ went to the ranch, he'd call Laitin frequently at about 11 to hear scuttlebutt on reporters traveling to Texas. Johnson felt particularly unfriendly toward one reporter for the old *New York Herald Tribune,* and Laitin was only too happy to regale the boss with tales of the reporter's after-hours activities. "At first I told true stories about him," Laitin has proudly recounted on several occasions, "but then I began making them up. I think the president knew I was making them up, but he loved it just the same."

That story, pathetic as it is, has been trotted out for years as testimony to Laitin's uncanny ability to survive. Of course, "serving the client" can also take the form of genuinely helping the boss, and Laitin was good at that, too. So good, in fact, that the Ford and Carter White Houses got angry at him because he made his clients, James Schlesinger under Ford and Michael Blumenthal under Carter, look good in the press at the expense of the president.

Take the time Treasury Secretary Blumenthal flew out to the Far East for meetings. As assistant secretary for public affairs, Laitin went too, fulfilling the classic survivalist dictum that you should always travel with the boss. (The logic, now a bit dated, being that if you and the chief happen upon certain naughty diversions, it makes it hard for him ever to fire you.) Anyway, Laitin, employing his gift, suddenly insisted that Blumenthal visit Shanghai, where the new treasury secretary had lived as a boy after escaping Nazism. "That's your log cabin," Laitin told him. Blumenthal made the trip and came away with enormous publicity, not to mention respect for Laitin. Was Laitin providing good information to the public about economic issues? That didn't matter to Blumenthal. Was the large section of the department for which he was responsible well run? That didn't matter either.

So Laitin, like countless other ring kissers, could hardly be blamed for sensing that all that really matters in surviving is pleasing those above you. As for subordinates, according to this model of survival they aren't especially relevant. That explains why reporters tend to like Laitin as a person and as a professional (in part because he leaked a lot), while a number of former subordinates show a decided lack of enthusiasm on the subject of their old chief. If Laitin was known around press haunts as a guy who never forgot the name of an important reporter or government official, at Treasury he spent so much time on the phone and out to lunch that he is said not to have known even the names of two of the secretaries in his own office. A few years earlier, while at the FAA, he walked into the office of one of his top staffers one day and the secretaries remarked that they had never even *seen* him before. But why should they have? Laitin wasn't building an empire; he was building a reputation — for service to superiors.

As you can imagine, such reputations don't often depend heavily on a person's beliefs. Like most public affairs officers — indeed, like most ring kissers who bounce from agency to agency — Laitin was not much of a policy man. To come across as one is considered bad form for survivors choosing this mode, the obvious reason being that the more closely associated you are with a particular policy, the worse off you'll be when administrations change. (The new guard can usually tell the difference between those who make policy and those who just mouth it.) On the other hand, if you don't identify with the administration at least partially, you could be out *before* the next election. So there's a balance to be struck.

A man who has spent the better part of a lifetime striking that balance is Dwight Ink, who for thirty years was a top manager at a half-dozen different agencies. Ink was a competent manager as managers go, but his greatest skill, according to several people who worked with him, was appearing neither too partisan nor too facelessly neutral. The latter is the way most career civil servants play it, and that's why few rise to be superbureaucrats at a political level. Ink was different. Whether he was at the AEC, or HUD, or OMB he could subtly — and without really saying anything — convey a sympathy with the prevailing political ideology, then just as effortlessly shed those few calculated ounces of conviction when bosses or administrations changed.

"If he knew what the secretary wanted, he'd help you get it," recalls Charles Haar, a Harvard law professor who was an assistant secretary of HUD in the late 1960s when Ink was assistant secretary for administration. "But he'd never move anything too fast; the instinct was for more paper, more copies, more dotted i's and crossed t's rather than for getting something done." The reason for that, as Haar and others have noted, is that getting something done too fast might have put him in a vulnerable position, and that kind of vulnerability is what the ring-kissing survivalist fears most.

Like many other administrators who endure for years, Ink is smart, hard working, and competent; that's his reputation, and it's one reason he gets tapped so frequently. The problem with the definition lies with that word "competence." More often than not, the word has come to mean a peculiarly calibrated type of bureaucratic performance that doesn't have much to do with commitment to goals. While sometimes sharing and acting upon the boss's goals, subordinates too often substitute for genuine aims the kind of "managerial" efficiencies that so many administrators mistakenly believe can be separated from issues of policy.

Thus, just as Joe Laitin never cared much about the politics of his clients as long as they sold briskly and reflected well on the salesman, so Dwight Ink never cared much about the prevailing philosophy of government as long as it allowed him to "do the job," whatever that meant. Given that, it was no big surprise when Ink accepted Reagan's offer last year to come out of retirement and coordinate the dismantling of the Community Services Administration, snuffing out some of the very same programs he once helped create while working at HUD. It wasn't that Ink had decided on long reflection that the programs didn't work. He simply did what good ring kissers believe they are supposed to do. He did what he was told.

Wind Sniffing

Now, in some ways it's a little unfair to single out Laitin and Ink. After all, they simply responded to the same ground rules for survival that most other upper-level bureaucrats, including many still in the government, subscribe to. Take William Heffelfinger of the Department of Energy. Reagan is planning to put DOE out of its misery, and Heffelfinger, as assistant secretary for management and administration, will do the bulk of the honors (the secretary, James Edwards, is a deferential sort of tooth puller). The fact that Heffelfinger held a similar job under

Carter when the department was *created* passes in Washington without notice. After all, the standard response goes, these are bureaucrats we're talking about, and they're supposed to be "professionals."

Heffelfinger's hard-nosed — many call it brutal — style of management is said to be the only reason he survives at all. A congressional subcommittee learned in 1978 that during his many earlier government incarnations he had falsified his resume by adding degrees and awards he never received, and had destroyed public documents, among other vices. When a man can undergo a full-scale congressional investigation and still get reappointed — and the reason he can get the new job is that he has a reputation for cracking the whip and otherwise pleasing whoever is boss — the legend of this route to survival grows stronger. This is true despite the fact that Heffelfinger does not appear to act like a timid ring kisser. He yells and screams and tries to be a "tough" manager who gets things done. Depending on whom you talk to, that may even be true. The point, though, is that he furthers the impression that the best strategy for getting ahead in the government is to do others' bidding rather than your own. Heffelfinger may have missed out on other survivalist secrets — a clean nose, for instance — but he remembered the one about sniffing the wind to catch the drift of one's superiors.

The current master of that art is Frank Carlucci, a hard-working, bright, former foreign service officer, ambassador, deputy director of the Office of Economic Opportunity, deputy director of OMB, deputy CIA director, and now deputy secretary of defense. Carlucci's legendary budget-cutting abilities, like those of his current boss, Cap (nee "the Knife") Weinberger, were dulled considerably once it became clear what *Weinberger's* boss — the president — really thought about defense spending. The quickness of Carlucci's response to Reagan's concerns about leaks testifies to this uncanny meteorological ability that is so often believed to be essential for ring-kissing survival. Carlucci embraced and implemented the order that lie detector tests be administered to senior defense officials. And like the good soldier he is, went first.

Ultimately, the lie detectors may prove far more destructive to Reagan than the leaks. As high-ranking Carter administration officials can attest, nothing so quickly breaks down basic loyalty to a president as this particular brand of faith in one's trustworthiness. But more to the point, the lie detectors prove once and for all that Carlucci belongs among the ring kissers. He apparently considers it a productive day's work to have humiliated colleagues and subordinates in order to keep the boss happy.

Persuasion by Polar Water

Of course in his heart of hearts, Frank Carlucci probably doesn't like ring kissing very much. In his line of work, ambition is not easily sublimated, and people who know him say that his will to survive is developing into a will to conquer. What Carlucci may be learning is that conquering can assure surviving, and that it makes some sense to develop empire-building skills, which in Washington means contacts in the press and on the Hill. These contacts are not meant to make your boss look good (the survival technique of a Laitin) but to make *you* look good, and to hell with your boss.

The greatest empire builder of recent years is Admiral Hyman G. Rickover, who as a captain after World War II came up with an idea — nuclear submarines — and in the next thirty-five years proceeded to shape almost every aspect of the U.S. navy: training, technology, surface ships, and so forth. The way he did it is a fascinating story, but equally interesting is the way he got away with it without losing his job.

It was in 1952 that Rickover first realized the classic ring-kissing route wouldn't work for him. He had already beaten the odds and made great progress on the development of the first nuclear submarine (it was eventually finished many years ahead of schedule), but that year a navy selection board passed him over for promotion from captain to rear admiral for the second time. Whether it was because of his Jewish background or simply that he already nettled navy brass, his career appeared over. Up to then, two rejections meant automatic retirement.

But Rickover was smart enough to know that if he could create enough interest outside the navy, he might have a fighting chance after all. In part because he had a sexy project (though it really wasn't much more newsworthy that year than a lot of what goes on in government today), he caught the attention of the press, particularly a young Pentagon correspondent for *Time* named Clay Blair. Blair knew a good story when he saw one, and Rickover knew how to be cooperative — he even lent the use of his office and his wife's editing skills for the book Blair eventually wrote about him. In later years, once safely ensconced, Rickover shunned reporters. But when it counted he played them masterfully, especially those journalists like Edward R. Murrow whom he knew could endow him with some of their own respectability.

Meanwhile, he wasted no time meeting the right people on the Hill. The year before the promotion controversy he happened to have been seated on an airplane next to a young politician named Henry Jackson. They became friends, and along with Representative Sidney Yates, Jackson led the charge that forced the navy to make Rickover a rear admiral, notwithstanding the selection board's decision. Rickover reached the mandatory retirement age for all navy personnel in 1963, but until last year (when at age eighty-one he almost sank a submarine while at the controls) he continually had been granted special two-year extensions, a biennial event that caused untold teeth gnashing among his superiors.

Why did Congress admire Rickover so much? Part was clever flattery. He took members on submarine rides, wrote them hundreds of handwritten notes while on historic sea trials (who wouldn't save a letter with the dateline, "At Sea, Submerged"?), and brought back "polar water" as gifts for their offices. But most important, according to his recent biographers, Norman Polmar and Thomas B. Allen, was a peculiar "chemistry" he developed with many congressmen that made them believe they actually were involved with the building of the world's first nuclear-powered submarine and, later, with the creation of a nuclear navy. That chemistry — a critical element in any kind of empire building — is really just the reflection of an ability to accomplish goals.

The fact that Congress and the press respond best to tangible achievement — as opposed to loyal ring kissing — has not always been a positive thing for the country. Just because reporters and congressmen can see it, touch it, and report it back home, doesn't mean the rest of us need it, as Rickover's success in winning support for a poorly conceived weapon like the Trident submarine suggests. But if this kind of congressional behavior can bring us bad weapons and wasteful pork barrel projects, it can also bring out the best in government employees — the desire to create and produce, and the understanding that if you do a good enough job in those areas, forces outside the bureaucracy will help you survive.

Rickover should be particularly inspirational to budding empire builders because he proves that rank plays no role in such survival. He was a *fourth-echelon* officer (as deputy commander for nuclear propulsion, Naval Ships System Command, he reported to the chief of naval materiel, who reported to the chief of naval operations, who reported to the president). That's not to say he didn't use what position he did have, but in Rickover's case this meant an additional position *outside* of the navy, at the Atomic Energy Commission (and later at the Department of Energy).

Many powerful survivors have donned two hats before — Richard J. Daley was both mayor of Chicago and chairman of the powerful party committee that slated candidates for mayor of Chicago — but Rickover elevated it into an art form. Admiral Elmo Zumwalt, who despised Rickover for upstaging him when Zumwalt was chief of naval operations, recalls that when a navy request irked Rickover, his standard practice was to reply on AEC stationery, which allowed him to distribute the copies of his position to congressional friends without going through the navy chain of command.

It was that chain of command that drove Rickover to distraction. Acting solicitous toward Congress and the press was one thing, the point being that it helped you accrue more autonomy for yourself. But performing like that every day for your boss was quite another (although Rickover expected it of *his* much-abused staff). "What was fatal to [General Wilhelm] Keitel [chief of Hitler's combined general staff] was not his weaknesses," Rickover lectured a congressional committee during

one of his more than 150 formal appearances on the Hill, "but his virtues —the virtues of a subordinate." Among such regrettable virtues,
Rickover believed, was a conception of the chain of command as something that entitled a bureaucrat to someday win perquisities. As far as he
was concerned, such niceties had nothing at all to do with power and
survival.

So where Frank Carlucci tends to want the best office space available,
Rickover worked for thirty years out of a converted ladies room with no
rug and flaking yellow plasterboard; where William Heffelfinger dines
most afternoons at the likes of Le Provencal, Rickover had canned soup,
cottage cheese, and skimmed milk at his desk; and where Joe Laitin,
while assistant secretary of defense, bragged that he sat ahead of the
generals in a motorcade, Rickover rarely wore a uniform and was indifferent to the idea of a fourth star. After all, he reasoned, what did organization charts have to do with building and keeping an empire?

Passport to Perpetuation

Now, not everybody in the government can, or should, think like
Hyman Rickover. If they did, we'd have a country of anarchists and
ulcers. But the fact remains that in almost any realm — military or civilian —chain of command tends to impede action. The best empire builders recognize this and risk angering others in the hierarchy who believe
individual initiative is a threat. Their power *and* their survival depend
on a base outside the normal line of authority.

The greatest practitioner of this art was J. Edgar Hoover. When Hoover took over the FBI in 1924, it was a weak, corrupt, politicized, highly
ineffective agency. When he died in 1972, the same thing might have
been said. But in between, the FBI was, in the words of Victor Navasky,
editor of the *Nation* and hardly a Hoover admirer, the "least corruptible,
most sophisticated investigative agency in the world." Hoover revolu-
tionized the science of crime detection — *legitimate* crime detection —by
sponsoring innovation in lab work and training and by creating a high
standard of performance for his agents.

The point is not to absolve this racist redbaiter of his crimes — against
Martin Luther King, Jean Seberg, and the Constitution in general — but
simply to make it clear that Hoover could not rely solely on his survivalist wits. If his cagey bureaucratic abilities had not been underlain by a
strong conviction on the part of outsiders that he was doing something
good, he wouldn't have made it.

But accomplishment, as any government official should know, takes
you only so far. Like Rickover, Hoover undertook a major effort to cultivate the press, particularly columnist Walter Winchell, and the Congress, particularly Representative John J. Rooney, who for twenty-five
years oversaw the FBI's budget. Equally important, he cultivated a pub-

lic image, by using gimmicks like the Ten Most Wanted List and a long-running television series. Efrem Zimbalist, Jr., may be reluctant to star in the TV version of "The FDA" (co-starring special agent James Beard?), but that doesn't mean heads of government agencies less dramatic than the FBI cannot borrow some of the imagination Hoover used to create a public constituency for his programs.

You don't have to be as famous as Rickover or Hoover in order to use such skills. Consider the case of a woman named Frances Knight, who ran the passport office at the state department for more than twenty years, largely over the objections of most of the secretaries of state she saw come and go. These men resented her fiefdom but were essentially powerless to do anything about it. (Finally, in 1977, the state department succeeded in turning the passport office into what the career people always wanted — a place to let foreign service officers punch their tickets while waiting for another overseas assignment.)

Knight was controversial, but she realized that controversy, because it keeps the press interested, can be the stuff of survival, even for those in seemingly modest positions. She also understood that the press and Congress respond best if they are fed and cared for. When Drew Pearson called one Christmas Eve to say he needed fifteen passports right away, she hustled down to the office. When a congressman had a problem with a constituent's passport, she took care of it within hours, an ability that members of Congress still recall with awe.

These survival skills, applied on the Hill and in the press, should not necessarily make us feel more cynical about the way the government works. As it happens, Knight often would extend the same service to anyone (airline clerks at international terminals across the country had her home phone number). But even if she hadn't, such cultivation of outside sources of power isn't objectionable in itself. What *is* objectionable is the use of such networks solely for the purpose of surviving. When the aim instead is survival as a way of accomplishing admirable goals — even if the goal is simply running an efficient passport office — well, then even the most dubious survival techniques can be put to good use.

To demonstrate the point, let's look at the most base and contemptible of those techniques, namely Hoover's use of blackmail. The conversation with a congressman usually went something like this:

"Hello, congressman. Edgar Hoover here. Terribly sorry to hear about this unfortunate matter."

"What do you mean?"

"Well, we've had some reports that have come into our field office in your district. Frankly, I personally find them very difficult to believe. The whole thing just doesn't sound like you. But I just wanted to alert you to the fact that some reports have indeed been filtering into the bureau."

"What reports?

"Believe me, congressman, this matter will be kept in strictest confidence between us. I've instructed the field office to route all the details of your case straight to the Director."

Whatever the congressman's little embarrassment — a drunken visit to a whorehouse, a son who happened to be a homosexual — Hoover knew how to use it to his advantage. The strategy, which didn't have to be employed too often to be effective, worked equally well with presidents. Hoover's reappointment was John Kennedy's first order of business after his election, and even after a feud broke out between Hoover and his nominal boss, Robert Kennedy (during which the director instructed tour guides at the FBI building to point out that he had become head of the bureau the year before the attorney general was born), JFK never even considered his removal. How could he? Hoover knew certain, uh, *details* about Kennedy's personal life. If William Sullivan, longtime number three man at the bureau, is to be believed, Hoover used this strategy even on Nixon of all people, after he and Bebe Rebozo were spotted in the company of a particular Chinese woman during trips to Hong Kong in the mid-1960s. By the early 1970s, Nixon, once a big Hoover booster, wanted him fired too, but like other presidents, he subscribed to Lyndon Johnson's memorable judgment that given the permeability of the administration's tent, it made more sense to have Hoover inside pissing out.

Honorable Blackmail

It doesn't require a deep sensitivity to fine moral distinctions to see that Hoover's form of persuasion constitutes the most reprehensible form of survivalism imaginable. But if you think about it a moment, you might realize that Hoover's blackmail, *sans* the prurient details, can be surprisingly instructive, especially to people who, unbelievable as it sounds, want to do good with their government service.

Suppose you hope to improve your program or agency, and that such improvement demands a certain level of performance from your boss. To the extent that you let the boss know that you are cognizant of what is wrong in this program or agency, and to the extent that he knows you care enough to do something about it, you have created in him a dependency not unlike that felt by presidents toward Hoover. This assumes, of course, that the boss is aware that you have attended to the fundamental empire-building duties of making contacts on the Hill and in the press that might allow you to make good on the implied threat of revelation, and it assumes that you have the guts to use those contacts. If the boss believes that you really are willing and able to go public, then he's more likely to want you inside his tent. That means you now have a powerful ability to pursue your own vision of how your agency or program should be run. Your boss, respecting this new power, will provide you more autonomy, which, assuming you maintain those essential outside contacts, could be the beginning of your own empire.

But what's remarkable is that even if you have no designs on an empire — even if you like your boss so much that you might be characterized as a ring kisser — you still can play a form of this game. In fact, the most effective user of constructive blackmail is the person who admires his superior, who wants to believe the best about him, who hopes that the boss soon realizes that his subordinates and all of the people who believe in his program will be disappointed if he doesn't shape up. What this really involves is a genuine, sincere version of what Hoover was disingenuously saying on the telephone to that congressman. It is an unconscious, unspoken way of playing not on the boss's fear of being exposed, but on his sense of guilt — guilt that he will disillusion those who share his goals.

Naturally, the only way the ring kisser can inspire that very positive form of guilt is if he does indeed share those goals. And if he does share them, he might not be such an objectionable ring kisser after all. Harry Hopkins (FDR's aide) and D. B. Hardeman (Sam Rayburn's aide) are examples of this better breed. Because they believed in what their bosses were trying to do, they shared in their bosses' accomplishments. Conversely, when ring kissers do not believe in what their superiors are trying to do — when they are simply determined to outlast them — then they do not share in their major accomplishments, except in the sense that they feel a little battered for having endured the long ride. Joe Laitin showed a keen sensitivity to this point when he admitted to the *Los Angeles Times* last year after his luck finally ran out that "I can't point to one thing I've accomplished, but my blood is all over this town for fighting for what I believe is right." What was "right," of course, was simply survival itself.

So the determining factor is not which strategy you choose to employ, but what you want to employ those survivalist techniques *for*. If survival is an end in itself, then none of the gambits are worthy of our respect. On the other hand, if survival is used as the means to genuine accomplishment, then ring kissing, currying favor with Congress and the press, even blackmail have their place when done constructively. That doesn't make all survival techniques equal in morality or even in plain tastefulness, but it can hook them to some larger purpose. The best survivors — the ones we all should learn something from — have made this essential connection.

To the Student:

Part of our job as educational publishers is to try to improve the textbooks we publish. Thus, when revising, we take into account the experience of both instructors and students with the previous edition. At some time your instructor will be asked to comment extensively on *Behind the Scenes in American Government: Personalities and Politics*, but right now we want to hear from you. After all, though your instructor assigned this book, you are the one who paid for it.

Please help by by completing this questionnaire and returning it to Political Science Editor, College Division, Little, Brown and Company, 34 Beacon Street, Boston, Massachusetts 02106.

School_____Course Title_____

Instructor's name_____

Other books assigned_____

		Liked best				Liked least	Didn't read
1.	Drew, Running	5	4	3	2	1	_____
2.	Andersen, Campaign 1984: Facing the Fatigue Factor	5	4	3	2	1	_____
3.	Thomas, Campaigning with Jesse Jackson: Pride and Prejudice	5	4	3	2	1	_____
4.	Cannon, Ronald Reagan: A Political Perspective	5	4	3	2	1	_____
5.	Royko, The Boss	5	4	3	2	1	_____
6.	Shipp, Will Loyalty Win the Ward Again?	5	4	3	2	1	_____
7.	Hunt, The Washington Power Brokers	5	4	3	2	1	_____
8.	Emerson, Dutton of Arabia	5	4	3	2	1	_____
9.	Egerton, Congressman Claude Pepper: Courtly Champion of America's Elderly	5	4	3	2	1	_____
10.	von Hoffman, The Washington Monocle: Scene of the Power Lunch	5	4	3	2	1	_____
11.	The Reverend Jerry Falwell and the Tide of Born Again	5	4	3	2	1	_____
12.	Whitehead, For Whom Caddell Polls	5	4	3	2	1	_____
13.	Blumenthal, Richard Viguerie: The Postmaster General of the Right	5	4	3	2	1	_____
14.	Powell, The Right to Lie	5	4	3	2	1	_____
15.	Weisman, Ronald Reagan's Magical Style	5	4	3	2	1	_____
16.	Babcock, The Rewards of Losing: Mondale Out of Office	5	4	3	2	1	_____
17.	Reedy, The White House Staff: A Personal Account	5	4	3	2	1	_____
18.	Dean, My First Day at the White House	5	4	3	2	1	_____
19.	Wise, Why the President's Men Stumble	5	4	3	2	1	_____
20.	McPhee, Senator Bill Bradley: Open Man	5	4	3	2	1	_____
21.	Feaver, The Secretary and the Senator	5	4	3	2	1	_____
22.	Evans and Novak, The Johnson System	5	4	3	2	1	_____
23.	Leamer, Robert Byrd and Edward Kennedy: Two Stories of the Senate	5	4	3	2	1	_____
24.	Latham, Russell Long	5	4	3	2	1	_____
25.	Breslin, The Politician	5	4	3	2	1	_____

(over)

	Liked best			Liked least		Didn't read
26. Kaplan, Going from Outsider to Insider on Capitol Hill: Les Aspin and the Case of the MX	5	4	3	2	1	_____
27. Woodward and Armstrong, The Brethren and the Abortion Decision	5	4	3	2	1	_____
28. Warren, A Case of Emotional Impact	5	4	3	2	1	_____
29. Ungar, The King: J. Edgar Hoover	5	4	3	2	1	_____
30. Alter, The Powers That Stay	5	4	3	2	1	_____

1. Are there any authors or political figures whom you would like to see represented?
   _____

2. Did you find the editor's introductions helpful?_____

3. Will you keep this book for your library?_____

4. Please add any comments or suggestions. _____
   _____
   _____

5. May we quote you in our promotional efforts for this book?
   _____yes_____no
   date_____signature_____
   mailing address_____